Assessing
the Elderly

Assessing the Elderly

A Practical Guide to Measurement

Rosalie A. Kane
Robert L. Kane
The Rand Corporation

LexingtonBooks
D.C. Heath and Company
Lexington, Massachusetts
Toronto

Library of Congress Cataloging in Publication Data

Kane, Rosalie A.
   Assessing the elderly.

   Includes bibliographical references and index.
   1. Aged—Medical care. 2. Aged—Care and hygiene. 3. Nursing
home care—Evaluation. 4. Long-term care of the sick—Evaluation.
5. Gerontology. I. Kane, Robert Lewis, 1940–   . II. Title.
RC954.3.K36   362.1'9897'0287   81–2389
ISBN 0–669–04551–9   AACR2
ISBN 0–669–09780–2 (pbk.)

Twelfth printing, April 1988

Published simultaneously in Canada

Printed in the United States of America on acid-free paper

International Standard Book Number: 0–669–04551–9 Casebound

International Standard Book Number: 0–669–09780–2 Paperbound

Library of Congress Catalog Card Number: 81–2389

Contents

List of Figures

List of Tables

Preface

This book evolved from our continuing efforts to articulate what is distinctive about geriatric practice and long-term care. The more we dealt with this subject, the more impressed we became that a major attribute of long-term care is the way providers define the reality of old people—a reality that they help to shape. From many quarters, the demand has mounted for techniques to describe and measure the problems, needs, strengths, and changes of elderly persons. Because the tools used for such tasks are pivotal to the way our views of the world are shaped, careful examination of the body of available measures is vital. We must strive to make a complex, multifactorial, multidimensional, multidisciplinary world more understandable and therefore, we hope, more amenable to change.

The targeted audience for this book is practitioners of all professions—persons who are motivated to make accurate and useful measurements but who are perhaps overwhelmed by the number of relevant variables and the variety of instruments that seem to be available. We envisage physicians, nurses, social workers, administrators, gerontologists, evaluators, and polyacronymic therapists of all types as potential users. At times we concentrate on the physician as a prototype caregiver, largely because it is the physician who may combine the greatest unfamiliarity with functional-measurement approaches with the greatest power. Moreover, we recognize that events that trigger changes in many aspects of life often begin with the identification of a health problem. Although measurement for physicians and other primary-health-care providers is emphasized, our intention is to provide a practical document for a much wider group of clinicians and researchers.

The release of this book coincides with multiple major public initiatives addressed to the needs of the frail elderly. Particular emphasis has been placed on achieving alternatives to the nursing home as we know it today. For these demonstration projects, measurement occurs on several levels. Assessments of individual clients and their families are a crucial part of case management. Program evaluation requires measures on the aggregate level to determine program effectiveness. We offer no simple solutions to long-term-care problems, but we do raise issues that should be considered in relation to the current concerns over assessment and case management.

We have approached this emotional topic with as much common sense as we can muster, trying to take nothing for granted and to question everything. We have also attempted to be as concrete as possible, filling these pages with specific examples of instruments and their variation. Indeed, we hope to have illustrated with actual measurements that the definition of reality provided by clinicians and policy-relevant researchers is a powerful shaper of the future. Because the same individuals are often involved in making measurements both for clinical and for program-evaluation purposes, we have also developed criteria for selecting measures according to their particular purpose.

If we have drawn attention to the potency and the potential of the measuring tool, this work will be amply rewarded.

Acknowledgments

This book has evolved as an indirect result of a number of past and present Rand Corporation research projects that stimulated us to focus on measurement in geriatrics and its problems. In 1978 and 1979, we performed an evaluation of ten demonstration projects in long-term-care review under a contract from the Health Standards Quality Bureau (HSQB) of the Health Care Financing Administration. During almost the same period, we participated in a Geriatric Manpower Policy Task Force, created under a grant from the Henry J. Kaiser Family Foundation; as part of this project, we made projections of geriatric-manpower needs and their implications for training. In the fall of 1979, we were awarded a grant from the National Center for Health Services Research (NCHSR) to develop methods of predicting the outcomes of nursing-home patients in a number of functional domains. Measurement was a common theme in all these projects, engaging us continuously in evaluating the state of that art.

We gratefully acknowledge the support of those three agencies and their encouragement as we became interested in the broader subject of measurement; particularly we thank Dr. Ruth Covell, our project officer from the HSQB; Dr. Robert Glaser, president of the Kaiser Family Foundation; and Mr. Julius Pellegrino, project officer for our current NCHSR grant. We also acknowledge the generous support of The Rand Corporation, which enabled us to develop the material further and to present it in this book form.

Over the years, we have absorbed the ideas, comments, and reactions of many colleagues and resource persons, both in the United States and abroad. Because we took every opportunity to discuss these issues, a listing of those who helped us would be formidably long, yet incomplete. Limiting our acknowledgments to those who worked with us directly, we extend appreciation to the other members of Rand's Geriatric Manpower Policy Task Force who participated in regular discussions of how to measure functional status in long-term care; these are David Solomon, John Beck, and Emmett Keeler. We are also grateful to Sandra Riegler, who, in the capacity of research assistant, assembled and organized voluminous materials for chapter 4 of this book. As always, our secretary, Janice Jones, made it all possible through her attention to detail in preparation of the manuscript. The opinions expressed, of course, are the responsibility of the authors, rather than of The Rand Corporation, any of Rand's sponsors, or any of our associates.

Finally, we gratefully acknowledge the support of the National Institute of Aging, which sponsors Robert Kane with a Geriatric Medicine Academic Award to support his commitment on the faculty of the University of California at Los Angeles in the Division of Geriatrics, School of Medicine.

This book has also benefited from the ideas, experiences, and materials that various scholars and long-term-care professionals have graciously shared with us over the past eighteen months. Although all the opinions and recommendations expressed here are our responsibility, we gratefully acknowledge the generosity and responsiveness of our colleagues. Among them, we particularly thank Dan Blazer, Larry Branch, Gerald Eggert, Angela Falcone, Charles Fogelman, Dolores Gallagher, Matilda Goldberg, Stewart Greathouse, Glen Gresham, Barry Gurland, Helen Hageboeck, Steven Hirsch, Joseph Hodgson, Barbara Ishizaki, Rene Jahiel, Sidney Katz, Iseli Kraus, M. Powell Lawton, George Maddox, David Mangen, Rudolph Moos, Eric Pfeiffer, David Reid, Robert Sanders, Sylvia Sherwood, and John Toner.

Assessing
the Elderly

1   Uses and Abuses of Measurement in Long-Term Care

Measurement is essential to good geriatric care. It is a crucial consideration for those developing, promoting, or practicing this still embryonic specialization. Any strategy for altering the health status of the elderly requires a technology for first assessing that health status and then detecting increments of progress. Training geriatricians or "gerontologized" practitioners requires accurate and appropriate assessment tools that can be introduced through the educational process.

The subject is topical and complex. Assessment has become somewhat of a buzzword in geriatric-policymaking groups. A comprehensive, individualized assessment of the elderly person's functioning has been proposed as the open sesame for access to expanded long-term-care (LTC) benefits. Once services have been marshaled on behalf of the individual, program accountability also depends on regular assessment of the program recipient. Integral to this process is an ability to make accurate measurements of factors selected as important. Unfortunately, no agreement has yet been achieved on two of the most crucial points: (1) the identification of important factors to be measured, and (2) the technology for making the measures.

Obviously those delivering medical care to the elderly need technical knowledge and skill derived from the medical subspecialties relevant for treating particular problems. Beyond that, they need a general perception about the well-being of the older person that transcends a particular diagnosis, problem, or specialization. Many authorities have pointed out the limitations of a diagnosis-centered approach to describing the health of the elderly (Kent, Kastenbaum, and Sherwood 1972; Sherwood 1975; Goran et al. 1976). Conventional wisdom now holds that: (1) the elderly are subject to multiple diagnoses; (2) the physical, mental, and social well-being of an elderly individual are very closely interrelated, so that multidimensional assessments of health status are necessary; and (3) measures of functional status that examine the ability to function independently despite disease, physical and mental disability, and social deprivation are the most useful overall indicators to assist those who care for the elderly.

Where does this leave the physician or other health-care provider? The mandate for a global assessment of functioning presents a formidable and elusive task. The clinician needs practical tools that will permit evaluation of individuals' status, prediction of their future course, and planning for their care. In a way, measurements are organizers, capable of turning amorphous

1

and expansive goals into a series of defined tasks. They are the means by which progress or lack of progress is noted. The bad image of geriatrics in the eyes of neophyte physicians may be attributed partly to a perception that the patients are not amendable to change in status. To dispel such notions, physicians can be equipped with accurate and trustworthy techniques to help focus their attention on the positive changes that are indeed possible.

Who Makes Measurements in Long-Term Care?

The choice of measurements for use in LTC depends on the role and purpose of the person using the measurements. At least four groups of users can be identified:

1. The physician, nurse, social worker, or other health-care provider who is not primarily a geriatric specialist but who encounters elderly persons in the course of clinical practice.
2. The geriatric specialist.
3. The case manager.
4. The researcher and/or program evaluator.

The Nongeriatric Practitioner

In their daily office and hospital practices, physicians encounter many patients over age 65 and over age 75 (Kane et al. 1981). In this context, the major purpose of a measurement of overall functioning is its assistance to the physician in organizing observations and ensuring that no important factor is omitted from consideration. Brevity and practicality are key features. As a generous estimate, one might expect the newly sensitized physician to spend a maximum of five extra minutes in consideration of the functional status of this patient beyond the particular complaint under immediate care. Alternatively or additionally, other systematic information might be collected by office personnel or through a self-completed series of questions given to the patient. In either case, the most-useful measurements will be those that can rather quickly help the provider assess the patient's total situation. As an outcome of such a measurement, the provider may turn attention to some problem amenable to medical assistance other than the one that brought the patient to him, or may seek consultation from a geriatric specialist, another member of the care team.

As medical educators seek to alert neophyte physicians to the complex needs of the geriatric patient, and to resocialize such physicians into a more-optimistic therapeutic stance toward the patient over age 75 with mutliple decrements in functioning, they will wish to equip new generations of physicians with convenient measuring tools that provide a frame of reference for treatment of their elderly patients. We might risk an analogy to the Apgar score for assessment of newborn children; although the score is recognized to be an accumulation of rather crude judgments, it has survived as a useful organizing tool with predictive validity. In the spirit of recognizing that we pay attention to what we can measure and that the very act of measuring reminds the physician that more than one action option is available, the search for appropriate brief measures for the nongeriatrician should be a priority.

Geriatric Specialists

The geriatric specialist is the individual whose chief practice concern is the elderly person with multiple physical, psychological, and social problems. Such a specialist will require a larger array of assessment tools and will need the capability of measuring rather small distinctions in functioning. In geriatric-assessment units, such specialists will make recommendations for future care in intensive rehabilitation settings or in LTC institutions on the basis of the patient's total functional (that is, physical, mental, and social) status and social supports. For the purposes of intensive rehabilitation, the specialist will wish to note progress toward goals such as mobility, transfer, and other skills of self-care. Later on we discuss some of the variations and refinements in existing functional-status measures. Informal discussions with geriatricians in Great Britain suggest that rate of change in functioning may be an important diagnostic and prognostic tool; the ability to evoke measures of change rates, in turn, depends on the ability to make repeated accurate measures in categories sufficiently fine to show change.

Practice in LTC institutions (or community programs serving the same population that currently resides in nursing homes) will be enhanced by an ability to measure differences at the lower end of the functional-status continuum. Although perhaps the majority of patients suffer impairments of physical functioning, and many are impaired in their mental abilities, all chronic LTC patients cannot be lumped together and assigned an identical and gloomy prognosis (which all too readily becomes a self-fulfilling prophecy). A further consideration is the morale of the staff who work with the chronically impaired, often in institutional settings. They, too, need to be shown how to observe small changes in functional abilities as a step toward engaging their participation in a team effort to promote the desired changes.

LTC institutions provide a drastic change of life-style for the residents. Ideally, such changes are recommended for the protection, care, and ultimate well-being of the older person. Because the setting of care imposes new conditions on the patient's life, it is incumbent on the provider to be able to measure effects on subjective states of happiness, morale or well-being as well as on objective states of social interaction and activity. Numerous technical problems arise in making such measurements, including: (1) the selection of instruments or indicators; (2) the difficulty in making attribution to the institutional environment without baseline information about psychological and social well-being prior to admission; and (3) the difficulty in getting valid information because of the physical and mental disabilities of the patients, on the one hand, and their dependence on the caretakers on the other.

Geriatricians cannot be expected to solve these measurement problems single-handedly, nor is it likely that they will be the primary measurers of psychological and social well-being among institutionalized elderly. In fact, some of this measurement falls under the rubric of program evaluation as discussed later on, involving as it does group measures rather than measures focused on the individual resident. In terms of the individual patient, however, the clinician needs to be aware of the possibility of untoward effects of treatment and to develop a manageable way of noting them. If he has followed the patient through earlier phases of care, he may, with the right tools, be in a position to measure changes in psychological and social functioning over time and from pre- to postinstitutional life.

Case Management

The case manager is responsible for decisions about the way resources are allocated to an individual patient on the basis of the patient's need; the presumed effects of various management strategies on the patient's well-being; and, of course, the availability of resources across the total community. Case management as a formal function is just coming into its own in geriatrics. Field tests of case-management systems such as ACCESS (Eggert and Bowlyow 1979; Eggert, Bowlyow, and Nichols 1980) and TRIAGE (Hodgson and Quinn 1980) have been mounted with the assistance of waivers that make available a more-flexible use of resources under Medicare and Medicaid funding. To a lesser extent, Professional Standards Review Organizations (PSROs) that have begun LTC review also engage in case management when they conduct a preadmission review to determine the appropriateness of nursing home for a patient; here, however, the PSROs are limited to the legalistic function of determining eligibility for funded services under the law rather than that of constructing ideal service packages. The National Channeling Demonstration, launched in 1980 under the auspices of the Health Care Financing Administration and the Administration on Aging, will test the effects of various models of case management on client outcomes, family outcomes, and costs of care.

The managerial function of the geriatrician has been emphasized in British literature (Anderson 1971; Brocklehurst et al. 1978). Such a function implies that a package of services is created for a patient based on an individualized assessment of needs and the likely benefit of services. A physician may not necessarily make all the assessments that lead to the service prescription, but it is argued that he serves a coordinating role. As formal case-management systems emerge in the United States as a means to control scarce resources, physicians are unlikely to be assigned the ultimate responsibility for assessment and placement. Especially where public dollars are concerned, other personnel—social workers, gerontologists, nurses, or some hybrid yet to emerge—may make the final choices. Even so, physicians (or substitute caregivers) will always have an important role in the case-management decisions and, in the private sector, may become de facto case managers, responsible for recommending a constellation of services to patients and their families.

What kind of measurement helps with the case-management role? Here a composite measure is required, constructed from an understanding of the patient's functional status, medical condition and prognosis, and social resources. Value decisions about preferred modes of treatment (for example, a value for treatment in the least-restrictive environment possible and for avoidance of institutional care) affect the way scores on such a scale are used as guides to action. Although cutoff scores on such scales could hardly be used as mechanical guides to specific actions, they can assist a case manager in reviewing the amount of care required by an individual, translating his functional limitations into practical factors relating to his capacity for self-care, considering the individual's affective state and social circumstances, and eventually reaching recommendations. Multidimensional assessment measures have also been used as tools to predict who will be able to remain in the community; to the extent that such scales have prognostic capability, they can be used to establish norms of the kinds and numbers of LTC services needed.

Case management does not cease, of course, when a patient becomes a resident in an LTC facility. Then, too, a measure of overall functioning across a number of dimensions can suggest a plan for the care of that individual; as will be shown later on, however, the instruments used may differ from those used for community-based-care management.

Furthermore, measurement of functional status may also be used as an indicator of the quality of care received (Aydelotte 1962). Although such measures must be suggestive rather than definitive, deterioration on functional-status measures that are sensitive to care provided should warn the case manager to reevaluate both the plan and its implementation. The PSROs have accumulated experience in identifying key patient-status variables that may be identified with substandard care (Kane et al. 1979).

Research and Evaluation

In the first stage of enlightenment about geriatrics, the neophyte is usually exposed to the burgeoning geriatric literature. Here he encounters many assertions about aging and subgroups of elderly persons, along with discussion of the relative merits of various approaches to achieving goals such as longevity, alleviation of depression, and improvement of functional status. The literature is replete with correlational studies reporting the relationship of demographic and other variables to the health status of the elderly; much less frequently, one also finds studies of cohorts of elderly persons over time. Such statements, although interesting to the geriatric specialist, cannot be evaluated without reference to the measurements on which the statements are based.

Recent reviews of measurements in LTC (Bloom 1975) or of classes of measurement such as measures of functional status (Katz, Hedrick, and Henderson 1979; Goga and Hambacher 1977); subjective well-being or happiness (Larson 1978; George 1979); life adjustment (Graney and Graney 1973); mental functioning or depression (Gallagher, Thompson, and Levy, 1980, Salzman et al. 1972a, b; Raskin and Jarvik 1979); and quality of life (George and Bearon 1980) indicate that measurements are numerous but often not thoroughly tested. In some instances, measures that were developed on youthful populations or for specialized populations (such as psychiatric patients) are applied to the elderly. In other instances, investigators have chosen to develop yet another instrument rather than use one that had already been fielded with an older population.

As a general rule, the clinician is not involved in methodological research designed to develop measures or in descriptive epidemiological studies of the aging process. Interface with the research and evaluation enterprise, however, occurs passively when the gerontological literature is read and more actively when measures are sought to study the effects of a clinical treatment or a management intervention on the general functioning and well-being of the patient. Some proportion of the geriatric specialists being trained for the future (especially those who will assume positions of leadership in teaching settings) will be engaged in clinical research and program evaluation. Choice of measurements determines the way reality is abstracted; the clinician cannot assume that all measures of concepts such as functional status, mental orientation, or adjustment really measure the same thing. In program evaluation, "measurement overkill" is an ever-present hazard; there is a tendency to include a large number of scales and composite measures that yield scores as a substitute for careful targeting of ways to measure the desired outcomes of the program.

Figure 1-1 depicts the relationship of measurement to research and evaluation in LTC. As the sequencing shows, the need to begin with characteristics that can be measured gives rise to a body of methodological research aimed primarily at ensuring the reliability and validity of the measurements themselves. Research should also be directed at showing how characteristics are correlated with each other and how they vary according to demographic or situational differences. A characteristic under scrutiny is conventionally called an *outcome* if it is sought as a treatment goal or encountered as an untoward result of treatment. Descriptive studies and longitudinal research, so important in the

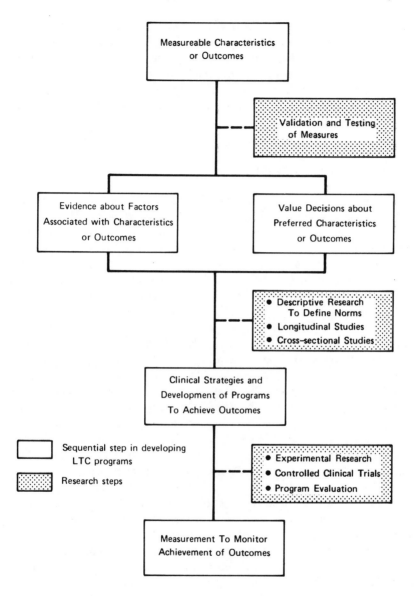

Figure 1-1. Schematic Representation of Relationship of Measurement to Research and Evaluation in Long-Term Care

development of understanding or normal aging and in making possible pre-liminary inferences about causality, are dependent on the initial adequacy of the measurements. The selection of clinical goals, however, depends not only on the body of research but also on value decisions about the preferred results of treatment. Such values may be either consciously defined and expressed or implicit; they may reflect preferences of the provider community, those of the elderly person, or some societal synthesis. On the basis of evidence about factors associated with aging and value statements about the kinds of characteristics deemed desirable as program outcomes, clinical strategies can be developed and tested.

Group Versus Individual Measures

Criteria for judging the adequacy of an instrument depend in part on whether that instrument is being used to assess the status of an individual or to describe a group of people. In making a clinical determination about the health of a particular person on which, in turn, we base recommendations for that person's care, we strive for the greatest accuracy possible. In so doing, we are likely to produce a large number of categorical distinctions growing out of the numerous possible variations on a human theme. On the other hand, estimations of the health status of groups of individuals are often needed to provide groundwork for program decisions; such decisions could occur at the level of a single organization (for example, an LTC center planning the differential expansion of programs and services) or at the level of a community, state, or larger region. In such instances a large number of observations of each individual would be both impractical and undesirable. Instead, one seeks a readily applicable instrument that suggests the extent and nature of need in the population.

Table 1-1 compares the desirable attributes of a group measure to those of an individual measure. Although the basic requirements for reliability and validity apply in both instances, our table shows some of the tradeoffs that might be made on the basis of the intended use of the data and the constraints imposed on their collection. In the case of the individual measures, we emphasize the detection of remediable problems and the documentation of small increments of change as a means of measure progress. In the case of group measures, we are more concerned with problems of inter-rater reliability and the identification of practical measures that can be aggregated. This distinction between individual and group measures becomes irrelevant when the sums of individual-change scores are used rather than a comparison of group means. To make the distinctions clearer, we draw the extreme contrast between a measure used by a planner in a broad population study with one used by a clinician planning for an individual elderly person. As later discussions show, these are not always clear-cut distinctions.

The points of contrast between group and individual measures represent not absolute differences but relative emphases. The community planner conducting a population study seeks an easily used instrument, which, in turn,

Table 1-1
Attributes Desired in Individual and Group Measures in LTC

Individual	*Group*
Reliability	Reliability
Across raters	Across raters
Over time	Over time
Validity	Validity
Minimizing false negatives	Capability of producing useful broad
Minimizing false positives	categories of functional ability across
Capability of documenting problems	whole spectrum of performance
amenable to intervention	Minimizing time and cost of administration
Capability of documenting conditions	Minimizing cost of analysis
requiring a service strategy	Portability—minimizing equipment required
Capability of documenting small changes	Reproduceability across geographical and
in functioning	cultural lines
Defensible strategy for sampling behaviors	Minimizing dependence on professional
measured	judgment or implicit criteria
	Defensible strategy for sampling from the
	population

suggests a self-administered questionnaire, an instrument amenable to group administration, or an instrument that can be personally administered in a fairly brief interview. The emphasis on volume means that an ideal instrument should not require a high level of professional education to administer and should lend itself to analysis with a minimal number of intermediate steps. To preserve flexibility of administration, it is best that it be independent of elaborate or expensive equipment. To preserve accuracy, it is best that the judgment of the raters be minimized. Such an instrument should be able to produce a manageable number of broad categories of ability across the full range-of-expected-performance spectrum. It is expected, however, that much specific information relating to a particular individual will be lost in developing general categories.

In contrast, a clinician must minimize both the false positives and the false negatives associated with the measure. Precision in terms of measuring the status of a particular individual will probably be more important than ease and economy of administration, analysis, and interpretation. The protection of the time of the professional personnel is also less relevant, particularly because those personnel will already be involved in a therapeutic and prescriptive sense. A functional-status measurement used in assessing impaired persons is sometimes needed to differentiate small changes at the lower end of the spectrum; this is particularly true in the case of stroke victims or mentally disoriented persons whose changes in status may be minute and slow. Further, a measurement should have some pragmatic application in the sense that it can document the problems and conditions that are most amenable to intervention and that would suggest a specific service strategy. Because an infinite amount of information could be collected about an elderly individual, it is important that the decisions about what to measure and the cutoff points used have practical utility. The practitioner, however, must not lose sight of the importance that small distinctions in functional ability can have for the quality of life of the geriatric patient. For example, the strength to sit up and the ability to do so for several hours makes an enormous difference to the patient. In another example, a small improvement in the use of a hand may be the key to communication.

Reliability and Validity

Reliability

Whether an instrument is designed to measure individual or group health status, reliability and validity are common concerns. Reliability refers to the ability (in the absence of real change) to obtain the same result with repeated measurements. Reliability is at particular risk when measures depend on raters' judgments. In LTC, many of the measurements of functional status in common use are, in fact, the cumulative observations of a professional or paraprofessional rater. Reported reliability data must be used with caution; such claims are pertinent only to the precise conditions under which a particular measure was tested.

Some organizations report high reliability among raters even when the tool used calls for many judgments; such inter-rater reliability is achieved through intensive training. It may be a fallacy to assume that instruments that were proved reliable when used at specialized centers for the study of aging will be reliable in the hands of other personnel in other programs. To the extent that an instrument calls for ratings based on explicit criteria using highly specific and observable categories, the inter-rater-reliability problem is minimized. Yet even with explicit criteria, reliability depends heavily on the stimulus provided by the tester. Often inter-rater reliability is tested by having two or more raters observe a subject simultaneously or conduct an interview together. Even if high agreement occurs between raters using such procedures, this still provides no assurance that the ratings would be reliable if the interviews had been conducted separately. Minimizing this very difficult problem necessitates explicit instructions about the conduct of testing.

Intra-rater reliability (or the ability of the same rater to achieve the same result with repeated measurements) is a vexing issue in LTC. Whether a test is self-completed or observer-completed, stability in the measurement over time is sought. If real changes occur in the subject between the two measurements, however, a change in score should indeed occur. (The same point applies to tests of inter-rater reliability unless observations can be made simultaneously by several raters.) Conventional clinical wisdom asserts that the elderly fluctuate in their functional abilities (partly because of factors such as fatigue or acute illness). The difficulty lies in distinguishing a change in a score that is a result of a real change in status from an artifact of the testing situation; for example, some tests of cognitive ability can be learned, so that one might expect successive improvements on retest, whereas others may become irritating to the respondent, so that one might expect a decrease of effort and cooperation. A catch-22 is presented: We cannot be certain about the degree that functional status fluctuates without reliable measurements, and we cannot readily test the measures for reliability without assuming some stability over time in the characteristic measured.

Peterson, Mangen, and Sanders (1978) discuss three types of reliability: time-bound, as in test-retest reliability; individual-bound, as in the case of inter-rater reliability; or item-bound, as in parallel forms, split-half techniques, or domain sampling to estimate internal consistency. Test-retest strategies are used to determine whether a measurement is stable, producing the same result with repeated applications. Interpreting the results of test-retest strategies is difficult because one cannot always tell whether a poor reliability coefficient means that the instrument is unstable or merely that it is sensitive to real change. The final form of reliability testing is a statistical examination of the internal consistency of the items, using techniques such as the coefficient alpha; quite often this is the only form of reliability testing available for LTC measures.

Validity

Validity, or the ability of a measure to reflect the characteristic it is intended to assess, is, of course, the ultimate requirement of all scales and tests. This is equally important whether the object of scrutiny is an individual elderly person or a population. Validity issues are discussed in subsequent chapters in the context of specific instruments, but a few comments are generally applicable. Many important outcomes of LTC are highly abstract (for example, morale or independence). Lay persons do not agree on the meaning of such terms, and there is a danger that instruments used to measure them will in fact measure only a limited aspect of what is commonly meant by the phenomenon. Worse, the measurement may reflect an idiosyncratic definition of the concept that would not be shared by many others.

The validity of a particular data set depends not only on internal characteristics of the measurements but also on the way the instrument is administered and the means of sampling. Obviously, a statement about the attributes of a group of elderly persons must be based on a sampling technique adequate to ensure representativeness and an information-collection strategy that does not bias the information received. The latter involves safeguards of confiden-tiality; creation of an environment permitting disclosure of feelings; and con-sideration of any particular limitations (hearing, speech, physical frailty) of the respondents that might affect the results. Less obviously, sampling is an important issue even when a clinician is measuring the status of one individual patient or elderly person. Here the key decisions involve the sampling of behaviors, the time window used, and the frequency of observation that is incorporated into a measure.

The Limitations of Scales

The overriding purpose of this book is to acquaint physicians, nurses, social workers in health settings, and other health providers with common and prac-tical approaches to assessing the general functioning of their patients. We urge that all primary providers develop routines for objectively assessing functional abilities and monitoring changes. Ironically, at the same time that we advocate increased use of measurement, we must raise cautions about the dangers of blind faith in measurement and scales. Measurements in long-term care can be dangerous if overinterpreted or misinterpreted. During a discussion of validity, we would be remiss to omit the pitfalls of scales, especially many relating to social/psychological constructs derived from the gerontological literature.

Once a scale is created to measure a complex and abstract quality (for example, socialization patterns, authoritarianism, perceptions of control over one's life, future orientation), some practitioners tend to reify the scores. They may forget that the name given to the scale is an arbitrary designation based on what the inventor believes it to reflect. But naming something does not always make it so. (A horse named "Speedster" can still come in last.) In other words, the users of the information may forget that the judgment about, say, "life satisfaction" was based on a pattern of response to a few questions and may come to regard the score as an absolute indicator of life satisfaction, just as a balance scale is an authoritative measure of body weight.

An imposing anthology of research measurements in aging (Mangen and Peterson, forthcoming) illustrates the point. In twenty-four categories (some as fine as "interspousal relations" or "cross-generational relations"), scholars have collected existing research instruments. An incredible proliferation of measure-ments and scales has been amassed, many very similar to one another. By the time a scale has a name, it can take on a concreteness unjustified by either its content or its original construction. For example, Anderson and Patten (forthcoming) cite the TRIAGE Quality of Life Scale (Doherty 1976); this scale is constructed from answers to seven interview questions such as "Are you happy?" and "Do you worry?" to which a respondent answers "never or rarely" (score 2); "sometimes" (score 1); and "regularly" (score 0). A score of 14 connotes a high quality of life. This scale was developed specifically for an evaluation of a comprehensive home-care program that compared 300 recipients of the service to 150 residents of a control community. The point is that, at best, such a scale corresponds to a narrow definition of "quality of life" and perhaps one at variance with usual perceptions. A scale with different items might produce an entirely different evaluation of the quality of a patient's life.

Because we advocate that providers systematically assess some important aspects of social functioning (loneliness, availability of a support system) and psychological functioning (depression, cognitive abilities), we also urge that instruments be chosen cautiously, based on a knowledge of the content of the instrument and the history of its use. "Readings" on a measure such as a loneliness scale should never be treated as concretely as, for example, readings on blood pressure. In the chapters that follow, we make recommendations about simple measures that seem to come closest to embodying the concepts originally intended.

Purposes of Long-Term-Care Measurements

To examine LTC measures in a somewhat different way, the major function of an instrument should be considered. Table 1-2 separates five functions: description, screening, assessment, monitoring, and prediction. For each, the major uses and characteristics of the desirable instrument are discussed.

Description

Description is a basic function that permits establishment of a body of information about the elderly population along selected parameters. It is important to be able to describe the population as a whole in order to develop normative data and to assess community needs. Additionally, at the level of the individual client, one needs to record the outcomes associated with care and to test hypotheses about the effectiveness of various interventions. For all this descriptive work, a bank of well-validated, reliable measures is required.

Screening

Screening is another function of measurement that is often advocated. By its very definition, screening is not expected to be error free; rather, it should indicate the need for further intensive assessment. Ideally, a screening instrument should be practical and inexpensive; this is especially true if the population

Table 1-2
Characteristics of Measures According to Function and Purpose

Function	Purposes	Characteristics
Description	Depict elderly population along selected parameters. Describe outcomes associated with various intervention forms. Develop normative data. Assess needs. Use as tool in hypothesis testing.	Reliability, face validity, and construct validity.
Screening	Identify from among populations at risk those individuals who should receive further assessment.	Reliable, easily administered, inexpensive measures of variables that have practical significance; minimize false negatives.
Assessment	Diagnosis. Assignment to interventive strategies.	Reliability, face and construct validity. Detailed measures that clearly delineate functioning in small units; practical significance; accuracy (that is, minimizing both false positives and false negatives); sufficient sampling of items measured to minimize error.
Monitoring	Reviewing progress of those receiving treatment. Observing change in untreated condition.	Reliability, face and construct validity. Does not need to be as detailed as assessment tool. Time intervals between monitoring selected on basis of likely change. Consideration of cost, time, and amenability to self-monitoring by patients.
Prediction	Make prognostic statements of expected outcomes on the basis of given conditions. Permit scientifically based clinical interventions. Add strength to case-management decisions.	Reliability of measurement. If a measurement predicts an outcome, it does not need to be tested for validity. Face validity, however, makes prediction more acceptable to users.

at risk is as large as is envisaged in discussions of screening for the elderly. (For example, it is sometimes suggested that all those over age 65 who are recently bereaved should be screened for depression or that all those over age 75 should be periodically screened for their coping ability, a composite measure of functional status balanced against social resources.) A screening instrument can rarely eliminate false positives and false negatives equally well. The relative merits of emphasizing one over the other will depend on the prevalence of the condition, its seriousness, the efficacy of available remedies, and the cost of further evaluation. At the screening level, minimizing false negatives would probably be best if, indeed, a helpful therapeutic or preventive intervention is available to be applied should further assessment indicate the need for services.

Assessment

Assessment involves a more detailed review than does screening and leads directly to diagnostic conclusions and assignment to interventive strategies. The terms *screening* and *assessment* are bandied about in the LTC field, often with no clear distinction between them. It may be that, especially in the psychosocial areas, very few measures are suitable for screening in long-term care but, rather, that periodic assessment is necessary. Certainly, LTC recipients are likely to change suddenly in important particulars. Although screening for some diseases and impairments (hypertension, glaucoma, hearing problems) could occur according to a fixed timetable with little likelihood of change between the intervals of measurement, the same assurance is not possible when screening for the majority of physical, psychological, and social problems. In fact, especially for psychosocial problems, screening might best be performed by examination of some very straightforward risk indicators (for example, recent bereavement as a risk factor for depression or social disruption) with a detailed assessment taking place on the first encounter with the individual at risk.

Assessment has become a keystone of geriatric practice. Each discipline claims its need to make particular assessments on dimensions that concern it most. Psychosocial assessments, mental-status examinations, physical-therapy assessments, occupational-therapy assessments, social-work assessments, and drug-regimen reviews are terms that connote the lack of clarity over whether assessments take their particular definition from the content focus or from the discipline performing the evaluation. There is no disputing that the assessment of the geriatric patient (or, on a community basis, the assessment of needs of the elderly) must be multifaceted and multidisciplinary. Recording formats have been developed for nursing-home records to facilitate an amalgamation of information systematically contributed from different disciplines. The best example of this is the PACE system developed by DHEW for assessment of nursing home patients (U.S. Department of Health, Education, and Welfare [DHEW] 1978a). Although designed as a case-management tool for nursing-home residents, the system does not contain rules for how the assessment team can use the information to develop specific plans based on combinations of observable factors.

Similarly, other multidimensional assessment tools have been developed that, although perhaps not requiring the literal involvement of an interdisciplinary team to collect the information, contain items that reflect functioning across many domains. In these cases, too, the multidimensional assessments may fail to provide a measure of overall functioning that takes into account the several dimensions; or, conversely, they may rely heavily on judgment for creating the overall estimate of functioning. Assessment of need for services must be made on the basis of composite measurements; it may be that an indicator such as physical functioning, although crucially important in itself, bears little direct relationship to the amount of care required from community services or the decision about the locus of such care.

Monitoring

Monitoring involves repeated measurements to assess change in status. Such monitoring may be undertaken as an adjunct to treatment or as an observation technique for noting change over time in a particular condition of an untreated patient. Monitoring of general functional status seldom requires as detailed measurement as does initial assessment because parameters of expected change are specified. Cost and convenience are important factors for consideration; it is an advantage if patients can perform the monitoring themselves. As obvious examples, most patients can weigh themselves or take their own blood pressure. Patients might also be taught to make important regular observations on functional-status dimensions, such as mobility and falls or continence. The development of measures that can readily be used by patients and their families as monitoring devices has not yet received much attention, and perhaps the ability of the elderly to participate in such a role has been underestimated.

Monitoring implies the importance of measuring change; therefore, the intervals between monitoring should be derived by some empirical notions of the rate of expected deterioration or improvement in the condition being monitored. Here we return to the more-basic measurement function: description. Until normal aging under a variety of circumstances is better described, it is rather difficult to know how often to measure or when the rate of change has reached alarming proportions.

Prognosis

The foregoing discussion leads to the last function of measurement, prognosis or prediction. To some extent, all clinical treatment involves prediction. At least informally, the clinician acts on a prediction that a given form of intervention will produce a desirable result. For a measure to be used as a prognosticator, it must be reliable and well designed. Longitudinal studies using these measurements have shown that certain outcomes are consistently associated with scores on the measures. Such studies may describe either the natural course of change in measurable attributes for categories of people or the change in measurable attributes associated with therapeutic intervention. If a measure can be used to predict an outcome, the association implies predictive validity. Nevertheless, if a measurement or a score has face validity (that is, if it makes common sense), practitioners are more willing to use it as a prognostic indicator. In LTC, examples can be given of discriminant analyses that have revealed rather implausible factors that predict outcomes such as likelihood of discharge from nursing homes (Gutkin et al. 1979). As Sherwood and Feldman assert (1970), statistical predictions may complement clinical judgments even if they do not explain reasons for associations. Occasionally the statistical predictors fly in the face of practice wisdom. In such cases, it is especially necessary that the initial findings be reproduced in replication studies.

Except in conditions of extreme limitation of physical functioning (as with comatose patients, for example), predictions in one domain of functioning must take into account the influence of other domains. Although predictive capability in measurement would lend comforting assurance to the work of case managers, the necessary studies of the relationships among aspects of overall functioning that would make detailed predictions feasible have not yet been done. Clinical experience suggests that a promising direction for improving our prognostic technology is to pursue measurement of rates of change in status rather than simply descriptions of a condition at any given point in time.

What to Measure?

As many writers have pointed out, long-term care embraces the spectrum of medico-social-psychological problems of persons aged 65 and over. An enormous number of variables are related to medical and physiological conditions; physical, intellectual, and psychological functioning, as well as social well-being, could conceivably be introduced into the clinician's routine measurement. Such an expansive approach to measurement would have disadvantages, however. It would be expensive and time consuming; it would impose a burden on patients; and, in the face of potential information overlap, might well obscure the distinctions between the important and the trivial.

An analogy to the health care of children serves to illustrate the problem. Clearly, one could collect voluminous information about the functioning of children, over and above information about the particular complaint, symptom, or problem that brought them to medical attention. Much of the information about the functioning of the developing child can be and has been expressed in terms of scores on particular scales. Thus it is possible to measure intelligence, cognitive development along a range of factors, body perceptions, health knowledge, school performance, motor functioning, relationships with peers, relationships with parents and siblings, communicativeness, affective states, and so on. No one has seriously suggested that such an assessment—using standard instruments, scales, and data-collection classification schemes—be used as part of a general pediatric workup. Yet some of the geronotological literature does seem to call for an elaborate list of measurements of elderly patients who come into LTC.

In measuring everything from sexual functioning to memory loss, from ability to do chores to church attendance, the LTC provider faces problems. First, few persons of any age wish to permit detailed and intrusive measures of their performance without perceiving clear relevance to their well-being. Practical and ethical problems are greater if the individuals being assessed are physically frail or intellectually unable to give consent to procedures. Additional practical and ethical problems are created if the measurement necessitates collecting information from persons collateral to the patient. Furthermore, an attempt to develop scales to measure every relevant concept in LTC may impede the refinement of measurement tools. The test of relevance in choosing items to measure is applicable to both the clinician and the researcher, although the latter may cast a somewhat wider net.

Not all observation results in a measurement or score. When information on a particular item is collected systematically along a continuum, a measurement can be said to have occurred. Classification systems that collect information on a range of items can contain a number of separate measurements but do not necessarily combine these measures in a predetermined way to form a score representing a higher level of abstraction. For example, many PSROs have begun collecting information on individual physical functioning (Kane et al. 1979), in some instances modeling their data collection on a classification system developed at Harvard University (Jones, McNitt, and McKnight 1974). Although no composite score is derived, each item of the classification scheme constitutes a measurement that could be tested for reliability and validity. In contrast, scales of functional status have been developed that merge observations on discrete items into an overall scale that is meant to describe physical functioning.

In clinical practice, not all items included in a social history, physical examination, or mental-status examination are incorporated as part of a systematic record; not all items incorporated in a systematic record lend themselves to continuous classification (checklists and individual items are also recorded); and not all classification is combined in a multiple-item scale. Decisions about what to measure also involve decisions about the way information can best be combined. Raising the level of abstraction embodied in a score increases convenience in management of disparate facts but adds risk of oversimplification and error.

In choosing what to measure, clinicians will first be concerned with those characteristics that they deliberately wish to change and, secondarily, with those characteristics that may be altered as a result of LTC. Because patient management requires decisions that often involve great shifts in the life-style of the patient, and because a patient sometimes enters a total institution in the name of LTC, the happiness or subjective well-being of that patient is often included in the array of LTC measures. This is true even though the primary reason for delivering care may be related to other goals, such as increasing life expectancy, minimizing discomfort, or improving the functional status of the patient. In contrast, acute care is perceived as a time-limited intervention that interrupts normal life activities; therefore, although one strives to deliver such care in a humane manner, the measurement of a person's happiness while under care is not a predominant concern. In LTC, the treatment or care interventions may be lifelong, forcing the clinician to ask whether the social and emotional costs of receiving care in the form offered justify the protection or prolongation of life. To develop some information about this disturbing line of thought, measurements of subjective well-being are necessary.

In deciding what should be measured beyond the physiological measures embodied in the laboratory or radiological tests appropriate to the medical problem, the clinician should consider the conditions common to LTC patients. The multiple diagnoses of the elderly patient result in a number of very common problems, which may occur singly or in combination. The most-common problems seen in LTC are immobility and falls, incontinence, and mental confusion. Stroke is an extremely common disorder and may be accompanied by any of the aforementioned sequelae as well as by severe communication difficulties. Hearing and vision defects, also common in old age, combine with social isolation, depression, and loss of social support systems. Physical, psychological, and social deficits are typically interactive so that it is difficult to distinguish what is causative; but it is clear that a spiral of exacerbations occurs. For example, the presenting picture of a mildly confused individual who walks with difficulty, has a hearing loss, is depressed, and lacks social contacts is not easily unraveled to reveal whether the sensory deficits and immobility have caused the confusion and what part the depression and dwindling social contacts play in the situation. This is the prototype of the patient who typically challenges the geriatrician or gerontologist; whatever measurements are taken should be targeted to the multiple disabling conditions of such patients and the limitations that these impose for independent daily life.

One of the greatest perils in geriatrics and gerontology (as well as in other forms of social research) is the great temptation to pick from the nearest branch or to pursue false economies of scale. Perhaps the most common pitfall is the "cafeteria" approach to measurement. The researcher identifies one or more areas or domains he would like to tap and shops through the literature to identify measures whose titles suggest that they cover the appropriate ground. If they come with appropriate psychometric pedigrees indicating high degrees of reliability and validity, they are almost certain to be adopted. Unfortunately, such measures may not always be suitable. They may be designed for a different population or may not measure the aspects of the attribute of interest that are of concern to the project at hand. For example, they may not reflect the aspects most directly targeted for intervention. Any frequenter of the buffet line knows that it is far easier to fill one's plate than to find just the food one really wants to eat.

Another frequent pitfall is the allure of false economy. This is perhaps most dramatically illustrated by efforts to combine classical care needs with those of research or evaluation. Such a marriage is possible only if both parties are prepared to compromise and to live with the consequences. Although there are needs in common and similar domains to be tapped, the specific requirements of clinical data and research data often differ. Clearly, the need for flexibility, the reliance on professional judgments, and the choice of measurement targets will be very different between the two types of activity. A marriage of convenience may well produce unstable offspring.

The remaining chapters contain reviews of instruments in categories of measurement that are important to the LTC provider:

1. *Measures of physical function.* These include the ability to perform tasks of daily living or self-care (bathing, feeding) and the ability to perform more-complex instrumental tasks (shopping, cooking). A measure of physical functioning is perhaps the most important measure required in LTC.

2. *Measures of mental functioning.* These are divided into measures of cognitive or intellectual abilities and measures of mental-health status, particularly affective functioning. This measure is also crucial because it involves the common problems of the LTC patient.

3. *Measures of social functioning.* A variety of terms, such as morale, life satisfaction, happiness, and adjustment, are used to connote subjective well-being; this is a legitimate concern of the long-term-care deliverer because his ministrations tend to be continuous and intrusive. Other social variables that need measuring include the extent and nature of family and social support, activity levels, and participation in satisfying human relationships.

4. *Multidimensional measures.* The distinctions among the preceding three measures are often blurred. At the lower level of functioning, the conceptual lines distinguishing mental abilities, appropriateness of social relationships, and physical abilities are often unclear. Even at higher levels of functioning, motivation rather than capacity may be at the root of some limitation, rendering categorization within a construct rather ambiguous. Many investigators have developed measures that tap several domains of functioning. Some are combined into a single functional-status score, whereas others yield a distinct score on each separate but related dimension of functioning.

Source of Measurements

LTC instruments already have been developed under a variety of auspices and for a range of purposes. Although a number of synthesizing efforts have been made, leading to review papers and even to major funded projects to examine measures, no single source is yet available. Some of the sources of measures in LTC are:

1. *Rehabilitation settings.* Intensive-rehabilitation settings for the elderly and the disabled (including paraplegics and stroke patients) have pioneered in the development of functional-status measures capable of documenting rehabilitation progress. Some of the most-common measures of ability to perform daily living and other functional-status scales are derived from this source.

2. *Geriatric centers and LTC facilities.* A number of geriatric centers have developed very sophisticated research programs directed toward improving treatment of the very frail and debilitated elderly. Typified by the work of researchers at the Hebrew Rehabilitation Center for Aged in Boston and the Philadelphia Geriatric Center, a body of measures has been developed that is particularly appropriate for use with the "old-old" (those aged 75 and over) in institutions. A major advantage of this systematic stream of work is that methodologists have been careful to build on previous research so that, over the years, the instruments have been refined considerably.

3. *Gerontology centers.* These centers have contributed to the development of instruments for the use of researchers and clinicians. In particular, the Older Americans Research and Service Center Instrument (OARS) developed at Duke University (1978), is a model of a much-used, relatively well-tested multidimensional instrument for assessing functional status in the community-dwelling elderly.

4. *Longitudinal or cross-sectional studies.* A number of instruments developed for particular studies have found their way into the LTC literature. Cross-national studies by Shanas and her colleagues (1968), for example, have produced instruments to measure the extent of natural support systems. The ambitious Comprehensive Assessment and Referral Evaluation (CARE) instrument (Gurland et al. 1977) was developed for assessment of functional status with an emphasis on mental-health status in urban populations in New York and London. Early studies of the effects of community care (Bloom and Blenkner 1970) produced creative ways of measuring subjective well-being. Perhaps special studies yield the largest number of instruments, ranging from large-sample surveys such as that used in the Harris poll on aging (1975) to brief measures designed to tap some aspect of life adjustment in a small number of persons in a particular setting. Such instruments vary greatly with respect to the care with which they are constructed. Some have been carefully tested

for reliability and then used repeatedly in longitudinal studies, whereas others have a brief appearance in the literature with very little information supplied about their use.

5. *Quality assurance in LTC.* The need to assess quality and appropriateness of nursing-home care has generated interest in developing standard classification system. Examples are the Patient Appraisal and Care Evaluation (PACE) system (U.S. DHEW 1978a), which was developed as a model for patient-care planning; the LTC Minimum Data Set (U.S. DHEW 1978b), developed by a technical consultant panel of the U.S. National Committee on Vital and Health Statistics; and the classification system for LTC pioneered by Densen and his colleagues at Harvard (Jones, McNitt, and McKnight 1974). Each of these systems includes careful definitions of terms to permit users to classify patients similarly across sites; each involves a series of measurements, generally on ordinal scales rather than composite scores. Some state health departments also developed classification schemes. When PSROs began assuming responsibility for LTC review (stimulated by HCFA demonstration projects of 1976-1978), they also developed assessment forms for use in reviewing nursing-home care. As reviewed recently (Kane et al. 1979), these measurements were shown to have many similarities to each other and yet to be illustrative of the small differences in the way categories are defined that make comparisons across the PSRO data sets almost impossible.

6. *Instrument Bank on Aging.* The University of Missouri-Kansas City was commissioned by the Administration on Aging to compile an instrument bank on aging and to disseminate various measures with their use history and reliability and validity data to prospective users (Peterson, Mangen, and Sanders 1978). As a result of the project, instruments on twenty-four topics and corresponding position papers and critiques will be available in a three-volume compendium on instruments for research in aging (Mangen and Peterson, forthcoming).

7. *Instruments developed for other purposes and applied to LTC.* A large number of instruments developed for the general population can be and have been used to measure the status of the elderly. Some have been borrowed without adaptation or comment, whereas others have undergone some testing for their suitability for use with an elderly population and modification when needed. Included in this category are various health and functional-status indexes developed for the population as a whole and a large number of mental-health measures, including projective tests. Rather commonly, measures developed for use in state mental hospitals have been applied to the geriatric population at large or especially to those living in nursing homes. Although there is some overlap in populations between the group presently served in nursing homes and those formerly served in state mental hospitals before the heyday of deinstitutionalization, the match is far from perfect; many problems

arise in the translation of measures of mental functioning and sociability from a psychiatric to a geriatric population.

Conclusion

Using all the sources indicated previously, we now examine four major areas of measurement (namely, physical functioning, mental functioning, social functioning, and composite measures). Each is treated separately and illustrated with selected examples that highlight problems in making measurements in that particular sphere. In considering the merits of given measures, we refer repeatedly to issues raised in this introductory chapter. Particularly important is the purpose of the measure in terms of the role of the user ("gerontologized" provider, specialist, researcher, or case manager) and the function of the measurement (description, screening, assessment, monitoring, or prediction). We also consider whether a measure is most appropriate as a clinical tool for individual care or for producing information about groups of persons for program-planning purposes, using the ideal criteria developed here for each kind of measurement. Finally, we separate the various components of the measurable construct as developed in each instrument, comparing them to the level of abstraction represented by the score. In the concluding chapter of the book, we return to a general discussion of practical issues associated with measurement in long-term care.

2 Measures of Physical Functioning in Long-Term Care

The intertwining of physical, psychological, and social well-being in the elderly makes independent measurement of physical functioning difficult. Yet such measurements are crucial to geriatric practice. Although authorities agree that a more-global assessment of physical health is needed than that provided by an unweighted list of diagnoses or impairments, there is little consensus about operational guidelines for such assessments. Assertions that an individual's health has improved or worsened or that someone enjoys physical functioning at a higher level than does someone else cannot be made without general assessment tools.

The Rand Corporation recently published a review of measures of physical functioning (Stewart et al. 1978). This work was undertaken to select the most-appropriate measures or composite of items to assess change over time in the physical functioning of a population aged 14 to 65. The investigators describe the difficulties they encountered in distinguishing physical functioning operationally from psychological or social functioning. They note, for example, that an indicator such as restricted-activity days or days in bed could be a reflection of willingness to enter the sick role, and performance of physical tasks could be a reflection of motivation and opportunity as well as of capacity. Self-report of physical symptoms could be a sign of psychological problems such as depression as well as a reflection of actual physical problems.

Problems in achieving conceptual clarity are magnified with an elderly group. Often older persons live in restricted environments where the opportunity to perform tasks included in measures of physical competence is very limited. In some nursing homes, for instance, residents are not permitted to walk alone on the grounds, to use public transportation, or even to take baths by themselves. Under such conditions, the assessment is sometimes based on hypothetical situations: The instrument assesses capability to perform the given task if the opportunity were present. Such a method requires judgments that compromise validity. On the other hand, the more-common rule of considering failure to perform a function for whatever reason as a functional limitation tends to introduce some extraneous content into the assessment of physical abilities and to overestimate disabilities because of sterile or restrictive environments. Items such as "restricted-activity days" are of dubious value when applied to persons whose days contain no demanding routines.

With few exceptions, the instruments used to measure physical functioning of general adult populations are severely limited when applied to elderly persons. For the most part, scales standardized on the general population not only are inadequate to distinguish the healthier from the more-debilitated elderly but also do not discriminate among levels of disability. This is particularly true for persons over 75 and is even more strikingly apparent with reference to institutional settings. Any instrument that depends on counting impairments, diagnoses, or even visits to the doctor will generally assign most persons over age 75 to the lowest scale category.

Our search, in contrast, is for measures of physical functioning particularly applicable to a long-term-care population. In addition to seeking instruments that distinguish groups in the community on the basis of physical health, we also sought instruments that might be used to identify subgroups from among fairly debilitated patients (such as those living in nursing homes).

Operational Components of Physical Health

A global measure of physical health could be derived from many different combinations of items. For convenience we separate these into three categories of measures: those that tap the construct of general physical health or absence of illness; those that measure the ability to perform basic self-care activities, sometimes called *activities of daily living* (ADL); and those that measure, in addition, the ability to perform some of the more-complex activities that are associated with independent life sometimes called *instrumental activities of daily living* (IADL). Table 2-1 lists selected concepts that might be included as part of the more-general construct; in the right-hand column, selected instruments that could be used to measure the more-general construct are listed and referenced. Few measures cover all the items on the left-hand side of the table; moreover, each of those items (for example, bed days or ability to bathe) is subject to varying definitions.

The instruments to be discussed do not fall perfectly into our three subcategories. When an instrument overlapped the categories (for example, included both ADL and IADL items), we allocated it to a category according to our perception of its predominant theme. A few of the instruments cited as examples strayed even further conceptually to include items related to other domains of functioning (for example, mental orientation). If we judged that an instrument primarily concerned physical functioning, we include it in this chapter. Finally, we also include discrete subsections of some multidimensional instruments, particularly the OARS (Duke University 1978) and the PACE II (U.S. DHEW, 1978a) instruments, even though these batteries are included in a later chapter on multidimensional measures.

The three subcategories that we list—general physical health, ADL, and IADL—roughly reflect a hierarchical approach. In a plea for a common concept

Table 2-1
Potential Items for Inclusion in Concept of Physical Health and Physical Functioning of the Long-Term-Care Patient and Selected Instruments for Measuring General Categories of Functional Status

General Category or Concept	Items that Could be Used to Measure the General Concept	Selected Instruments Measuring Concept	Reference
Physical health	Bed days Restricted-activity days Hospitalizations Physician visits Pain and discomfort Symptoms Signs on physical exam Physiological indicators (for example, lab tests, X-rays, pulmonary function, cardiac function) Permanent impairments (for example, vision, hearing, speech, paralysis, amputations, dental status) Diseases/diagnoses Self-ratings of health Physician ratings of health Predicted life expectancy	Cornell Medical Index Health Index Patient Classification Form: Section III: Impairments[a] PACE II: Medical Data Section[a] OARS: Physical Health Section, Questions 37–55[a] Cumulative Illness Rating Scale	Monroe et al. 1965 Rosencranz and Philbad 1970 Jones, McNitt, and McKnight 1974 U.S. DHEW 1978[a] Duke University 1978 Linn, Linn, and Gurel 1968
Activities of daily living	Feeding Bathing Toileting Dressing Ambulation Transfer from bed Transfer from toilet Bowel and bladder control Grooming Communication Visual acuity Upper extremities (for example, grasping objects, picking up objects) Range of motion of limbs	Pulses[b] Index of ADL Kenny Self-Care Evaluation Barthel Index Barthel Self-Care Ratings Range of Motion PACE II: Physical Functioning[a] OARS: Physical ADL[a] Functional Health Status Index for Institutionalized Elderly (ADL-A) Rapid Disability Rating Scale	Moscowitz and McCann 1957 Katz et al. 1963 Schoening et al. 1965 Mahoney and Barthel 1965 (in Sherwood et al. 1977 Granger 1974 U.S. DHEW 1978[a] Duke 1978 Mossey and Tisdale 1979 Linn 1967

Table 2-1 (continued)

General Category or Concept	Items that Could be Used to Measure the General Concept	Selected Instruments Measuring Concept	Reference
Ability to perform instrumental activities of daily living (IADL)	Cooking Cleaning Using telephone Writing Reading Shopping Laundry Managing medications Using public transportation Walking outdoors Climbing stairs Outside work (for example, gardening, snow shoveling) Ability to perform in paid employment Managing money Traveling out of town	Rosow Functional Health Scale PGC Instrumental Activities of Daily Living PGC Instrumental Role Maintenance Scale PACE II: Ability to Carry Out IADLs[a] OARS: Instrumental ADL Questions 56–62[a] Caro Functioning for Independent Living Scale (FIL)[b] PGAP Functional Assessment Instrument	Rosow and Breslau 1966 Lawton 1972a Lawton 1972 U.S. DHEW 1978a Duke University, 1978 Gross-Andrew and Zimmer 1978 Jette and Deniston 1978

[a]A discrete section of a larger multidimensional instrument.

[b]Instrument primarily addresses category indicated but includes some items that refer to other concepts.

of functional capacity in the elderly, Leering (1979) proposed a four-order hierarchy consisting of:

1. Autonomic nervous system (responsible for excretion, production of saliva and intestinal juices, body-temperature regulation, and maintenance of blood pressure).
2. ADL (bathing/washing, dressing, toileting, eating, and continence).
3. Mobility (bed activities, rising and standing, walking or wheelchair management).
4. Household activities (such as cleaning, laundry, shopping, meal preparation, and bedmaking).

Except for raising the issue of whether continence should be considered an ADL function, as is now conventional, or whether it is more appropriately a function of the autonomic nervous system (or, more accurately, of other homeostatic mechanisms), Leering suggests that each level requires a higher order of functioning than the preceding one. A practical problem is created, however, when one comes to measure the performance of the activities inherent in each level; here one must resort to the observation of behavior. Any failure to perform could be interpreted several ways. If an individual does not wash himself, for example, does this automatically signify a lower level of physical or mental functioning, or does it reflect depression, apathy, or plain distaste for soap and water?

Physical Health

As table 2-1 shows, a plethora of indicators can be and have been used for general health status. Conventional wisdom recognizes that physical health is not a unidimensional concept. Commonly used indicators of physical health do not always yield identical results. This is particularly true with ratings of health; self-ratings sometimes differ substantially from physician ratings (Maddox 1962), with individuals often rating themselves more positively than do their physicians (Tissue 1972).

If diagnoses or illnesses cannot be treated additively to indicate relative health status, then how should self-reported diagnostic information be used? About twenty years ago, Shanas (1962) grappled with this issue in interpreting data gathered in a large-scale interview survey of noninstitutionalized elderly persons. In an effort to use "degree of fitness" rather than a pathology-oriented measure, she constructed an Illness Index that took into account the number and severity of self-reported conditions and the degree of associated functional limitations. Shanas's formula was:

Question	*Answer*	*Points*
Illness in past four weeks (mentioned with open-ended question)	Neoplasms, cardiovascular heart disease	2 each
	All others	1 each
Current health problems not mentioned earlier (interviewer read a list of twenty-three problems)[a]	Paralysis, heart trouble	2 each
	All others	1 each
Past history of an illness (not a current problem)	Neoplasms, cardiovascular, heart trouble	1 each
	If in past one to three months	1 each
Time in bed or wheelchair	One to three months	1 each
	Three or more months but not constantly	2 each
	Constantly	3 each

Using this formula, Shanas found scores ranging from 0 to 22. She constructed six index categories based on the scores; an index of 1 or 2 (scores of 0 to 2) for those who were essentially in good health; an index of 3, 4, or 5 (scores of 3 to 8) for those who had diseases and illnesses but were considered to have minimally impaired functioning; and an index of 6 (scores of 9 or more) for those viewed as very sick. Of the sample, 10 percent had an Illness Index of 6; when Shanas added to this group those sampled but not interviewed because they were too sick to participate, she estimated that 14 percent of the non-institutionalized elderly were very sick.

In this early example of a health index, we note that self-perception of health problems would figure highly in the accumulation of a score. In self-reported data, moreover, some subjects telescope a variety of symptoms and discomforts into a single illness, whereas others subdivide the complaints. If the purpose of estimating the health of the population is to determine the expected demand on services, dependence on self-identified health problems may be appropriate. Those who perceive themselves as having a lot of health problems will be likely to seek out more care. Other strategies employ a mix of self-reported problems and structured care-giver observations (including laboratory tests) to gauge the fitness of an elderly population.

Lawton, Ward, and Yaffee (1967) present an articulate discussion of the

---

[a]The list includes hearing trouble, eye trouble, cough, diarrhea, constipation, dizziness, headaches, shortness of breath, asthma, weight loss for no reason, arthritis or rheumatism, diabetes, stomach trouble, gall bladder, heart trouble, high blood pressure, kidney trouble, paralysis, piles, sinus trouble, varicose viens, female trouble, prostate trouble.

advantages and disadvantages of the various items that could be used to indicate health status. A summary of their major points includes:

1. Diagnoses alone present an inadequate index of health because the range of severity within a diagnosis is often greater than that among diagnoses.
2. Number of hospital days is too gross an indicator to tap the health of the general aged public.
3. Treatment by a physician can reflect ability to pay, accessibility of services, and emotional states as well as physical health.
4. Self-ratings of health are subject to distortion by psychological mechanisms such as denial or hypochrondriasis.
5. Laboratory and physiological measures require interpretation within the context of other information and, compared to other indexes, tend to be removed from functional ability.
6. Pain and discomfort is an important dimension that has not received enough attention from those measuring the health status of the elderly.
7. Information on physical functioning can be derived from physicians (or other health-care providers), from patients, or from medical records; at present, there is some merit in considering information from all three sources.
8. An inverse relationship presently exists between the objectivity of a health measurement and its comprehensiveness as an indicator of functional ability. For example, an objective and reliable laboratory test may have almost perfect validity as an indicator of a diagnosis but poor validity as an indicator of functional level. Because functional level may be better predicted by a composite of items including diagnosis, self-ratings of health, physician ratings of health, and fulfillment of personal and social roles, more opportunity for error is introduced into the comprehensive measure.

Lawton's observations of a decade ago are still pertinent today. An update might note that, stimulated by the hospice movement and the development of palliative-care units, much recent attention has been given to the measurement of the nature of pain, as perceived by the sufferer. The McGill Pain Questionnaire (Melzack 1975) provides a good example of such a technique. For the most part, however, these instruments have been developed as tools for the management of pain in cancer patients. Whether they can usefully be translated to the measurement of differences in pain and discomfort in a geriatric population that suffers from a wide range of painful and uncomfortable conditions remains undemonstrated.

Asking the person most concerned seems an intuitively satisfying way of finding out about physical health. Unfortunately, the answers to the simple question "how would you rate your health" are difficult to interpret. Consumers may mean something different than providers do when they speak of being in good health. Subgroups may behave differently in self-ratings. For example, very old people tend to rate their health more positively than do those in the immediate postretirement decade. Does this mean that the older one gets, the more one exaggerates one's good health? Or are those who survive into very old age "biologically elite"? Are self-reports to be trusted?

A recent study (Linn and Linn 1980) suggests that self-reports correspond to objective health indicators. Almost 300 people were asked to rate their health on a five-point scale from excellent to poor; then these ratings were compared to the number of physican visits, number of days in bed, number of days in the hospital, number of surgical operations, number of medications, number of diagnoses, total disability, and total impairment. (Total disability and total impairment were measured by scores on scales that are discussed later in this chapter.) All but days in bed and number of surgical operations were correlated with self-assessed health. Age itself was not an important variable, although those 65 to 74 years old tended to use more medications, whereas the older group tended to have more operations. These findings are compatible with Ferraro's analysis of the relationship between self-reported health and objective health in 3,000 low-income respondents (Ferraro 1980). Apparently, the self-assessments of the elderly provide a good clue to their overall physical health. Nevertheless, a global self-report is a crude screening device at best and would need to be followed by a more-specific approach.

Physician predictions of life expectancy, another item proposed to measure general health, may be subject to some systematic error in addition to the limitations imposed by the predictive power of medical science. In multiple-physician ratings of the likelihood of death for fifty-one patients (Kastenbaum 1965), no physician predicted any deaths in the next twelve months. This was true even though available statistics showed that 26 percent of patients admitted to the institution under study died within a year of their admission.

Given the vulnerability of each set of items to charges of invalidity as measures of functional status, the temptation is to fall back on the systematic history and physical examination as a way of periodically measuring the physical health of the elderly. Undoubtedly measurement is no substitute for clinical diagnosis. Brocklehurst and his colleagues (1978) screened 100 applicants for admission to old-age homes; each subject received (at a minimum) a history, a physical examination, urine tests, a chest X-ray, hemoglobin, serum iron, vitamin B-12, folate, urea, electrolytes, a biochemical profile, and a short mental-status test. Based on these tests, admission to an old-age home was deemed inappropriate in one-third of the cases. Half of the inappropriate group (16 percent) were considered more suitable for remaining at home or in sheltered housing, and the other 16 percent were advised to enter the hospital for active investigation and treatment of a problem. Presumably some of this latter group would enter old-age accommodations at a later time, whereas others would return home. Even more significantly, 137 previously unrecorded treatable physical disorders were identified in these 100 patients. The findings led the investigators to suggest that the occasion of a proposed dramatic life change, such as admission to an old-age home, might be an appropriate time for medical screening.

Certainly the physical history and examination can be made more systematic. In a series of Edinburgh studies, Milne and his colleagues (1972) determined that nonphysicians can make accurate and reliable determinations of physical- and mental-health parameters using a questionnaire and a few simple examination procedures. The entire process was estimated to take about twenty-five minutes. The physical-health questions were keyed to conditions prevalent among the elderly, with the wording of questions carefully designed to minimize confusion and to be compatible with colloquial patterns of speech (for example, "Have you ever had pain in your joints?" proved better than a direct question about rheumatism or arthritis because those terms are used loosely to refer to many aches and pains). The questionnaire was constructed to include screening questions that have had good sensivitity and specificity in pinpointing various disease states. The physical examination included blood pressure, height and weight, triceps skinfold thickness, peak expiratory flow rate, handgrip, and examination of joints.

Currie field tested a simple checklist approach to health screening for the elderly (Currie et al. 1974). The health visitor or nurse applied this technique to 259 elderly persons in their homes. They discovered 790 diseases or disabilities (an average of 3.5 per patient), of which about 20 percent were previously unknown to the geriatricians. Very little physical or psychological disease was missed in this screening, as shown by physician verification later.

Despite the impressive evidence that a thorough physical and physiological workup can identify treatable problems among the elderly, the need for measures of general physical health and functioning remains. First, some general indicators are necessary for application on a community-wide basis because intensive physicals and batteries of tests are impractical. More importantly, although intensive physical assessments identify pathology and suggest corresponding treatment recommendations, including hospitalizations, they do not provide all the information about physical functioning that medical advisors need. Recommendations for the least-restrictive living environment compatible with an individual's health needs required a judgment of the limitations imposed by the constellation of medical problems and disabilities. To make such determinations as free as possible from arbitrary and idiosyncratic judgments, the struggle to develop measurements of physical functioning continues.

Table 2-2 considers selected measurements of physical health with particular reference to the items included in the instrument, the type of scaling, and the administration of the test, as well as information on reliability and validity insofar as these were available in published material. The instruments (presented chronologically) represented different approaches to the problems of assessing physical functioning.

Table 2-2
Characteristics of Selected Measures of Physical Health

Name of Measure (Reference)	Items Included	Type of Scale	Administration	Reliability	Validity
Cornell Medical Index (Brodman et al. 1951)	195 items in 12 categories of physical health and 51 items in 6 categories of mental health.	Yes–no answers; each answer reflecting a health symptom, problem, or concern gets a points. In community-based sample of elders, mean score of 16.2 for men and 22.2 for women.	Self-completed by subjects. Takes about 20 minutes.		
Cumulative Illness Rating Scale (Linn, Linn, and Gurel 1968)	13 organ systems: heart, vascular; respiratory; EENT; upper GI; lower GI; hepatic; renal; other GU; musculoskeletal; neurologic; psychiatric; endocrine-metabolic.	Each organ system scored on 5-point scale for severity of impairment (none to extremely severe); sub-scores are derived for impairment on 5 systems—for example, cardiovascular or gastrointestinal.	Physician ratings with brief instructions.	Interrater reliability ranges from .91 to .83 on various sets of ratings.	Review of 472 health histories showed that cumulative-impairment scores predict death better than chronological age.
Health Index (Rosencranz and Pihlblad 1970)	40 common ailments listed and subject asked about duration of problem; also asked about illnesses that have confined them to bed, to house, or to hospital in past month.	4 points for each major illness and 4 more for each that confined patient in past month; 2 points for each minor illness and 2 for confining patient; added points for severity and duration of confinement.	Administered to subject by interviewer.		5 classes developed on basis of scores; these correlate well with self-perceptions of health and functional-status indicators.

Table 2-2 (continued)

Name of Measure (Reference)	Items Included	Type of Scale	Administration	Reliability	Validity
PACE II: Medical Data (U.S. DHEW 1978a)	Checklist of 22 diagnostic categories and medical-status measures including height, weight, blood pressure, pulse, respiration, 4 blood tests, 3 urine tests, stool test.	No score derived.	Review of history; conduct of physical examination and tests.		
Patient Classification for LTC: Impairments and Medical Status (Jones, McNitt, and McKnight 1974)	Impairments = sight, hearing, speech, fractures, joint motion, missing limbs, paralysis and dentation; risk factors = height, weight, blood pressure, BUN, blood cholesterol, albuminurea, and smoking; 14 medically defined conditions listed.	3-point classification for impairments with checklist for ways of compensating; all others checklist; no score derived.	Physician or nurse giving care completes items.		
OARS: Physical Health (Duke University 1978)	Doctor visits, sick days, hospital days, nursing-home days; 18 categories of medications; 26 illnesses; disabilities; vision; hearing; prostheses used; drinking; exercise; self-ratings of health.	Some Likert scales; medications, illnesses and prostheses on checklists; overall physical health scored as 1–6, ranging from excellent physical health to totally physically impaired.	Interview with subject.	See Chapter 5	

Cornell Medical Index

Because it is one of the oldest instruments for the assessment of general health, the Cornell Medical Index (CMI) (Monroe et al. 1965) has been included as a frame of reference. It also exemplifies a questionnaire strategy.

The index consists of 195 questions—twelve sections of 144 questions concerning body symptoms and six sections of 51 questions concerning moods, feelings, and mental symptoms. It can be completed by an elderly person in approximately twenty minutes; each question requires only a yes or no answer.

When the index was administered to a volunteer group of 520 persons over age 65, the investigators found that: (1) the respondents within this elderly sample did not show more health problems with advancing age; (2) controlling for age within the sample, women reported more health problems than men; and (3) the self-report of problems rose with educational levels.

At best the Cornell Medical Index scores reflect feelings about health, rather than health itself. Items require interpretation (for example, the definition of a severe headache). A number of items in the Cornell Medical Index query the subjects about illnesses or symptoms in their family; the higher scores of women have been interpreted as reflective of nurturant roles and the likelihood that women will be more aware of family medical history. The inclusion of items on family history, however, suggests that the health score of the individual will be confounded by items that really reflect risk factors rather than health status.

It is not clear precisely how age might affect performance on an instrument such as the Cornell Medical Index. Clinicians indicate that elderly persons sometimes understate their symptomatology because of a belief that certain problems are a natural part of old age rather than health problems (Anderson 1974). Memory losses might also lead to inaccuracies and understatements of general health problems. Finally, it is possible that elderly persons in the community might fear disclosing the degree of their health problems on a general checklist because of the danger that some disruptive social recommendation might follow. On the other hand, because of the accumulation of illnesses, symptoms, and problems over a lifetime, older persons can earn higher scores than their present health would warrant.

Cumulative Illness Rating Score

In contrast to the Cornell Medical Index, the Cumulative Illness Rating Score (Linn, Linn, and Gurel 1968) is a clinical approach to a measure of overall health of the elderly. Its developers perceived a need for some way to summarize the physician's diagnostic and prognostic judgments on the severity of illnesses. They therefore designed an approach based on the degree of impairment for each of thirteen organ systems. For example, upper-gastrointestinal

(GI) impairment is rated on a five-point scale from none (0) to extremely severe (4); if an individual has more than one upper-GI diagnosis (perhaps a stomach and a pancreatic disease), the rater is instructed to base the score on the total impairment to that organ group. Some diseases (such as metastatic cancer) may be rated on more than one organ system. Some specific definitions are provided with which raters needed to be familiar; for example, *hernia* is identified as a disorder of the lower gastrointestinal tract.

The Cumulative Illness Rating Scale can be performed either against the history of the patient to produce a measure of the amount of lifetime bodily impairment or, more usefully, as a measure of current severity of impairment. In any event, a score is derived for each of thirteen organ systems and for overall pathology.

Linn, Linn, and Gurel (1968) report that inter-rater reliability was high, despite the obvious role that judgment plays in the ratings. Further, they claim that retrospective application of the scale to case records showed that scale scores were correlated with survival. They argue with some merit that such a scale would be a much better predictor of life expectancy than chronological age itself.

We are somewhat skeptical about the reliability of this scale when applied away from the particular Veterans Administration setting in which it was developed. In any event, it can be used only when a very detailed information base is available on each patient, thus limiting its utility to hospital and equivalent settings.

Health Index

The Rosencranz Health Index objectifies the information sought, thereby avoiding some of the ambiguities of self-report embodied in the Cornell Medical Index. For each of forty common ailments, subjects are asked whether they have suffered from any of them and, if so, to what extent the ailment was responsible for confining them to bed, house, or hospital during the past month. The score is weighted to take into account both the existence of ailments and the extent of intrusion of those problems into the respondents' daily lives. The score is further weighted to give more points to major illnesses (defined as heart trouble, high blood pressure, hardening of the arteries, stoke, tumor, cancer, and paralysis) than to minor ailments (including, among others, arthritis, sinus trouble, uncorrectable visual defects, hearing problems, back trouble, and gall-bladder complaints).

In testing this instrument with 1,700 elderly respondents, Rosencranz and Pihlblad (1970) found scores ranging from 0 to 45.5 (the latter for an individual with seventeen conditions who had been in the hospital for the entire month prior to the interview). Empirically, five classifications were developed, based on the scores:

Class I: 0 for none of the ailments.

Class II: 0.5-2 typically for those mentioning one minor ailment but having no health problem in the last month.

Class III: 2.5-14, typified by those with two or more medical conditions and perhaps a short-term illness in the last month.

Class IV: 14.5-21, typified by those with two or more serious ailments and definite illnesses during the last month.

Class V: 21.5 and above, usually signifying some period of hospital confinement as well as serious illness.

About 10 percent of the sample fell in Class I, and 25 percent of the males and 20 percent of the females scored in either Class I or II, signifying good health. Slightly more than half of both sexes fell into Class III, the average-health classification.

This index may prove a promising tool for assessing the general health and the need for medical care of a population of elderly persons at home. It is easy to administer, the questions are clear and linked to a definite time window, and the authors suggest that the scores correlate well with other indicators such as self-report of general health and measures of functional status. We have not identified any further reports of the use of this instrument in the published literature.

PACE II and Patient Classification Form (PCF) for LTC

PACE II (U.S. DHEW 1978a) and the Patient Classification Form (PCF) (Jones, McNitt, and McKnight 1974) from which it is derived provide comprehensive tools for considering the physical health of nursing-home patients. Both classification systems lean heavily on checklists to identify the presence of diagnostically defined conditions, abnormal laboratory or other test results, risk factors, or impairments. The PCF permits a three-category classification for impairments that differentiates between complete and partial impairment (for example, vision is categorized as "no impairment," "legally blind," or "impaired"). A second-level checklist is provided for noting the comparable means used by those in the partially impaired category (for example, "glasses," "contact lenses," "large print," "other"). Similarly, under each medically defined condition, the rater indicates something further about the duration of the problem and, when appropriate, more about the type or location.

Both PACE and PCF are patient-planning tools rather than instruments that yield a score. The value of the information that they record depends on the thoroughness with which the observations are made. Completing the appropriate sections of these forms on medical conditions and impairments requires a review of the history and test results and the performance of a physical examination. To the extent that these classification systems provide organizing tools to ensure that information is collected, they are useful for the geriatric provider or equivalent in institutional settings.

OARS: Physical Health

The OARS instrument (Duke University 1978) contains a relatively comprehensive section on physical health, which includes items on doctor visits, sick days, hospital days, nursing-home days, presence of an alcohol problem, and participation in vigorous exercise. Checklists are provided for eighteen categories of medication use, twenty-six illnesses, three impairments, and use of ten prosthetic devices. Likert scales are used to rate overall health, relationship of present to past health, and the degree to which health problems stand in the way of desired activities.

After collecting all the information that is part of the OARS questionnaire, the interviewer scores the respondent from 1 to 6 on a global rating of physical health; descriptive anchors are provided for each rating. The OARS instrument is discussed in considerable detail in a later chapter; here we note only that it is perhaps the most widely tested method of getting a comprehensive measure of physical health for a community sample without using actual physical examinations and physiological tests as part of the data base.

Activities of Daily Living (ADL) or Physical Functioning

As already stated, general-health measures have limited value in indicating the degree of independence an individual can attain despite diseases or impairments. Gerontologists, geriatricians, and rehabilitative specialists have therefore had considerable interest in developing measures that tap practical dimensions. Table 2-3 lists a selection of the resulting instruments. Some included on this table deal solely with basic self-care or ADL activities; some deal solely with mobility; others combine both elements into a physical-functioning measure.

Substantial consensus can be reached about the items that indicate ADL activities; almost all scales include some combination of dressing, bathing, toileting, transfer, and feeding. Although a question has been raised about whether continence should legitimately be considered an ADL rather than a physiological function (Leering 1979), most scales also include continence. Sometimes continence is further divided into separate items for bowel and bladder control. Mobility is often added to ADL instruments. Those instruments developed in rehabilitative settings tend to include alternative items

Table 2-3
Characteristics of Selected Measures of Ability to Perform Activities of Daily Living or Physical Functioning

Name of Measure (Reference)	Items Included	Type of Scale	Administration	Reliability	Validity
PULSES (Moscowitz and McCann 1957, as referenced by Granger et al. 1975)	*Physical conditions; Upper limbs (self-care); Lower limb (mobility); Sensory components; Excretory functions; Social problems.*	Each item on 4-point Likert Scale from independent to dependent; score ranges from 6/6 for intact to 6/24 for complete dependence.			Correlates with Barthel and patient outcomes (Granger and Greer 1976).
Index of ADL (Katz et al. 1963)	Bathing; dressing; going to toilet; transfer; continence; feeding. Order of items reflects natural progression in loss and regaining of function.	Dichotomous rating of independence or dependence on each item; forms 6-level Guttman scale.	Professional raters using detailed anchoring statements.	Simultaneous observations; differences in less than 1 of 20 evaluations.	Correlated with mobility and house confinement after discharge.
Kenny Self-Care Evaluation (Schoening et al. 1965	17 activities in 6 categories: bed activities; transfers; locomotion; personal hygiene; dressing; feeding.	Each activity rated on 4-point scale: 0 = complete dependence, 4 = complete independence. An average score is created for each category, making total score = 24. Bottom and top points of scale precise with an expanded middle interval that patients pass through quickly.	Ratings by rehabilitation staff. Score constructed on basis of observations of how many of the substeps on each task the patient can perform.	Figures not quoted but subtasks and decision rules are precise so that reliability is encouraged.	Face and content validity; using scale, one can plot learning curves that predict total rehabilitation time and suggest when to discharge (Schoening and Iversen 1968).
Barthel Index (Mahoney and Barthel 1965)	Feeding; moving to bed; grooming; toileting; bathing; walking (propelling wheelchair; stair climbing; bladder control; bowel control.	Partial scores for performing with help, full score for independent performance; items weighted; full score of 100 signifies ability to do all tasks independently.	Rehabilitation-center staff perform ratings.		Scores and changes in scores correlate with clinical judgment; low scores predict mortality (Wylie 1967).

	Description	Scoring	Rater	Reliability/Validity
Rapid Disability Rating Scale (Linn 1967)	16 items: eating, diet, medication, speech, hearing, sight, walking, bathing, dressing, incontinence, shaving, safety supervision, confined to bed, mentally confused, uncooperative, depression.	Each item has value of 1, 2, or 3, with 3 indicating the greatest severity or occurrence. Scores range from 16 to 48.	Medically oriented raters (such as nurses) rate on first-hand information about patient. Instructed not to use record. Takes 2-3 minutes.	Scores correlated with physician's prognoses, number of previous hospitalization, length of stay, and 6-month mortality.
Barthel Self-Care Ratings (as adapted by Sherwood et al. 1977)	Drink from cup; feed from dish; dress upper body; dress lower body; don brace or prosthesis; groom self; wash or bathe; bladder continence; bowel continence; care of perineum/clothing at toilet; transfer chair; transfer toilet; transfer tub/shower; walk 50 yards; stairs; wheelchair; walk outside.	Each item on 4-point scale; Likert scale of intact, limited, helper, and null.	Ratings of staff; detailed descriptions for anchoring.	Sherwood et al. 1977 report alpha reliabilities of .95 for 3 separate samples of rehabilitation patients.
Range of Motion (Granger 1974)	32 items dealing with specific motions of the shoulders, elbows, wrists, fingers, thumbs, hips, knees and ankles.	Each item classified as: performs against resistance; performs not against resistance; passive motion only; combination of active and passive motion.	Patient demonstrates and staff rates.	
PACE II: Physical Function (U.S. DHEW 1978a)	ADL section includes: goes outside; walking; climbing stairs; transferring; wheeling; bathes/showers; toileting; dressing; grooming; eating; range of motion on 17 items including left and right digits, wrist, elbow, shoulder, ankle, knee, and hip, head and trunk; 8 items on strength, balance and coordination (such as grasping, rolling).	ADL items classified as: mechanical aid; human help; does not perform. Rehabilitation potential for each item also classified. No overall score derived. Range of motion requires checklist for motion subject cannot perform; strength, balance and coordination items have yes/no subparts.	Rated by nurse examiner; ADLs rated on basis of usual performance in last 2 weeks; other items rated by asking patient to perform task.	Inter-rater reliability and test-retest reliability are very high.

Table 2-3 (continued)

Name of Measure (Reference)	Items Included	Type of Scale	Administration	Reliability	Validity
OARS: Physical ADL (Duke University 1978)	Eating; dressing; grooming; walking; getting in and out of bed; bathing/showering; getting to bathroom on time; continence.	Each item rated on 3-point scale for ability to perform independently; a global ADL/IADL score (range: 1-6 assigned, or from excellent to completely impaired.	Interview with respondent.	See chapter 5	
Functional Health Status of the Institutionalized Elderly (ADL-A) (Mossey and Tisdale 1979)	Getting out of bed; eating; drinking; walking; bathing; dressing; toilet use.	Each of 7 items on 4-point scale, from 0 = never needs help to 3 = always needs help; analysis of total scores + ability to eat and drink independently produced 9 categories that more specifically reveal patterns of dependency.	Investigators constructed index from secondary data from the Survey of Institutionalized Persons. Nursing-home personnel completed original instrument for sample.	Cannot assess interrater reliability. Coefficient of reproduceability = .958; high internal consistency of items; coefficient alpha = .94.	Correlates with independent criteria from same study—for example, bed confinement, ability to walk, blindness, and items suggesting admission for social reasons.

dealing with mobility in a wheelchair. Sometimes these wheelchair-related items are quite detailed.

Scores on ADL usually are based on the degree of independence attained for each function. The individual who needs a corrective device to perform the function or who requires the help of another person is assigned an intermediate position between independence and dependence. Sometimes these two forms of dependency are equated and receive the same score; more often, however, the ability to perform with a device is rated as a higher level of independence than the ability to perform with human help. This decision rule seems sound (has face validity) because people dependent on a device have more control over their own lives than those dependent on another person. Indeed, therapeutic progress may be achieved by equipping patients with mechanical devices that substitute for human help.

Definitions of independent functioning on a given item are important. To return to the example of bathing, independence might be defined as the ability to lather and rinse the whole body, including the back and all extremities. Few persons of any age can reach their backs without the help of a long scrub brush, and the elderly will have reduced skills. An overly rigid definition of ability for independent functioning in bathing would defeat the purpose. Similarly, caregivers must guard against rating the ability to dress independently by applying stringent criteria for neatness and grooming. Timing may also be a part of the definition. Some of the scales provide no time frame for the completion of the activity, whereas others rate the performance as less than fully independent if its completion is inordinately slow.

Data for ADL scales are most commonly collected by direct observation. Sometimes the rating is performed on the basis of immediate observations and sometimes on the basis of performance during a designated time window prior to completion of the instrument. If the latter decision is used, clear instructions should be given about whether the rating should be made on the basis of average performance over the time period or that of best performance. Certainly an "average" is difficult to reach when performance fluctuates; therefore, "best performance" may have more precision. Using a retrospective time frame creates the problem of dependence on the memory and judgment of the rater, but using a here-and-now evaluation may produce a result that is not a valid reflection of performance apart from the test situation.

Another decision rule that must be incorporated into the instrument is a procedure for identifying activities that are inapplicable for a particular person. One strategy is to consider all items applicable and to rate the subject as dependent if he does not perform an activity, even if the reason reflects lack of motivation or opportunity rather than lack of capacity. Some instruments designed for use in nursing homes, such as PACE II, deal with this constraint on the test by allowing "against nursing-home policy" as a response for various ADL measures. The classic case in point is bathing; in many institutional settings, unsupervised baths are forbidden. Speculation about abilities is likely to be inaccurate under these circumstances.

If an elderly person lacks opportunity for an activity, how should this information be used in a total ADL scale? It is no more reasonable to assume an inability than to assume an ability. One strategy is to ask the patient to demonstrate the skill. In addition to the practical difficulties in demonstrating a skill such as bathing, a dilemma is posed when artificial tests are used to compose scores. The person who is not permitted to venture outside or who is too depressed to do so is functionally homebound. We resolve this problem by emphasizing the purpose of the measurement. Tests that are used to make placement decisions must measure demonstrable capacity to perform; otherwise we create a catch-22 for nursing-home patients seeking discharge. On the other hand, if the test is used to assess quality of care in an institution, then the lack of an opportunity to use the functional ability is equivalent to dysfunction. In any case, judgments about hypothetical abilities must be suspect.

An infinite amount of detail could conceivably be incorporated into ADL measures. For example, some practitioners indicate that mere division into those dependent on devices for ambulation does not separate the person who uses a cane occasionally on rugged terrain from the person who is entirely dependent on a walker or wheelchair. Similarly, indication that a subject requires personal help to transfer does not distinguish a need for one person's arm from the need to be carried by two strong people. The possible variation applies not only to refinements of scaling but also to refinements of items; feeding, for example, could further be broken down into drinking and eating; each of those, in turn, could be broken down into further subtasks, each of which could be scaled separately. The amount of actual detail required depends on the setting in which the measurement is being taken and the importance of the distinctions that more refinements of scaling or of items permit.

This discussion is best illustrated by a brief discussion of some of the measures on table 2-3. (Again, the scales are not listed in any particular order of importance).

PULSES Profile

An early measure developed by Moskowitz and McCann (1957) and later modified by Granger (Sherwood et al. 1977), the PULSES profile actually taps a wider dimension than physical functioning. The "P" in the acronym refers to a rating of physical condition based on the need for medical or nursing monitoring; the second "S" refers to a rating of social factors, including emotional and intellectual adaptability, social support from family, and financial ability. The other dimensions to complete the acronym are *U*pper limbs (self-care abilities), *L*ower limbs (ambulation), and *S*ensory abilities.

No information was available to us about the reliability of the measure; an inspection of the items, however, suggests that a number of concepts are embedded in single items. This, in turn, might affect reliability adversely. For example, the first "S" refers to sensory components, particularly speech, vision, and hearing. Granger and his colleagues have shown that the modified PULSES profile correlates with the Barthel Index and other outcomes when used with stroke patients (Granger and Greer 1976; Granger et al. 1975); however, these reports do not suggest that the PULSES profile adds very much to distinguish it from the Barthel Index itself.

Katz Index of ADL

The Katz Index of ADL is one of the best-known and most carefully studied ADL tests. The measure calls for a dichtomous rating of six ADL functions (in order of decreasing dependency): bathing, dressing, going to the toilet, transfer, continence, and feeding. One point is given for each item of dependency. In the order given, these items form a Guttman scale, meaning that the score indicates the exact pattern of responses (Katz et al. 1963). In various studies, Katz and his colleagues have shown that there is a natural progression in both the loss of ADL capacities and the return of these abilities upon recovery or rehabilitation.

Although the eventual rating is dichotomous, the form on which observations are made allows a differentiation of those able to perform the activity with human help. For the purpose of the score, however, only those who can perform it without human help are rated as independent; the worksheet with its extra categories serves to remind the rater of how the final determination is made. (See table 2-4 for the actual Katz scale and accompanying worksheet.) Staff of the Hebrew Rehabilitation Center for Aged report in unpublished data (Sherwood et al. 1977) that the Guttman scale is highly reproducible with coefficients of reproducibility of .948 for patients in the Worcester Home Care Study and .976 for the Fall River Sheltered Housing sample. The coefficients become even better when the item on continence is dropped.

Although originally reported as a Guttman scale based on six dichotomous items, the concept of the Katz ADL scale has also been adapted in a different way. The basic idea appears in other contexts as a Likert-type scale with each item assigned points according to a defined decision rule (for example, 0 = no help needed; 1 = uses a device; 2 = needs human assistance; 3 = completely dependent). The sum of all the items is then used to describe ADL activities.

Barthel Index and Barthel Self-Care Ratings

Another well-established instrument for measuring functional status, the Barthel Index (Mahoney and Barthel 1965) provides a score based on ratings of the

Table 2-4
Katz Index of ADL

Index of Independence in
Activities of Daily Living

The Index of Independence in Activities of Daily Living is based on an evaluation of the functional independence or dependence of patients in bathing, dressing, going to the toilet, transferring, continence, and feeding. Specific definitions of functional independence and dependence appear below the index.

A   Independent in feeding, continence, transferring, going to toilet, dressing, and bathing.
B   Independent in all but one of these functions.
C   Independent in all but bathing and one additional function.
D   Independent in all but bathing, dressing, and one additional function.
E   Independent in all but bathing, dressing, going to toilet, and one additional function.
F   Independent in all but bathing, dressing, going to toilet, transferring, and one additional function.
G   Dependent in all six functions.
Other   Dependent in at least two functions, but not classifiable as C, D, E, or F.

Independence means without supervision, direction, or active personal assistance, except as specifically noted below. This is based on actual status and not on ability. A patient who refuses to perform a function is considered as not performing the function, even though he is deemed able.

BATHING (Sponge, shower or Tub)
Independent: assistance only in bathing a
 single part (as back or disabled extremity)
 or bathes self completely
Dependent: assistance in bathing more than
 one part of body; assistance in getting in
 or out of tub or does not bathe self

DRESSING
Independent: gets clothes from closets and
 drawers; puts on clothes, outer garments,
 braces; manages fasteners; act of tying
 shoes is excluded
Dependent: does not dress self or remains
 partly undressed

GOING TO TOILET
Independent: gets to toilet; gets on and off
 toilet; arranges clothes, cleans organs of
 excretion; (may manage own bedpan used
 at night only and may or may not be using
 mechanical supports)
Dependent: uses bedpan or commode or
 receives assistance in getting to and using
 toilet

TRANSFER
Independent: moves in and out of bed
 independently and moves in and out
 of chair independently (may or may
 not be using mechanical supports)
Dependent: assistance in moving in or
 out of bed and/or chair; does not perform one or more transfers

CONTINENCE
Independent: urination and defecation
 entirely self-controlled
Dependent: partial or total incontinence
 in urination or defecation partial or
 total control by enemas, catheters, or
 regulated use of urinals and/or bedpans

FEEDING
Independent: gets food from plate or its
 equivalent into mouth; (precutting of
 meat and preparation of food, as
 buttering bread, are excluded from
 evaluation).
Dependent: assistance in act of feeding
 (see above); does not eat at all or
 parenteral feeding.

Source: S.Katz, A.B. Ford, R.W. Moskowitz, B.A. Jackson, and M.W. Jaffee, "Studies of Illness in the Aged. The Index of ADL: A Standardized Measure of Biological and Psycho-social Function," *Journal of the American Medical Association* 185 (1963):94 ff.

Table 2-4 (continued)

Evaluation Form

Name ——————————— Date of Evaluation —————

For each area of functioning listed below, check description that applies. (The word *assistance* means supervision, direction of personal assistance.)

BATHING—either sponge bath, tub bath, or shower

☐ | ☐ | ☐

Receives no assistance (gets in and out of tub by self if tub is usual means of bathing)	Receives assistance in bathing only one part of body (such as back or a leg)	Receives assistance in bathing more than one part of body (or not bathed)

DRESSING—gets clothes from closets and drawers—including underclothes, outer garments and using fasteners (including braces, if worn)

☐ | ☐ | ☐

Gets clothes and gets completely dressed without assistance	Gets clothes and gets dressed without assistance except for assistance in tying shoes	Receives assistance in getting clothes or in getting dressed, or stays partly or completely undressed

TOILETING—going to the "toilet room" for bowel and urine elimination; cleaning self after elimination and arranging clothes

☐ | ☐ | ☐

Goes to "toilet room," cleans self, and arranges clothes without assistance (may use object for support such as cane, walker, or wheelchair and may manage night bedpan or commode, emptying same in morning)	Receives assistance in going to "toilet room" or in cleansing self or in arranging clothes after elimination or in use of night bedpan or commode	Doesn't go to room termed "toilet" for the elimination process

TRANSFER—

☐ | ☐ | ☐

Moves in and out of bed as well as in and out of chair without assistance (may be using object for support such as cane or walker)	Moves in or out of bed or chair with assistance	Doesn't get out of bed.

CONTINENCE—

☐ | ☐ | ☐

Controls urination and bowel movement completely by self	Has occasional "accidents"	Supervision helps keep urine or bowel control; catheter is used or is incontinent

FEEDING—

☐ | ☐ | ☐

Feeds self without assistance	Feeds self except for getting assistance in cutting meat or buttering bread	Receives assistance in feeding or is fed partly or completely by using tubes or intravenous fluids

ability to feed onself, groom oneself, bathe, go to the toilet, walk (or propel a wheelchair), climb stairs, control bladder, and control bowels (see table 2-5). On each item the individual is given points for being able to perform it independently and fewer points for performance with help. The score values are weighted and may be 15, 10, 5, or 0. For example, 10 points are given for independent feeding and 5 points for requiring help (including cutting of food), whereas 15 points are given for independent ambulation and 10 for ambulation with help. On two items (bathing and going to the toilet) full independence earns only 5 points and requirements for some help receive 0 points. The highest possible Barthel score of 100 signifies independence on all items, although the originators of the instrument make clear that this does not mean the subject could live alone without social assistance. (He might need help, for example, with cooking or cleaning). The Barthel score reflects ability to perform ADL activities without a personal care attendant. In rehabilitation settings, the Barthel Index correlates well with clinical judgment and has been shown to predict mortality (Wylie 1967) and ability to be discharged to less-restrictive settings (Granger and Greer 1976).

Granger adapted the Barthel Index into a series of ordinal scales (Sherwood et al. 1977). The resulting instrument is called the Barthel Self-Care Ratings. Some additional items have been added to the original group and each is rated on a four-point scale of intact/limited/helper required/null. An

Table 2-5
Barthel Index

Activities Rated by Examiner	Points for Performance[a]	
	Independently	With Help
1. Feeding (if food needs to be cut = help)	10	5
2. Moving from wheelchair to bed (includes sitting up in bed)	15	10-5
3. Personal toilet (wash face, comb hair, shave, clean teeth)	5	0
4. Getting on and off toilet (handling clothes, wipe, flush)	10	5
5. Bathing self	5	0
6. Walking on level surface	15	10
Propel wheelchair (score only if unable to walk)	5	0
7. Ascend and descend stairs	10	5
8. Dressing (includes tying shoes, fastening fasteners)	10	5
9. Controlling bowels	10	5
10. Controlling bladder	10	5

Source: Extrapolated from F.I. Mahoney and D.W. Barthel, "Functional Evaluation: The Barthel Index," *Maryland State Medical Journal* 14 (1965):61–65.

[a]Total possible points = 100

intact rating implies that the activity can be completed independently under normal circumstances in a reasonable amount of time. Limited ratings are given if special aids or devices are needed or if the subject needs an inordinate amount of time.

The items on the Barthel self-care ratings are meticulously defined to include all the steps of the particular functional activity. Under bowel and bladder care, those who are able to manage catheters, ileal appliances, or colostomy bags by themselves are considered to be almost intact. To take another example, for those who are not ambulatory, wheelchair activities are described in detail. The items on the Barthel Self-Care Rating scale appeared in table 2-3. Table 2-6 illustrates the level of detail contained in the descriptive anchor points with examples of four items. The Barthel Index is an ADL scale with instructions for including the time it takes a subject to perform a task as a dimension of ability, although phrases such as "reasonable time" are open to interpretation.

Test-retest reliabilities have not been reported for the Barthel scales. Sherwood and her colleagues (1977) report high alpha reliabilities (ranging from .953 to .965) for three samples of hospital patients, suggesting that the test is consistent internally as a measure of self-care activities. In a personal communication (1980), Lawton speculates that the original weighted scale of the Barthel Index is most useful for rehabilitation-center patients but that the Likert self-care scales are a better measure for geriatric patients.

Rapid Disability Rating Scale (RDRS)

The Rapid Disability Rating Scale (Linn 1967) resembles Linn's Cumulative Illness Rating. The instrument contains sixteen items that are rated by medically oriented staff on a three-point scale; the scale points depict no impairment or no special help (1), moderate impairment or assistance needed (2), and substantial or complete impairment or assistance needed (3). Linn claims that a nurse can complete the scale from first-hand knowledge of the patient in about two minutes. High inter-rater and test-retest reliabilities are reported for this scale within a hospital context. Furthermore, Linn reports that when hospital nurses used the scale on a group of patients entering nursing homes and the same patients were rerated by nursing home personnel about three days later, the mean scores of the two groups were almost identical. (This is suggestive of a high reliability between the two raters, although the paper does not report on the degree of consensus on cumulative scores or particular items for individual patients.)

Linn argues that the primary purpose of the RDRS is to facilitate research. She and her colleagues have subsequently used the scale in a study of the reactions of Veterans Administration patients to nursing-home placement (Ogren

Table 2-6
Examples of Items from Barthel Self-Care Ratings

Score	Items
	Transfer/chair
0 Intact	Able to approach, sit down, or get up from a regular chair safely; if in wheelchair, able to approach a bed or another chair, lock brakes, lift foot rest, and safely perform either a standing pivot or sliding transfer; able to return safely, changing the position of the wheelchair if necessary; able to remove and replace arm rest if necessary.
1 Limited	As above but requires adaptive or assistive devices such as a sliding board or a lift, or takes more than a reasonable time but does not require assistance.
2 Helper	Minimal assistance or lifting is required.
	Dress upper body
0 Intact	Able to dress and undress upper body, including obtaining clothes from their customary places such as drawers and closets; able to handle bra, slip, pullover garment and front-opening garment, as well as manage zippers, button, and snaps.
1 Limited	Requires prior retrieval or arrangement of clothes, or able to dress presentably in spite of omission of some of above or through use of special closures, or takes more than a reasonable time.
2 Helper	Patient performs at least half the effort himself.
	Bladder continence
0 Intact	Complete voluntary and elective control of bladder (never incontinent).
1 Limited	Has catheter, urinary collecting device or urinary diversion; able to clean, sterilize, and set up the equipment for irrigation without assistance; able to assemble and apply condom drainage or an ileal appliance without assistance; able to empty, put on, remove and clean leg bag or empty and clean ileal appliance bag; no accidents. May have bladder urgency.
2 Helper	Needs assistance with external device, or has occasional accidents, or cannot wait to get bed pan or to the toilet in time.
3 Null	Incontinent despite aids or assistance.
	Bowel continence
0 Intact	Complete voluntary and elective control of the bowels (never incontinent).
1 Limited	Regularly requires stool softeners, digital stimulation, suppository, laxative, or enema, but does not require assistance; has colostomy but does not require assistance; no accidents. May have bowel urgency.
2 Helper	Needs assistance using suppository or taking an enema or has occasional accidents.
3 Null	Incontinent despite aids or assistance.

Source: S.J. Sherwood, J. Morris, V. Mor, and C. Gutkin, "Compendium of Measures for Describing and Assessing Long Term Care Populations" (Boston: Hebrew Rehabilitation Center for Aged, 1977, mimeographed).

and Linn 1971) and on a large-scale study of patient outcome as a quality-of-care indicator for nursing homes (Linn, Gurel, and Linn 1977). In the latter study, scores on the RDRS were used to define improvement or deterioration of functional status of nursing-home patients six months after placement, with the patient assigned to a new status if the difference between the first and second scores exceeded two points. One problem of this method is its inherent assumption that all sixteen items have equal weight; for example, the need for a special diet would not seem to connote impairment equal to that signified by an inability to make oneself understood. Furthermore, the investigators concluded that, because nursing-home personnel and hospital personnel rated patients similarly around the time of patient transfer, any changes six months later would be real changes rather than artifacts of distinctive rating styles. It is not clear, however, that observations of continuing patients by nursing-home personnel are of the same quantity and quality as their observations of new patients. The RDRS lacks the definitional rigor that one prefers in a research instrument.

Range of Motion

Moving away from ADL activities, the Granger Range of Motion Scale develops a rather precise rating of thirty-two items of specific body motion; the patient demonstrates whether or not he can perform the movement of the particular body part, and each item is classified according to whether he performs it "against resistance," "without resistance," "in passive motion only," or "in combination of active and passive motion." As far as can be determined from periodical literature, this produces a nominal scale only and does not yield a total score. Sherwood and her colleagues (1977) report on Granger's Active Motion of Limbs scale, which rates each limb (left and right, upper and lower) as "good," "fair," "poor," or "null" according to the ability of all muscle groups of the limb to perform the full range of motion against varying levels of resistance and the degree of limitation imposed by contracture, spasticity, or pain.

Staff at Hebrew Rehabilitation Center for Aged have also reported their experience with the internal reliability of the Granger instruments. Here they report alpha reliabilities of .868 and .861 for the Worcester Home Care and the Fall River housing samples, respectively.

Kenny Self-Care Evaluation

The Kenny Self-Care Evaluation is designed to tap the ability to perform the purely physical activities involved in self-care at home or in a similar closed environment. It includes seventeen activities, each of which is allocated to one of six categories: bed activities, transfers, locomotion, personal hygiene, dressing, or feeding. Personal hygiene has five subitems (washing face and arms, washing trunk and perineum, washing lower extremities, bowel program, and bladder program). Bed activities has two subitems (moving in bed and rising and sitting in bed), whereas ability to feed oneself is a single item. Each item is rated on a five-point Likert Scale (0 to 4), and a score for each category is derived by summing the subsocres and dividing by the number of items. In this way, the five-item category on personal hygiene is weighted equally with the single-item category on feeding.

Schoening and his colleagues have reported some interesting elaborations on the Kenny instrument (Schoening et al. 1965); Schoening and Iversen 1968). They gave their raters specific instructions for the completion of the Likert scale based on an analysis of the substeps involved in each activity. For example, seven distinct steps are involved in making a standing transfer from a wheelchair; an individual performing all the steps is rated 4, and a person unable to perform any of the steps is rated 0. A person who can perform all but one or two steps independently and the remaining ones with help is rated 3; one who performs one or two steps with help and is unable to perform any of the others is rated 1. All other possible combinations are rated 2. Not only does this add precision to the rating procedure, but also the investigators were able to demonstrate that the learning curve is such that most patients move very quickly through the expanded midpoint of the scale (the 2 rating), so that the length of the interval in terms of component parts is not important to the utility of the scale. Further, different learning curves have been identified and associated empirically with different problems (stroke versus paralysis, for example). This has utility for discharge planning from rehabilitation settings; if one knows that the expected learning curve is such that many weeks are likely to elapse before an individual moves from a 3 to a 4 on a given item, then one would be unlikely to postpone discharge in order to try to facilitate that small gain.

PACE II

PACE II (the patient-care-planning tool already mentioned) has both an ADL and a range-of-motion section. All ADL items are classified as "mechanical aid," "human help," or "does not perform"; additionally, the rehabilitation potential on each item is judged. No overall score is derived. The range-of-motion section provides checklists of motions that the subject can perform; in addition, items are developed on strength, balance, and coordination. The nurse examiner is instructed to rate the ADL items on the basis of the usual performance in the past two weeks and to observe the patient performing the other tasks. In keeping with the purpose of PACE II as a patient-planning instrument, the list is comprehensive; however, the state of the art of ADL assessment would seem to have gone beyond a simple classification scheme to permit some kind of composite score more useful for nursing-home personnel.

OARS

The OARS instrument contains a physical ADL section, which rates eating, dressing, grooming, walking, getting in and out of bed, getting to the bathroom on time, and continence on a three-point scale based on the ability to perform the activity independently. Essentially, the OARS scale picks up the six Katz ADL items (bathing, dressing, feeding, transfer, continence, and toileting) and adds walking and grooming. The distinction is that the Katz information is based on a caregiver's observation of best performance, whereas the OARS uses self-report by the subject or a relative (if the subject is incompetent).

Because of the prominence of the OARS instrument in community-based gerontological research, this ADL measure has perhaps been used most widely with the general population. One might suppose that some items will be very sensitive to the social circumstances of the elderly person. (For example, getting to the bathroom on time will be influenced by the number of persons sharing the bathroom and the location of the bathroom in terms of stairs and other factors.) Perhaps, too, the interview approach tends to produce socially acceptable answers.

Although a global rating is made for "Ability to Perform Activities of Daily Living" on a scale of 1 to 6 (analogous to the OARS global rating of physical health already discussed), this scaling on the OARS instrument reflects a composite of both the ADL and IADL sections and thus cannot be compared to scores based solely on ADL. The OARS instrument has no instructions for summing on its composite ADL score.

ADL-A

Finally, Mossey and Tisdale (1979) are currently working on the scaling of ADL items. Using the questions on the Survey of Institutionalized Persons (U.S. Department of Commerce 1978), they have constructed an index in such a way that the score rather precisely suggests the pattern of problems experienced by the subjects. Using seven items (getting out of bed, eating, drinking, walking, bathing, dressing, and toilet use) rated on four points from "never needs help" (0) to "always needs help" (3), they developed six categories based on cutoff points of total scores (possible range: 0 to 21). They then introduced distinctions within the categories according to whether dependency exists in eating or drinking. (This is considered to impose more dependency than do the other categories.) This procedure yielded nine ADL-A levels with considerable specificity about the abilities of the individual. Claims for the validity of these measures are based on the correlation of ADL-A levels with other criteria from the same study, such as bed confinement, ability to walk, and blindness. Of course, the inter-rater reliability of an ADL-A scale could not be tested because the investigators were using secondary data collected by nursing-home staffs from facilities participating in the Survey of Institutionalized Persons.

General Comment

The choice of ADL scale may influence results. Those doing research or interpreting data need to be aware that findings yielded from different instruments may not be comparable. Donaldson, Wagner, and Gresham (1973) evaluated 100 patients in such a way that they could generate a Kenny Self-Care Score, a Barthel Self-Care Score, and a Katz ADL score.[b] The patients were reevaluated one month later, allowing the investigators to demonstrate that changes in the three scales moved in a parallel fashion for 68 of the patients. In 32 score divergences, the expected hierarchy of sensitivity prevailed; that is, the Kenny was most sensitive to change, followed by the Barthel and then by the Katz. Most of the eight unexpected patterns were accounted for because the most sensitive scale, the Kenny, does not include continence.

The choice of an ADL instrument surely will depend on setting. Perhaps the Katz scale is adequate for a family practitioner or internist evaluating a hospital patient, but the Barthel is more useful for a nursing-home or rehabilitation setting. In outpatient settings, where observation is more difficult, a physician may need to rely on a self-report analogous to the OARS ADL questions.

Whatever method is used, the caregiver should not neglect to get systematic information about the commonly agreed-on ADL variables. Furthermore, in so doing or in relying on ADL information collected by care attendants and others, those planning the care must be aware of the pitfalls inherent in defining in an operational way seemingly straightforward terms such as "bathing" and "feeding." Perhaps a good rule of thumb for a care planner is to make rather detailed inquiries, in order to be sure that he and the informant are using the same language when they discuss these matters. Another practical strategy is to ensure that all members of multidisciplinary care teams use the same definitions and that nursing aides and attendants are clearly instructed in the correct

---

[b]The format for programming the three scores was printed in a booklet issued by the Department of Physical and Rehabilitative Medicine at Tufts University in 1971. It is now available from Dr. Gresham at the SUNY Buffalo.

way to make ADL observations. Because the terms seem so obvious, these steps may be overlooked.

Instrumental Activities of Daily Living (IADL)

The IADL Concept

The IADL concept includes a range of activities more complex than those needed for personal self-care. At the same time, the potential bias introduced by motivation and opportunity is probably exacerbated, and the items are likely to be even more sensitive to variations in mood and emotional health. A depressed person who believes life is not worth living might be less likely to neglect ADL activities (such as using the toilet) than IADL activities such as cooking and cleaning.

IADL items are difficult to measure in most institutional settings in the United States because the opportunity for household activities in institutions is rather limited. If model kitchens and laundries are available, it might be possible to test the abilities empirically. Perhaps an even better test would be trial home visits where the individual is thrust into the reality of independent living in a more-familiar environment. On the other hand, when IADL abilities are measured in the community, the score may reflect the social situation rather than the innate ability level. Usually questions are phrased as "Do you perform this activity"; to take an example, doing laundry would vary in difficulty depending on whether laundry facilities were available in the housing unit, within the same building, or only in public facilities down the street.

IADL scales have been said to overemphasize tasks customarily performed by women (Lawton 1972). This may be a valid criticism, particularly for the cohorts now elderly. On the other hand, perhaps the survival skills of cooking, cleaning, and shopping are equally relevant whether one has been socialized to them as a woman or is learning them as a man. Of course, if a man living with a fit spouse indicates that he does not perform most of the IADL tasks, this may not reflect any limitation in his abilities. One must also remember the old story about the patient who complained after hand surgery that he couldn't play the piano; such a problem is relevant only if he could previously play the piano. Inability to cook, launder, or sew, if one has never learned those skills, does not reflect impaired capacity. Widowed men may well be able to learn some straightforward "survival skills" rather than be forced into protected settings for social reasons.

Identification of items that tap social-role performance in retired men is an important priority. The use of items such as "fixing things around the house" or "gardening" has not been exploited in IADL scales.

All IADL scaling suffers, of course, from the difficulty in conceptualizing role activities apart from the work situation. The Sarno Functional Life Scale (FLS), developed in a rehabilitation setting, illustrates this problem (Sarno, Sarno, and Levita 1973). It contains some items that address activities representing upper levels of functioning, such as attending the theater, taking unaccompanied long trips, or playing solo games like chess. Such items are hard to apply. Little consensus is available about normally independent functioning on matters such as attending the theater or traveling out of the city. Furthermore, the activities themselves might be broken up into dozens of subtasks performed over a long period. Going to the theater could involve selecting the play, buying tickets, preparing for attendance, transporting oneself, sitting through three acts, and understanding the content. Many social, physical, and economic factors converge to determine whether the activity is performed; much judgment would be needed to decide what constituted "independence." Because the task is complex and interpretation of the response is equivocal, perhaps IADL is better measured through such constrained tasks as using the telephone or watering plants.

We do not include the FLS in our tables because information on its scoring is scant and because, despite Ernst and Ernst (forthcoming), we question its utility for geriatrics. But the FLS illustrates another dilemma: how much information to include about an activity. The FLS requires raters to rate each of forty-four items four times, according to: (1) speed, (2) frequency, (3) self-initiation, and (4) overall efficiency. All four ratings are combined additively, making a score of 16 possible on some items. But does one gain more information through this method, or does the score simply become more difficult to understand and impossible to interpret? Is there really any point in rating an item such as "turning on the television" according to initiation, frequency, speed, and efficiency? Doing all four ratings on "going to the theater" (for example, deciding how to handle the component of speed) might involve enormous and inappropriate judgments.

Scale developers must decide whether to incorporate into the measure information with etiological implications. In the previous example, "self-initiation" ratings were meant to suggest a motivational factor in performance or an overprotectiveness in the environment that encouraged the patient to be passive. Similarly, a decision is needed about whether to include information about the quality of performance by separate measures such as the speed and efficiency scales. Other investigators may choose to emphasize information about the amount of pain that performing the activity costs the subject. An alternative is simply to measure whether the activity is performed independently and to rely on other indicators to deduce the etiology of reduced performance. When this latter strategy is employed, decision rules are needed to indicate when speed has become so diminished or frequency so low that the rating should be "does not perform independently."

Like the ADL measures, the IADL skills can be assessed through caregiver ratings of usual performance, through self-report of usual performance, through demonstrated abilities, and through theoretical abilities to perform. The last strategy (for example, "If you needed to cook, would you be able to do so?") is the least satisfactory. The demonstration of abilities seems the most-sensible way to proceed, but even this has pitfalls. Performance of many of the IADL functions depends on mental capacity as well as psychomotor skills. An individual who might readily make a cup of tea in an artificial test situation might, in the real world, forget to prepare meals.

The interpretation of IADL results is also difficult because not all persons are required to manage skills at the same level of complexity. Some have more of the advantages of modern devices and human help than do others. In geriatric-rehabilitation settings in England, caregivers sometimes handle this by tailoring the expected performance to the individual's home environment. In these cases, those with automatic washing machines use them in the rehabilitation setting, whereas others wash by hand; likewise, those with high kitchen cabinets or gas stoves practice under these familiar conditions. Success is thus measured by performance relative to the actual home environment rather than by an absolute set of skills. An alternative strategy is to prepare individuals for self-care in specially constructed or modified environments.

Long-term-care settings in the United States do not tend to provide the elderly with the chance to use and demonstrate IADL skills. Yet such settings do have kitchenettes, laundries, telephones, public transportation on nearby corners, and other resources that, we suggest, could be made available to residents. Certainly one's own room is available to be decorated and cared for. The paradigm for helplessness is the television set located above the patient's head, its remote controls firmly ensconced with equally remote nursing personnel; the bedroom door without a lock; or the bedside cabinet without even a door.

Ironically, individuals who are temporarily placed in these environments are likely to lose their IADL skills permanently. Our plea to geriatric caregivers is that they be sensitive to assessing the more-complex self-care functions and that, as persons who plan and work in congregate settings, they make sure that the elderly are not housed in environments stripped of IADL demands.

Case managers in particular need to appreciate the nuances of information contained in an IADL scale and to experiment with the least-restrictive solution. If an individual cannot clean windows, perhaps dirty windows can be tolerated. If an individual cannot take medicines because of failing memory or eyesight, perhaps some simple memory aids can be prepared. If cooking cannot be accomplished because meals are forgotten, a telephone reminder might work. Step-saving devices such as automatic door openers are also feasible.

The present, rather one-sided approach to using IADL data involves holding the medical regimen constant. Once the medical advice has been given, a patient cannot manage the regimen of medications, instructions, injections, and return visits, then a more-sheltered environment is considered. It is time to wonder whether such cures are not worse than the disease. Perhaps IADL tests should be used as a basis for decisions to simplify regimens, to involve visiting nurses or meal services, or to modify the medical treatment in some way rather than to modify the social situation so drastically.

Long ago, Zeman (1947) argued persuasively that physicians must become conditioned to providing general classifications of the functional ability of elderly patients. Taking into account all physical and mental limitations, he proposed the following rough scheme:

Class A: Individuals capable of unlimited and unsupervised activity, to be trusted to go about the city in safety.

Class B: Individuals capable of moderate activity, to be trusted in the neighborhood of home, but who may require the escort of a younger person for extended or tiring trips.

Class C: Individuals whose capabilities are limited and whose activities need both assistance and supervision; require escort on the street; practically housebound.

Class D: Individuals who are confined to bed or its immediate vicinity.

Class E: Individuals who are totally blind, or whose vision is so impaired that they cannot take care of themselves.

In addition, the numeral 1 indicates a specialized manual skill, the numeral 2 indicates ordinary skills, and the numeral 3 indicates no skills or a handicap of some type. The combination of letter and numeral in the patient's chart conveys a great deal of information for planning purposes that cannot be derived from the history, physical, and diagnosis.

Zeman suggested that those in class A or B should almost never be housed in institutions. Social workers and physical or occupational therapists can make use of the combined functional-ability/skill ratings to suggest alternatives to institutionalization or to plan a meaningful program within a congregate setting for those in class C, D, or E who require such a setting.

A generalized judgment of functional capacity such as Zeman suggests is one extreme of IADL determination. It is a step in the right direction for physicians to think in such terms, although the end result could be dangerous if the classification is based on guessing and subjective bias rather than on empirical fact. A number of IADL scales permit examination of instrumental abilities in more detail.

Examples of IADL Scales

Table 2-7 lists selected scales for IADL activities. Because mental capacity (particularly memory) is linked to the performance of many of these activities, some of the scales contain items that relate directly to mental abilities. The table includes three Guttman scales. The first, the Functional Health Status test (Rosow and Breslau 1966), is an extremely simple measure designed for use in a general population. A short twenty-five-question instrument was found to contain six items with Guttman-scale properties showing ascending dependency. The maximum-independence item is an affirmative response to a question about the ability to do heavy work such as shoveling snow (this question seems weighted against women, rather than the reverse as is usually the case). The greatest dependency is signified by a negative response to a question about being able to go out to a movie, church meeting, or similar activity. Between these two extremes are items reflecting, in descending order, no physical disability or condition now, no limitations in activities now, ability to walk half a mile (eight blocks), and ability to climb stairs. Obviously, this scale would have very limited utility with a severely debilitated population, and its reliability and validity have not been established.

The two other Guttman scales (Lawton 1972), both developed at the Philadelphia Geriatric Center, use items more pertinent to a geriatric, disabled population (such as meal preparation, laundry, cleaning, or telephone use). One of these instruments was designed for self-report of subjects: the Instrumental Role Maintenance Scale. It rates the *frequency* of shopping and frequency of meal preparation (other than breakfast) rather than the *capacity* to do the activities; presumably, the frequency provides a more-objective and more-relevant measure.

PACE II and OARS each have IADL sections. PACE II rates each item as "no problem," "performs with human help," or "does not perform." Realistically, the possibility is provided that nursing-home policy may prohibit or provide no opportunity for performance of the items included: using the telephone, handling money, securing personal items, tidying up, and preparing simple meals. The OARS instrument includes additional items in the battery such as taking one's own medicine. When OARS is administered in a nursing home, the interviewer is instructed to ask the respondent whether he could perform the task if it were necessary; the validity of this procedure is not certain. As already indicated, an overall activities-of-daily-living score is developed in the OARS instrument with consideration of both ADL/IADL batteries combined rather than of each separately.

The Functioning for Independent Living Scale (FIL) was developed by Francis Caro of Community Service Society of New York City (Gross-Andrew and Zimmer 1978). This includes eleven items, each developed on an ordinal

Table 2-7
Characteristics of Selected Measures of Ability to Perform Instrumental Activities of Daily Living

Name of Measure (Reference)	Items Included	Type of Scale	Administration	Reliability	Validity
Functional Health Status (Rosow and Breslau 1966)	Doing heavy work (such as snow shoveling); no physical illness or condition *now*; not limited in any activities; able to walk half a mile; climb stairs; go out to a movie or meeting.	6 items listed from Guttman scale in order of increasing difficulty.	Short instrument with 25 questions administered to subject; items making Guttman scale imbedded in questionnaire.	Reproducibility coefficient = .91; test-retest reliability not reported.	Not reported; validity of self-reports assumed from earlier studies.
PGC Instrumental Activities of Daily Living (Lawton 1972)	Using telephone; shopping; food preparation; housekeeping; laundry; public transportation; taking medications; handling finances.	Most items on 3-point scale; no instructions on summing items; effort to create a Guttman scale.	Observer ratings.	Reproducibility coefficient = .94; interrater reliability not reported.	Investigator comments that measure does not tap full content of IADL and is more suitable for women.
Instrumental Role Maintenance Scale (Lawton 1972)	Frequency of meal preparation other than breakfast; frequency of shopping; distance of shopping from residence; manner of doing laundry.	Guttman scale.	Self-report questionnaire to use with women who apply for nursing-home admission.	Reproducibility coefficient = .94; test-retest reliability not reported.	Investigator comments that measure does not tap full content of IADL and is more suitable for women.
PACE II: IADLs (U.S. DHEW 1978a)	Using telephone; handling money; securing personal items; tidying up; preparing meals.	No problem; performs with human help (indicate how many helpers); or does not perform; no instructions on summing.	Completed by staff of institution or by appraiser.		Possibility that some items will be prohibited by nursing-home policy.

Measure	Items	Scoring	Administration	Reliability/Validity
OARS: Instrumental ADL (Duke University 1978)	Using telephone; shopping for groceries or clothes; transport self to places out of walking distance; prepare meals; do housework; take medicine; handle own money.	Each item rated as: without help, with help, or unable to perform; a global score of ADL and IADL made on 6 points, ranging from excellent to completely impaired.	Interview with subject.	See chapter 5
Functioning for Independent Living (Gross-Andrew and Zimmer 1978)	Vision; hearing and speech; mobility; bowel and bladder control; confused behavior; knowledge of identity; ability to make self understood; wandering; extent of nonconventional behavior.	Choices within items are keyed to tasks relevant to independent living (for example, sees well enough to recognize household objects but not to cross streets); items weighted; total possible score of 47 reflects maximum disability.	Professional ratings based on observation and asking client or family member.	
Performance Activities of Daily Living (PADL) (Kuriansky and Gurland 1976)	16 activities: drink from cup; wipe nose; comb hair; file nails; shave; eat with spoon; turn faucet on and off; turn light switch on and off; take jacket with buttons on and off; put on and remove slippers; brush teeth (real or false); make telephone call; sign name; turn key in lock; tell time; stand up and walk and sit down.	Tasks are rated as 0 (performed without help) or 1 (unable to perform without help). A 9 indicated task did not apply or wasn't requested. No allowance made for disability, lack of cooperation, or lack of comprehension.	Tests administered with props; subject performs each task in order of difficulty; paraprofessional can administer.	Interviewer and observer reliabilities were high (.9) in a pilot study. Predictive validity claimed in terms of disposition and mortality.

Table 2-7 (continued)

Name of Measure (Reference)	Items Included	Type of Scale	Administration	Reliability	Validity
Pilot Geriatric Arthritis Project Functional Status Measure (PGAP) (Deniston and Jette 1980)	12 mobility items (driving, shopping, walking inside, walking outside, stairs into home, other stairs, curbs, transfer bed, transfer chair, transfer car, transfer toilet, transfer bath); 17 personal care items (telephone; writing; cutting food; drinking; washing self; turning faucets; teeth care; shaving; combing hair; setting hair; donning shoes, hose/pants, underclothes, shirt/blouse; buttoning/zipping sweater/coat); 15 work items (employment; stove/oven/refrigerator; sink/faucets; reading; cupboards; lifting pots; peeling/cutting; opening containers; laundry; sweeping/mopping; making beds; washing dishes; cleaning bathroom: washing windows/home repair; yardwork.	For each of 44 items, 3 ratings are made: a dependency rating (0 = independent, 1 = mechanical help, 2 = human help, 3 = both kinds of help, 4 = cannot perform); a pain rating (1 = no pain, 2 = mild, 3 = moderate, 4 = severe); and a difficulty rating (same scale as pain rating). Scores are summed and 2 subscores are created for mobility, personal care, and work.	Rating on basis of patient self-report.	Repeated measures of same person by different interviewers produced same score 85 percent of time; interrater reliability best with dependency items and worst with difficulty items; reliability best at lowest level of functional ability and worst for midpoints of scales.	Scores correlated with clients' ratings of (1) their joint status and (2) their ability to deal with their arthritis and associated problems. Scores did *not* correlate with professional ratings of their clients' joint status or ability to deal with their arthritis.

scale, with scoring according to weightings assigned to the items. The item descriptors are particularly practical. For example, vision is scaled as follows:

Score

A. Sees well enough with or without glasses to recognize all common   0
    household objects and/or negotiate street crossings.
B. Sees well enough with or without glasses to recognize most house-   2
    hold objects, but cannot discriminate well enough to read labels
    on common objects.
C. Sees well enough with or without glasses to recognize most house-   2
    hold objects but cannot see well enough to negotiate street
    crossings.
D. Sees well enough with or without glasses to recognize most house-   4
    hold objects but cannot see well enough to discriminate among
    labels on common objects or to negotiate street crossings.
E. Does not see well enough with or without glasses to recognize   5
    most household objects.

Similar specificity is offered in other items; for example, hand movement is assessed in terms of common household tasks. Several items are included on memory (in terms of remembering meal preparations or appointments), identity (in terms of knowing name and address), wandering (ability to leave and return home without getting lost), and nonconventional behavior (related to dress and hygiene). Such items usually are not included on an IADL scale because they are related to mental capacity, yet here they are keyed specifically to functional abilities related to independence. According to findings on a project involving provision of support for relatives of disabled elderly persons in the community, the cutting scores established for the FIL have some validity in separating those whose relatives require few services.

The Performance Activities of Daily Living Scale (PADL) was designed to overcome the confounding of capacity to perform functions and opportunity to perform them in the environmental setting. The subjects demonstrate their ability to complete a series of sixteen tasks, arranged in ascending order of difficulty, such as drinking from a cup, lifting food onto a spoon and into the mouth, turning a water faucet off and on, making a telephone call, turning a key in a lock, and telling time. The authors suggest that "on face value, the test appears to measure apraxia; i.e., the inability to know how to use common objects, which is a recognized symptom of organicity." In this test, however, no allowances are made for noncooperation; any nonperformance is recorded as inability to perform, although the conjectured reasons are recorded separately. The final score is a percentage of administered tasks that the subject could complete independently. A patient was classified as moderately dependent if the score fell between 99 and 75 percent and as severely dependent when the score was under 75 percent.

Kuriansky and her colleagues (1976) used the PADL in a study of fifty hospitalized psychiatric geriatric patients, reporting that the PADL results were more consistent with informant reports, psychiatric diagnosis, and physical condition than were self-reports of functional abilities. Furthermore, the PADL had a higher predictive validity in terms of disposition or mortality three months later than did either informant of self-reports. Finally, the test was highly acceptable to the subjects and was easy to explain even to those with communication or language barriers. All this makes the PADL seem a promising tool. More work is required to determine whether the test is now presented in its most-economical form. Some of the items in the version available to us seem duplicative, and it may be that the PADL can be shortened without loss of information.

The last item of table 2-7, the PGAP, was developed in a model project for arthritis patients (Jette and Deniston 1978; Deniston and Jette 1980). It is noteworthy in two respects: (1) it expands the repertoire of ADL and IADL items to many practical indicators not usually included (such as lifting pots and opening containers); and (2) more importantly, it adds two additional dimensions to the standard performance rating: pain and difficulty. The scales achieved best inter-rater reliability with the basic dependency ratings and least with the difficulty ratings. This approach indicates an attempt to expand the amount of information beyond a statement of ability to perform a task to include other relevant information.

Comparisons of Physical-Function Measures

In the introductory chapter we discussed measures in long-term care along several dimensions: giving consideration to the user of the measure (who might be a nongeriatric medical provider, a geriatric specialist, a case manager, or a researcher); and to the purpose of making the measurement (in terms of description, screening, monitoring, assessment, or prognosis). In table 2-8 we review the measures that have been included in this chapter along these dimensions. Although the allocations to categories are admittedly disputable, the principle of the importance of these considerations to the choice of measures is not. We have also gone so far as to make some recommendations, albeit idiosyncratic ones, on the utility of the instruments included.

Review of the table shows that the measures of physical functioning and ADL are most suited to measuring differences in individuals and therefore are most amendable to use in a clinical context. Of course, any of these measures might be employed in large-scale studies; but they were allocated to the individual-measurement category because of the practical problems that use entails. Most of them depend on direct observation, either at the moment of making the assessment or over a period of weeks prior to the measurement; some require

Table 2-8
Selected Measures of Physical Functioning by User, Purpose, and Recommendations

Measure	User[a]	Purpose[b]	Recommendations
Cornell Medical Index	n, r	d, s	Not recommended
Health Index	r	d, a, m	Promising self-report on health
PACE II and Patient Classification Form (relevant sections)	g	d, a	Record-keeping system only
OARS (relevant sections)	n, g, c, r	d, a	Community-based assessment when observation is impractical
Cumulative Illness Rating Scale	n, g	d, a, p	Not recommended
PULSES	g, c	d, a, p	Not recommended
Katz Index of ADL	n, g	d, a, m, p	Useful general tool
Barthel Index	n, g	d, a, m, p	Useful when sensitive tool needed
Disability Rating Scale	n, r	d, p	Not recommended
Kenny Self-Care Evaluation[c]	g	d, a, m, p	Useful in rehabilitation settings
Granger Range of Motion	n, g	d, a, m	Useful in rehabilitation settings
Rosow Functional Health Scale	r	d	For group information only
PGC IADL	g, c	d, s, a	Promising tool, best for women
PGC Instrumental Role Maintenance	g, c	d, s, a	Promising tool, best for women
Caro Functioning for Independent Living Scale	c	d, s	Promising tool, practical
Performance ADL	n, g, e	d, m, a, p	Promising tool, depends on demonstration
PGAP Functional Assessment Instrument	g	d, m, a,	Promising tool, offers added dimensions of ADL and IADL

[a]User: n = nongeriatric provider; g = geriatric provider; c = case manager; r = researcher.

[b]Purpose: d = description; s = screening; a = assessment; m = monitoring; p = prognosis.

[c]As refined by H.A. Schoening, L. Anderegg, D. Bergstrom, M. Fonda, N. Steinke, and P. Ulrich, "Numerical Scoring of Self-Care Status of Patients," *Archives of Physical Medicine and Rehabilitation* 46 (1965):689–697.

that professional personnel make the determinations and/or that the determinations be made on the basis of extensive clinical evaluations. Those based on self-report, such as the OARS ADL or physical-health scales and the Philadelphia Geriatric Center Instrumental Role Maintenance Scale, seem more suitable for large-scale studies even though they are capable of generating clinical or case-management distinctions pertient to the care of an individual.

The determination of potential users of an instrument depends to some extent on the amount of detail it is capable of generating. Some instruments (Katz ADL, Granger Range of Motion) are useful for both the geriatric specialist and the nonspecialist provider. (The former might use the measure as a first-line screen prior to more detailed studies, whereas the latter could use it as a quick check on the overall status of the patient.) Indeed, the field would profit by the establishment of some common, easily learned and used measures that might provide a common vocabulary for the generalist and the geriatric specialist. On the other hand, instruments such as PACE II or the Kenny scale as refined by Schoening are either so lengthy or require so much training in their use that they seem more suited to the rehabilitation specialist.

Although table 2-8 credits a number of the instruments with utility as predictors, we emphasize that "predictive potential" might be a better term. Also, the predictability is usually achieved within a narrow and specific context. The Cumulative Illness Rating Scale, for example, claims to predict mortality; several other instruments (Kenny, Granger, and Barthel, for example) have been shown to predict discharge status. The Katz ADL scale is a predictor in the sense that an individual's score on the six-point Guttman scale should help a clinician predict the status for similar measures in subsequent stages.

Only a few of the instruments mentioned here seemed suited to large-scale administration; among these, the OARS is by far the best tested. None of the instruments is credited as yet with the power to be used as a predictor of the need for future services in a community (probably the most important kind of prediction one would want to make on the basis of group data). Studies conducted with the OARS instrument in Cleveland (U.S. Comptroller General 1977, 1979), however, may enhance our confidence in using it to assert something about the adequacy of service levels. Recently Glassman and his colleagues (1976) have suggested that information across a community of elderly persons about the ability to perform five basic tasks (go out of doors, climb stairs, get about the house, wash and bathe without help, and dress and put on shoes) can be used for community planning. In other words, the percentage of persons unable to dress and put on shoes, for instance, is a useful indicator of need for services for noninstitutionalized persons. Glassman urges the incorporation of such indicators into census or other general data collection that occurs on a large-scale basis.

Conclusion

We recommend that all physicians, nurses, and social workers who provide direct care to the elderly incorporate ADL and IADL indicators into their routine assessments. Particularly for the latter measures, some baseline information is important so that a caregiver will know whether a particular finding represents a change for the individual in question. The Katz ADL items and the Lawton or OARS IADL items would seem adequate for most general purposes, although those who are hospital based or treating patients with chronic long-term-care needs and multiple disabilities should be familiar with more-detailed breakdowns of ADL functioning such as the Barthel Self-Care Ratings. Furthermore, the approach pioneered in the Performance ADL (PADL) Scale should be considered in making decisions about discharge from hospital and extended-care facilities. The advantage of the PADL, with its kit of practical props, is that its ratings are independent of the life circumstances of the institution where they are made.

Brief assessments of ADL and IADL functioning will never become part of the general repertoire of caregivers unless neophyte professionals are made aware of their importance. Because the hospital is the site of most education for health-care providers, the infusion of these concepts into medical records, ward-round commentary, and the reflexes of those who serve as role models for students is essential. In any event, the treatment of old people in hospitals is an aspect of LTC delivery, even though (paradoxically) such care is given in acute settings. All care delivered to elderly persons with multiple disabilities should be planned in the context of their functional abilities; in this respect, a dichotomy between hospital-based and community-based assessment is artificial and damaging. Acceptance of the principle that hospital care can be considered one aspect of an LTC program will pave the way for introducing ADL and IADL concepts to students.

3 Measures of Mental Functioning in Long-Term Care

Geriatric specialists and primary-care providers alike are frequently required to judge the mental status of the elderly. As we indicated elsewhere (Kane et al. 1981), general practitioners and internists treat numerous old people in the course of their routine practice. Although extensive psychological testing would be prohibitively costly, beyond the skill of the physicians, and often inappropriate, some measuring tools can be usefully applied to assessments of the mental functioning of older persons in the community. The geriatric medical specialist, and certainly the geropsychiatrist, need a broader armamentarium of measures at their command. In addition, they must be well versed enough to collaborate with psychologists and to interpret psychological-test results in the light of the current limitations of many standard batteries with reference to elderly persons.

Primary-care providers who assess mental status usually must assess both cognitive and affective functioning. They need to determine whether an impairment in intellectual ability or a depressive state exists and, if so, its extent. Both cognitive impairment and depression are prevalent in the elderly and have practical implications for self-care abilities. Beyond this, the practitioner may at times need to conduct a general "mental-health" screening, perhaps with particular concern for whether a psychotic condition is suspected and a full mental-health assessment is required.

The primary-care provider may be the first recourse for relatives concerned about the ability of an older person to care for himself in the community. Under our current nursing-home-placement system, physician decisions are critical in declaring patients eligible for institutional care, often because of mental impairments. Other physicians, nurses, and assorted health-care providers monitor these determinations as part of the utilization review required under Medicare and Medicaid. It is difficult to determine how often institutional placements are made on grounds of mental incapacity because of the simultaneous presence of multiple diagnoses. Also, it is almost impossible to extrapolate admission status from cross-sectional data on nursing-home residents. Commonly, two-thirds of nursing-home residents are said to be "senile" (Kovar 1977a, b). The accuracy of these all-important assessments depends on refinements in measurement capability.

Berger (1980) proposes a practical method for classifying senility on the basis of severity. His six-interval scale extends from least severe (class I), where the patient can function in any surrounding but forgetfulness often disrupts

69

daily activities, to the patient confined to bed or chair and responsive only to tactile stimuli (class VI). Although no data are offered on its use and the classifications are arbitrary, the author claims that his distinction between needing direction (class III) and needing assistance (class IV) is a clinically significant one.

Even when the stake is not as dramatic as nursing-home placement or guardianship procedures, a physician or primary-health-care provider is often asked whether a patient has the capacity to function in a particular environment or to perform certain activities. Simply to judge whether a patient can manage a medical regimen requires an assessment of that patient's memory and orientation.

Assessment also determines who can best benefit from scarce resources. (Case-management programs, emerging to facilitate judicious use of services, require differential assessment of need.) For example, despondency among the bereaved elderly is "normal," but a measurement that identifies the members of this high-risk group most in need of special services such as day care, congregate meals, or psychotherapy would be useful. Such allocations may be based on scaling the severity of the problem or the expected benefit from the intervention.

Objective instruments are available to help the practitioner make uniform asseessments of mental status. Often the most-telling sign is a change in intellectual or affective functioning, rather than a description of the functioning itself. Change increments are best reported through reliance on objective measures rather than on the memory of the provider.

To complicate the issue further, the primary-care provider often receives reports of changes in mental status from observers other than the patient. In such cases, the provider must be able to evaluate the probable accuracy of the observations through his understanding of the informant's motivation, capacity, and opportunity to observe. Numerous observer-rating scales systematize and, to some extent, objectify the observations of others; these vary greatly in their detail and reliability. The physician caring for institutional residents can use some of these tools to help care attendants provide reliable information about the progress of persons under their care.

Measurements of mental functioning are also important for documenting the effects of care. Here the geriatric specialist may require an instrument that picks up rather small increments of deterioration or improvement. This would be especially true for those attempting to improve the status or at least prevent the deterioration of patients already known to be disoriented or confused.

Geriatric providers, of course, are not presented with neatly arranged problems already sorted into the physical and mental spheres. Rather, they are presented with symptoms and behaviors and are challenged to use history, examination, and assessment to sort out the etiology as well as possible. Similarly, when determining whether an individual is capable of self-care, the ability to perform a particular constellation of tasks is the key concern, regardless of the reason for incapacity. Certainly the instrumental activities-of-daily-living (ADL) measures discussed in the previous chapter depend on mental as well as physical capacity. For example, the skills required to use a telephone, write a letter, boil an egg, or take a bus obviously demand some threshold of mental as well as physical health.

General Inssues in Measuring Mental Status of the Old

Relationship of Physical and Mental Status

Physical and mental functioning are known to be interdependent states (Habot and Libow 1980). This truism takes on particular poignancy for the elderly. Physical impairments are often responsible for diminished performance on mental tests. The clues for unraveling the physical and mental components of the functional problem are often obscured. However, the repercussions of a judgment that an individual is mentally incapacitated may have far-reaching negative consequences for the quality of the rest of his life.

Common sense suggests the interrelationship between physical and mental impairments in the elderly. Signs of mental problems (such as confusion, memory loss, fatigue, appetite reduction, anxiety, blunted affect, personality changes, irritability, and even paranoia) can be linked to acute and chronic illnesses. For example, cardiac arrhythmias, brain tumors, fevers, or even infections may cause changes in mental functioning. Hearing losses have notoriously been associated with confusion and paranoia in all age groups, and uncorrected hearing deficits are very common among the elderly. Visual problems compound the lack of sensory stimulation (perhaps already heightened because of the absence of meaningful routines). Some investigators (Ernst et al. 1977a, b) maintain that sensory deprivation produces symptoms of chronic brain syndrome. Then, too, the side effects of medications used to treat physical illnesses may create the signs of mental problems. Particularly if medical care is episodic and fragmentary, iatrogenic mental dysfunctioning can be easily overlooked.

Relationship of Cognitive and Affective Status

Not only are physical and mental problems likely to be confounded in the elderly, but mental problems are also confounded with each other. Cognitive and affective impairments are partciularly hard to distinguish. Although they occur separately, they also coexist in the same individual, and at times it is important to determine which problem is primary.

Overuse of catchall labels such as "senility" or "dementia" to depict a wide range of late-onset mental problems has been a pervasive deterrent to the development of individualized treatment plans. At the extreme, the label can become a self-fulfilling prophecy. A person diagnosed as senile, placed in an environment with others similarly diagnosed, and relieved of decision-making responsibilities and prerogatives is likely to deteriorate rapidly. Some authorities (Eisdorfer and Friedel 1977) recommend that, in their unmodified forms, the terms "senility" and "dementia" both be dropped from the working vocabularies of those caring for the elderly. Then, too, it is important to recognize, as Kastenbaum and Sherwood (1972) point out, that the term "senile dementia," even if appropriately used, does not describe the wide variation in performance abilities related to different subcategories of cognitive functioning. For example, some persons maintain social skills intact, although recent memory is lost; such nuances, which have importance for self-care, can be captured through functional assessment.

Like persons of all ages, the elderly are vulnerable to reversible psychotic disorders and to endogenous depression. Perhaps even more than younger persons, they are at risk of substance abuse (either of alcohol or of prescription drugs). The prevalence of reactive depression is high, even among older persons preselected as physically and mentally healthy (Perlin and Butler 1963; Birren et al. 1963). Suicide is a real risk; in 1975, 23 percent of suicides were committed by persons over age 65; and the risk of suicide for males continues to increase with age into the eighties (Miller 1978). The suicide attempts of the elderly are often successful, perhaps because of some combination of more-serious intention, frailer physical condition, and more-isolated social circumstances than those of their younger counterparts. One suspects that suicide among elderly residents of institutions is underreported or, in the case of passive self-neglect, unrecognized. Thus the mental-health problems of the elderly are numerous and various; they tend to be undertreated, particularly by classic mental-health organizations. The overworking of the term "senility" further exaggerates the problems in getting appropriate help to patients in a timely fashion.

Stereotyped thinking of care givers is not the only problem in differential assessments of mental status. Distinguishing between intellectual impairment and depression is realistically complicated because some depressions of the elderly present themselves as "pseudodementias." When this phenomenon is compared to actual Alzheimer's disease (Salzman and Shader 1979), the differences are imprecise and a matter of degree.

In pseudodementia, the sleep and appetite disturbances and the depressive affect are somewhat more pronounced, whereas in Alzheimer's disease the disorientation and impairment of recent memory are accentuated. In addition, pseudodementia is characterized by rapid onset, with mood disturbances occurring *before* the disorientation and memory loss; the persons most at risk are those with a low premorbid intelligence. On the other hand, highly intelligent and intellectually oriented persons are said to be vulnerable to depressions that are *secondary* to a failing memory.

In the last analysis, a diagnosis of pseudodementia is sometimes confirmed only by observing a patient's response to a trial of antidepressive drugs or electric-shock therapy. This discussion provides one example of why a *change* in mental functioning may be a more-important measurement than the mental capacity itself, a point emphasized throughout this chapter. Encouraging work by Gurland and his colleagues (1979) promises to specify criteria for the diagnosis of "pervasive dementia" in a way that guards against overuse of the term. Particularly promising is their specification of the concept of "positive cognition." They offer a list of circumstances, behaviors, and abilities that seem inconsistent with pervasive dementia and therefore would suggest that the diagnosis be reconsidered.

Relationship of Mental and Social Well-Being

Just as physical and mental functioning are difficult to distinguish operationally, so, too, do the constructs of mental and social functioning become blurred. Screening batteries designed to tap emotional-system psychopathology may, in fact, be measuring the extent to which an individual is bereft of social relationships and meaningful activities. Loneliness may be based on reality; expressions of anxiety may represent prudent fears based on life in a high-crime area. "Paranoia" and suspicion could be an awareness that plans are being made to appropriate an elderly person's resources.

Social functioning is indirectly related to mental status in the sense that both are products of the environment. Weinstock and Bennett (1971) showed that intellectual performance measured by the Wechsler Adult Intelligence Scale (WAIS) was better for newly admitted residents in a home for the aged than for otherwise comparable long-term residents. Moreover, the extent of deterioration in WAIS scores over time was greater for this group than for either former waiting-list patients or long-term residents.

Chapter 4 describes measurement of social functioning. Concepts often considered important under this rubric are "morale," "life satisfaction," "contentment," and "social involvement." In practical terms, however, measurements of depression and of morale overlap substantially, although the latter avoid tapping the psychophysiological indicators of depression. These issues are discussed further in chapter 4; here we note that mental-health measures, especially of affective functioning or of general mental health, must be examined critically lest they really be measuring social deprivations that require social solutions. On the other hand, involvement in social relationships and social activities is often used as a tangible indicator of mental well-being.

Personality Traits and Mental Functioning

Mental functioning is viewed as a characteristic that improves or deteriorates. In contrast, certain attributes are thought to be fixed human personality traits that depict life-long patterns of decision making, personal style, and reaction to stress. This chapter does not deal with the measurement of personality except insofar as it becomes confounded with mental-status measures.

From her review of personality tests in the elderly, Dye (forthcoming), concludes that most individuals show "stability and continuity" of personality over the life span. Nevertheless, certain characteristics often attributed to the elderly (such as cautiousness) may be cohort specific (and, therefore, limited to a particular generation) because most studies are cross-sectional rather than longitudinal.

Personality may be an important intervening variable to explain health behavior or response to treatment. For example, locus of control, defined as the extent to which an individual takes direction from himself (internal) or from others (external), may be linked to observation of good health habits or maintenance of independence, even in situations where the environment discourages personal decision making. In a more down-to-earth example, Kleban and Brody (1972) demonstrated a connection between personality traits such as "belligerence" and "cantankerousness" and improvement in treatment outcomes. These personality traits (deemed disagreeable by nursing-home staff) were identified by relatives as lifelong characteristics, which stood their owners in good stead under the stresses of long-term care.

The confusion between measures of personality traits and measures of mental well-being arises when observer-rating scales for mental functioning include items such as "irritability," "bothersomeness," or "sociability" as well as more-classic components of mental status such as "anxiety," "depressed mood," or "delusional statements." When such items are summed together to form a score, there is danger that stable personality traits will contribute to the totals. The line between paranoia and suspicion as symptoms and irritability as a trait is undoubtedly quite fine.

Measuring Mental Functioning in the Elderly

Mental functioning is assessed in a variety of ways; these include unstructured "mental-status examinations" administered by clinicians, semistructured interviews that permit scores to be derived from responses of the subjects and observations of the interviewer, self-completed questionnaires, observer ratings, and formal psychological tests. This last group, in turn, may include cognitive tests and projective tests designed to assess emotional states.

Unstructured and Semistructured Interviews

The "mental-status examination" is a time-honored method by which psychiatrists and other mental-health personnel form judgments about mental functioning in the context of a clinical interview. Typically, the clinician observes behavior, emotions, and reactions; analyzes the content of the subject's speech; and perhaps administers a scattering of quick tests and routine questions designed to probe a particular area. Thus fairly standard questions about sleep and eating disturbances and suicidal ideation often become part of a workup to rule out depression. Similarly, orientation is often assessed through routine questions about "time, place, and person"; and higher cognitive abilities are assessed through quick tests of vocabulary, proverb interpretation, or mathematical computation. The final conclusions of the clinician are expert judgments based on the entire interview and perhaps on history and background information obtained from other sources. Although on a case-by-case basis the clinician may be able to explain how the interview information is used to reach conclusions, it is more than likely that no explicit decision-making rules are applied.

A discussion of the reliability and validity of mental-status examinations in general is beyond the scope of this book. We note, however, that the reliability of psychiatric diagnosis is notoriously poor, although it is enhanced by training, detailed instructions, and diminution of the number of categories permitted to the clinician (Kendell 1975). For example, inter-rater reliability will be better when the clinician sorts his observations into broad groupings (such as psychotic or nonpsychotic, oriented or disoriented) rather than into finer diagnostic categories. In the case of examinations of the elderly, Perlin and Butler (1963) reported high inter-rater reliability among three psychiatrists who based their conclusions on identical observations of subjects in a research project; conditions were thus ideal for consensus. However, one of the reasons that mental-status-examination results are often unreliable is that two clinicians are unlikely to pose exactly the same questions in the same manner. Even when using more-objective tools such as proverb interpretation, for example, individual clinicians may choose proverbs of varying difficulty and accept varying answers as adequate.

The validity of the mental-status examination depends on whether the clinician's judgments accurately reflect the constructs measured (for example, dementia, paranoia, depression, schizophrenia). If such judgments cannot be shown to have inter-rater reliability, then by definition they are not valid. Additionally, validity is affected if the sample of behavior observed by the clinician does not accurately reflect the capacity or customary behavior of the subject. Elderly persons may become anxious and disoriented by the test situation itself, especially if the test is administered in strange surroundings. Other threats to validity are presented if the tester represents a different frame of reference from the subject, perhaps because of age and cultural differences. To take extreme examples, the tester might interpret reticence as withdrawal, or religious expression as delusion. As stated earlier, the examiner may also fail to distinguish apparent cognitive and affective disturbances that are actually the manifestations of sensory deficits such as poor hearing.

Structured interviews for assessing mental functioning minimize reliability and validity problems by ensuring that each judgment is based on very similar content. Some structured mental-health interviews designed for the elderly also organize the examiner's thoughts by collecting information about possible physical or social problems that could bias results; information about drug use, hearing ability, or recent losses would thus be included in the interview format and the interviewer instructed to probe the reality base for apparent delusional or paranoid ideation. (For example, if the subject indicates that people are trying to harm him, the interviewer asks for more detail and then rates the likelihood that the concern is based on reality.) A further advantage of a semistructured approach is that less-expensive personnel with lesser qualifications may be taught to conduct the examinations.

Structural interview approaches may even include an optional scoring format. An example is the FROMAJE approach (Libow 1977), developed to assist physicians in assessing the mental status of the elderly. The acronym stands for *F*unction, *R*easoning, *O*rientation, *M*emory, *A*rithmetic, *J*udgment, and *E*motional Status. Function refers to impediments to self-care *for mental reasons*; the information for the rating is elicited from relatives. Reasoning is tested through proverb interpretation; orientation through inquiry about time, place, and person; memory by a question to tap distant memory, recent memory, and immediate memory; and arithmetic by asking the patient to count forward, count backward, and subtract serial sevens. To tap judgment, a realistic problem is given; for example, "If you need help at night, how would you obtain it?" Finally, emotional state is assessed on the basis of general behavior during the interview and some probes about crying, hallucinations, mood swings, and so on. During a fifteen- to twenty-minute interview, each component is tested and scored individually. A score of 1 is awarded for no problem, 2 for a moderate problem, and 3 for a severe problem.

The FROMAJE technique allows latitude for the clinician to establish a relationship and evolve a personal testing style. At the same time, it organizes the interview and provides a screen for dementia. (A score of 9-10 is said to signify mild dementia or emotional illness; 11-12, moderate dementia or emotional illness; 13 or more, a severe condition.) Libow carefully points out that this technique is inappropriate for aphasic patients, who would show false positives for dementia. Clearly, so much judgment is allowed the individual clinician in selecting the question and interpreting the responses that the FROMAJE is not a measurement in the usual sense of the word. Indeed, the author points out that the final rating "is a product of the examiner's subjective assessment" (Habot and Libow 1980, p. 702).

Unstructured and semistructured interviews to assess the mental functioning of the elderly have several disadvantages. Both depend on a cooperative subject who can communicate in some manner. The interviews tend to be lengthy and therefore expensive to collect and process. To varying degrees, most interview batteries rely on judgment, either for particular items (for example, ratings of the appropriateness of the subject, the nature of the affect); overall assessments;

or both. We cannot replace the rich observation of the one-to-one clinical interview with an objective instrument, nor would we desire it. Screening tools to determine the need for clinical assessment will be impractical, however, unless they minimize judgment more than do typical structured-interview approaches.

Self-Administered Instruments

Numerous self-administered scales are available to measure psychological conditions such as depression and anxiety. These range from multidimensional batteries such as the Minnesota Multiphasic Personality Inventory (MMPI) to brief scales designed to tap single dimensions. Self-ratings have the advantage that the subject does not need to disclose sensitive information directly to the interviewer and, likewise, that interviewer personality and behavior do not influence test results. The disadvantage is that the tester cannot explain or clarify any of the items or protect against responses based on misunderstanding.

With elderly populations, self-administered scales also have drawbacks. Visual or motor impairments may prevent self-completion of a test. In some instances, language and format developed with a younger group in mind, may be unfamiliar or distasteful to the older individual. Then, too, if the work of interpreting the tests (validating them against clinical judgment and establishing norms) was done with a younger group, the test may not accurately measure the particular attribute in older subjects.

In practice, tests developed for self-administration are sometimes administered to elderly subjects in an interview format. Although this change in procedure may be necessary because of physical limitations of the subject (including reading difficulties), it can produce unsatisfactory results. For example, a respondent can consider a much larger number of response categories on a written questionnaire than in an oral presentation. Furthermore, some items that seem appropriate when read silently sound awkward, intrusive, or both when read aloud. This is often the case with true-or-false formats. The process of reading the items aloud may focus undue attention on each item, whereas the intention of the tester was that the subject go quickly down the list, indicating his first reaction. Self-administered batteries are often "subtly" modified for oral administration, and the results of such changes on validity are unclear.

Observer Ratings

Observer-rating scales are widely used to supplement information gained from the subject or as a sole source of information when the subject cannot communicate. Typically, such instruments use Likert-type scales or checklists for the observer to indicate the presence or absence of various forms of psycho-pathology or problematic behaviors. Such devices are used in mental hospitals and institutions in an attempt to codify and systematize the observations of caregivers.

Because observer-rating scales tend to be used to assess physical, mental, and social functioning simultaneously, discussions of most of the instruments themselves are reserved for chapter 5, where global measures of functioning are discussed. Here we note only that observer ratings of mental functioning present problems of rater subjectivity, lack of reliability, and uncertain validity. Observers are subject to biases in the directions of both under- and overstatement. On the one hand, nurses may wish to reflect positively on their own care provision; on the other hand, they may be overly critical of a disliked patient. To the extent that such scales are specific about the behavior observed, they are more likely to be used reliably. The difficulty occurs when constellations of observed behaviors are grouped under labels such as "paranoia" or "belligerence."

Observer-rating scales also require decisions about the appropriate time frame for the observations. Scales based on observations made at the moment of completing the rating may use an inadequate or biased sampling of behavior, whereas scales based on ratings of the subject over a more-extended period of time may be dependent on selective recall by the rater or may ignore the fact that the rater's opportunities for observations are really quite limited. Many data sets, including those used to form popular understanding of the characteristics of persons currently in nursing homes (U.S. Department of Commerce 1978), are, in fact, based on ratings of nursing attendants and are riddled with these problems. Very few observer-rating scales based on a random or even a systematic sampling of observations were identified.

Psychological Testing

Gerontologists have been pointing out for some time that the standard testing batteries, particularly those used to test intelligence, have only limited applicability to the elderly (Botwinick 1977; Schaie and Schaie 1977a). Although a full discussion of the problems is beyond the scope of this work, a partial listing of difficulties includes:

1. Intelligence tests have been developed and standardized on much younger groups and are therefore subject to cultural and educational bias; they may also be more pertinent to academic skills than reflective of the practical abilities of elderly persons.
2. Intelligence tests may unfairly penalize a person who is physically disabled or frail. This is especially true because testing tends to be a long, arduous process and is often timed for speed.

3. Tests are standardized on a particular cohort of individuals. A test that measures the intelligence of those who are 20 years old in 1940 may be a meaningful measure for those who are 60 years old in 1980 but not at all suitable for a cohort aged 40 in 1920, aged 60 in 1960, or aged 80 in 1980. This suggestion that tests also age and may not be applicable to any cohort other than the one used to standardize the instrument complicates interpretation of the results of psychological tests.

Full-scale psychological testing of cognitive functioning is interesting to developmental theorists and scientific researchers but is not a practical or desirable course for most geriatricians, primary-care physicians, social workers, or nurses who need to understand something about the mental abilities of their clients. Moreover, in the case of geriatricians, they are not particularly interested in intelligence quotient itself but, rather, in whether the patient is undergoing a rapid decline that might be an indication of pathology or might influence capacity for self-care. Fortunately, current work is pinpointing subtests in intelligence-test batteries that do not seem to decline with normal aging. Such information, in turn, suggests useful brief tests that might predict increasing dependence and even mortality.

Because standardized batteries that test cognitive functioning are onerous for both tester and subject and require special skill and equipment, a tendency has developed to use certain subtests that correlate with the overall score, reflect items considered predictive of outcomes for elderly patients, or do both. Some apparently useful techniques derived originally from standardized tests have worked their way into clinical practice; examples are digit span forward and backward, similarities and other vocabulary tests, and mathematical tasks such as "serial 7s." As such techniques are handed down through apprentice training of practitioners, the idea may lose its original rigor. If the practitioners are consistent in administering the test, it can be used to compare their own patients and to document changes in particular patients over time; but it cannot be used to compare groups of patients tested by other caregivers. Practitioners who are not consistent in their own testing methods cannot use their results even for these more-limited purposes.

In an effort to combine simplicity with some standardization, special tests have been developed for cognitive assessment of the elderly. Two opposite approaches to test development are prevalent: (1) construction of a test that reflects a single cognitive dimension such as memory, orientation, or visual-motor coordination; or (2) more commonly, construction of a test that samples items reflective of different attributes of the cognitive domain. The latter procedure is economical—it permits the physician or other caregiver to assess quickly a variety of cognitive functions. On the other hand, the practitioner needs to be cautious in interpreting summed scores on short tests that sample multiple constructs. Disentangling the meaning of a final score is often difficult.

Unless substantial work on the properties of the scale is available, the clinician may need to consider the items separately and to view the entire test as only a crude screening device.

Many of the problems in using standardized intelligence tests apply also to the common projective tests of psychological functioning. Lawton, Whelihan, and Belsky (1980) concluded that the state of the art is inauspicious for application to the elderly. Deterrents include the length of the tests, their physical demands on a group with limited eyesight and stamina, and educational and cultural differences associated with age that make interpretation difficult. If the individuals involved have minimal or moderate cognitive impairments, interpretation of projective tests is even more difficult. These tests—located in the realm of the trained psychologist—need study before they can be used to diagnose the mental health of the elderly. Some projective tests have been developed particularly for elderly subjects; in these cases the stimulus is usually adapted to elicit feelings thought to be associated with aging, but problems in administration remain.

Selected Measures

Measures of cognitive function have largely been developed on young subjects, and measures of mental status have generally been developed on psychiatric patients. A growing number of instruments, however, have been adapted or created afresh to measure mental status in older subjects. In the remainder of this chapter we discuss a selection of these instruments. We further refer the reader to the comprehensive handbook of mental health and aging (Birren and Sloane 1980) for discussions of assessment from a variety of perspectives including cognitive (Miller 1980); neurological (Drachman 1980); personality (Lawton, Whelihan, and Belsky 1980); and organic brain syndrome (Sloane 1980). In the same volume, Gurland (1980) treats assessment of mental health status of the elderly from the perspectives of both clinician and client, making explicit some of the nonmeasurement considerations involve in forming a helpful relationship and winning the client's confidence.

Table 3-1 divides the subject matter into three general concepts of importance to the primary-care provider treating an elderly patient, to the geriatric specialist, or to the researcher, namely, cognitive functioning, affective functioning, and general mental health. General mental health, in addition to including an assessment of cognitive and affective states, also encompasses other psychiatric conditions. For some purposes, especially screening, a general measure of mental health may be sufficient.

The table illustrates the highly abstract nature of concepts such as cognitive functioning, affective functioning, and mental health. Each concept can be further subdivided into component parts that are also abstractions requiring operational definition. For example, cognitive ability further sorts into components such as orientation, memory, perception, judgment, and so on, each of which is a complex phenomenon in its own right. The middle column of the table lists some of the specific items characteristically used to measure cognitive and

Table 3-1
Concepts Often Included in Measurement of Mental Functioning of the Long-Term-Care Patient and Items Commonly Used to Measure Concepts

General Concept	Selected Items Used to Measure Concept[a]	Selected Instruments Tapping General Concept[b]
Cognitive functioning		
Orientation	Knowledge of own name	VIRO Orientation Scale (Kastenbaum and Sherwood 1972)
Memory: recent	Knowledge of place	Mental Status Questionnaire (MSQ) (Kahn et al. 1960b)
Memory: distant	Knowledge of time	Face-Hand Test (Kahn et al. 1960b)
Perceptual ability	Knowledge of recent news events	Short Portable MSQ (Duke University 1978)
Psychomotor ability	Knowledge of distant news events	Set Test (Isaacs and Kennie 1973)
Attention span/concentration	Recall of birth date	Memory and Information Test (Kay 1977)
Problem solving/judgment	Recall of distant personal information (mother's maiden name)	Dementia Rating Scale (Kay 1977)
Social intactness	Recall of messages	PGC Mental Status (Fishback 1977)
Reaction time	Appropriateness of observed behaviors	PGC Extended Mental Status Questionnaire (Lawton 1968)
Learning ability	Vocabulary tests	Visual Counting Test (Fishback 1977)
Intelligence	Puzzles, word problems	Extended Dementia Scale (Hersch, Krai, and Palmer 1978)
	Mathematical problems	Misplaced Objects Test (Crook, Ferris, and McCarthy 1979)
	Block designs	WAIS complete and shortened form (Britton and Savage 1966)
	Simulated situations	Wechsler Memory Scale (Wechsler 1945)
		Geriatric Interpersonal Evaluation Scale (GIES) (Plutchik, Conte, and Lieberman 1971)
		Mini-Mental State (MMS) (Folstein, Folstein, and McHugh 1975)
		Quick Test (Ammons and Ammons 1962)
Affective functioning		
Depression, reactive	Appetite disturbances	Zung Self-Rating Depression Scale (Zung 1967)
Depression, endogenous	Sleep disturbances	Beck Depression Index (Beck et al. 1961)
Suicidal risk	Psychophysiological symptoms (heart beating, dizziness, constipation, faintness)	Hopkins Symptom Checklist (Derogatis et al. 1974)
Demoralization	Withdrawal, apathy	Affect Balance Scale (Moriwaki 1974)
	Tearfulness, sadness	
	Suicidal thoughts	
	Sense of failure	

Table 3-2 (continued)

General Concept	Selected Items Used to Measure Concept[a]	Selected Instruments Tapping General Concept[b]

General mental health
  Cognitive impairment
  Affective impairment
  Paranoia
  Substance abuse
  Presence of Psychopathology
	Numerous items gathered through clinical observation, questionnaire, or projective testing	OARS[c] Mental Health Section (Duke University 1978)
		Screening Score of Psychiatric Symptoms (Langner 1962)
		Emotional Problems Questionnaire (Ernst et al. 1977a,b)
		Gerontological Apperception Test (GAT) (Wolk 1972)
		Senior Apperception Test (SAT) (Bellak and Bellak 1973)
		Geriatric Mental State Examination (Copeland et al. 1976)
		Sandoz Clinical Assessment–Geriatric (SCAG) (Shader, Harmatz, and Salzman 1974)
		Savage–Britton Index (Britton and Savage 1966)
		London Psychogeriatric Rating Scale (Hersch, Kral, and Palmer 1978)
		Psychological Well-Being Interview (Lawton, n.d.)
		Nurses Observation for Inpatient Evaluation (NOSIE) (Honigfeld and Klett 1965)

[a]The selected items listed in this column are not to be linked to the subcategories in the left-hand column but only to the major concept, that is, cognitive functioning, affective functioning, or general mental functioning.

[b]The selected instruments listed in this column are not to be linked to specific items in either of the other columns but only to the major concepts, that is, cognitive functioning, affective functioning, or general mental functioning.

[c]A multidimensional tool, which is discussed in its entirety in chapter 5.

affective functioning operationally; because general mental health includes so many components, we made no attempt to list specific items. Finally, the right column of the table indicates a selection of instruments that have been used to measure general mental health in the elderly. The listed instruments vary widely; some are most suitable as screening tools, whereas others are designed to be part of a more-definitive assessment.

Cognitive Functioning

We have already indicated that assessments of cognitive functioning have practical implications for long-term care of the elderly. Clinicians making such determinations generally weigh the history, information on recent functioning gleaned from informants, and their own observations to reach conclusions about an elderly patient's overall competence. As table 3-1 shows, a variety of subcategories are included under the general construct "cognitive functioning," ranging from simple orientation to time, place, and person to the ability to perform feats of abstract reasoning and problem solving.

An assessment need not include all the dimensions of cognitive functioning listed in the table. Moreover, some higher-reasoning abilities may be assumed to be absent in the presence of severe disorientation and memory loss; similarly, some lower threshold of abilities may be presumed to have been reached in individuals capable of complex tasks. Presumably, an assessment of cognitive functioning is most useful if it branches to suit the quickly demonstrated ability of the patient. Not only are such procedures efficient, but they also avoid frustrating some subjects with items that are too difficult and annoying others with items that are too simple. The latter problem is sometimes addressed by conducting a brief orientation test in the context of gathering identifying information (name, age, birth date) from the patient. Another issue is that the factual information used in these tests must be subject to some verification. In the absence of external verification, one strategy is to repeat the question and consider consistent responses to be correct.

The circumstances for assessment of cognitive functioning are not always ideal. Potential problems include the following:

1. A reliable informant may not be available.
2. The opportunity for direct observation may be limited.
3. The clinician may be required to make determinations at a time when mental deterioration is suspected, yet may lack baseline data on the functioning of a particular individual.
4. The problem of lack of baselines is exacerbated when no performance norms for persons over 65 are available for a particular measure. Unfortunately, adequate norms are not available for many such tests.

Table 3-2 summarizes some of the instruments that have been developed for, or used extensively in, measurement of cognitive functioning of the elderly.

Table 3-2
Comparison of Measures of Cognitive Functioning

Name of Measure	Items	Score	Administration	Reliability	Validity
VIRO Orientation Scale	See table 3-3.	Perfect score = 24; partial score offered for partly correct responses; (see table 3-3).	Structured interview.	Alpha reliability of about .7 ; coefficients improved for first six questions.	
Mental Status Questionnaire (MSQ)	See table 3-3.	Errors counted, yielding score of 0–10; three levels of disability determined on basis of cutoff (see table 3-3).	Interview.	Alpha reliability of .84 and test-retest reliability of .8.	Correlated with clinical diagnosis of organic brain syndrome.
SPMSQ from OARS	See table 3-3.	Errors counted, yielding score of 0–10; four levels of disability determined on basis of score cutoff; standard adjustments for education and race.	Interview.	Test-retest reliability better than .8. (Pfeiffer 1975)	Correlated with clinical diagnosis of organic brain syndrome; good correlation but more false negatives than positives with this criterion.
PGH Mental Status Questionnaire	See table 3-3.	Errors counted, yielding 0–35 score; five levels of disability determined based on score (see table 3-3).	Interview and some questions to nursing personnel.		Face validity for some items; no information on test as a whole.
PGH Extended Mental Status Questionnaire	26 questions similar to PGH MSQ but no physical-disability items; unique items include: "Who was Hitler?" "On what day do we not eat?" "When is a boy Bar Mitzvah?" and, "What happened to President Kennedy?"	Not indicated.	Administered to patients in Jewish Home for the Aged; some verification from record needed.		Face validity of items; particularly developed for an elderly Jewish group.

Test	Description	Scoring	Mode	Comments
Memory and Information Test	Age, month, and date of birth, year of birth, today's date, 2 items of recent news, past and present monarch, past and present prime minister, date of beginning and end of World Wars I and II.	Items worth 1 or 2 points—depending on difficulty—to maximum score of 20.	Interview.	Used in Newcastle-upon-Tyne studies, cutoff point between 12 and 13 produced best discrimination between dementia and nondementia; scores correlated with 4-year mortality rates (Kay 1977).
Dementia Rating Scale (DRS)	Ability to perform household tasks; cope with small sums of money; remember 3-item list; find way about indoors and familiar streets; grasp explanations; recall recent events; tendency to dwell in past; eating, dressing, and excretory habits.	1 point each for presence of problems in each of first 8 areas with half points allowed; the 3 ADL functions are rated on a 3-point scale; maximum disability = score of 17.	Questions addressed to reliable informant and refer to usual functioning over past 6 months.	Used in Newcastle-upon-Tyne studies; few senile subjects score over 7; DRS scores correlated with 4-year mortality rates (Kay 1977).
Extended Scale for Dementia	23 items—commands; digits; naming; repeating; movements; graphomotor; block design; similarities; identities; sentences; orientation (time and place); information; count A's; count backwards; count by 3s; verbal recognition and memory; design recognition and memory; 14 items borrowed from Mattes Dementia Scale (Coblentz et al. 1973).	Each item has subparts; maximum scores per total item range from 5 to 18 points and for single question from 1/2 to 4 points. Points awarded so that each item is weighted to account for an equal part of total possible score of 250. Mean score of demented patients is somewhat less than 100.	Questions arranged hierarchically within each item group. If patient can perform most-difficult item, it is assumed that he can do all easier ones in the subcategory.	Test-retest reliability at 6-week interval showed Pearson-r of 194. No factorial structure found; high level of internal consistency for scale as a whole. Score distinguishes "demented" from "nondemented" patients among psychogeriatric inpatients; dementia patients showed significant decline on retests over time. Some items (counting backwards, block design, verbal recognition and memory, arithmetic) were most useful for predicting diagnoses of dementia and other items (orientation—time, naming, sentence construction) were useful for predicting severity of dementia.

Table 3-2 (continued)

Name of Measure	Items	Score	Administration	Reliability	Validity
Face–Hands Test	Patient touched on hands and cheek simultaneously in 10 trials (4 contra-lateral, 4 ipsilateral, and 2 symmetric stimuli interspersed).	Patient rated negative if errors persist in last 4 trials after the 2 symmetric stimuli.	Interview with cueing to help patient recognize that he may have been touched twice; eyes may be open or closed.	Demonstrated by Fink, Green, and Bender (1952) to be a reliable test of brain damage.	Correlates with clinical diagnosis of organic brain syndrome.
Visual Counting Test	Examiner holds up fingers in 4 different combinations and asks subject to indicate number of fingers.	25 points for each correct response.	If subject is blind, fingers are placed in his hand; not suitable for deaf or aphasic subjects.		Correlated with PGH MSQ, but higher scores are achieved on the former if administered after visual counting test.
Set Test	Subject asked to name as many animals, colors, fruits, and towns as possible.	One point awarded for each item in category, up to 10 per category; full points = 40; a score under 15 is abnormal.	Administered quickly in interview; not suitable for deaf or aphasic patient.		Norms developed in healthy old people who had mean score of 31.2, and 95 percent of scores were above 15 (Isaacs and Akhtar 1972). In sample of 189 subjects, score of 15 or less closely correlated with diagnosis of dementia and scores of 25+ with no dementia. Physical illness, depression, and social class did not influence test.

Test	Description	Scoring	Administration	Reliability	Validity
Misplaced Objects Test	Ability to recall where one has placed representations of common objects in a model of a house.	Point for each object correctly recalled.	10 magnetized objects and board depicting 7-room house used; subject places each object, but no more than 2 objects may be placed in a room; 5 to 30 min. later the board is presented again and subject replaces objects in the rooms previously chosen. Instructed to guess if they can't recall. In interval, subject is distracted from continuous rehearsal.	Test-retest reliability on successive days equaled .84.	Test has face validity. In test with elderly subjects with memory impairment (based on self-report and Guild Memory Scale subtests) and those with no memory impairment, and young subjects with no memory impairment, test correctly sorted most persons when 2 or more errors used as criterion. Vocabulary subtests of WAIS were held constant.
WAIS Short Form	Four subtests of the WAIS: Vocabulary (V), Comprehension (C), Block Design (BD), and Object Assembly (OA).	Personally administered by tester. Verbal IQ, performance IQ and full-scale IQ are calculated by prorating and using age norms in WAIS manual 1955.[a]	Individually administered by tester.	Reliability of WAIS.	Correlates highly with full version of WAIS.
Wechsler Memory Test	Seven subtests: personal and current information; orientation; mental control (backwards counting, alphabet, and counting by 30); logical memory (2 passages read and subject scored on average	Memory-quotient scores corrected for age. Some suggestion that scoring most useful on 3 factors: memory, attention, and concentration. Scoring instructions in Wechsler (1945) or Klonoff and	Individual administration.	Two forms of tests may not be reliably interchangeable.	Discussion in Kramer and Jarvik (1979), and in Erickson and Scott (1977). Questions on validity center on whether test measures motivation, cooperation, and willingness

Table 3-2 (continued)

Name of Measure	Items	Score	Administration	Reliability	Validity
	number of items retained in repeating); digit span (forward and backward); visual reproduction (draw geometric figures from memory); and associate learning (learning 10 word pairs in 3 trials).	Kennedy (1965) show norms for persons in eighties and nineties.			to memorize material of little value rather than recall of learned material. Scale does not discriminate among various patient groups. Age norms are available, and some correlations with IQ has been shown.
Quick Test (QT)	4 drawings shown on a card; 50 words listed that apply to one of the 4 drawings. Examiner reads words, and subject identifies appropriate picture associated with the word. 3 alternative forms of test available.	Score is total answered correctly in reaching the criteria of 6 consecutive failures plus all items easier than the easiest item passed. Scores can be converted into percentile norms and IQ norms for adults. Corrections for those over age 45.	Tester asks words until obtains 6 consecutive misses; takes 10 minutes to administer with elderly.	Test-retest reliability reported as adequate for screening; 3 forms of test well correlated.	Face validity and good correlation with full-scale WAIS (Ammons and Ammons 1962). In test with 50 elderly subjects (Levine 1971), QT well correlated with WAIS. In another trial (Gendreau, Roach, and Gendreau 1973), QT was found suitable for testing the very old, including some senile subjects. The 3 forms were found to be correlated with each other in aged sample.

	Description	Scoring	Administration	Reliability	Validity
Mini-Mental State	See table 3-4. Test covers orientation, memory; attention; ability to name, to follow verbal and written commands, to write a sentence spontaneously, and to copy a figure.	See table 3-4. Total of 30 points; score of 21 or less found only in patients with dementia, schizophrenia, delirium, or affective disorder.	Takes 5-10 minutes to administer; more detail on administration and scoring available; context of good rapport important.	Test-retest reliability at 24-hour intervals better than .8 with some different examiners; test-retest in 28 days for patients thought clinically stable .98.	Separates patients with and without cognitive disturbance; scores improve with change in function; correlates with WAIS and clinical judgment.
Geriatric Interpersonal Evaluation Scale (GIES)	See table 3-5; 16 items tapping cognitive and perceptual abilities, some with subparts.	Pluses are summed for a possible score of 46.	Personal administration.	Split-half reliability equaled .93.	Content validity on basis of selecting behaviors identified by ward staff as relevant; correlation between scores on GIES and on Geriatric Rating Scale (a measure of physical and social functioning); item analyses done with "highest" and "lowest" scorers and all but 6 of subitems discriminated.

[a]The formulas for calculating IQs from the shortened version of the WAIS are (Britton and Savage 1966):

$$\text{Verbal Scaled Score} = 3\,(V + C)$$

$$\text{Performance Scaled Score} = \frac{5\,(BD + OA)}{2}$$

The list, which is by no means exhaustive, includes instruments that tap a single dimension and multidimensional test batteries; instruments that are completed in interview with the subject and those that are completed through ratings of performance; instruments suitable for the measurement of differences both at the lower end of the cognitive-functioning spectrum and at the upper end.

Because orientation and memory are extremely important areas in geriatric assessment, it is not surprising that quick-assessment tools have been developed to tap those dimensions. The first six measures listed on table 3–2 are quick-assessment tools to measure orientation and related cognitive abilities; the specific items on four of these tests are reproduced in table 3–3. Taken together, our examples illustrate the similarity among brief screening instruments used to measure basic cogntivie abilities. The differences generally reflect the differences in the expected performance of the group for whom the test was designed.

Before we touch briefly on each instrument, some general comments about reliability and validity are appropriate. As indicated earlier, reliability falls into categories including test-retest, inter-rater, and item-bound reliability (that is, tests of the internal consistency of the measure). Inter-rater reliability tests, designed to determine whether the results are consistent despite variations in interview styles and techniques, have generally not been reported for these measures of cognitive functioning. Test-retest reliabilities with the same interviewer are also rarely described. Interpretation of the results of a test-retest strategy is particularly problematic in measures of mental orientation because the characteristic is believed to fluctuate with changes in physical status and even with the time of day. As far as can be determined, none of the orientation instruments described here have been studied to determine whether the time and circumstances of the testing can be correlated with test results. The most-common form of reliability testing for measures in this domain is the statistical test of internal consistency of the items. In the case of mental-status-screening questionnaires, however, the most widely used instruments are purposely designed to include items that represent a variety of domains. In such cases, one would not expect the instrument to be internally consistent. In most cases, more work is needed to determine what pattern of responses typically makes up the total score.

We repeatedly stress that, although reliability is a prerequisite of validity, it is insufficient by itself. The validation of most of the mental-status-questionnaires (MSQs) rests on a correlation of their results with a clinical diagnosis of organic brain syndrome or senile dementia. Here the knottiest problem of all emerges; a clinical diagnosis of senile dementia is highly unsatisfactory as a criterion measure unless the diagnosis itself is reliable and valid. At a minimum, some control must be exerted over the definitions leading to that diagnosis.

Unfortunately, many studies rely on a diagnosis of dementia as found on a medical chart or provide insufficient information about who made the diagnosis and under what definitions and conditions. If a particular MSQ does not correlate well with a clinical diagnosis of dementia, one is still left wondering whether the test or the criterion measure is at fault.

Some cognitive tests seem to be predictive of increased mortality. If this is true, the tests have a utility for prognosis; but such predictive validity still does not assure us that the phenomenon being measured is really disorientation and cognitive impairment. In instances when a measure seems to perform consistently to predict outcomes, perhaps its name is less important than are further efforts to understand the basis for its predictive power.

Although we tend to view clinical diagnosis as a validity criterion, it is well to consider that the ability of a mental-status instrument to duplicate a clinical label is not its only important function. There is indeed a place for face validity in mental-status testing. The need to replicate a clinical diagnosis is most important when the choice of therapy is diagnosis specific. In other cases, specific diagnosis may be less important than identification of dysfunction. For example, depression may need to be clearly defined before antidepressants are used or their effectiveness tested, but social support and counseling can be used once a state of unhappiness or sadness is established.

The VIRO Orientation Scale

The VIRO Orientation Scale (Kastenbaum and Sherwood 1972) was designed for use as part of a method for rating the Vigor, Intactness, Relationships, and Orientation of geriatric patients on the basis of their responses and reactions during an interview situation. (See chapter 4 for a dicussion of the test as a whole.) As the scoring format indicates, it is suitable for developing a spread of scores in very regressed patients. For example, the respondent is awarded partial points for identifying the current year and his own age if he comes within ten years of the correct responses. As befits its name, the orientation scale does not really tap dimensions reflecting more-advanced cognitive abilities or even distant memory; memory is assessed through a test of whether the subject can remember the examiner's name (given clearly at the outset of the contact) and whether he can estimate the length of the total interview. Otherwise the questions are straightforward orientation items about age, dage of the week, month, year, community, and street.

Table 3-3
Four Mental-Status Tests

Viro Orientation Scale[a]

		Score
1. Knows age	Precisely	3
	Within 2 yrs	2
	Within 10 yrs	1
2. Knows day of week	Yes	3
	No	0
3. Knows month	Yes	3
	No	0
4. Knows year	Precisely	3
	Within 2 yrs	2
	Within 10 yrs	1
	All else	0
5. Knows name of community	Yes	3
	No	0
6. Knows street	Yes	3
	No	0
7. Remembers examiner's name	Yes	3
	Partially	2
	No	0
8. Estimation of interview length	Within 5 mins	2
	Within 10 mins	2
	Within 30 mins	1
	All else	0

Perfect Score = 24

Short Portable Mental Status Questionnaire (SPMSQ)[b]

1. What is the date today (month/day/year)?
2. What day of the week is it?
3. What is the name of this place?
4. What is your telephone number? (If no telephone, what is your street address?)
5. How old are you?
6. When were you born (month/day/year)?
7. Who is the current president of the United States?
8. Who was the president just before him?
9. What was your mother's maiden name?
10. Subtract 3 from 20 and keep subtracting each new number you get, all the way down.

0-2 errors   = intact
3-4 errors   = mild intellectual impairment
5-7 errors   = moderate intellectual impairment
8-10 errors = severe intellectual impairment

Allow one more error if subject had only grade school education.
Allow one fewer error if subject has had education beyond high school.
Allow one more error for blacks, regardless of education criteria.

Mental Status Questionnaire (MSQ)[c]

1. What is this place?
2. Where is this place located?
3. What day in the month is it today?

Table 3-3 (continued)

4. What day of the week is it?
5. What year is it?
6. How old are you?
7. When is your birthday?
8. In what year were you born?
9. What is the name of the president?
10. Who was president before this one?

Score shows severity of brain syndrome

0-2 errors   =   none or minimal
3-8 errors   =   moderate
9-10 errors =   severe

Philadelphia Geriatric Center Mental Status Questionnaire[d]

1. What is your name?
2. Who am I (point to self)?
3. Who is that (point to nurse)?
4. Are you married or single?
5. If married, do you have children?
6. If yes, what are their names? (incorrect if not known)
7. Where is your room?
8. What is your room number?
9. What is the name of this place?
10. What floor is this?
11. Where is the bathroom?
12. Where do you eat your meals?
13. What meal did you eat last?
14. What is today and what is the date?
15. What month is it now?
16. What year is this?
17. What season is this? (accept either if season is changing)
18. What is the weather outdoors now?
19. How old are you?
20. When were you born (month)?
21. What year were you born?
22. What is your mother's first name?
23. What is your father's first name?
24. Who is the president of the United States?
25. Who was the president of the United States before him?
26. Do you wear glasses?
27. Where are they now?
28. Do you have your own teeth?
29. If not, do you have plates or dentures?
30. Where are they now?
31. Do you dress yourself? (Note if capable.)
32. Do you feed yourself? (Observe if patient uses cutlery or fingers.)
33. Bladder and bowel continence (ask nurse).
34. Family recognition (ask nurse).
35. Is it now morning or afternoon?

One point for each correct answer

0 = total loss	21-33 = mild
1-10 = severe loss	34-35 = not impaired
11-20 = moderate	

[a]Adapted from R. Kastenbaum and S. Sherwood, "VIRO: A Scale for Assessing the Interview Behavior of Elderly People," in *Research, Planning and Action for the Elderly*, ed.
D.P. Kent, R. Kastenbaum, and S. Sherwood (New York: Behavioral Publications, 1972).

[b]Adapted from Duke University, *Multidimensional Functional Assessment: The OARS
Methodology* Durham, N.C.: Duke University, 1978.

[c]From R.L. Kahn, A.I. Goldfarb, M. Pollack, and A. Peck, "Brief Objective Measures for
the Determination of Mental Status in the Aged," *American Journal of Psychiatry* 117
(1960b):326-328.

[d]D.B. Fishback, "Mental Status Questionnaire for Organic Brain Syndrome, with a New
Visual Counting Test," *Journal of the American Geriatric Society* 25 (1977):167-170.

The Hebrew Rehabilitation Center for the Aged ran reliability tests of the
VIRO scale using two community-based samples of 382 subjects in Worcester,
Massachusetts and 140 in Fall River, Massachusetts (Sherwood, et al 1977).
The alpha coefficients were .75 and .67, respectively; these reliabilities improved to .814 and .718, respectively, when the two items on the examiner's
name and the length of interview were dropped from the scale. This suggests
that the last two items may indeed tap a somewhat different phenomenon.

Mental Status Questionnaire (MSQ)

The MSQ (Kahn et al 1960a, b) has been extensively used in geriatric research
and practice. Its ten questions contain many of the same items as the VIRO
orientation scale, although, unlike the VIRO, it does not permit partial scores.
The last two items on the name of the president and the immediate past president tap awareness of current events and memory for more-distant events.
Although this question recurs in various forms on mental-status tests, some
critics suggest that it probes memory with items that are increasingly irrelevant to the elderly, particularly those residing in institutions. Kahn reports
that test-retest reliability is better than .8 and the Hebrew Rehabilitation Center
for the Aged, using the two samples previously mentioned, reports alpha reliabilities of .84.

Short Portable MSQ (SPMSQ)

The SPMSQ (Duke University 1978) is a part of the larger OARS battery, a
multidimensional tool for community-based assessment discussed in chapter 5.
The SPMSQ, however, is suitable for administration apart from the more-
extensive battery; and much work has been done to develop norms for the
scale. In addition to borrowing a number of orientation and memory items

from the MSQ already cited, the SPMSQ also taps other spheres. The item on "mother's maiden name" is a test of remote memory, which, unlike the questions about past presidents, is almost certain to probe material that was once learned. The ability to remember a telephone number (or street address) is a test of practical survival skills for self-care in the community. The last question, serial subtraction from 20 by 3s, provides an indicator of mathematical ability.

The SPMSQ is more difficult than the previously discussed scales; for example, the subject must know the day, month, and year before being awarded points for birth date or current date. Despite the test's relative difficulty, it generates a spread of scores from 0 to 10, even in nursing-home populations, and is seemingly inoffensive when administered to a community-based sample. A decided advantage of the SPMSQ is that the norms, adjusted for race and education, have been developed (Pfeiffer 1975).

Fillenbaum (1980) found that the MSQ and SPMSQ were highly correlated. However, both must be viewed as only screening tests subject to error. When scores were compared to the results of psychiatric interviews with eighty-three patients, twenty-nine of whom were diagnosed as having organic brain syndrome, a score of two errors on the MSQ and a similar score for the SPMSQ yielded a true positive (sensitivity) rate of 55 percent and a true negative (specificity) rate of 96 percent.

Philadelphia Geriatric Center (PGC)
Mental Status Questionnaire

Fishback (1977) reports the development of a mental-functioning test that is capable of producing a spread of scores among those who would receive a 0 on the MSQ or SPMSQ. It contains all the items of the MSQ (although subdivided so that partial scores are possible) and, in addition, has items thought to be more pertinent to the situation of the nursing-home patient, such as the location of various places in the facility, the season of the year, the day's weather, and the last meal eaten. Some items refer to ability to perform ADL functions and the ability to locate glasses and dentures. No further work with this scale is reported in the literature. On the face of it, the inclusion of items about ability to perform ADL activities may compromise the measure; the instructions do not clarify whether the subject loses points on these items if the limitations are based on physical problems.

PGC Extended Mental Status Questionnaire

An earlier extended mental status questionnaire was developed at PGC by Lawton (1968). Like Fishback's later version, it expands the MSQ to include items that might be simpler for regressed patients and more meaningful to residents in nursing homes. Among its remote-memory questions are items requiring the first names only of mother, father, and (if applicable) children. This instrument does not include ADL Items and thus remains free of the possible confounding of the Fishback test. Of particular interest are questions that are designed especially for the population being assessed—in this case, residents in a Jewish home for the aged. Thus items on Jewish observances are included, and subjects are asked, "Who was Hitler?" Elsewhere, Lawton (1972) has argued that patterns of memory retention and loss may be socially and culturally determined. Interestingly, the 1968 version of the Extended MSQ available to us contains the item, "What happened to President Kennedy?" Such a question may be pertinent to a narrow age cohort only and yet be very discriminating for that particular group.

Memory and Information Test (MIT)

The MIT is a British test, adapted by Kay (1977) for use in the Newcastle-upon-Tyne population studies. Its eleven questions contain seven items that require orientation to the world around one; subjects are asked for two recent news events, the name of the monarch, the former monarch, the prime minister, the former prime minister, and the dates of World Wars I and II. (The last two items require both beginning and ending dates.) Although this test seems more difficult than either the MSQ or the SPMSQ, in the British context it was used (with a cutoff between 12 and 13) to discriminate those with the clinical diagnosis of dementia, and was even correlated with four-year mortality rates.

Face–Hand Test and Visual Counting Tests

The next two tests are tests of organicity that have the advantage of being minimally influenced by language, culture, and verbal skills. Face–Hand Test (Fink, Green, and Bender 1952) is based on the ability of the individual to recognize simultaneous tactile stimulation on cheek and palm. Its administration permits a rehearsal so that the individual can become familiar with the test; only the last four of ten paired stimuli count for the score. This test has been widely used in gerontological research (Kahn et al. 1960a), although results are mixed on whether the Face–Hand Test adds additional information to a mental-status battery (Kramer and Jarvik 1979). The Face–Hand Test apparently is useful for distinguishing psychotic patients from those with brain damage; although hallucinating patients might perform poorly on MSQ tests, they apparently will not make errors on identifying the locus of the tactile stimulation.

The Visual Counting Test, suggested by Fishback (1977), is based on the assumption that counting extended fingers is one of the first skills learned by a child and one of the last to disappear in disoriented adults. It has the advantage of being a simple test, insensitive to culture and language, and easy to administer to all but deaf patients. Fishback found that this test correlated well with his own PGC Mental Status Questionnaire, but no further use of the Visual Counting Test can be found in the literature.

Set Test

The Set Test (Isaacs and Kennie 1973) is an easily used test that identifies the presence and level of senile dementia. The subject is simply asked to name as many examples of animals, fruits, colors, and towns as possible. One point is awarded for each, up to ten in each category. Those with organic brain damage demonstrate sufficient categorical fluency to perform this task. In a population study, 95 percent of the scores were above 15; in a later study of long-term-care patients, a score under 15 very closely approximated diagnoses of senile dementia. This test has entered the black bags of many British geriatricians as a working clinical tool but has not yet been reported in the United States.

Dementia Rating Scale (DRS)

The Dementia Rating Scale, another British measure, was used in the Newcastle-upon-Tyne studies (Kay 1977). A reliable informant rates the subject over the past six months regarding the propensity to dwell in the past or the inability to do the following: cope with small sums of money, remember a three-item list, find his way about indoors, find his way around familiar streets, grasp explanations, recall recent events. One point is awarded for a problem in each of these areas, with half the points permitted for partial problems. In addition, eating, dressing, and excretory habits are rated on a three-point scale. This test has the merit of containing some practical items that might be known to an informant who is in close contact with the subject; it is unsuitable, however, if no such informant is available. Out of a possible score of 17, the Newcastle studies showed that few persons diagnosed as senile scored over 7; furthermore, the DRS was correlated with four-year mortality. False positives identified through the DRS fell into borderline categories where differential psychiatric diagnosis was difficult.

As used by Kay, the DRS was treated as a straightforward rating scale, whereas in an earlier study by Blessed, Tomlinson, and Roth (1968), problems in performance of ADL functions were included in the dementia score only if no organic cause for the limitation could be identified. When those rules were used, the DRS was more closely associated with post-mortem cortical pathology than was the MIT, perhaps because the latter picks up acute confusional states, whereas the former gathers information that presumably reflects functioning over a longer period.

The Misplaced Objects Test

The Misplaced Objects Test (Crook, Ferris, and McCarthy 1979) is an example of a measure that approximates the tasks of the real world. It requires subjects to place magnetized representations of common objects (for example, pen, key, umbrella) in a model representation of a seven-room house. After five to thirty minutes of intervening distractions, the subject is asked to replace the articles as they were before. This test is suitable for detecting mild as well as more-serious memory impairment. Its game-like format is apparently well tolerated by the subject, perhaps because absentmindedness is socially acceptable. Because the test is a relatively new one, little information is available about its use. No specific instructions are given about how to vary the time interval, nor was the length of that interval incorporated into the score. The authors of the test report a good test-retest reliability (.84) with retesting on successive days; however, they caution that, in the absence of alternative forms, subjects might learn associations and achieve a better score on repeated administrations. The Misplaced Objects Test is worthy of further exploration to develop norms and refinements of scoring.

Extended Scale for Dementia

The next group of measures is based on subsets of standardized psychological tests developed originally for younger respondents. The Extended Scale for Dementia (Hersch, Kral, and Palmer 1978), developed in London, Ontario, was adapted from the Mattis Dementia Rating Scale (Coblentz et al. 1973). The battery contains twenty-three items (each with subitems) derived from the Wechsler Adult Intelligence Test (WAIS). The items include Digits, Naming, Repeating, Movements, Graphomotor, Block design, Similarities, Identities, Sentences, Orientation (time), Orientation (place), information, Count A's, Count Backwards, Count by 3s, Design recognition and memory, and Verbal recognition and memory. The investigators developed a scoring system based on empirical analysis of item difficulty. The goal was to ensure that each general item has an equal chance of contributing to a total score of 250. With this system, the subitem maximum scores ranged from 0.5 to 4 points, and the item maximum scores from 5 to 18 points. The mean score of those diagnosed as demented was less than 100. A test such as the Extended Dementia Rating Scale requires time, equipment, and skilled administration and thus is unsuitable for screening purposes. The originator of the scale point out, however, that within each item the subitems are arranged in order of difficulty, rendering it unnecessary to administer an easier item if the individual can perform a more difficult one.

WAIS Short Form

Britton and Savage (1966) describe their experience with a shortened version of the WAIS. Four subtests were used: vocabulary and comprehension subtests were combined to produce a verbal IQ, and block design and object assembly to produce a performance IQ. Investigators comparing the IQ scores (verbal, performance, and full scale) generated from the entire WAIS to those generated by the abbreviated version found a high correlation. Clearly, the shorter version is much more convenient.

Wechsler Memory Test

The Wechsler Memory Test is a battery designed to measure memory function apart from intelligence; the objective was to create a measure that correlated well with intelligence tests but did not duplicate them. As Erickson and Scott (1977) point out, one hazard in developing memory tests on the basis of informational questions is that the original learning of that information might not have occurred. Even questions about former presidents (common on mental-status questionnaires) assume that the information was once learned, but not all individuals have equal interest in acquiring such information. Other approaches to testing memory that avoid the assumption of original learning require the subject to demonstrate learning of new material. Here, however, because the cooperation of the subject is crucial, failure to remember may be a function of motivation rather than of ability. This is particularly true if the test requires memorization of meaningless material and sequences. The Wechsler Memory Test has been included on the list as a example of an early attempt to measure memory that has been used with elderly subjects. Its advantage is that it is a clearly described, easy-to-use test that differentiates aspects of memory. As Kramer and Jarvik's (1979) review shows, the measure has not been entirely satisfactory. The timed feature has been a problem with elderly subjects, and some critics suggest that the two forms of the test are not comparable.

Klonoff and Kennedy (1965) studied the Wechsler Test with a sample of 172 community-dwelling subjects in their eighties and nineties. Norms have been developed from this study for memory patterns of the old-old (aged

75 and over). For example, the rank order of intactness of memory was mentation, personal information, digit span, mental control, associate learning, visual reproduction, and logical memory. The mean score for digits forward was 6.12 and, for digits backward, 4.01. In mental control, ability to repeat the alphabet was most intact, followed by counting backwards and then by counting by 3s. Associate learning is a task involving presentation of ten word pairs (some easy, such as "north/south," and some difficult, such as "cabbage/pen") and then requiring the subject to supply the missing one from the pair. The elderly subjects did quite well with this after the permissible three trials. Out of a possible 13 on the paired associates, the mean score for the same was 10.11 and for those age 86 and over, 9.56. Logical memory requires the subject to remember twenty-four ideas from a logical paragraph read aloud. Out of a possible 24 points, the mean for the same was about 3.

Summarizing these findings, the Wechsler results showed greater loss in immediate than in remote memory, in logical than in rote memory, and in visual than in auditory retention. A direct relationship was found between Weschler scores and rating of activity levels (on a three-point scale from "very active" to "minimally active").

Quick Test (QT)

The Quick Test (Ammons and Ammons 1962) provides a means of assessing vocabulary ability in a rapid and pleasant format. The QT correlates well with both the verbal and the pull-scale IQ on the WAIS. The subject is shown a card with four pictures and, for each of a series of words, is asked to designate the most-relevant scene. Although fifty vocabulary words are provided for each version of the test, the tester does not repeat them all; rather, he enters the test at what he would judge to be an appropriate level for the subject and continues until six successive misses are made. The test takes about three minutes with younger subjects and about ten minutes with older ones. In a number of trials of this test with elderly subjects (Levine 1971; Gendreau, Roach, and Gendreau 1973), the correlations with the WAIS held up; even with senile patients, some score could usually be obtained.

As in all vocabulary tests and tests of verbal ability, the QT is influenced by the educational levels of the subjects. Therefore, it would not be suitable for testing a group of educationally or culturally deprived individuals. Nor would it be a useful test for a population composed largely of brain-damaged and deteriorated individuals because, in this context, it would not yield much information beyond confirmation of the original diagnosis. For establishing the abilities of the general population of elderly persons over time, however, this test might have utility because of its ease of administration, minimal dependence on hearing, and acceptability to the subjects.

Vocabulary is considered to be an attribute of crystallized intelligence (Horn 1970); that is, it is an "overlearned" behavior that does not decline with normal aging but rather increases or remains constant. Gerontological researchers (Birren 1968; Schaie and Schaie 1977a) have convincingly shown that seeming declines on vocabulary tests with age are artifacts of cross-sectional studies (reflecting differences in learned vocabulary among cohorts). Such differences disappear with longitudinal studies and elimination of speed tests. A sudden drop in vocabulary ability may therefore be an indicator of serious difficulties. To explore such hypotheses further, the Quick Test may be a promising vehicle.

Mini-Mental State Examination

The WAIS and its subtests, the Wechsler Memory Scale, and other test batteries not included here (such as the Bender Gestalt, the Primary Mental Abilities Test, and the Shipley–Hartford Institute of Living Scale) introduce some disadvantages for the long-term-care provider. Their use presupposes a sophistication with psychological test batteries and their implications. The "testiness" of these batteries renders them inhospitable to physicians, nurses, and social workers who may be searching for a general measure of cognitive functioning that is convenient and has obvious relevance to decisions that need to be made about care of the elderly. Furthermore, although the administration of a large battery of tests is prohibitively expensive, time consuming, and intrusive, the selection of a few subtests (for example, digit span) may inadequately sample the domain of cognitive functioning.

Folstein and his colleagues (1975) developed the Mini-Mental State Examination (MMS) partly to address these issues. It is "mini" in the sense that only cognitive functioning is measured; within that realm, however, the test was designed to be thorough. At the same time, the test takes only five to ten minutes to administer; and, because its items are so similar to those of a clinical mental-state examination, its relevance is immediately apparent. For this reason, the authors suggest that psychiatric trainees could profitably be exposed to the test.

Table 3–4 shows the items of the MMS. The latter part of the test involves reading and writing and may therefore be difficult for subjects with visual problems. Nevertheless, the tester can minimize such problems by writing in very large, bold print. No prepared materials are needed. Considerable work was done to establish that the MMS distinguishes among those with the diagnoses of dementia, depression, and schizophrenia, and elderly control subjects without psychiatric diagnosis. Depressed patients presenting with pseudodementia are reported to show improvements on the MMS as the depression is ameliorated.

Table 3–4
Items of Mini-Mental State Examination

Maximum Score	
	Orientation
5	What is the (year) (season) (date) (day) (month)?
5	Where are we (state) (county) (hospital) (floor)?
	Registration
3	Name three objects: One second to say each. Then ask the patient all three after you have said them. Give one point for each correct answer. Repeat them until he learns all three. Count trials and record number.
	Number of trials
	Attention and calculation
5	Begin with 100 and count backwards by 7 (stop after five answers). Alternatively, spell "world" backwards.
	Recall
3	Ask for the three objects repeated above. Give one point for each correct answer.
	Language
2	Show a pencil and a watch and ask subject to name them.
1	Repeat the following: "No 'if's,' 'and's,' or 'but's.' "
3	A three-stage command, "Take a paper in your right hand; fold it in half and put it on the floor."
1	Read and obey the following: (show subject the written item).
	CLOSE YOUR EYES
1	Write a sentence.
1	Copy a design (complex polygon as in Bender-Gestalt).
30	Total score possible

Source: Adapted from M.F. Folstein, S. Folstein, and P.R. McHugh, "Mini-Mental State: A Practical Method for Grading the Cognitive State of Patients for the Clinician," *Journal of Psychiatric Research* 12 (1975):189–198.

Geriatric Interpersonal Evaluation Scale (GIES)

Table 3-5 shows the items of the GIES (Plutchik, Conte, and Lieberman 1971), a test developed at the Bronx State Hospital to test cognitive and perceptual functioning. Like the Folstein test, it is designed to sample the cognitive domain thoroughly, has face validity, and is administered quickly. The items include

Table 3-5
Items of the Geriatric Interpersonal Rating Scale

1. Rater offers patient a seat. Score plus if patient sits with no further urging.

2. Rater indicates, "I'd like to ask you some questions to find out how you are doing," and scores plus for each correct answer:

   "What day of the week is it today?"
   "What month is it?"
   "What is today's date?"
   "What year is it?"
   "What season is it?"
   "What was your last meal—breakfast, lunch, or supper?"

3. Rater places pad in front of patient, offers him a pencil saying, "Will you take the pencil please." Score plus if patient accepts without further urging.

4. Rater shows patient a drawing of a three-inch square with diagonals and asks patient to copy it onto the paper.

   Score plus if the patient draws anything.
   Score plus if the patient draws a four-sided figure.
   Score plus if the patient draws a four-sided figure with diagonals.

5. Rater tells the patient he is going to say some numbers, asks the patient to listen carefully and repeat them. If the patient answers correctly to a given length of the first set, score plus and go on to the next length of that set. If he fails a given length in the first set, repeat that same length in set 2. Stop when any length is failed twice.

Set 1	Set 2
7-2	4-9
3-7-6	6-2-5
8-7-2-1	9-6-5-3
8-1-2-9-3	6-5-4-7-3
9-1-2-8-5-3	9-4-1-8-7-2

6. "Whom did the United States fight in World War II?" Score plus for Germany, Italy, or Japan.

7. "Whom did the United States fight in World War I?" Score plus for Germany.

8. "Now I am going to ask you if two words mean the same thing or if they are different." Score plus for each correct answer.

   "Does talk mean the same as speak?"
   "Does stop mean the same as go?"
   "Does bug mean the same as insect?"
   "Does automobile mean the same as train?"
   "Does boast mean the same as brag?"

9. "I am going to name some objects and what they could be used for. If I am right, you say 'Yes' and if I am wrong, you say 'No.'" Score plus for each correct answer.

   "A fork is for eating."
   "A train is for traveling."
   "A pen is for cutting."
   "A gun is for shooting."
   "A saw is for writing."

10. "Okay. Now we have some number questions." Score plus for each correct answer. Stop after two consecutive items are missed.

"What is 2 × 3?"	"What is 2 × 192?"
"What is 2 × 6?"	"What is 2 × 384?"
"What is 2 × 12?"	"What is 2 × 786?"
"What is 2 × 24?"	"What is 2 × 1536?"
"What is 2 × 48?"	"What is 2 × 3072?"
"What is 2 × 96?"	

Table 3-5 (continued)

11. Rater shows patient two cartoons and asks, "Do you think either of these is funny?" Score plus if either is considered funny. Score plus if patient gives an adequate reason why.

12. Asks patient to tell a joke. Score plus if patient can do so.

13. Rater takes all the picture cards from two decks and arranges them randomly in front of patient. In the context of a game, rater draws a red card, places it in the center and asks subject to find a card of the same color and place it on top of this card. Score plus if patient can do so.

14. Rater draws a jack; asks patient to find a card with the same picture and put it on top of his. Score plus if patient can do so.

15. Rater draws queen of spades and asks patient to find card with both the same picture and the same color and put it on top of his. Score plus if patient can do so.

16. Rater separates the two sets of cards, putting one in front of patient and one in front of himself, both sets arranged randomly. He asks patient to "put one of your cards between us and I will put one of mine exactly like it on top." Rater purposely puts the wrong card on patient's. Score plus if patient indicates that rater made a mistake.

Scoring: All pluses summed for a possible score of 46.

Source: Adapted from R. Plutchik, H. Conte, and M. Lieberman, "Development of a Scale (GIES) for Assessment of Cognitive and Perceptual Functioning in Geriatric Patients," *Journal of the American Geriatric Society* 19(1971):614–623. Precise wording has been abbreviated somewhat in the interests of space.

simple orientation questions, tests of appropriate social behavior in the testing situation, a perceptual motor task (item 4), tests of immediate and remote memory (items 6 and 7), and tests of the quantitative and verbal aspects of cognitive functioning. Four points in the test are awarded for the ability to categorize playing cards on the basis of color, shape, and both color and shape together. (This test may be easier for subjects familiar with card games such as gin rummy or canasta.) The GIES also contains a digits-forward sequence, an item that may have prognostic significance because a rapid decline in this ability has been associated with mortality (Schaie and Schaie 1977a, b).

Because the authors developed the items for the GIES after discussions with personnel in geriatrics, the test is anchored in reasonable expectations for the patient's performance. The test is designed to produce some score even among highly regressed patients. Item analysis suggests that most items are useful for discriminating those with high and low scores. In his review of the use of psychiatric scales in drug studies, Kochansky (1979) found only one example in which the GIES was used as a measure, with, as it happened, no difference between the drug and the placebo group. No further examples have been found in which the GIES was used to measure change occurring as a result of treatment, although the test would seem useful for that purpose.

For both the MMS and the GIES, the tester might profitably examine performance on individual items because the measures tap a variety of items in the cognitive dimension.

An Evaluation of a Cognitive Functioning Scale

In a study sponsored by the Royal College of Physicians, Hodkinson (1972) performed a detailed analysis of a cognitive-funcitoning test. Physicians and staff members in participating hospitals administered the test to over 700 British hospital patients over age 65 within the first four days of their hospitalization. The original twenty-six-item test is reproduced in the left-hand column of table 3–6. Earlier studies had shown that a score of 25 to 34 signified normal mental functioning. Although lower scores were associated with mental impariment, the test did not differentiate acute confusional states from dementia.

The investigator performed a series of analyses to refine the scale. For example, a comparison of low-score-discriminating and high-score-discriminating questions identified some questions that were either so easy or so difficult that they accounted for variance only at the extremes of the score range. Other clusters of questions, such as those concerning time orientation, personal background information, or orientation to place duplicated each other; that is, the questions tapped similar dimensions and behaved almost identically across the sample. Table 3–6 also shows the new version of the test after less-useful or redundant items were eliminated. The results on the ten items of the abbreviated test were found to conform very closely to the results on the longer twenty-six-item version. Calling for more work on the test, the author indicates that the abbreviated test has not yet demonstrated itself to be satisfactory for helping a diagnostician recognize progressive or abrupt changes suggestive of confusional states. Repeated applications are required to make this claim.

The most noteworthy aspect of the Royal College study is that it represents a cooperative effort among physicians to forge practical measuring tools for geriatrics that could be applied in clinical settings. Analogous work is not as evident at health-care-delivery sites in the United States.

Affective Functioning

Measuring affective functioning is one of the great challenges in geriatric care. Although depression is almost universally acknowledged to be important, both as an outcome in itself and as an independent variable influencing outcomes, little consensus has emerged on how to measure depression in the elderly.

Table 3-6
Evaluation and Revision of Hodkinson's Mental Test Based on 700 Hospital Inpatients

Original Test Items	Score	Reason for Dropping Item	New Test Items
1. Name	1	Too easy; only dropped marks on those scoring under 5	
2. Age	1	Retained	Age
3. Time to nearest hour	1	Retained	Time to nearest hour
4. Time of day	1	Duplicated #3	
5. Name and address for 5-minute recall:		Retained but simplified	Address recall for end of test: 42 West Street
Mr. John Brown	1 or 2		
42 West Street	1 or 2		
Gateshead	1		
6. Day of week	1	Duplicated #9	
7. Date (day of month)	1	Duplicated #9 but also difficult	
8. Month	1	Duplicated #9	
9. Year	1	Retained	Year
10. Type of place (for example, hospital)	1	Duplicated #11	
11. Name of hospital	1	Retained	Name of hospital
12. Name of ward	1	Duplicated #11	
13. Name of town	1	Duplicated #11	
14. Recognition of 2 persons (for example, doctor, nurse)	1 or 2	Retained	Recognition of 2 persons
15. Date of birth	1	Retained	Date of birth
16. Birthplace	1	Duplicated #15	
17. School attended	1	Duplicated #15	
18. Former occupation	1	Duplicated #15	
19. Next of kin	1	Duplicated #15	
20. Date of World War I	1	Retained	Date of World War I
21. Date of World War II	1	Duplicated #20	
22. Name of present monarch	1	Retained	Name of present monarch
23. Name of present prime minister	1	Duplicated #22	
24. Months of year backwards	1 or 2	Too difficult	
25. Count 1–20	1 or 2	Too easy	
26. Count backwards 20–1	1 or 2	Retained	Count backwards 20–1
Full points = 34 *Normal range* = 25–34			*Score*: 1 point per correct item *Full points* = 1

Source: Developed on the basis of information in H.M. Hodkinson, "Evaluation of a Mental Test Score for the Assessment of Mental Impairment in the Elderly," *Age and Ageing* 1(1972):233–238.

- *reactive*
- *endogenous*
- *psychotic* (impaired reality)
- *neurotic*

Some very useful reviews highlight the problems (Salzman and Shader 1979; Gallagher, Thompson, and Levy 1980).

The complications in measuring depression in the elderly are similar to those confronting the measurer in other domains. Briefly summarized, they include:

1. *Ambiguity of the term.* Depression is a loosely used term that has entered the common language to depict a gloomy mood state that could be transient or prolonged, reality based or without obvious reason. The clinician, however, usually reserves the term for profound affective disturbances characterized by a variety of symptoms such as feelings of worthlessness, psychosomatic complaints, lethargy, sleep and appetite problems, crying jags, and suicidal thoughts. Even then, clinicians make other distinctions, differentiating reactive depression (that is, reality-based) from endogenous depression (that is, a persistent pattern of depressive cycles) and psychotic depression (that is, depression accompanied by impaired reality testing) from neurotic depression. Such distinctions are used to determine the severity of the problem, including degree of suicidal risk, and to suggest treatment plans. Because depression is such as imprecise term, one cannot always be confident that the clinical diagnosis produces a useful or consistent criterion measure to validate scales.

2. *Relevance of present diagnostic categories to the elderly.* At present we cannot be confident that distinctions between reactive and endogenous depression or between psychotic and neurotic depression have practical relevance with an elderly population, particularly persons with severe reality problems. If, in fact, a person is faced with a future that seems to offer much pain and little hope of personal pleasure or fulfillment, then suicidal plans may develop despite excellent reality testing and no previous history of cyclical depression. The mental-health professionals have failed to generate information about the clinical attitudes of elderly persons who perceive (and act on) such despair. Without epidemiological studies, we cannot be certain what signs and symptoms accompany the mood states of elderly persons who are at high risk of self-destructive behavior.

3. *Relevance of standard diagnostic criteria in elderly groups.* The third edition of the *Diagnostic and Statistical Manual* (DSM III) provides a considerably tightened set of operational diagnostic criteria for depression (American Psychiatric Association 1978). These were conceptualized as follows:

1. Dysphoric mood or loss of interest or pleasure in all or almost all usual activities and pastimes. The dysphoric mood is characterized by descriptors such as depressed, sad, blue, hopeless, low, down in the dumps, irritable, worried. The disturbance must be prominent and relatively persistent but is not necessarily the most-dominant symptom. It does not include momentary shifts from one dysphoric mood to another (for example, from anxiety to depression to anger), such as are seen in states of actual psychotic turmoil.

2. The illness has had a duration of at least two weeks, during which, for most of the time, at least four of the following symptoms have persisted and have been present to a significant degree:
    a. Poor appetite or significant weight loss (when not dieting) or increased appetite or significant weight gain.
    b. Insomnia or hypersomnia.
    c. Loss of energy, fatigability, or tiredness.
    d. Psychomotor agitation or retardation (but not mere subjective feelings of restlessness or being slowed down).
    e. Loss of interest or pleasure in usual activities, or decrease in sexual drive (do not include if limited to a period when delusional or hallucinating).
    f. Feelings of self-reproach or excessive or inappropriate guilt (either may be delusional).
    g. Complaints or evidence of diminished ability to think or concentrate, such as slowed thinking or indecisiveness (do not include if associated with obvious formal thought disorder).
    h. Suicidal ideation or wishes to be dead, or any suicide attempt.
3. Not superimposed on either schizophrenia, schizophreniform disorder, or a paranoid disorder.
4. None of the following dominates the clinical picture for more than three months after the onset of the depressive episode:
    a. Preoccupation with a mood-incongruent delusion or hallucination.
    b. Marked formal thought disorder.
    c. Bizarre or grossly disorganized behavior.

Blazer (1980) tested the extent to which the DSM III criteria were workable for identifying elderly persons diagnosed as depressed. Using existing community-survey data, he identified eighteen questions appearing in the first edition of the OARS instrument that reflect the DSM III criteria. These eighteen questions were labeled the OARS Depressive Scale (ODS). The ODS performed well in identifying hospital patients with well-established psychiatric diagnoses of depression but was less satisfactory in the community sample. In this latter group, dysphoric mood (worry, sadness, dissatisfaction) did not consistently correlate with symptoms of depression such as difficulty concentrating, restlessness, feelings of uselessness, and sluggish thinking. One suggested explanation is that the diagnosis of depressive reaction is often made in elderly persons on the basis of mild depressive symptomatology. Growing out of this work, Blazer suggests that distinct subgroups might be identified: namely, those who meet the DSM III category for depressive disorders; those who meet the DSM III category for depressive disorders but, in addition, have some other significant mental disturbance such as thought disorders; and those with dysphoric symptoms that are perhaps related to medical disorders and other problems. The new specificity of the DSM III provides a good jumping-off point for considering ways of objectively identifying depression in the elderly. Work with these criteria should render psychiatric diagnosis of depression more reliable for the population as a whole, and studies such as Blazer's will ensure that any necessary modifications or amplifications of the criteria be made for application to the elderly. A newly developed Diagnostic Interview Schedule, designed to generate the diagnostic categories of the DSM III, is currently being tested with an oversampling of elderly persons.

4. *Lack of norms.* As with the preceding point, little information is available about the incidence and prevalence of depression among the aged in the community and in particular among the aged in institutions. Keller (1979) found existing literature to be inconclusive and contradictory. Scales, therefore, do not have norms adequate for elderly persons. As Gallagher, Thompson, and Levy (1980) suggest: ". . . a useful scale for assessing depressive symptoms in older adults should focus on the symptoms characteristic of depression in this age group and be able to differentiate the latter from the dementias of old age." They state that no scales have been designed with these requirements in mind; indeed, we would suggest that the knowledge is still insufficient to design a scale to those specifications.

5. *Construct validity.* Depression scales (and clinical workups for depression) rely heavily ont he presence of somatic indicators of a depressed mood state. These include insomnia and early-morning wakefulness, poor appetitite, weight loss, constipation, headaches, rapid heartbeàts, and dizziness. Such phenomena could be due to poor physical health rather than to depression. Little information is available about the extent to which those who already have poor health experience an increase in somatic symptoms attributable to mood states. To support such assertions, data are required that show a fluctuation of the somatic items on depression scales in the elderly while observable health indicators remain constant. Similarly, depression measures often contain items that query whether the subject is preoccupied with death or with his own health. Such items may indicate morbid thoughts in a younger age group and yet have much-less-negative significance for persons near the end of the life span. Other typical items may not reflect the construct of depression as well with the elderly as they do with younger age groups. Many depression scales contain items about loss of libido, operationalized as having less interest in sex. Those items have been criticized because many elderly persons within and outside institutions have narrowed opportunity for sexual expression and, therefore, a socially determined lack of interest. In administering a depression test recently, we found that the sexuality item might have implications for mood that are the reverse of the test maker's intention. An 87-year-old nursing-home resident who selected the response, "I have lost interest in sex completely," went on the say thoughtfully that probably this was a good thing because she would hate to have "that torment" added to her other problems.

6. *State/trait distinction.* Levitt and Lubin (1975) present a cogent

discussion of the distinction between "trait" and "state" in measurement of affect. A trait measure taps a condition that has been stable for a considerable period of time, whereas a state measure taps an immediate mood. Measures that use the here and now as a time reference are, of course, state measures; to take an extreme example, an individual who is clearly distressed and tearful at the time of interview is in a depressed state but might not, in fact, be characterized as depressed on a trait measure. Test-retest reliabilities are sometimes considered inappropriate for state measures because the phenomenon captured is ephemeral. Trait measures, however, suffer from the problem that present mood colors one's view of past mood.

As always, the purpose of the measurement dictates the choice. The state measurement may have face validity for the moment, yet not reflect the needs of the individual long-term-care patient whose pattern of mood may be at variance with the single observation. When mood is measured for a group of long-term-care patients, perhaps to determine the outcome of care, then the mean scores on measures of depression would seem adequate. For example, if the majority of nursing-home patients were in a depressed state, the cumulated evidence would leave little doubt that the mood of the patients was low, despite the use of a state measure.

7. *Cohort effect.* Ours is an introspective, psychologically oriented generation. The past twenty-five years, during which most depression scales were developed, have been characterized by increasing attention to mood states. It is by no means clear that an 80-year-old man would call himself "worried" or "tense" in describing the kind or degree of feeling that a 40-year-old man would describe in those terms. Moreover, some language may simply be unclear because of the generation gap, and older persons may have different inhibitions than do younger persons about expressing mood states.

8. *Administration problems.* Many depression scales are complex instruments. Questions have lengthy stems and require that the respondent choose among many responses. The more reading entailed in the test, the more difficult is self-completion for the elderly subjects. In any event, when self-administration is not feasible because of physical or sensory impairments, the test must be administered orally. Oral administration may militate against socially unacceptable responses. Also, for oral administration, the items usually require simplification of both the stems and the response choices.

Salzman and his colleagues (1972b) reviewed mood-rating scales presenting information about eleven adjective inventories to assess mood states, fifteen depression inventories, four anxiety and hostility inventories, and nine morale inventories. They cite difficulties in applying many of the instruments to geriatric patients because of length and other administrative factors. Additionally, many of the instruments were developed for other populations and either have thus far failed to register change in studies of elderly patients or have not yet been used in such studies. The authors conclude that, because mood is a private experience, its accuracy can be reported only with a cooperative subject. For a geriatric group, the criterion of cooperation is more likely to be achieved if the scale is brief, clearly stated, and relevant to the respondent's current life situation.

Table 3-7 describes four examples of scales that are currently available to assess depression in the elderly, and table 3-8 presents the actual items of the tests. Among them, the Zung Self-Rating Depression Scale (SDS) and the Beck Depression Inventory are keyed quite closely to the clinical symptoms of depression, whereas the Hopkins Symptom Checklist (Depression Items) is designed to tape the existence of a dysphoric mood state with minimal emphasis on the psychophysiological symptoms associated with depression. The Affect-Balance Scale, the fourth instrument included, is a brief screening device that not only taps dysphoric mood but also yields a measure of the other extreme, that is, of positive affect or elation. All four instruments require responses from cooperative subjects; we have excluded assessments of mood that require a rating by caregivers or significant others. We also omitted the depression scale of the MMPI because, with its sixty questions, it seemed to have no advantages over other scales that would outweigh its considerable practical disadvantages.

Zung SDS

The Zung Self-Rating Depression Scale has been used quite widely in geriatric research and has attracted substantial critical comment (Salzman and Shader 1979). The scale choices, ranging from "a little of the time" to "most of the time," seem inappropriate for community-based groups without psychiatric disturbance. Elderly persons have been antagonized by the need to select from those choices on items such as "I feel that others would be better off if I were dead." Oral administration increases the sensitivity of the questions. Some users advocate changing the first response category to "none or a little of the time" to avoid offending the respondents. In any event, the Zung instrument is somewhat cumbersome for oral administration.

Blumenthal's (1975) factor analysis of the SDS yielded four subscales: a well-being index, a depressed-mood index, an optimism index, and a somatic-symptoms index. The latter contained two items: "My heart beats faster than usual," and "I get tired for no reason at all." Steuer and her colleagues (1980) identified six additional somatic items in the SDS; these dealt with diurnal variation, insomnia, appetite, enjoyment of sex, weight loss, and constipation.

The items in the Zung scale were derived from clinical observations associated with depression; many have a substantial psychophysiological component, and some gerontologists (Morris, Wolf, and Klerman 1975) suggest dropping the item on sexual libido entirely. Not enough information is available to assert

Table 3-7
Comparison of Measures of Affective Functioning

Name of Measure	Items	Score	Administration	Reliability	Validity
Zung Self-Rating Depression Scale (SDS)	20 statements that subjects rate as applicable to themselves "a little of the time," "some of the time," "a good part of the time," or "most of the time" (see table 3-8 for exact items).	Likert scales with total raw score of 80 possible. Index ranging from 0.25–0.100 is calculated by dividing sum of the raw score by 80 × 100.	Designed for self-administration; with elderly it has also been administered orally.		Face validity because items are based on clinical diagnostic criteria for depression. Mean scores of depressed patient before Rx were 0.74 compared to 0.39 after treatment and 0.33 in control group. (Zung 1965). Morris, Wolf, and Klerman (1975) produced 2 factors (agitation and self-satisfaction) and showed correlation with morale scales.
Beck Depression Index	21 sets of 4–5 graded statements, each set ordered to show increasing depression; subject chooses the response most appropriate for self (see table 3-8 for exact items).	Each choice given a weighted score; 3 points possible per item.	Statements are read to subject, who chooses the one most applicable to self; subjects are given a copy of the statements to refer to during interview.	Alpha reliabilities are high; inter-rater reliability tested indirectly by seeing if scale correlations with clinical judgments differed by rater.	Face validity because items were selected to represent clinically observed behaviors; scale scores correlated with clinical impressions of *severity* of depression; scores will reflect change as clinical judgments of depression severely change.

Hopkins Symptom Checklist	13 symptoms—subject rates degree of symptoms on 5-point scale from "not at all" to "extremely" (see table 3–8 for exact items).	Depression items are interspersed in a 90-question self-report mental-health battery.	Likert-type score—each item ranges from 0 to 4, total score for depression = 52.	Gallagher, Thompson, and Levy (forthcoming) report that it is sensitive to change in elderly depressed psychotherapy clients. Face validity for dysphoric mood; relatively few psychophysiological items.
Affect-Balance Scale	10 short yes-no questions that reflect positive (5 items) or negative (5 items) affect over past few weeks (see table 3–8 for exact items).	Interview.	Positive Affect Scale (PAS) is sum of positive items, and Negative Affect Scale (NAS) is sum of negative items; Overall Affect Balance Scale is the sum of positive items minus sum of negative items; a constant of 5 is added, producing ABS scores of 0–10.	Bradburn (1969) reported test-retest reliability on the items ranging from .80 to .97. He reported, too, that the PAS and NAS are independent of each other, and this was confirmed in elderly samples.	Gaitz and Scott (1972) administered ABS to 1,441 community residents and found that older subjects scored lower on both PAS and NAS, but that ABS had no correlation with age. ABS correlated with global self-appraisals of happiness and life-satisfaction. Moriwaki (1974) showed that all 3 scales discriminated elderly psychiatric outpatients from normal subjects. Scores of ABS, PAS, and NAS were correlated for both groups with degree of role loss, mental health, morale, and avowed happiness.

Table 3-8

Examples of Scales to Measure Affective Status

Zung SDS
1. I feel downhearted and blue.[a]
2. Morning is when I feel the best.
3. I have crying spells or feel like it.
4. I have trouble sleeping at night.
5. I can eat as much as I used to.
6. I still enjoy sex.
7. I notice that I am losing weight.
8. I have trouble with constipation.
9. My heart beats faster than usual.
10. I get tired for no reason.
11. My mind is as clear as it used to be.
12. I find it easy to do the things I used to.
13. I am restless and can't keep still.
14. I feel hopeful about the future.
15. I am more irritable than usual.
16. I find it easy to make decisions.
17. I feel that I am useful and needed.
18. My life is pretty full.
19. I feel that others would be better off if I were dead.
20. I still enjoy the things I used to do.

Modified Beck Depression Inventory[b]
1. I do not feel sad.[c]
   I feel sad.
   I am sad all the time and can't snap out of it.
   I am so sad or unhappy that I can't stand it.
2. I am not particularly discouraged about the future.[c]
3. I do feel like a failure.[c,d]
4. I get as much satisfaction out of things as I used to.[c]
5. I don't feel particularly guilty.[c,d]
6. I don't feel I am being punished.
7. I don't feel disappointed in myself.
8. I don't feel I am any worse than anyone else.
9. I don't have thoughts of killing myself.[c,d]
10. I don't cry any more than usual.
11. I am no more irritated now than I ever am.
12. I have not lost interest in other people.
13. I make decisions about as well as I ever could.[c]
14. I don't worry that I look worse than I used to.
15. I can work about as well as I used to.
16. I can sleep as well as usual.
17. I don't get any more tired than usual.
18. My appetite is no worse than usual.
19. I haven't lost much weight, if any, lately.
20. I am no more worried about my health than usual.
21. I have not noticed any recent change in my interest in sex.

Table 3-8 (continued)

Hopkins Symptom Check List–Depression Items

How much discomfort has this problem caused you during the past _____, including today?[e]

How much were you distressed by _____?

1. Loss of sexual interest or pleasure.
2. Feeling low in energy or slowed down.
3. Thoughts of ending your life.
4. Crying easily.
5. Feeling of being caught or trapped.
6. Blaming yourself for things.
7. Feeling lonely.
8. Feeling blue.
9. Worrying too much about things.
10. Feeling no interest in things.
11. Feeling hopeless about the future.
12. Feeling everything is an effort.
13. Feelings of worthlessness.

Bradburn Affect Balance Scale

Looking at your present situation, have you ever felt:

		Yes	No
1.	Particularly excited or interested in something?	___	___
2.	So restless you couldn't sit long in a chair?	___	___
3.	Proud because someone complimented you on something you had done?	___	___
4.	Very lonely or remote from other people?	___	___
5.	Pleased about having accomplished something?	___	___
6.	Bored?	___	___
7.	On top of the world?	___	___
8.	Depressed or very unhappy?	___	___
9.	That things were going your way?	___	___
10.	Upset because someone criticized you?	___	___

Sources: For Zung: adapted from W.W.K. Zung, "A Self-Rating Depression Scale," *Archives of General Psychiatry* 12(1965):63–70. For Hopkins: adapted from L.R. Derogatis, R.S. Lipma, K. Rickels, E.H. Uhlenhuth, and L. Covi, "The Hopkins Symptom Checklist (HSCL): A Measure of Primary Symptom Dimensions," *Pharmacopsychiatry* 7(1974):79–110. For Beck: A.T. Beck, C.H. Ward, M. Mendelson, J. Mock, and J. Erbaugh, "An Inventory for Measuring Depression," *Archives of General Psychiatry* 4(1961):53–63, as modified by Dolores Gallagher, Andrus Gerontology Center, University of Southern California, 1979. For Bradburn: adapted from S.Y. Moriwaki, "The Affect Balance Scale: A Validity Study with Aged Samples," *Journal of Gerontology* 29(1974):73–78.

[a]For each item, the respondent rates the statement as "a little of the time," "some of the time," "good part of the time," or "most of the time."

[b]Each item has 4–5 responses, representing a range of mood; the respondent picks the one most appropriate. We included all four responses only for item no. 1.

[c]Used on a seven-item scale developed by Sherwood et. al. (1977) to measure rejection, guit, and despair.

[d]Used on a three-item scale developed by Sherwood et. al. (1977) to measure rejection, guilt, and despair.

[e]Choices: not at all; a little bit; moderately; quite a bit; extremely.

whether psychophysiological systems and libido loss differentiate depression in the elderly.

A study by Steuer and her colleagues (1980) has suggested, however, that physical-health status may not unduly confound SDS scores in the elderly. Using a sample of sixty elderly participants in a clinical trial of antidepressive medication, they correlated physicians' health ratings, SDS scores, and somatic-item-subscale scores, finding no association between physician ratings and SDS scores. The Blumenthal two-item somatic subscale, especially the single item of fatigability, was significantly related to physicians' ratings and to total SDS scores. With the elderly patients, however, the nonsomatic items correlated better with the SDS scores than did the somatic. The somatic items showed relatively weak associations, with two items (tachycardia and constipation) failing to achieve significance. In contrast, the other thirteen items were all significantly associated with the total scores, with seven exceeding .50. The authors suggest that their findings challenge clinical folklore that "emphasizes somatization as an important aspect of depression in the elderly" (p. 687). This type of work on the properties of a scale as applied to an elderly population is a model for the type of methodological research that could increase our confidence in transferring measures for the general population to the elderly.

Beck Depression Inventory

The items on the Beck Depression Inventory are also clinically derived; the twenty-one items shown on table 3–8 are designed to reflect (in this order) mood, pessimism, sense of failure, lack of satisfaction, guilt feelings, sense of self-punishment, self-hate, self-accusations, self-punitive wishes, crying spells, irritability, social withdrawal, indecisiveness, body image, work inhibition, sleep disturbance, fatigability, loss of appetitie, weight loss, somatic preoccupation, and loss of libido. For these attitudes, a series of graded statements was produced, with numerical values of 0 to 3 assigned to each. Some statements are assigned identical weightings. The statements are read to the subject, who selects the one in each set that is most personally pertinent. (The subject refers to a copy of the test during the administration.)

Beck and his colleagues (1961) report extensive work on the reliability and validity of the inventory. In order to validate the scale against clinical judgment, the investigators were challenged to show that clinical judgment itself is reliable when rating the depth of depression (regardless of diagnosis) even when a diagnosis of depression in itself does not produce consensus. Using the depth of depression as a criterion, the Beck inventory discriminated effectively among groups of patients. It also registered changes in intensity of depression over time.

The experience of the Beck scale with elderly subjects is fairly encouraging. With a small sample of aged persons, Gallagher showed that psychotherapy could lead to measurable improvement in the Beck scale (Gallagher, Thompson, and Levy, 1980). The wording of items shown in table 3–8 follows Gallagher's suggestions for oral administration to the elderly; reading along is difficult for many of the elderly, and simplification of the statements has made the choices easier to remember.

In our own work with nursing-home residents, we have found that some respondents become fatigued by the full-scale Beck instrument. As shown in table 3–8, Sherwood and her colleagues (1977) developed two shortened versions: a seven-item scale and a three-item scale. Alpha reliabilities for both shortened scales were performed for two samples, a home-care population and a rehabilitation-center population. In all scases, the scales were homogeneous with the three-item scale performing better. The items retained in that scale (expressed in the most-depressed form) were: "I feel I am a complete failure"; "I feel as though I am very bad and worthless"; and "I would kill myself if I got the chance."

Beck and Weissman (1974) also developed a "hopelessness scale" that is similar to the depression inventory. Although it may tap the trait of pessimism rather than a changeable state, the explanation of future orientation seems particularly appropriate for an elderly population. In at least one study of an elderly institutionalized group, improvements were noted on the Beck Hopelessness Scale after an intervention designed to increase perceived control (Mercer and Kane 1979). As far as we know, however, this scale has not been used in other studies with elderly subjects.

Hopkins Symptom Checklist

The Hopkins Symptom Checklist is a series of statements developed originally from the Cornell Medical Index. The subject rates, on a five-point scale, the amount of discomfort he has been caused by each of the ninety problems.

Factor analysis has revealed four clusters, labeled anxiety, depression, anger/hostility, and obsessive/compulsive/phobic (Derogatis et al. 1974). The thirteen depression items on this questionnaire are easily administered to aged subjects. Gallagher and her colleagues (1980) argue that it is a promising instrument for measuring the existence of a dysphoric mood apart from psychophysiologic symptoms.

Affect-Balance Scale

The Affect-Balance Scale is a simple test designed to tap the affective status of the general population. As table 3-8 shows, it consists of five questions tapping negative affect and five tapping positive; altogether, three scores are generated: a positive-affect score (PAS), a negative-affect score (NAS), and an affect-balance score (calculated by PAS − NAS + 5). Gaitz and Scott (1972) demonstrated that the affect-balance score does not change with age but that both the PAS and NAS scores are lower in the elderly: both positive and negative affect were blunted with age in this cross-sectional study. Moriwaki (1974) showed that, despite the blunting of affect with age, all three scales discriminated elderly psychiatric outpatients from normal elderly subjects. Furthermore, in this elderly sample, lower scores on all three scales were associated with role loss, morale, and self-rating of overall happiness.

The Affect-Balance Scale would seem to be a useful screening tool for the general population, particularly because it taps the positive domain. On the face of it, however, the scale would not be promising for eliciting the severity of depressive states; and, in fact, the negative-affect items tap dimensions other than depression (boredom, restlessness, and sensitivity to criticism).

General Mental Health

At times the geriatric provider needs to make a generalized assessment of mental health. We have already seen that more-focused concepts such as cognitive functioning or affective functioning are actually multidimensional. Those attempting to assess general mental health are faced with even more problems created by the sheer multiplicity of dimensions to be tapped.

In table 3-9 we present a selection of instruments that have been used to measure the mental functioning of the elderly. Those chosen represent different strategies, which could be employed for different purposes. Some of the instruments are brief and fairly crude screening tools; these would not assist a provider in reaching diagnostic specificity, nor would they differentiate between mild symptomatology and full-bown pathology. At the opposite end of the spectrum are detailed interview schedules from which a series of scales can be derived. Two projective tests developed for the elderly are also represented in the table. Finally, we include examples of mental-health scales based on observer rating.

Table 3-9
Comparison of Measures of General Mental Health

	Items	Administration	Score	Reliability	Validity
OARS Mental Health Screening	15 yes–no questions (see table 3–10).	Part of longer OARS schedule administered by personal interview	No score produced; interviewer uses the answers to these questions and others to produce a 5-point rating of overall mental health.	See chapter 5	Questions derived from MMPI.
Screening Score	22 yes–no questions (see table 3–10).	Interview developed as part of 2-hour midtown-Manhattan study	1 point for each symptom; a cutoff score of 4+ had only 1% false positives and about 25% false negatives; a screening score of 7+ is recommended to eliminate false positives.		Questions derived from MMPI and other batteries. Questions discriminate between psychiatric-patient groups and group judged as psychiatrically intact. Questions correlate highly with those psychiatrists use to judge mental health. Gaitz and Scott (1972) showed no age differences on total score in cross-sectional study, but older people had higher proportion of somatic and memory problems and lower proportion of compliants of alienation, restlessness, and hopelessness.
Emotional Problems Questionnaire	10 questions to screen for depression and "psychotic complaints" (see table 3–10)	Interview	4+ complaints viewed as indication of affective or psychotic symptoms.		Ernst et al. (1977b) show changes in emotional-problems score in small nursing-home sample; sensory stimulation led to increase in cognitive abilities and increase in depression as well, measured by this scale.

Table 3-9 (continued)

	Items	Administration	Score	Reliability	Validity
Savage-Britten Index	15 yes-no questions (see table 3-10).	MMPI questions adapted for oral administration in interview.	Newcastle-upon-Tyne studies suggest cutoff of 6+ as abnormal score; this cutoff produces more false positives than false negatives.		Questions selected on the basis of (1) correlating well with full MMPI in large population-study; (2) high loading on general mental illness factor derived from MMPI; and (3) high correlation with psychiatric diagnosis; validated on small sample ($N = 30$) of psychiatric normals and abnormals.
Sandoz Clinical Assessment Geriatrics	18 items rated on 7-point scale from "not present" to "severe."	Rating by professionals.	Likert scale with possible 7 on each item; complete norms not published; overall rating ≤3 was judged normal.	Small inter-rater reliability showed good reliability in most items but poor reliability on fatigue, irritability, appetite, and anxiety.	Tentative suggestion that ratings reflect changes after drug Rx (Kochansky 1979), expecially attitude or mood items and cognitive-impairment items. Shader, Harmatz, and Salzman (1974) suggest SCAG scores do correspond with professional judgments.
London (Ontario) Psychogeriatric Rating Scale (LPRS)	36-item questionnaire with scale of 0–2 for each item as severity increases. Four subtests are: mental disability, physical disability, socially irritating behavior, and disengagement.	Ratings by 2 ward staff members on psychogeriatric unit; raters blind to the way items form subscales.	Average of 2 raters' scores used; total score and subscale scores are expressed as percentages; cutoff scores for each subscale predict suitability for group psychotherapy.	Inter-rater reliability not reported, but 2 raters are always used and agreement is said to be high.	LPRS scores highly predictive of outcomes of psychogeriatric patients (death, discharge to a nursing home, discharge home); LPRS also differentiates diagnostic subgroups in psychiatric population.

Gerontological Apperception Test (GAT)	14 cards, each depicting an older person in common situations; subject asked to associate to picture.	Examiner presents subject with one card at a time and asks for a story about it with a beginning, middle and end. Not all cards need to be used. Stories recorded verbatim and analyzed.	No norms established; scores may be developed by individual users.	Reliability problematic; in TAT (from which GAT is derived), reliability depends on use of a predetermined specified scoring system and training.	Validity of notion that these age-specific stimuli evoke richer responses unproved. Dye (forthcoming) suggests that test is overweighted with depressive themes.
Senior Apperception Test (SAT)	16 cards with drawings of older people in life situations.	Subject asked to present story for each card. The last card is presented as a person dreaming and subject is asked to describe dream "and make it lively." Five minutes maximum per card is recommended and not all need to be used. Stories recorded verbatim and analyzed.	No system of scoring developed; norms for length of stories have been developed on small samples.	Same problems as GAT above.	Kahana (1978) summarized published and unpublished studies supporting the contention that SAT stimuli are useful with elderly population.
Geriatric Mental State Examination	Standardized psychiatric interview yielding 541 ratings, most on 5-point scales.	Psychiatric interview with content and probes structured; requires 30–40 minutes; suggested that interviewers be trained through 20 joint interviews.	Details not provided; factor analysis has yielded scales, and use of instrument assists psychiatrists in reaching reliable diagnosis.	Reliability assessed through a second psychiatric rating as observer and test-retest; reliability of individual items and total scores quite high; "observational" items least reliable (Copeland et al. 1976).	Analysis of data from 100 geriatric psychiatric patients in London and New York yielded 21 factors: depression; anxiety; impaired memory; retarded speech; hypermania; somatic concerns; observed belligerence; reported belligerence; obsessions; drug/alcohol; cortical dysfunction; disorientation; lack of insight; depersonalization; paranoid delusion; disordered thought; visual hallucination. auditory hallucination; abnormal motor movements; nonsocial speech; and incomprehensibility (Gurland et al. 1976).

Table 3-9 (continued)

	Items	Administration	Score	Reliability	Validity
Psychological Well-Being Interview	98 questions; 32 yes–no; 40 on 5-point scale; others on 3- or 4-point scale.	Personal interview for community-based group of elderly.			Factor analysis has yielded 21 factors.
Nurses Observation Scale for Inpatient Evaluation (NOSIE)	80 items describing patient, each rated on 5-point scale from 0 ("never") to 4 ("always"). Examples of items: "Shaves himself"; "Can be drawn into conversation"; "Helps when asked"; "Shouts and yells"; a 30-item version is also available.	Nurse rates based on observations over last "three days."	Scores are additive; norms have been published for the 7 factors (Honigfeld and Klett 1965).	Dye (forthcoming) summarizes inter-rater reliabilities for separate factors; they are very high (above .8).	Factor analysis produces 7 factors: social competence; personal neatness; irritability; manifest psychosis; psychotic depression; cooperation; social interest; scale sensitive to change in double-blind drug studies.

Despite the difficulties inherent in asking a third person to rate someone's mental health, some systematic methods are required for assessing the mental well-being of those persons who are too disoriented to complete a more-conventional interview or questionnaire.

Screening Scales

Three of the four screening scales shown in full in table 3-10 (OARS Mental Health Screening, Langer Twenty-two-Question Screening Score, and the Savage-Britton Index) have roots in the Minnesota Multiphasic Screening Examination (MMPI). Despite efforts to understand its factorial structure with the elderly (Britton and Savage 1969), the MMPI itself with its 500 questions is not a practical instrument for wide use with LTC patients. The Mini-Mult (Kincannon 1968) is a reduced 71-question version of the MMPI that permits sex-adjusted scores on eleven subscales and generates a profile analogous to that produced by the full instrument. Fillenbaum and Pfeiffer (1976) tested the Mini-Mult with about 1,000 community residents.

On the basis of this work, they raise a number of issues. First, of 997 participants, only 640, or somewhat less than two-thirds, could complete the 71 questions necessary to generate the scores. The ability to complete the questionnaire was correlated with age, education, and organicity as measured by the Short Portable MSQ. Based on the data from the 640 for whom scores could be derived, Fillenbaum and Pfeiffer found that scores adjusted for sex according to instructions showed males to be more impaired than females on five subscales. Corrections for race were also problematic. The reliability of the Mini-Mult on a test-retest at a five-week interval was not impressive with a subsample of 30 subjects. Finally, the validity of the Mini-Mult scores was also called into question. On the basis of answers to other questions, 19 "superbly well" individuals were identified from the 640; Mini-Mult scores were no better for this group than for the sample as a whole. Because an instrument with properties like the MMPI would be useful for the elderly, the authors recommend that further work be done to establish appropriate sex and race corrections and standardized norms for the elderly.

Even without its imperfections, the Mini-Mult clearly posed difficulties for more than one-third of the community-based sample and, for a more-impaired sample, would be even less useful. The screening devices shown in table 3-9 are designed for ease of completion. The OARS fifteen-question mental-health-screening tool does not pinpoint pathology in any precise way, nor does it generate scales. When used as part of the OARS Multidimensional Battery, it forms part of the data base for global mental-health ratings. Used alone, the questions form a crude screen. No instructions for interpreting responses are given.

The Langer Twenty-two-Question Screening Score was developed for the midtown Manhattan study of the mental health of community residents. Some

Table 3-10
Examples of Scales to Measure General Mental Health

Screening Score[a]

1. I feel weak all over much of the time.
2. I have periods of days, weeks, or months when I can't take care of things because I can't get going.
3. In general, would you say that most of the time you are in high (very good) spirits, good spirits, low spirits, or very low spirits?
4. Every so often I suddenly feel hot all over.
5. Have you ever been bothered by your heart beating hard? (Often, sometimes, or never)
6. Would you say your appetite is poor, fair, good, or too good?
7. I have periods of such great restlessness that I cannot sit long in a chair (cannot sit still very long).
8. Are you the worrying type (a worrier)?
9. Have you ever been bothered by shortness of breath when you were *not* exercising or working hard? (Often, sometimes, never)
10. Are you ever bothered by nervousness (irritable, fidgety, tense)? (Often, sometimes, never)
11. Have you ever had any fainting spells (lost consciousness)? (Never, a few times, more than a few times)
12. Do you ever have any trouble in getting to sleep or staying asleep? (Often, sometimes, never)
13. I am bothered by acid (sour) stomach several times a week.
14. My memory seems to be all right (good).
15. Have you ever been bothered by "cold sweats"? (Often, sometimes, never)
16. Do your hands ever tremble enough to bother you? (Often, sometimes, never)
17. There seems to be a fullness (clogging) in my head or nose much of the time.
18. I have personal worries that get me down physically (make me physically ill).
19. Do you feel somewhat apart (isolated, alone), even among friends?
20. Nothing ever turns out for me the way I want it to.
21. Are you ever troubled by headaches or pains in the head? (Often, sometimes, never)
22. You sometimes can't help wondering if anything is worthwhile anymore.

OARS Mental Health Screening Questions[b]

1. Do you wake up fresh and rested most mornings?
2. Is your daily life full of things that keep you interested?
3. Have you at times very much wanted to leave home?
4. Does it seem that no one understands you?
5. Have you had periods of days, weeks, or months when you couldn't take care of things because you couldn't "get going"?
6. Is your sleep fitful and disturbed?
7. Are you happy most of the time?
8. Are you being plotted against?
9. Do you certainly feel useless at times?
10. During the last few years, have you been well most of the time?
11. Do you feel weak all over much of the time?
12. Are you troubled by headaches?
13. Have you had difficulty in keeping your balance in walking?
14. Are you troubled by your heart pounding and a shortness of breath?
15. Even when you are with people, do you feel lonely much of the time?

Emotional Problems Questionnaire[c]

1. How do you sleep (well, so-so, badly)?
2. How are your bowel movements (constipated, OK, sometimes constipated)?

Table 3-10 (continued)

3. Is it hard for you to get up in the morning?
4. Do you feel better in the afternoon than in the morning?
5. How do you feel generally?
6. Do you think people like you?
7. Do you think people hate you?
8. Do you think that people are trying to run your life?
9. Are you sociable?
10. Are you lonely?

Sandoz Clinical Assessment-Geriatric[d]

1. Mood depression
2. Confusion
3. Mental alertness
4. Motivation, initiative
5. Irritability
6. Hostility
7. Bothersomeness
8. Indifference to surroundings
9. Unsociability
10. Uncooperativeness
11. Emotional lability
12. Fatigue
13. Self-care
14. Appetite
15. Dizziness
16. Anxiety
17. Impairment of recent memory
18. Disorientation

Overall impression of the patient

Rating: 7-point scale from 1 (not present) to 7 (severe).

Savage-Britton Index[e]

1. Have you been well most of the time during the last few years?
2. Do you often worry about your health?
3. Do you have many headaches?
4. Have you had any dizzy spells lately?
5. Does your hand often shake when you try to do something?
6. Do you have little or no trouble with your muscles twitching or jumping?
7. Would you say that you have few or no pains?
8. Do you have numbness in one or more regions of your skin?
9. Are your hands and feet usually warm enough?
10. Is your sleep fitful or disturbed?
11. Do you go to sleep on most nights without thoughts or ideas bothering you?
12. Do you enjoy social gatherings just to be with people?
13. Have you frequently found yourself worrying about something?
14. Are you sometimes full of energy?
15. Do you feel useless at times?

[a]Adapted from T.S. Langner, "A Twenty-two Item Screening Score of Psychiatric Symptoms Indicating Impairment," *Journal of Health and Human Behavior* 3(1962):269-276.

[b]From Duke University Center for the Study of Aging and Human Development, Multidimensional Functional Assessment: The OARS Methodology (Durham, N.C.: Duke University, 1978).

Table 3-10 (continued)

[c]Adapted from P. Ernst, D. Badash, B. Beran, R. Kosovsky, and M. Kleinhauz, "Incidence of Mental Illness in the Aged: Unmasking the Effects of a Diagnosis of Chronic Brain Syndrome," *Journal of the American Geriatric Society* 25(1977a):371-375; and P. Ernst, B. Bera, D. Badesh, R. Kosovsky, and M. Kleinhauz, "Treatment of the Aged Mentally Ill: Further Unmasking of the Effects of a Diagnosis of Chronic Brain Syndrome," *Journal of the American Geriatric Society* 25(1977b):446-469.

[d]Adapted from R.I. Shader, J.S. Harmatz, and C. Salzman, "A New Scale for Clinical Assessment in Geriatric Populations: Sandoz Clinical Assessment–Geriatric (SCAG)," *Journal of the American Geriatric Society* 22(1974):107-113.

[e]From R.D. Savage and P.G. Britton, "A Short Scale for the Assessment of Mental Health in the Community Aged," *British Journal of Psychiatry* 113(1967):521-523.

work has been done with the scale to suggest a cutoff point separating those who merit further psychiatric evaluation. The Savage-Britton Index is a fifteen-item screening instrument developed as a result of the analysis of the Newcastle-upon-Tyne community studies for which the complete MMPI was administered to the entire sample. The fifteen screening items were selected because they correlated well with the overall MMPI scores, had a high loading on the mental-illness factor derived from the MMPI scores with that elderly sample, and had a high correlation with psychiatric diagnosis. The authors then validated the screening scale on a small sample of normal and abnormal subjects.

The Ernst Emotional Problems Questionnaire is an even more-simplified tool for assessing mental health. Its items are very simply worded (for example, "Are you lonely?") with five items designed to tap depressive symptomatology interdigited with five items designed to tap psychotic behavior. Despite the seeming simplicity of the tool, it was used effectively to demonstrate improvements among a small group of cognitively impaired subjects who experimentally received sensory stimulation. The Ernst Emotional Problems Quesionnaire would seem suitable for a nursing home or equivalent population, although we have located no further reports of experience with it.

Observer-Rating Scales

The Sandoz Clinical Assessment–Geriatrics (SCAG) was developed by Sandoz Chemicals for use in psychopharmaceutical research. As table 3-10 shows, it requires a rating of the subject on eighteen specific dimensions and a rating of overall impression; each item is rated on a seven-point scale.

Shader, Harmatz, and Salzman (1974) analyzed the SCAG in detail; their work pinpoints problems in studying the validity and reliability of such scales. Validity was claimed because the SCAG subscores correlated highly with the analogous subscores of the Mental Status Examination Record and the SCAG ratings themselves differentiated among four groups: a healthy group (N = 20), a minimally demented group (N = 5), a severely demented group of psychiatric inpatients (N = 15), and a group of psychiatric inpatients with primary affective disorders (N = 11). The mean scores for overall impression were 1.9 for the healthy, 2.6 for the minimally demented, 4.6 for the affective disorders, and 6 for the severely demented. As might be expected, the depressed group had high mean scores on the item "mood depression." Reliability was measured by an inter-rater-reliability procedure that involved four psychiatrists and eight patients; all psychiatrists attended a clinical interview and rated independently from the same clinical observations. The average coefficient of reliability across all items was .75. Most items achieved satisfactory reliability under this method, with notable exceptions for irritability (.39), fatigue (.27), appetite (.24), and anxiety (.32). No inter-rater reliabilities based on independent clinical interviews were reported.

The problem posed by the SCAG is that the scores, even if reliable under conditions of independent rating of the same clinical interview, are highly dependent on (1) the stimuli presented to the subject and (2) the empirical referents used to anchor the seven points of the scale. Reliability is not adquate unless independent raters conducting independent clinical interviews achieve agreement. Even if this level of inter-rater reliability were achieved, however, validity still remains at issue. If the clinical interview, an artificial situation at best, is the basis for the SCAG ratings, then the stimuli provided to the patient in terms of the questions asked become crucial to the meaning of the ratings. If, however, the questions asked are specified in detail with scale anchor points established on the basis of response patterns, then the observation scale becomes little different from a structured-interview guide and presents the problem that some elderly respondents will not be able to complete it.

The Nurses Observation Scale for Inpatient Evaluation (NOSIE) is similar to the SCAG but is based on nursing observations over a three-day period rather than on a clinical interview. Although judgment is still required, the NOSIE shows an effort to express the items in objective terms. For example, items such as "has temper tantrums," "talks freely with volunteer workers or other visitors," "hoards things," or "claims that he is being controlled by unusual forces" are observable events. The scale choices ("never," "sometimes," "often," "usually," and "always") do not seem appropriate for many of the items. For example, an item such as "plays cards with others" or "reads newspapers or magazines" would hardly be amenable to the choices "usually" or "always" unless those had a specialized meaning such as "usually during waking, noneating hours" or "usually, when an unread magazine or newspaper is available."

The NOSIE scale was designed particularly for use with older, chronic-schizophrenic patients, a group that, according to Honigfeld and Klett (1965) "is relatively asymptomatic, characterized by apathy and indifference, and is often inadequately described by symptom rating scales." (p. 65) The scale was pruned from an original 100 items to eliminate those that were not reliable. Factor analysis of the scale yielded seven factors: social competence, social interest, cooperation, personal neatness, irritability, manifest psychosis, and psychotic depression. It is not clear whether this scale can be transferred, without further modification, from a chronic-mental-hospital population to an elderly institutionalized (or equivalent) population. Among observer-rating scales, the NOSIE shows promise.

The London Psychogeriatric Rating Scale (LPRS) (Hersch, Kral, and Palmer 1978) was developed specifically to fill a need for "assessing the untestable as well as the testable patient" on a psychogeriatric hospital unit. The authors adapted two multidimensional geriatric-rating scales, the Stockton Geriatric Rating Scale and the Physical and Mental Impairment-of-Function Evaluation (PAMIE) (briefly discussed in chapter 5), to fit the psychiatric context; major modifications were the inclusion of a mental-status measure and a general simplification.

The LPRS has thirty-six items divided into mental disorganization/confusion (36 percent of the total score), physical disability (25 percent), socially irritating behavior (22 percent), and disengagement (17 percent). Each is rated on a three-point scale ("always," "sometimes," or "never"), producing a score range of 0 to 2. Each subscore is converted into a percentage figure. Examples of items from the mental-disorganization/confusion scale are: "The patient has trouble remembering things," and, "The patient doesn't make much sense when he talks." The socially-irritating-behavior-scale items include: "The patient threatens harm to others," and, "The patient takes his clothes off at the wrong time or place." The six disengagement items include: "The patient keeps himself occupied in constructive or useful activity," and, "The patient helps out on the ward." The physical items include the standard ADL items.

The investigators report that scores on the LPRS and its subscales can distinguish patients with dementia from those with psychotic disorders; over an eighteen-month period the former deteriorate, whereas the latter improve or stay the same. Furthermore, the initial scores predicted outcomes eighteen months later in terms of discharge status (to home or residential home, to nursing home, remained in hospital, or death). Tentative norms have also been developed for a psychogeriatric population on each of the subscales, and the authors suggest that the scores can be used to predict suitability for participation in group therapy. This relatively new scale emerges among psychogeriatric rating scales because systematic work has been done to describe its practical applicability in the treatment context.

Projective Tests

Table 3-9 includes two projective tests particularly developed for older persons: the Senior Apperception Test (SAT) and the Gerontological Apperception Test

(GAT). Both these tests are modifications of the Thematic Apperception Test (TAT), a format that requires subjects to develop a story suggested by a pictorial stimulus on a card. The SAT and GAT are both based on the assumption that elderly persons will respond more fully to stimuli that present older persons in typical situations. This contention is unproven; Kahana (1978) presents evidence on both sides of the question. Dye (forthcoming) suggests that these scales, particularly the GAT, might be overweighted with depressive themes, leading to the production of more depressive content and the judgment that the elderly are depressive.

In any event, projective tests (of which these TAT offshoots are just two examples) are problematic in their interpretation. If such scales are used in research, then investigators must establish rules for scoring based on observable phenomena such as the quantity of ideas produced and a systematic content analysis of the themes. Usually a qualified psychologist is required to administer and interpret the tests.

Structured Interview or Questionnaire

The Geriatric Mental State Examination is perhaps the best example of a structured-interview approach to determining the mental health of an elderly population. It models a psychiatric interview with a series of standard questions, structured branching probes, and specific observations, ensuring that a common data base will be collected in psychiatric interviews. The interview consumes a substantial investment of high-priced time; each interview requires at least half an hour, and the constructors of the scale suggest that a new interviewer should be trained through at least twenty joint interviews. Inter-rater reliability was shown to be good for the items that involved direct patient response but not as good for the observational items.

The Geriatric Mental State Examination has now been subsumed in the multidimensional assessment known as CARE (discussed in chapter 5), which includes an assessment of physical and social as well as mental functioning.

In another interview approach to assessing mental health, Lawton has generated ninety-eight questions on personal well-being that are posed directly to elderly respondents.[a] Some questions are measured on five-, four-, or three-point scales, whereas others are dichotomous. A scoring system for the interview has not yet been published, but factor analysis has produced twenty-one factors. Examples include happiness, negative affect, residential satisfaction, self-rated health, conflicted irritability, and social ease. In this approach, shorter scales can be produced by using the "best" items in each factored scale. As yet, this material is available only through mimeographed materials from the Hebrew Rehabilitation Center for the Aged. The Lawton Psychological Well-Being Scale

---

[a]Available from M.P. Lawton, Philadelphia Geriatric Center, 5301 Old York Road, Philadelphia, Pennsylvania 19141.

does have the potential advantage that, as opposed to pathology-oriented scales, it could produce some measure of positive mental health. This would be compatible with Lawton's emphasis on the "competencies" of older persons in a number of domains (Lawton 1972, 1974).

Comparison of Measures of Mental Functioning

Table 3-11 classifies most of the instruments contained in this chapter by user, purpose, and function, according to definitions already established in earlier chapters. Again, some of the choices were necessarily rather arbitrary and thus are presented to provoke thought rather than as definitive statements. Furthermore, the division of the instruments into categories according to their practical utility begs for the moment the question of the reliability and validity of many of these tools. In the right-hand column, we make some recommendations.

Most of the instruments are amenable to use by either a geriatric specialist or a generalist serving the elderly. Some of the instruments, however, must be administered by psychiatrists; others require persons skilled in psychological testing, thus reducing their applicability even when a geriatric specialist is not needed. More of the devices were judged useful for screening and quick monitoring than for assessment. Assessment on which treatment plans might be based seems difficult to manage systematically in psychogeriatrics; exceptions are the Geriatric Mental State Exam and some of the standardized psychological tests that pinpoint problem areas in cognitive functioning. Tests that can readily be learned by the subject are not suitable for periodic monitoring; therefore, the Misplaced Objects Test would not be recommended for use as a monitoring device until alternative forms are developed.

Those few tests credited with prediction are, for the most part, modest in their predictive promise; and further study is needed to replicate earlier findings. With these caveats, however, two British cognitive tests, the MIT and the DRS, predicted mortality; the Mini-Mental State examination predicted those who would improve over time, and the LPRS predicted discharge status from psychiatric hospitals and suitability for group therapy.

Many of the tests are cumbersome for research purposes, requiring extensive training of users, a lengthy observation period, and/or special equipment. Unfortunately, most of the instruments designated as useful for research purposes are those that must be completed by written or orally administered questionnaire; these have obvious limitations for those functioning at the lower end of the continuum. For most of the instruments, experience is insufficient to generate norms or to explain how the instrument performs over a large sample of elderly persons. Such information is useful for a research instrument. Exceptions to this limitation are the OARS SPMSQ, which has been widely used in population studies; the Langer Twenty-two-Question Screening Score, from the Midtown Manhattan Study; and the MIT and DRS, both used in the Newcastle-upon-Tyne studies.

Table 3-11
Selected Measures of Mental Functioning by User, Purpose, and Recommendations

Measure	User[a]	Purpose[b]	Recommendations
VIRO Orientation Scale	n, g	d, s, m	Acceptable for nursing-home population
Mental Status Questionnaire	n, g, r	d, s, m	Acceptable
Face-Hand Test	n, g, r, c	d, s, m	Helpful to establish organicity
SPMSQ (OARS)	n, g, r, s	d, s, m	Recommended, highly reliable
Set Test	n, g, r, c	d, s, m	Acceptable
Memory and Information Test	n, g, r	d, s, m, p	Not recommended for United States
Dementia Rating Scale	n, g, r	d, s, m, p	Not recommended for United States
PGH Extended Mental Status Examination	g	d, a, m	Needs work, promising
Extended Dementia Scale[c]	f	d, a	Detailed approach for psychogeriatric settings
Misplaced Objects Test	g	d, a	Promising test of memory
WAIS (Short Form)[c]	n, g	d, a	Not generally useful for LTC
Weschler Memory Scale[c]	g	d, a	Not generally useful for LTC
Geriatric Interpersonal Evaluation	n, g, c	d, s, a, m	Promising
Mini-Mental State Examination	n, g, c	d, s, a, m, p	Promising
Quick Test	n, g	d, s, m	Promising
Zung Self-Rating Depression Scale	n	d, s, m	Not recommended
Beck Depression Scale	n, t, r	d, s, m	Promising
Hopkins Symptom Checklist	n, g, c, r	d, s, m	Promising
Affect Balance Scale	n, g, r	d, s	Very simple tool, not sensitive
OARS Mental Health Screening Scale	n, g, c, r	d, s, m	Recommended for screening
Langner Screening Score	n, g, c, r	d, s, m	
Emotional Problems Questionnaire	n, g	d, s, m	Not recommended
GAT, SAT[c]	g	d, a	Limited applicability
Geriatric Mental State Examination	g	d, a	Not generally useful
Sandoz Clinical Assessment-Geriatric (SCAG)[c]	n, g, r	d, s, m, a	Judgmental
London Psychogeriatric Rating Scale	n, g, r	d, s, m, a, p	Promising; needs more study
Nurses Observation Scale for Evaluation of Inpatients (NOSIE)	n, g, r	s, m, a	Judgmental but useful when subjects cannot respond

[a]User: n = nongeriatric provider; g = geriatric provider; c = case manager; r = researcher.

[b]Purpose: d = description; s = screening; a = assessment; m = monitoring; p = prediction.

[c]Psychiatric expertise or expertise in psychological testing is required.

Among the mental-status tests, the OARS SPMSQ stands out as the most universally useful. It is simple to administer, reliable, and has norms available. With the SPMSQ, people can be sorted into categories highly suggestive of their cognitive abilities. To make distinctions among those who achieve very low scores on the SPMSQ, however, other techniques, such as the Extended Dementia Scale, the Mini-Mental Status, or the GIES, are useful. The Misplaced Objects Test is a promising test of memory for community-based subjects. An important caveat is that brief screening tests for cognitive functioning should not be used as diagnostic indicators but, rather, to identify those needing a diagnostic assessment.

On the affective side, one cannot be sanguine in recommending instruments to measure depression. The Zung SDS seems to have many limitations, leaving the Beck and Hopkins as most promising. However, more work is needed to understand depression in the elderly before a scale is finally adopted. As the studies by Gurland and his colleagues continue, we hope that the essential aspects of depression in the elderly will be objectively identified, permitting the creation of more-precise measures.

4 Measures of Social Functioning in Long-Term Care

Rhetoric about "treating the whole person" pervades today's medical world, especially primary-care fields. Nevertheless, holistic person-centered health care remains a vague ideal. The term *holistic*, which is rarely well specified, connotes caregivers who are mindful of the patient's physical, emotional, and social circumstances when making a diagnosis or recommending a course of action. Providers with this philosophy are expected to remember that patients are not diseased objects but people with families who live in communities and who view their health needs in the larger context of their social structure and personal life. Presumably, physicians who treat the whole person are sensitive in their approach and realistic in their advice.

The hallmark of long-term care (LTC) is a fusion (and sometimes a confusion) of health and social care. In fact, the bulk of long-term care is delivered not by professionals but by family and friends. Geriatric providers, therefore, have the responsibility to assess social functioning, including the strength of support systems, with a precision approaching that applied in physical and psychological domains. Objective indicators of social well-being must replace clinical hunches and subjective judgments.

In the last analysis, geriatrics is a matter of management. On an individual level, this means management of physical and mental problems in a way that compromises social functioning as little as possible. On a societal or planning level, this means promoting social and familial structures that maintain the frail elderly while minimizing the care burdens of individuals and the tax burdens of the citizenry. Therefore, purposeful patient management in long-term care requires systematic social assessment.

Finding an efficient and accurate way of assessing the social well-being of elderly patients is a formidable challenge. The gerontological literature has spawned an abundant supply of instruments purporting to measure social functioning, but many have not gone beyond the embryonic stage. A quick review of any compilation of sociological measurements for research in aging (Peterson, Magnen, and Sanders 1978; Binstock and Shanas 1976; George and Bearon 1980) shows that, although many aspects of social functioning are measured, the available tools often overlap or employ dissimilar items to measure variables with the same name. Furthermore, the mere existence of large numbers of measurement tools does not address the practical choices involved in applying such measures to LTC delivery.

Social functioning is a broad concept, embracing all human relationships and activities in society. The geriatric provider must decide which aspects of social functioning are important as part of a geriatric data base, how trustworthy information can be gathered, the degree of detail that should be sought, and the way that social information should be interpreted and used.

Because presentation of long arrays of instruments that measure some aspect of social functioning would introduce content extraneous to geriatric practice, this chapter's format differs from that of those on physical and mental functioning. Although the list of possible instruments is long, recommendations for the LTC practitioner are few and tentative. The discussion concentrates on the rationale for measuring social functioning in LTC and the problems inherent in defining the concepts operationally and making valid measures. In this context, we describe current available measurement tools as examples without attempting to offer an exhaustive survey.

Rationale

The LTC practitioner should screen, assess, and monitor social functioning for several reasons:

1. Social functioning is correlated with physical and mental functioning. Change in patterns of activities or relationships can adversely affect physical or mental health and vice versa. For example, activity levels, socialization patterns, or morale can be directly associated with sensory deprivation, depression, and diminished ability to perform tasks. In order to determine whether an individual's social functioning is impaired, the geriatric provider needs a structured way of making observations and a rationale for interpreting the data.

2. Social well-being enhances the ability to cope with health problems and to maintain autonomy despite functional limitations. The geriatric provider must try to determine whether the social resources and supports are adequate to sustain an individual in a medical emergency. Although the strength of such reources may be impossible to ascertain on a hypothetical basis in the absence of an actual need for care, we might possibly identify those with tenuous or nonexistent support systems as a first step in taking preventive measures to strengthen the individual's social resources.

3. Adequate social functioning is an important outcome in itself. Admittedly, LTC cannot reasonably be charged with improving lifelong social circumstances. It should not be expected to turn the friendless into popular figures or make joiners out of social isolates. On the other hand, receipt of LTC services should not force individuals into lower levels of social functioning. When a change in social circumstances (such as a move to congregate housing, the introduction of a home-health team into a patient's environment, or—even more drastically—a relocation in an LTC facility) is ordered for health reasons, the

care system becomes responsible for the effect of that change on the patient's social functioning. Caregivers are morally obligated to consider whether the measures they implement to protect and prolong life rob that life of meaning. Perhaps for this reason, recent rhetoric has emphasized the "quality of life" of the elderly as an important operational consideration. Although quality of life clearly overlaps with social functioning, the phrase is difficult to reduce to measurement. George and Bearon (1980) suggest four component dimensions to quality of life: life-satisfaction measures; self-esteem measures; general-health and functional-status measures; and socioeconomic-status measures. Life-satisfaction and socioeconomic-status measures are embraced in our term *social functioning,* which we perceive as pivotal to quality of life.

4. On a more-positive note, one of the benefits of diagnosing and treating chronic illness may be an increase in social activity and interaction. Adequate social measures permit LTC programs to be assessed in terms of their social benefits as well as their social costs.

Summarizing these four points, the geriatric provider measures social functioning because it is an intervening factor affecting the ability to cope independently despite functional limitations, because it is an intervening variable in the development of physical problems, and because it is an important outcome in itself that might be adversely or positively affected by implementation of the LTC plan.

What to Measure

Social functioning is a comprehensive construct. Researchers concur in their definitions at a tautological level only. For example, social functioning has been defined as the degree to which people function adequately as members of the community (Donald et al. 1978). So vague a definition permits disagreement about which aspects of social functioning are important and what constitutes an adequate performance.

We divide the amorphous area of social functioning into three component concepts: (1) social interactions and resources; (2) personal coping and subjective well-being; and (3) environmental fit. At some risk of arbitrariness, we classify social-functioning instruments into one of these categories. Each category lends itself to further subdivision into component concepts to extract those elements most useful for LTC.

Social Interactions and Resources

Under this rubric we include measures of the existence, nature, frequency, and subjective importance of social interactions and of social activities, as well as the extent of social resources.

Social interactions occur within families; within friendship and neighborhood groupings; and within the community (through clubs, social organizations, religious affiliations, or work-related affiliations). The term *social network* has evolved to refer to all the sets of formal and informal interactions developed to fill social and emotional needs. The patterns of social networks may vary through the life cycle in focus, number, intensity, and complexity, with resulting variation in the amount of emotional satisfaction and practical support that the social network affords the individual. Among elderly individuals, at least three predictable events commonly disrupt and challenge the social network:

1. Retirement from the work force eliminates or reduces many of the social contacts and role relationships taken for granted during a lifetime.
2. Bereavements create voids in an individual's social and family structure.
3. Diminishing health, mobility, energy levels, and financial resources reduce an individual's continuation of social interactions or development of new contacts and relationships.

To complicate the measurement problem, variation in social interactions occurs not only within the life cycle of individuals but also among individuals. Patterns of social contacts and relationships, for example, differ markedly according to differences in marital patterns, social class, occupation, and personal inclination. Therefore, although social interactions can be counted, classified, and empirically described, their meaning to the individual is necessarily subjective. One can describe or try to predict the amount of tangible sustenance an individual receives from the world around him, but only the individual can determine whether the extent and nature of that support meets expectations and is emotionally satisfying. Duff and Hong (in press) found recently that the quality of interactions with friends and relatives was more associated with global expressions of happiness and life satisfaction than was the frequency of those contacts. Similarly Brown (1980) showed an association between availability of a trusted confidant and mental well-being (measured by anxiety and depression scales).

Activities also vary across individuals and across the life cycle. Some activities require more physical or intellectual energy than others, some are more dependent than others on the participation of other persons, and some are more costly than others. Some activities involve social interaction, and some are solitary. Some people engage in a wide range of pleasurable activities and interests, whereas others limit themselves to a few favored activities. Consider, for instance, the differential demands and constraints of activities such as playing cards, reading, traveling, going to the theater, watching television, gardening, sewing, volunteering in social agencies, hunting or fishing, raising animals, and visiting friends.

Just as social interactions have both an objective and subjective component, so too do social activities. Activities can be observed and described objectively, but the satisfaction or dissatisfaction they produce is subjective. The challenge for the geriatric provider is to develop a practical way of assessing and monitoring the adequacy of social relationships and social activities while making allowances for individual variation in expectation and preference.

Conventional wisdom about what constitutes a desirable social-support system may need revision. Considerable research suggests that frequency of contact with adult children bears no relation to subjective well-being (Arling 1976; Lee 1979; Mancini 1979), and a recent study extends the inferences to suggest that frequency of interaction with siblings is not related to subjective well-being (Lee and Ihinger-Tallman 1980). Similarly, in a study that defined a functional-support system as continuous or frequent contact with a functional spouse, a functional sibling, a functional other relative, a functional friend, or a functional neighbor, Adler, Cantor, and Johnson (1978) found that availability of a support system thus defined was not correlated with adjustment. To explore further such leads in understanding the importance of social contact to elderly individuals, measurement techniques for both social interactions and subjective well-being must be clearly specified and, when possible, consistent from study to study. We also note that social support in terms of social interaction may not be correlated with morale in community-dwelling populations. Rather, it may be correlated with ability to live in the community; and, in turn, community dwelling may be associated with greater subjective well-being than is institutional dwelling.

Coping and Subjective Well-Being

In this category we include the adaptive or coping abilities of the individual and the subjective states that result from successful or unsuccessful coping skills. Scales in this category measure abstractions such as life satisfaction, happiness, morale, coping abilities, adaptability, contentment, hopefulness, future orientation, and personal fulfillment. Each of these terms has a slightly different connotation. George (1979) suggests, for example, that life satisfaction is an expression of a positive comparison between one's initial aspirations and one's achievements, whereas happiness is a current mood state of gaiety and morale is a feeling state characterized by courage, discipline, confidence, and enthusiasm in the face of hardship. If such distinctions are reflected in measurement devices, these dimensions could vary independently in a single individual (for example, an individual could theoretically have low life satisfaction, have high morale, and be moderately happy).

Unfortunately, scales purporting to measure various aspects of personal functioning overlap. Larson (1978) suggests that the high intercorrelation of measures within this area is attributable to a shared underlying dimension, which he labels "subjective well-being." On the other hand, Cutler (1979) argues that such correlations occur because scales intended to measure different concepts contain almost identical items and because the construction of scales to tap a definable domain is often inadequate. In any event, Lohman's work (1977) shows that correlations between life satisfaction, morale, and adjustment measures, although present, are imperfect. Morris, Wolf, and Klerman (1975) have demonstrated correlations between scales measuring depression (discussed in chapter 3) and those measuring morale or subjective well-being.

The practitioner, then, is faced with a morass of instruments of uncertain reliability and validity. Geriatric practitioners are not (nor need they be) psychometricians; they use measurements to make meaningful distinctions, not to test and refine measurement capability for its own sake. The crucial questions for the practitioner are whether personal adjustment is a practically important variable to measure apart from emotional well-being, and whether the technology exists to measure it.

As we have already emphasized, a measure is important to a provider if it can be used to either (1) assist in LTC decision making or (2) monitor outcomes of care. By these criteria, measures of personal social functioning have uncertain utility. Quite possibly knowledge of a client's coping abilities and styles might help a provider or case manager predict the ability of a person to function independently. If measurements of this dimension suggest differential management plans, then they are justified on the first criterion. At present, however, no longitudinal data linking coping abilities to outcomes is available. More research to establish the predictive utility of various promising measures is indicated before they are routinely applied to practice. Measures of morale, happiness, or life satisfaction, on the other hand, represent outcomes of care and could address the second purpose. Here, however, the geriatric provider must guard against grandiosity. Life satisfaction, defined as perception of life accomplishments balanced against goals, could hardly be altered much by LTC, especially in a positive direction.

Some patients entering LTC are unhappy because of multiple losses. Some may have a lifelong pattern of low morale in response to difficulties. Again, the lack of longitudinal data to describe the stability of these traits over time, coupled with the paucity of large-scale studies to develop norms for institutionalized and noninstitutionalized elderly persons, makes interpretation of any finding about subjective well-being difficult. This also makes an evaluator uncertain about when to hold a care program responsible for poor morale.

Despite these caveats, geriatric providers must know when persons under their care are actively unhappy, and especially when such distress marks a change for the worse. This responsibility is greatest when the social circumstances have been entirely directed by the care plan. Such knowledge serves as the basis for efforts to improve the social situation, stimulate interests, and promote positive interactions. The consistently positive responses of institutional patients, in particular, to a wide range of experimental interventions suggest that the attention and stimulation itself may produce the change as much as the specific independent variable. Caregivers should at least probe to determine whether subjective well-being has fallen below an acceptable threshold. Also, possible remedies themselves can be tested and improved through a conscious effort to improve subjective well-being and monitor results.

Environmental Fit

Our final category concerns the impact of the environment on social interactions and personal functioning. As Moos (1974) indicates:

> Human behavior cannot be understood apart from the environmental context in which it occurs. . . . accurate predictions of behavior or of treatment outcome cannot be made solely from the information about individuals; information about their environments is essential. (p. 21)

All persons experience environmental constraints. Each society imposes rules, regulations, and structures under which social beings must function. These constraints will change across the life cycle as social roles and responsibilities change. The degree of environmental constraint experienced by community-dwelling elderly persons is influenced by their functional abilities. They may be confined to a single city, to a neighborhood, to an age-segregated housing unit, or even to a single room.

As elderly persons move from the general community to a more-sheltered environment and as their functional abilities decrease, the constraints imposed by their environment increase. When an individual enters an institution, the rules, regulations, and routines of the environment may well become the central factors affecting social functioning for the dependent population. Brody (1973) drew the chilling metaphor of "Procrustean beds," likening the nursing home to the iron beds of the legendary highwayman who stretched or chopped his victims to fit the standard length of the bed.

The human relationship to the environment can be expressed along a continuum. In their full vigor, some individuals influence the environment, whereas others adapt creatively to environmental demands. At either extreme of the life cycle, an individual's actions tend to be determined by the environment rather than the reverse. The activist may influence the environment for better or for worse, just as the adapter may have a good or poor adjustment. Strategies for influencing one's environment include active efforts to bring about structural changes, attempts to motivate people toward one's point of view, or even a careful selection of more hospitable surroundings. As they become more dependent, the elderly have less and less opportunity to shape an environment to meet their particular needs. Adaptation then seems to be the major option.

If this is the case, care providers have a responsibility to promote the kind of environment that meets the preferences of the LTC recipient and minimizes the individual's need to make difficult adaptations. One approach to this task focuses on the environment itself as the unit of assessment and measurement. Numerous descriptive tools have been developed to classify care settings, and rating forms are available that produce scores with this kind of information (Anderson and Patten, forthcoming). Others have been produced as part of the quality-assurance programs of Professional Standards Review Organizations (PSROs) and state licensing programs (Kane et al. 1979). Objective-standard setting in terms of life-safety codes and basic amenities is crucial and uncontroversial. At some minimum threshold, measures of environmental standards are applicable to all persons.

Measures of specific physical or programmatic aspects of institutions or environments (such as degree of "homelikeness" or "resource availability") are incomplete gauges of how an environment might meet the needs of a particular individual. Although these undoubtedly depict a necessary floor for personal satisfaction, they are far from sufficient. Individual well-being requires that the environment match the particular expectations and desires of the individual. Measures of environmental fit attempt to capture the interaction between the individual and the environment and to produce some indication of their compatibility. A subtype of special importance here consists of measures of satisfaction with institutional and other care. In this chapter we ignore the measures of environments themselves in order to concentrate on measures of environmental fit.

Problems in Measuring Social Functioning

Before illustrating the three categories of social functioning measures (that is, social interactions and resources, coping and subjective well-being, and environmental fit), some general concerns arise. These cross all three of our subgroups and are in turn divided into conceptual issues and practical issues.

The measurement of social functioning in the elderly presents challenges similar to those of measuring physical or mental functioning. Abstract concepts need to be defined, distinguished from similar concepts, and quantified. Strategies for information collection must be developed and reliability sought (even when a subset of informants may be intrinsically unreliable because of cognitive impairments). Interpretation of information is always difficult in the absence of age norms or of longitudinal studies that associate certain scores on scales with later outcomes or events. All these problems are exaggerated for measurements in the social sphere.

As indicated earlier, measurements of physical or mental capabilities may be distorted because of social factors. For example, a person may test as mentally disoriented when thrust into strange social settings or may test as limited in mobility when, in fact, a constricted social circle has led to demoralization, lack of motivation, and disuse of skills. The ability to perform ADL and IADL functions, as shown in chapter 2, is heavily influenced by social opportunity as well as by individual capacity. Thus a host of social variables, including socioeconomic status, ethnicity, geography, income, family and social supports, and culturally derived role expectations intervene to influence physical and mental status.

Obviously, the reverse relationship also occurs; physical or mental impairments affect social functioning, not only because they limit the functional abilities of the subject but also because they evoke reaction in others. Mental disorientation brings about a sharp reduction in social skills. Abilities to participate in solitary and group leisure activities, to conduct casual or meaningful conversations, or to engage in reciprocal social relationships are impaired. This in turn creates severe emotional and practical stress for those in the social orbit, and interactions become problematic. As another example, depression is obviously associated with social isolation and withdrawal. The cause-and-effect relationship here is difficult to determine, although a history might indicate whether the social withdrawal was voluntary and secondary to the depressed mood.

The infinite number of specific social facts that intervene to distort results of health assessments similarly complicate the measurement of social functioning itself. Social measurements are justified on the basis that some social states are more desirable than others, that some support systems are more supportive, and that some coping skills are better designed to fend off the insults of time. Many of the conceptual questions raised in measuring social health stem from the need to make value judgments on matters such as the strength of social supports or the adequacy of social relationships. Additional difficulty is encountered in developing a continous scale on which to evaluate such information. Consequently, large social-functioning batteries are often purely descriptive; that is, they provide for collection of sociodemographic information according to standardized definitions and procedures without offering a formula for weighting the responses.

Problems that complicate quantification of social functioning are as follows.

Vague Concepts

The concepts included in social health or social functioning are often exceedingly general. Universal agreement has not been achieved on the components of the concepts; identical measures are sometimes purported to measure different constructs, or different measures are used to define the same construct. The overlapping of scales precludes comparisons and complicates the establishment of norms for friendship ties, solitude, presence of a confidant, and other such scales in the social sphere.

Lack of Norms

Longitudinal studies that tie scores on social scales to later outcomes are also sparse, making interpretation of any given score difficult and limiting the prognostic significance of the measures. Norms are not available for many of the measures.

Interactive Nature of Variable

Social functioning is an interactive variable. It involves people in interaction with each other, people filling social roles, people in relationship to their environment, and people coping with socially derived stress. All participants in the interaction can contribute their own perspectives. Resolution of discrepancies is a problem, as is the initial decision about the source of the information.

Because social functioning is interactive, the predictive capability of measures is compromised. Subjective well-being may plummet because of the behavior of others in the patient's life. Relationships may disappear and resources diminish. Of course, unpredictable events hamper predictions in the physical domain as well (for example, a stroke can drastically alter functional abilities); but the events and circumstances that could positively or negatively affect social functioning are countless, difficult to categorize, and more often than not under control of those other than the patient.

On the other hand, in some ways the elderly person does influence the responses of others. Sometimes his or her current behavior (pleasant, querulous, helpful, demanding) is the determining factor; sometimes, especially for families, past relationships are the key. Isaacs, Livingstone, and Neville (1972) in Britain and Brody and Spark (1966) in the United States show that those neglected in their old age may have been neglecting or abusing when they were at the other end of the dependency relationship.

Difficulty in Constructing a Continuum

The wide variation among social attributes impedes the development of a single continuum. For example, is the individual who has daily contact with one close friend and confidant as well supported emotionally as the person with a large circle of less-intense friendships? Is the person with six close friends twice as well supported as the person with three, or is such arithmetic meaningless? How does the geographic proximity of the "significant others" enter the equation? Do a wide range of contacts by mail and telephone serve a function similar to that of personal contact? How should all the factual information be combined to develop a scale or several scales depicting friendship and social relationships?

Examples come readily to mind. For instance, in rating relationships between parents and offspring, what dimensions are important? Is mutual exchange of services a key, or is reciprocity less meaningful than the ability of the older person to depend on the younger? How should the practical and the emotional component of the relationship be balanced? How does one compare the older person who has four affectionate and caring children scattered around the continental United States to the person who has a friction-laden relationship with several local children who nevertheless provide some practical assistance? What if the favored child has rejected the parent, but a disliked child is in constant attendance?

To take another example, how does a caregiver decide when an individual is insufficiently stimulated or active? Is a person better off in a congregate facility with a full activity program and plentiful company, or in his own home alone and with no anticipated activities beyond immediate self-care? When should a provider intervene to prescribe, as it were, a social diet?

Subjective Component

As with the preceding point, social behavior and social facts have subjective meaning as well as objective reality. When the focus is on overt behavior (as in frequency of social participation), data from observers can be assembled even though they are hard to combine into a score. When the focus is on an individual's subjective perception of the behavior (for example, satisfaction with activities), an internal dimension is sought that can only be supplied by the subject. A complete measure of most concepts within social functioning would necessarily include an objective or external component and a subjective or internal component. Combining such information into a score is again very difficult. Suppose a subject expresses high satisfaction with an isolated and constricted life-style. Suppose an individual expresses dissatisfaction with what objectively seems to be a large cadre of family members who are providing practical care.

Two scores can be developed, one for the external and one for the internal component of the dimension being measured. Even if the problem of combining the elements to compose these scores were solved (for example, by reaching a quantitative general measure of satisfaction with social participation when some activities are satisfying and some are not), the problem of how to use the information remains. Should subjective satisfaction be the key information? Some would argue that caregivers must refrain from imposing values, that a day full of despised activities should not be viewed as good social participation. On the other hand, persons whose expectations for themselves in old age are modest may express satisfaction with meager and limited social lives, whereas those with higher expectations may be dissatisfied.

Socioeconomic and Cultural Determinants

Expectations of social activities and relationships, the pleasure derived from them, and the nature of the activities and relationships themselves are culturally and socioeconomically determined. This also complicates the construction of scales to measure and evaluate these dimensions. The very definition of a family member differs in different subgroups. Checklists of activities may not translate very well from one culture to another, particularly for the cohort now elderly. Useful work is in progress to define the value preferences of elderly persons (Flanagan 1978; Reid and Ziegler 1977). These studies may yield the information needed to combine objective and subjective measures into a single observation and might be especially useful for community planning.

For example, if investigators determine what most older persons prefer (for example, to live apart from adult children or to walk outdoors each day), then social observations could be weighted according to general preferences. Unfortunately, consensus is easier to reach on rather global preferences, such as the wish to be useful, than on specification of the detail of activity perceived as useful. In any event, the value preferences of the elderly derived from one population would need to be reproduced in other studies. The generalizability of such information is somewhat suspect, given the huge number of variables that shape personal values. One must even question whether any preference norms derived from groups can profitably be applied to the individual. It may be a fallacy to infer individual preferences from those of the larger group.

Lack of Societal-Role Expectations for the Elderly

Role expectations for the elderly have not been defined societally. The work relationship shapes the social activity and participation of adults in the preretirement years. For the cohort now old, this is especially true for men and unmarried women; the married woman's social role, however, was also shaped by homemaking tasks and the social expectations associated with her husband's occupation. A definition of a good worker could be developed based on observable characteristics such as absenteeism, disposition on the job, and quality and quantity of performance. Relationships between spouses or with young children are dictated by custom, and thus normative standards can be applied to those role performances. Even though these standards are influenced by cultural variables and are reworked with each generation according to prevailing ideas of male–female relationships or parental roles, most people can conjure up a definition of a good mother or a good wife.

In sharp contrast, the role definitions for the retirement years are incomplete and contradictory. What is a good grandparent? A good retiree? Should the latter be an active volunteer, an avid consumer of leisure-time activities, a doting grandparent? Is the role best conceived in terms of the family or of the entire community? How should a widow or widower behave? What are the expectations for sexual behavior, courting, or making new friends in retirement years? The lack of conventional wisdom on these points is heightened when, in fact, younger caregivers are in the position of making judgments about the social adjustment of people in a different generation.

Multiplicity of Patterns of Satisfactory Social Functioning

Finally, more than one road leads to Rome. Activities and relationships are seemingly substitutable, although the precise conditions under which substitution is satisfactory is still a matter for research. Weiss (1969) has suggested that each person may have a "fund of sociability" (which can be replenished in a variety of combinations). This optimistic theory maintains that individuals need to achieve a threshold of companionship and that losses of important lifelong relationships can be compensated for, at least in part, in new social relationships. Certainly more than one pattern of socialization seems to satisfy human needs. Rosow (1967) studied compensatory socialization patterns empirically, finding that some substitution of relationships with neighbors for relationships with children did occur under considerations of residential propinquity, but that substitution of relationships was not automatic. In validating instruments in the social domain, more than one observable pattern should surely be considered equally adequate.

A geriatrician needs guidelines for choosing and interpreting measurements in a domain where the number of observable facts is almost infinite and where social values are so prevalent. Three rules of thumb are suggested:

1. *Remember the purpose of the measurement.* For example, if social relationships are being assessed as a gauge of the patient's emergency-reserve support system, this purpose dictates the selection of items, the strategy for collecting information, and the scaling that would be useful.

2. *Think in terms of thresholds and cutoff points.* Because social functioning does not lend itself to interval scaling and because so many patterns of relationships could exist, the major concern of the LTC provider is whether a threshold has been crossed (for example, in terms of social isolation or inadequate social support), rendering the individual vulnerable. The functional abilities of the patient will influence the threshold considered satisfactory in the immediate

future. An ambulatory, mentally oriented person might require less social-support provision; however, shifting circumstances (for example, a broken hip) could quickly make a support system essential. To judge social support as adequte because no additional support is needed immediately would be fallacious.

3. *Consider changes in social functioning.* Given the diversity of human social conditions and life-styles, preferences for social functioning are almost infinite. The geriatric provider should be especially alert to any changes, especially those in the direction of diminished contact or stimulation. An ideal (and perhaps idealistic) approach is to establish baseline information. More often, however, the change in social functioning needs to be documented retroactively at the time service is requested; those instruments measuring social functioning that build in comparisons between present and former states are especially useful here.

Practical Problems in Measuring Social Functioning

Choosing an Informant

Many social-functioning measures concern interactions between people. Who should supply the information in these situations? Do we ask an elderly person, for example, what help he expects to receive from his daughter, or do we ask the daughter what help she is prepared to offer? Some social-functioning instruments depend heavily on second-person comment about the activities, preferences, and relationships of the elderly person; this seems unsatisfactory unless the subject is definitely an unreliable informant. Seeking out all relevant informants is both expensive and impractical, and raises ethical issues about privacy. Furthermore, even if multiple informants could be tapped, the resolution of discrepancies is difficult.

Limits of Self-Report

A socially desirable response set, a desire to defend family members, or mere wishful thinking might lead someone to exaggerate the quantity and quality of attention received from family or the extent of social resources. Memory is also a problem; persons of all ages are prone to underestimate or overestimate events of the past and increasingly do so if the events are (1) remote, and (2) routine. Even mild memory loss could complicate the problem further. Therefore, reports on such facts as frequency and duration of visits, incoming and outgoing telephone calls, numbers of activities, or time spent alone might well be consciously or unconsciously distorted. Direct verification of many such phenomena is almost impossible.

One strategy to reduce forgetting is the diary or log. This is workable over a relatively short period of time but would be intrusive for more than a few weeks. The log, of course, is likely to influence the phenomenon measured. The very act of recording telephone calls might, for example, stimulate use of the telephone, creating a problem in a research design. In clinical practice, where presumably the goal is increased social participation, the influence of the measure on the phenomenon would be a problem only if the desired behavior were to cease after the device was discontinued. Direct observation (such as visiting in the subject's home or observation in an institutional day room) may influence the social behavior measured and thus be of questionable validity as a gauge of habitual behavior. However, interactive strategies can be used to measure social skills, especially in regressed subjects.

Another problem of self-report is that most interview formats use poorly defined terms. Questions such as, "How many conversations did you have this week?" might be answered differently, depending on what the informant included as a conversation. Does one count passing greetings, business transactions, and so on? Questions about how many times one engaged in certain activities (playing cards, for example) are open to interpretation about the end point of one episode the beginning of another. The term *friend* is open to interpretation, as is the term *relative*. Yet constant definition of terms in an interview format would both increase the time and decrease the conversational flow.

Choice of Time Window

Related to the foregoing point is the choice of a time frame for the questions. A recent time window (such as "yesterday" or "in the last week" or even "in the last month") will increase the likelihood of accuracy but decrease the meaning of the information, at least in individual terms. For research purposes or for evaluation of an institution's quality of care, one might well ask a large number of persons to comment on their activities of the last twenty-four hours. Unless the day chosen were highly atypical (for example, Christmas Day or a day with unusual weather conditions), one could safely extrapolate something about the average activity level of the population studied. But information about the past twenty-four hours in the life of a single individual will not give the provider any sense of that person's social participation. In addition, some infrequent but important events such as the visit of a distant child would not be tapped at all. This strategy is flawed, even for comparing LTC facilities, when the activities are infrequent and distributed according to a schedule rather than at random. (For example, if an excursion or a group meeting had not been scheduled for the previous day, the entire sample from a particular nursing home might appear deficient compared to a group from a home that had just finished a scheduled event.)

The time window must be carefully considered and a choice based on the likely frequency of the event and the likelihood of the individual remembering. Some instruments combine a short time window for detailed recall with a longer one for selected questions. This strategy is costly in terms of time and poses the risk of confusing the informant.

Degree of Specificity

The measurer confronts a dilemma in selecting quantitative response categories. Here the challenge is to find a method that is reliable, acceptable to the client, and valid in terms of the concept being measured. Terms such as "often," "seldom," or "very frequently" depend on the respondent's judgment and cannot be as readily interpreted as can numerical categories such as "one to three times" or "more than twice a week." Conversely, informants might be fatigued and irritated by having to quantify events that are not usually treated that way (for example, "How many times did you go out of your house?"). The vaguer response categories are more likely to be reliable than are more-precise counts, yet the validity is questionable except in terms of the respondent's perception. Another aspect of quantification is the decision about whether the events should be counted as discrete events, whether some estimation of duration is reported, or both. For example, in answer to the question, "How many times did you leave the house yesterday?" a person who collected the newspaper in the morning and walked around the block in the afternoon would score 2, whereas the person who was on an excursion all day would score 1. Bearing in mind that a threshold of information is most useful for clinical practice, perhaps these instruments should use numerical quantifiers but should limit the number of response categories to reflect categories with clinical meaning. On the other hand, some research designs may call for finer distinctions and a scale that will show a wide gamut of functioning.

Dealing with the Hypothetical

Measurements to predict social performance under stress often include hypothetical questions. With measures of social support, the provider or case manager sometimes needs to assess the resources and relationships that would be brought to bear in an emergency; this forces informants to make guesses and judgments. Patients and their relatives can be asked, "What would you do if . . ."; but the information gained is hard to interpret unless follow-up studies have confirmed that the suggested scenarios really do come to pass. Then, too, questions about whether a daughter could give help or care to her mother often do not specify the kind of assistance (money, errands, company, personal-health care); the frequency of the services; their duration; or the social cost that would be incurred by the caregiving family member. Such factors can differ substantially from case to case and circumstance to circumstance. Hypothetical questions also invite socially desirable responses.

Despite these caveats, direct questioning can yield useful data. Kulys and Tobin (1980) examined the relationship between community-dwelling elderly persons and the individual whom the respondents had designated as responsible in case of emergency. Individuals varied markedly in the confidence they expressed in this "responsible other" and in the degree to which the responsibility had been made explicit. Some people named individuals whom they had not seen for years and who did not know that they were so designated. About one-third of the sample refused to have their "responsible others" interviewed for fear of angering them. When the rest of the responsible others were asked to participate in an interview, one-third of this group declined, many for lack of interest. Because relatives were chosen over friends for responsibility, some elderly informants whose relationship with the responsible other was literally and/or figuratively distant could name someone else who satisfied their emotional needs on a more-regular basis. However, 10 percent had no real support system at all in case of emergencies; a larger group had no second line of defense if help from the designated person was not forthcoming. The point here is that, when the hypothetical situation is explored in greater depth, the caregiver's confidence that a support system is available may evaporate. Studies such as this one suggest that measures of social support might incorporate items designed to screen for that subgroup that is poorly defended against medical or social crisis.

Measures of environmental fit also delve into the hypothetical with attempts to match persons to environments. In this instance the questions are, "How would you like . . .?" applied to various activities and situations that could be outside the informant's experience. Another approach is to elicit agreement or disagreement with a series of statements (about aging, privacy, the younger generation, and so on) and extrapolate from the responses whether the individual prefers an active or sedentary environment, age integration or age segregation, and so on. This strategy raises questions to an even higher level of abstraction.

Another of our categories of measures containing scales that gauge coping abilities and subjective well-being also struggles with making predictions based on responses to hypothetical situations. Here the questions are, "How would you handle it if . . .?" Obviously, responses are influenced neither by the emotional reactions engendered by the crisis nor by the interaction with interested other people who they make it easier or more difficult to cope.

Some might argue that the hypothetical should be avoided entirely in favor of descriptive information. In some cases, items about help rendered in the past or past coping styles might elicit useful information. However, not everyone has had the need to test resources or skills in the same way. Furthermore, at least for coping abilities, a rationale can be built for getting all respondents to react to the same hypothetical stimuli.

Measuring Social Functioning in the Cognitively Impaired

Gathering data from the cognitively impaired presents a challenge to measurement that has not been satisfactorily solved. Some individuals are so disoriented that they provide inaccurate objective information and inconsistent subjective reports about preferences. In such situations, the provider would do better to abandon self-report approaches. Some measurements can be made on an observational basis, but they are limited. Interactions, activities, visits, and other observable events can be counted if the opportunity to observe is present. Emotional reactions can also be observed; constant crying and moaning or combativeness might be extrapolated to mean unhappiness or anger; the regular selection of certain activities or company might be interpreted as a preference.

In all likelihood, however, some self-report is possible from most of the cognitively impaired, especially if the questions are important, concrete, and asked in the presence of the stimulus. Logically, one would expect persons to be able to indicate whether they like or dislike a particular meal set in front of them even when memory is greatly eroded. However, little systematic work has been done to determine under what conditions cognitively impaired persons can reliably supply information about personal preferences. On the contrary, assumptions are made about the degree to which the environment retains importance for the cognitively impaired; it is possible that some of the behaviors considered bizarre and disruptive would abate if the individual could structure his or her own time and activities. Many rating scales have been developed that rely on the care attendants to judge the social behavior of regressed patients. Items such as "happy and cheerful," "enjoys his activities," or "friendly with other patients" are typical. Besides the dubious likelihood that the rater has had the opportunity to make the observations, these scales also overlook the possibility that the raters themselves may elicit a particular social behavior from the subject being rated. Such rating scales are worse than futile. They may actually detract from the real challenge of finding indicators of subjective well-being among the mentally impaired.

Measuring Small Increments of Social Functioning

We have already suggested that a threshold of adequate functioning should be defined to identify persons in need of preventive or restorative social services. On the other hand, once a person has been identified as experiencing severe social limitations that also run counter to his or her expectations and preferences, then small social differences should not be discounted; they may, in fact, have enormous significance for social well-being. The experience of the stroke clubs in England suggests that the social supports provided by volunteers (who often receive little positive feedback at the time) is later appreciated and cited as a factor in recovery; if so, doubling the visiting from once to twice a day may be an important increment in social support. Experience in the United States indicates that the added social support of a simple and brief daily telephone reassurance contact makes a great difference in the ability to function independently (Sherwood and Morris 1980). Within institutions, persons who communicate poorly for physical or mental reasons nevertheless may experience sujective reactions to their social network (largely, the care personnel) that enormously influence subjective well-being; although up to now this phenomenon has been described largely in novels (Sarton 1973; Tulloch 1975; Laird 1979), it is an important area for future clinical study. Before definitive pronouncements can be made, the social input needs to be capable of characterization and quantification.

In the remainder of the chapter, thre three categories of social measurement (social interaction and resources, subjective well-being and coping, and environmental fit) are discussed with selected examples of measurement approaches. The conceptual and practical problems discussed in this section are well illustrated by the various instruments. At the end of the chapter, we illustrate some techniques for measuring the social function of the cognitively impaired.

Measures of Social Interactions and Resources

For the most part, the practitioner meets the elderly person in a caregiving setting. Even if a visit is made to a subject's home, observation of an individual's interaction within the environment is inevitably limited and does not always represent the person's behavior in less-artificial circumstances. Yet the clinician needs to assess whether the social environment provides adequate support for present care needs and likely support for prospective care needs.

If extensive care is required, an understanding of the patient's resources and social life-style forms the basis for prescriptive action. If the elderly person is lonely, isolated, or unstimulated (especially if these circumstances represent a deterioration), or if the patient is alienating his circle of caregivers and supporters, the practitioner needs to be aware of it. If one elderly person receives social support at the expense of the physical and mental well-being of another (such as a spouse, a sibling, or even a parent or child), this too must be known. Only then can the intervention be tailored to the particular needs.

Table 4-1 lists a number of instruments that measure social interactions and indicates briefly the scope and strategy of each. This selected group of tools includes ambitious attempts to describe the full range of social interaction of a

Table 4-1
Overview of Selected Measures of Social Interactions and Resources

Measure	*Description*
1. Network Analysis Profile (Cohen and Sokolovsky 1979)	Respondents in single-room-occupancy hotel are interviewed on the content, frequency, duration, intensity, directionality and importance of all their social interactions with other tenants and nontenants in a one-year period; no scaling information.
2. Social Networks Assessment Questionnaire (Froland et al. 1979)	Subjects applying for mental-health treatment are interviewed about proximity to, contacts, exchange of assistance, and emotional relationship with family and friends; no scaling information.
3. Role Activity Scales (Havighurst and Albrecht 1953)	Interviewer rates 13 social roles of elderly people; 10 degrees of activity are defined for each role and scored 0–9. Inter-rater reliability is reported as high items for Role Activity as a Parent Scale shown in table 4-2.
4. Mutual Support Index (Kerckhoff 1965)	Six questions on exchange of help across generations are used for a mutual-support score; one question is used for a geographic-propinquity score (see table 4-2 for items). Mutual-help levels and propinquity are combined in an undescribed way to classify families into four types.
5. Family Structure and Contact Battery (Shanas et al. 1968)	Structured interview with older persons on family composition, physical proximity of relatives, and frequency of kinds of contacts between family members and exchanges of assistance. Used in cross-national study with three waves of interviewing. Norms have been established. No scaling information.
6. Exchanges between the Generations Index (Hill 1970)	Two-hour interview with the wife in an elderly household; detailed questions on social activities and rituals and exchange of monetary help across the generations. No scaling information.
7. Family Structure and Contact Battery (Lopata 1972)	Structured interview tapping frequency and nature of contacts with relatives, friends, and in-laws since death of spouse. Adapted from Shanas et al. (1968). Includes 36 statements about widowhood with which respondent agrees or disagrees. Lopata states that scales were derived: role of mother; social isolation, frequency of contact; and a relations-restrictive scale. Each is expressed as high, medium, or low; no information about scale construction is given.
8. Exchanges of Support and Assistance Index (Harris 1975)	Twenty-one questions (used in interview with elderly about assistance given to children or grandchildren; response categories are "do," "don't do," "not applicable/not necessary," and "not sure." Subject then asked ten questions about help received from children or grandchildren, with the same response categories (see table 4-2 for items). Used in large Harris poll; no scoring provided.
9. HRCA Social Interaction Inventory (Sherwood et al. 1977)	Frequency of telephone and personal contact with children and grandchildren and visits to children or grandchildren; frequency of telephone and personal contact with siblings, other relatives, and friends (see table 4-2 for items).

Table 4-1 (continued)

Measure	*Description*
10. Bennett Social Isolation Scales (described in Anderson and Patten, forthcoming)	Semistructured interview used to probe 9 categories of contact (for example, children, siblings, friends, spouse, organizations) on a scale of 0–4 with 4 equaling the most contact. A Preentry Isolation Index has also been developed with 6 categories of contact, each with a possible score of 0–2. Another version, the Last Month Isolation Index, uses 0–2 scales; the total theoretical score depends on the number of categories of contact used.
11. Family APGAR (Smilkstein 1978)	Patient rates satisfaction with family on 3-point scale ("almost always," "some of the time," "hardly ever") on 5 dimensions: help received in times of trouble; common problem solving; acceptance of change in himself; expression of and response to affection; amount of time spent together. Total score = 10. Score of 10–7 = highly functional family; score of 0–3 = very dysfunctional family See table 4–2 for items.
12. OARS Social Resources Scale (Duke University 1978)	Structured interview asks questions about family composition, personal and telephone contacts, and availability of care. Interviewer then rates social resources on 6-point scale. See table 4–3 for questions and rating scale.
13. Social Dysfunction Rating Scale (Linn et al. 1969)	Professional rates client on 6-point scale (from "not present" to "very severe") on 21 items of social functioning. See table 4–4 for items. Yields overall score and three subscores.
14. Social Behavior Assessment Schedule (Platt et al. 1980)	A semistructured interview (taking 45 minutes) with relative or friend closest to mental patient. Major sections deal with (1) patient behaviors, (2) patient's social performance, (3) subjective burden on family, and (4) concurrent events placing a burden on household. Under behavior, 22 specified behaviors are rated according to degree of disturbance, onset, and distress occasioned for the informant. For social performance, 12 dimensions (for example, household tasks, household management, daily conversation) are rated for objective performance, amount of change reflected, onset of change, and distress occasioned for informant. Concurrent life events are rated for recency of onset and likely connection to patient. Six summary scores are created for patient's disturbed behavior, patient's social performance, objective burden, and distress arising from each of the first three.
15. HRCA Reduced Activities Inventory (Sherwood et al. 1977)	For 8 listed activities (reading, watching television, listening to radio or music, hobbies, receiving and reading mail, going for walks, writing letters, informal group activities such as cards, taking rides), subjects are asked to rate their interest on a 5-point scale ("very interested" to "not at all") and their current participation on a 7-point scale ("daily" to "once a year or less").
16. Activity Scale (Graney and Graney 1974)	Nine questions tapping television viewing, reading, and listening to the radio (hours yesterday), telephone use (number of calls received and made yesterday), visiting in the building, visiting in the city, church or synagogue attendance, club membership and club attendance.

Table 4-1 (continued)

Measure	*Description*
17. Usual Day (Schonfield 1973)	Subjects questioned about usual number of hours awake and typical breakdown of their time in active pursuits (domestic, active hobby, active social activity) and passive pursuits.

$$\text{Usual Day Score} = \frac{\text{Hours spent in active pursuits}}{\text{Hours awake} \times 7} \times 100$$

| 18. Future Activity Scores (Schonfield 1973) | The future-diary questionnaire calculates the percentage of the waking hours of the next 7 days for which the subject has commitments for special future activities (other than routine meals and self-care. |

$$\text{Future Activity Score} = \frac{\text{Committed Hours}}{\text{Hours awake} \times 7} \times 100$$

particular individual; questionnaire approaches to determine the kinds of exchanges of assistance and support that prevail among the generations; professional ratings of social functioning; self-reported activity questionnaires; and, finally, a diary-style approach to the "usual day."

Although instruments measuring income and social class are excluded from this review, we note that even assessing the economic well-being of an elderly person is complex. What income is to be considered? How are property assets counted? Should we include only the individual's own income or average the family income where he resides? If economic well-being is to be measured in order to allocate resources where they are most needed, these questions must be resolved. The real income of the elderly may be distorted by the decisions reached; in the absence of clear decision rules, statistics may not be comparable. George and Bearon (1980) illustrated this problem in a discussion of measures of socioeconomic well-being; they also raised unanswered questions about the utility of measures of social class (based on education and occupation) to make useful distinctions about persons in postretirement years.

Social Networks

The first two items in table 4-1 represent two different approaches to examining social networks. The term *social network* has come into prominence without benefit of an agreed-on definition. One authority suggests that

> Social networks in its usual definition describes the direct and indirect ties linking a group of individuals over certain definable criteria, such as kinship, friendship, acquaintance . . . , providing the structural framework within which support may or may not be accessible to an individual. [Lin, Dean, and Ensel 1979, p. 2]

Mitchell and Trickett's (1980) account of the definitions of social network used in the research of the 1970s points out that the term *personal network* was originally used to refer to the linkages with others surrounding a single focal individual, whereas *social network* was used to refer to all the linkages of members of a particular population. By that rule, one could refer to the personal network of an elderly nursing-home resident and to the social network of the retirement community or nursing home wherein he or she resides. Subsequently, this distinction came to be blunted; the later literature uses the term *social network* to refer to both patterns.

A social network provides the potential for the *social support system*. The latter has been defined as "a set of relations involving the giving and receiving of objects, services, and social and emotional supports defined by the giver and the receiver as necessary, or at least helpful in maintaining a style of life" (Lopata 1975, p. 41). We cannot assume a direct correlation between the size and density of the social network and the amount of support experienced by the individual. In fact, the relationship between social network and social support is an important area for intensive study.

Social networks vary on multiple dimensions, producing a wide array of patterns. Relevant characteristics include size, density, intensity of interactions, durability, multidimensionality, directedness of interactions, geographical dispersion, frequency of interaction, and homogeneity of members. Each of these dimensions is difficult to define and quantify. For example, homogeneity is a complex attribute to scale, given the many ways that people can be alike or can differ (by age, education, income, ethnicity and culture, social values, and so forth). Although the phenomenon of social networks is captured in descriptive approaches, measurement has not extended to scales that capture an entire social structure.

Essentially, there are two possible approaches to the methodical description of social networks. The first method makes an entire environment the focus of attention, and all the relationships and contacts within that environment are examined. The second approach focuses on a particular individual and examines that person's network of relationships and contacts. In the latter approach, attention may be limited to a particular kind of network (family and kinship, friendship, neighborhood, or work). Clearly, the first approach is more feasible when a limited number of variables are under consideration for a small population, whereas the second approach is more appropriate when a large number of variables concerning a single individual are of interest.

The Network Analysis Profile (Cohen and Sokolovsky 1979) was developed to study the nature of the social networks developed by elderly residents in single-room-occupancy hotels. The format uses a structured interview of each resident to prepare a profile of his or her interactions in six fields: tenant–tenant, tenant–nontenant, tenant–kin, tenant–hotel staff, tenant–agency staff, and tenant–social institution. Within each interactional field, the tenant's relationships are depicted according to content, frequency, duration, intensity, and directional flow of the interaction. For example, the in-hotel tenant–tenant relationships are divided into the following content areas: visits to the room, meetings in the lounge, informal conversations, money/loans, drinking/drugs, food aid, medical aid, eating out together, other social outings, sexual activities, and jobs. Within each of these content fields, the interactions between network members are categorized according to direction and frequency. Then the importance of the relationship and the degree of intimacy between two individuals is rated globally. The complexity of such a tool and the vast number of operational decisions required (definition of terms, establishing time frames, collapsing the information into scales) renders the reliability and validity of such instruments problematic. Furthermore, even if the information is collected meticulously (with checks for accuracy and reliability), any scoring system that used a fraction of the information would require computer-assisted techniques. Actual information about how the Network Analysis Profile is scored is not available.

In another example, Froland and his colleagues (1979) developed the Social Networks Assessment Questionnaire (SNAQ) to examine the social networks of mental patients. Through self-report, the patient supplies information about proximity to, contact with, exchange of assistance with, and emotional relationships with all family, friends, and "significant others." Questions about former relationships presumably permit an estimation of the stability of the individual's network. The authors claim that "the characteristics defining structure, interaction, and stability" (p. 84) were measured through the SNAQ, but no formula for making the calculations is provided.

Network assessment, a popular concept in the community-mental-health movement, has been proposed as a possible diagnostic technique in LTC. Therapeutic intervention to alter patterns of interaction and to render social networks more supportive (sometimes known as *networking*) has become a fad. A comprehensive review of the various approaches to defining and measuring social networks is beyond the scope of this work. In general, however, network-assessment questionnaires tend to be "purpose-built," rendering comparison of findings about the relationship between social networks and social supports difficult. As a practical clinical tool, network assessment is ambitious and rather unwieldy.

Measures of Intergenerational Support and Role Performance

Items 3 through 11 in table 4-1 are approaches to measuring intergenerational contacts and support. (Five of these measures are detailed in table 4-2.) The Role Activity Scales (Havighurst and Albrecht 1953) represent an early effort to gauge intergenerational relationships. Thirteen role activities of older adults are rated, each according to nine categories. For example, the Role Activities as a

Parent Scale (table 4-2) arrays the role of parent according to the extent and nature of dependency relationships, including those characterized both by dependency of the parent on the child and by the reverse. The scoring does not reflect a continuum, however, but rather the assignment to a discrete category. The scale attempts to capture affectional as well as interactional variables, but, in so doing, fails to include all possible combinations.

The Role Activity Scales were developed for a landmark study of aging in a Midwestern community; a field worker made the ratings on the basis of responses to a structured interview. The authors tested the reliability of the thirteen role scales by examining the percentage of agreement among the field worker and three other raters who read the written report of the interview. By this method, the percentage of complete agreement ranged from 79 percent on Role Activities as a Grandparent to 45 percent on Leisure Time Activities. For only two of the scales did the level of agreement within one deviation on the scale fall below 80 percent. This form of reliability testing has two problems:

1. A difference of one degree in these particular scales could imply a great divergence. For example, a rating of 4 on the Role Activities of a Parent Scale means "shares children's home, somewhat burdensome," whereas a rating of 5 means "shares children's home, a help rather than a burden." Here a discrepancy of one degree connotes a diametrically opposite meaning for the subjective component of the item.
2. More importantly, the inter-rater reliability achieved is based on ratings of a prepared interview report and a completed questionnaire. What remains untested is whether more than one field interviewer would have produced identical materials from which the ratings could be derived.

In summary, the Role Activities Scales present both conceptual problems, in terms of the failure of the nine items in each category to form logical continua, and practical problems, in terms of achieving reliability and interpreting the scores. Admittedly, these early measures lack some of the sophistication of psychometric tools today. Nevertheless, the problems exemplified by these scales persist in many of their more modern counterparts.

Other approaches largely eliminate the rater's judgment. Shanas and her colleagues (1968) developed their Family Structure and Contact Battery for use in a cross-national study. The format requires an interview with an elderly household member. The content focuses on living arrangements and proximity of the subject to living children. Proximity to children is measured in terms of the amount of time it would take the particular child to reach the subject using his or her usual means of transportation (the categories are: share a household; 10 minutes or less; 11–30 minutes; 31–60 minutes; more than an hour; or one day or longer). Additionally, the subject is asked when he last saw his children. Exchanges of most kinds of assistance and support are measured through a checklist

Table 4-2
Examples of Measures of Intergenerational Support

Mutual Support Index[a]

Mutual Support (2 points if need present and met; 1 if no need for this help; 0 if need present and unmet)

1. Have any of your children helped out when either of you were sick?
2. Have any of your children given advice on business or money matters?
3. Have you helped your children in any way when someone was sick in their family?
4. Have you given any of your children advice on business or money matters?
5. Have any of your children ever offered you financial assistance?
6. How willing would you say that your children are to make sacrifices for you?

Propinquity Distance of each child from parental home is noted and average distance taken for propinquity.

Supportiveness and propinquity indicators are combined to produce four categories of family types:

    extended family = near family/high mutual support
    modified extended = near family/low mutual support
    nucleated = distant family/high mutual support
    individuated family = distant family/low mutual support

Family APGAR[b]

Adaptation
1. I am satisfied with the help that I receive from my family when something is troubling me.

Partnership
2. I am satisfied with the way my family discusses items of common interest and shares problem-solving with me.

Growth
3. I find that my family accepts my wishes to take on new activities and make changes in my life-style.

Affection
4. I am satisfied with the way my family expresses affection and responds to my feelings such as anger, sorrow and love.

Resolve
5. I am satisfied with the way my family and I share time together.

Scoring: (2) almost always; (1) some of the time; (0) hardly ever

Short HRCA Social Contact Inventory[c]

Ask for A and B for the following categories of persons: children; other relatives; friends; other residents of this facility.

A. *How often do you see your . . . ?*
    (Code each category or person separately.)

    0 Inapp.; R has no (children, relative, friends)
    1 Never, almost never
    2 Once a year or less
    3 Several times a year
    4 Monthly
    5 Several times a month
    6 Weekly
    7 Several times a week
    8 Daily
    9 DK/NA

Table 4-2 (continued)

B. *Would you like to see . . . more often than you do?*

  1 More often
  2 Same
  3 Less often
  0 Inapp.; R has no (child, siblings, etc.)

Exchanges of Support and Assistance Index[d]

Do you ever help either your children or grandchildren in any of the following ways?[e]

(For younger generation) Do your parents or grandparents every help you in any of the following ways?

  1. Help out when someone is ill.
  2. Take care of small children.
  3. Give advice on running a home.
  4. Give advice on bringing up children.
  5. Shop or run errands.
  6. Give you/them gifts.
  7. Help out with money.
  8. Fix things around your/their house or keep house for you/them.
  9. Give advice on job or business matters.
10. Give general advice on how to deal with some of life's problems.
11. Take grandchildren, nieces, or nephews into their/your home to live with them/you.

(For older generation) Do your children or grandchildren ever help you in any of the following ways?

(For younger generation) Do you ever help your parents or grandparents in any of the following ways?

  1. Help out when someone is ill.
  2. Give advice on money matters.
  3. Shop or run errands for them.
  4. Give them/you gifts.
  5. Help fix things around the house or keep house for you/them.
  6. Help out with money.
  7. Take them/you places such as the doctor, shopping, church.
  8. Give advice on running their/your home.
  9. Give advice on job or business matters.
10. Give general advice on how to deal with some of life's problems.

Role Activities in Later Maturity Ratings[f]

Role Activities as a Parent[g]

0 Never visited by children. No interest in them. Rejects them.
1 No interest in children; too old or too ill to care.
2 Knows little about children, where they are, etc. Seldom hears from them.
3 Sees children occasionally or depends on them.
4 Shares children's home; somewhat burdensome.
5 Shares children's home; a help rather than a burden.
6 Slight dependence on the part of children; some responsibility for them.
7 Responsible for children full or part time (children dependent).
8 Independent; occasional advice to children or needs their advice. Children may live with parent.
9 Mutual independence but close social and affectional relationship.

---

[a]Adapted from A.C. Kerckhoff, "Nuclear and Extended-Family Relationships: A Normative and Behavioral Analysis," in *Social Structure and Family: Generational Relations*, ed. E. Shanas and G. Streib (Englewood Cliffs, N.J.: Prentice-Hall, 1965).

Table 4-2 (continued)

[b]Adapted from G. Smilkstein, "The Family APGAR: A Proposal for a Family Function Test and Its Use by Physicians," *Journal of Family Practice* 6(1978):1231–1239.

[c]From S.J. Sherwood, J. Morris, V. Mor, and C. Gutkin, "Compendium of Measures for Describing and Assessing Long Term Care Populations" (Boston: Hebrew Rehabilitation Center for Aged, 1977, mimeographed).

[d]Adapted from Louis Harris and Associates, *The Myth and Reality of Aging in America* (Washington, D.C.: National Council on Aging, 1975).

[e]Response choices are: "do," "don't do," "no need/not applicable," "not sure."

[f]Adapted from R.J. Havighurst and R. Albrecht, *Older People* (New York: Longmans, Green, and Company, 1953).

[g]Nine-category scale is used to rate 12 other role activities: as great-grandparents; grandparents; home responsibilities; kinship group; social clubs; business clubs; church activities; peer relationships; small-group activities or cliques; civic activities; community activities; and business or occupation.

of the kinds of assistance the respondents have given to or received from their children in the past month. Children's help with medical bills or household expenses, in contrast, is tapped on a twelve-month time frame.

It is not clear how the information in the Family Structure and Contact Battery is collapsed when each child presents a different profile in terms of proximity, recency of last contact, and exchange of assistance. In any such inquiry, the decision rules about analysis should depend on the purpose of the measure. For example, one might be interested in the total amount of filial contact experienced by the elderly, the degree to which the middle generation remains in contact with and supportive of the parental generation, or the extent to which each elderly person with children enjoys some threshold level of contact and support from them. Depending on its purpose, the analysis might total the contact hours of all children and the cumulative amount of assistance, or be expressed as a ratio of the amount of assistance divided by number of living children with some adjustment for distance, or use the figures pertinent to the child who is closest geographically or who gives the most assistance.

MacDonald's Exchanges Between the Generations Index (Hill 1970) is developed from semistructured interviews with the wives in elderly households. A retrospective record of all exchanges of assistance in the past year is produced. The kinds of help received or given are subdivided into financial help, goods, services, and knowledge assistance. All categories of receivers or givers are included—immediate family members, extended kin, friends, neighbors, and community organizations. Each type of assistance is further coded according to the circumstances prompting the help and the conditions of the help. "Associational solidarity" across the generation is also tapped through a matrix including the kinds of persons (immediate household family, husband or wife only, married children, married grandchildren, wife's parents) with whom common activities, such as birthdays, special holidays, vacations, and dining out, are shared. Like the Shanas questionnaire, the MacDonald instrument has been used to report frequencies and percentages in gerontological research; but no information is given about how the information might be scaled. Although the questionnaire has the potential to produce a voluminous amount of information, no information is available about its reliability. One wonders whether the informant would be able to supply accurate information about exchanges of goods and services over an entire year, especially when the items extend to exchanges of advice, sympathy, and small practical services, including loans of equipment.

Lopata (1972) developed an extensive Family Structure and Contact Battery for her study of the adjustment of widows in the Chicago area. Based closely on Shanas's battery, the Lopata instrument is particularly adapted to elicit information about the period after the death of a spouse. Respondents' attitudes about widowhood are tapped by thirty-six true-or-false questions. Lopata indicates that four scales were derived from her instrument (role of mother, social isolation, frequency of contact, and "relations–restrictive"); but her book provides no information about the nature of or rationale for the scales.

In contrast to the more-detailed batteries of Shanas, MacDonald, and Lopata, more-streamlined approaches have been developed to gauge intergenerational relationships. A relatively old example is Kerckhoff's Mutual Support Index, shown in table 4–2 (Kerckhoff 1965). The approach involves six simple questions about categories of help received or offered from children. In answering the questions, the respondent refers to all of his or her children as a category and uses a broad time window (for example, "Have any of your children ever offered you financial assistance?"). Possible scores on each item range from 0 to 2, with 2 points signifying that the need is present, 1 point connoting no need for that type of help, and a score of 0 indicating an unmet need. Kerckhoff and colleagues combine this information with a single question about the geographical propinquity of each child in relationship to the respondent and, based on the answers, propose four types of family structure. The extended family is characterized by geographical closeness and high mutual family support, the modified extended family is geographically close but shows low mutual support, the nucleated family is geographically distant but highly supportive, and the individuated family is geographically separated and unsupportive. The notion of developing new categories of family types that take into account various mixes of mobility and affectional ties is attractive. Precise information about how the scores on the six questions were combined to connote high or low support was not available. The propinquity figure is based on the average distance between respondent and adult children, permitting one very distant child to distort the rating.

The Short HRCA Social Contact Inventory (see table 4–2) was designed primarily for use in institutional or congregate-living facilities (Sherwood et al.

1977). It is particularly attractive because it combines an objective measure ("How often do you see children, other relatives, friends, other residents of this facility?") with a subjective measure, which, for each category, probes whether that class of contact is more frequent, less frequent, or just as frequent as the respondent would prefer. The format is deceptively simple; in administering a version of this scale in a current nursing-home study, we found that respondents could not readily think in categories such as children and other relatives without differentiating among them. Moreover, the eight response categories, ranging from "never/almost never" to "daily" caused difficulties for respondents with memory losses, compounded by the difficulty in gauging time in an institutional setting.

Bennett and her colleagues have used a similar series of scales to measure social isolation. As summarized in a recent review (Anderson and Patten, forthcoming), the Adult Isolation Index taps lifelong patterns of isolation in terms of nine categories of social contact (for example, children, siblings, organizations). Other variations of the scale have been developed to measure isolation prior to entering a congregate-living facility (Preentry Isolation Index) and isolation over the past month. Bennett and her colleagues have evolved these instruments through successive studies (Tec and Granick [Bennett] 1960; Weinstock and Bennett 1971; Bennett 1973a, b). The ability to measure social isolation permits this variable to be linked to the cognitive functioning of the individual and to organizational characteristics of the institution. In a 1967 study, Nahemow and Bennett found that the mean Adult Isolation Index scores (out of a possible 36, signifying maximum contact) were 13.48 for residents of a voluntary home for the aged; 19.90 for residents of a proprietary nursing home; and 16.20 for residents of a public-housing complex. The Adult Isolation Index has the advantage of clear scoring rules; however, the validity of the score is based on an assumption that the more categories of social contact the individual has, the less isolated he is. It does not take into account that an individual who scores 4 points in several areas (for example, children and friends) may have sufficient contact within those categories to compensate for low scores in other categories (such as siblings, organizations). The Adult Isolation Scale has been incorporated into the multifunctional CARE instrument, discussed in chapter 5.

The Exchanges of Support and Assistance Index (see table 4-2) was developed for a 1975 Harris poll. Eleven types of assistance emanating from the older generation to the younger are listed, along with ten emanating from the younger to the older generation. The respondent indicates whether he has given or received any of those categories of help. Depending on the age of the informant, he or she replies in terms of help given to and received from parents and grandparents or children and grandchildren.

Rating Scales

The next four items on table 4-1 illustrate three quite different approaches to rating social functioning (or dysfunctioning). The Family APGAR (Smilkstein 1978), which was not developed particularly for a elderly population, represents an intriguing attempt to develop a screening instrument for family practitioners to use in gaining a systematic impression of "family health" from the perspective of each family member (see table 4-2 for items). Straining somewhat to preserve the familiar acronym for gauging the well being of neonates, the six categories rated are labeled *A*daptation, *P*artnership, *G*rowth, *A*ffection, and *R*esolve. In order, they refer to the subject's satisfaction with: (1) the way family members assist each other or elicit community assistance in times of need; (2) the way family members communicate about decisions and problems; (3) the way family members assist each other in facilitating their own desired personal growth or change; (4) the way family members respond to emotional expressions such as love, anger, and sorrow; and (5) the way family members share resources, especially time, space, and money. The family member is asked to check his or her satisfaction with each item on a 0–2 scale ("almost always," "some of the time," "hardly ever"); or, alternatively, the physician can ask leading questions in order to make a rating. The authors suggest that a score of 3 or less (out of a possible 10) suggests a highly dysfunctional family for the particular individual and that a score of 4 to 6 suggests a moderately dysfunctional family. If family members show discrepancies in the way they complete the Family APGAR, or if they receive low scores, the physician is urged to explore the situation further.

The validity of the Family APGAR has been tested by comparing the scores of thirty-eight adults in married students' housing quarters with those of twenty adults in psychotherapy (Good et al. 1979). A mean score of 8.24 for the non-clinical group was compared to 5.89 for the psychotherapy group. In the latter group, the ratings of spouses were highly correlated. In addition, the Family APGAR scores were correlated with Pless–Satterwhite Family Function Questionnaire (1975) and with clinical judgment of the therapists. Information about reliability in terms of reproducibility of the instrument is not yet available. Clearly, the validity must also be established with a larger number of subjects who represent a wider age spectrum. Although we do not yet endorse the author's view that the Family APGAR is a valid and useful instrument for clinical practice and research, we present it because of its novel approach to providing a practical tool for physicians that at least taps a patient's perception of family functioning. If such a technique were to be adapted for rating the family units of elderly patients (which sometimes traverse households), the variables would require rethinking.

Table 4–3 presents the Social Dysfunction Rating Scale (SDRS) (Linn et al. 1969), which is similar in style to the Cumulative Illness Rating and the Rapid

Table 4-3
Social Dysfunctioning Rating Scale

Directions: Score each of the items as follows:
1. Not present   3. Mild   5. Severe
2. Very mild   4. Moderate   6. Very severe

Self-esteem

1. ____ Low self concept (feelings of inadequacy, not measuring up to self-ideal).

2. ____ Goallessness (lack of inner motivation and sense of future orientation).

3. ____ Lack of a satisfying philosophy or meaning of life (a conceptual framework for integrating past and present experiences).

4. ____ Self-health concern (preoccupation with physical health, somatic concerns).

Interpersonal system

5. ____ Emotional withdrawal (degree of deficiency in relating to others).

6. ____ Hostility (degree of aggression toward others).

7. ____ Manipulation (exploiting of environment, controlling at other's expense).

8. ____ Overdependency (degree of parasitic attachment to others).

9. ____ Anxiety (degree of feeling of uneasiness, impending doom).

10. ____ Suspiciousness (degree of distrust or paranoid ideation).

Performance System

11. ____ Lack of satisfying relationships with significant persons (spouse, children, kin, significant persons serving in a family role).

12. ____ Lack of friends, social contacts.

13. ____ Expressed need for more friends, social contacts.

14. ____ Lack of work (remunerative or nonremunerative, productive work activities that normally give a sense of usefulness, status, confidence).

15. ____ Lack of satisfaction from work.

16. ____ Lack of leisure time activities.

17. ____ Expressed need for more leisure, self-enhancing, and satisfying activities.

18. ____ Lack of participation in community activities.

19. ____ Lack of interest in community affairs and activities that influence others.

20. ____ Financial insecurity.

21. ____ Adaptive rigidity (lack of complex coping patterns to stress).

Patient: _____ *Rater*: _____ *Date*: ____

Source: M.W. Linn, W.B. Sculthorpe, M. Evje, P.H. Slater, and S.P. Goodman, "A Social Dysfunction Rating Scale," *Journal of Psychiatric Research* 6(1969):299–306.

Disability Rating Scales by the same author (see chapter 2). The rater is instructed to rate each of the twenty-one items on a six-point scale (from "not present" to "very severe"). The scale contains both objective and subjective items; for example, "lack of friends and social contacts" is rated as one item and "expressed need for more friends and social contact" as another. Validity has been tested in terms of the ability of the scale to discriminate between 80 psychiatric and nonpsychiatric outpatients; 92 percent of the patients were correctly classified using the scale. SDRS scores were also correlated with global judgments of local workers, unfamiliar with the scale, who did unstructured interviews; a product-moment correlation of .89 was achieved.

Item reliability was tested by two independent raters with reliability varying from .86 on "lack of friends, social contacts" to .54 on "manipulation." This latter item was defined as evidence during the interview that the subject uses or exploits others for his or her own satisfaction, leading to an adverse effect on others in the environment. A very high inter-rater reliability for overall scores was found when seven raters used the same interview material on which to base the scores. Factor analysis has identified five factors (apathetic detachment, dissatisfaction, hostility, health/finance concern, and manipulative dependency). The authors suggest that both the factor scores and the overall scores could be used for rapid appraisal of social functioning. However, we would urge caution in using a scale that calls for judgment at such a level of abstraction, at least until more-solid inter-rater reliability information can be produced.

The OARS Social Resource Scale, part of the larger OARS battery, is perhaps the best-known general measure of social functioning for the elderly. As table 4-4 shows, the questions elicit information about family structure, patterns of friendship and visiting, availability of a confidant, and availability of a helper should the need arise. A different version of the questions (shown in italics in table 4-4) is used when the respondent lives in an institution. On the basis of the responses to the questions, the interviewer rates the social resources of the individual according to a six-point scale, ranging from "excellent social resources" to "totally socially impaired." The entire OARS technique is discussed in the next chapter, which treats multidimensional measures.

The Social Behavior Assessment Schedule (SBAS) was designed to elicit information about social functioning using the patient's most-involved relative or friend as respondent (Platt et al. 1980). Developed in a British psychiatry department, the technique uses a standardized, semistructured interview dealing with the patient's behavior and social functioning and its adverse effects on the household. The authors envisaged the SBAS as a practical tool, useful not only for basic research but also for evaluating the effects of therapeutic regimens. Although developed for the relatives of acutely ill psychiatric patients, it could be adapted for the chronically ill, including the psychogeriatric patient. A detailed manual (Platt, Weyman, and Hirsch 1978) accompanies the instrument, ensuring some degree of standardization in its use.

The SBAS has the following sections:

1. *Introduction.* A brief section designed to gather background information about both the patient and the respondent.
2. *Patient's behavior.* Here twenty-two patient behaviors are considered: misery, withdrawal, slowness, forgetfulness, underactivity, overdependency, indecisiveness, worrying, fearfulness, obsessionality, odd ideas, overactivity, unpredictability, irritability, rudeness, violence, parasuicide, offensive behavior,

Table 4-4
OARS Social Resource Scale

Now I'd like to ask you some questions about your family and friends.

Are you single, married, widowed, divorced or separated?
  1   Single
  2   Married
  3   Widowed
  4   Divorced
  5   Separated
  —   Not answered

  (Inst.)
  (If "2" ask a)

  a. *Does your spouse live here also?*
     1   Yes
     2   No
     —   Not answered

  Inst: *Do not ask following. Ask following (Inst.) instead*

Who lives with you?
[Check "yes" or "no" for each of the following.]

Yes   No

____   ____ No one
____   ____ Husband or wife
____   ____ Children
____   ____ Granchildren
____   ____ Parents
____   ____ Grandparents
____   ____ Brothers and sisters
____   ____ Other relatives (does not include inlaws covered in the above categories)
____   ____ Friends
____   ____ Nonrelated paid help (includes free room)
____   ____ Others (specify)   _____

(Inst.): In the past year about how often did you leave here to visit your family and/or friends for weekends or holidays, or to go on shopping trips or outings?
  1   Once a week or more
  2   1-3 times a month
  3   Less than once a month or only on holidays
  4   Never
  —   Not answered

How many people do you know well enough to visit with in their homes?
  3   Five or more
  2   Three to four
  1   One to two
  0   None
  —   Not answered

About how many times did you talk to someone-friends, relatives or others—on the telephone in the past week (either you called them or they called you)? [IF SUBJECT HAS NO PHONE, QUESTION STILL APPLIES.]
  3   Once a day or more
  2   2-times
  1   Once
  0   Not at all
  —   Not answered

Table 4–4 (continued)

(Inst.): Substitute italicized paragraph.

How many times during the past week did you spend some time with someone who does not live with you; that is, you went to see them, or they came to visit you, or you went out to do things together?

How many times in the past week did you visit with someone, either with people who live here or people who visited you here?

    3 Once a day or more
    2 2–6 times
    1 Once
    0 Not at all
    – Not answered

Do you have someone you can trust and confide in?

    2 Yes
    0 No
    – Not answered

Do you find yourself feeling lonely quite often, sometimes, or almost never?

    0 Quite often
    1 Sometimes
    2 Almost never
    – Not answered

Do you see your relatives and friends as often as you want to, or are you somewhat unhappy about how little you see them?

    1 As often as wants to
    2 Somewhat unhappy about how little
    – Not answered

Is there someone *(Inst.: outside this place)* who would give you any help at all if you were sick or disabled; for example, your husband/wife, a member of your family, or a friend?

    1 Yes
    0 No one willing and able to help
    – Not answered

If "yes" ask a and b.

  a. Is there someone *(Inst.: Outside this place)* who would take care of you as long as needed, or only for a short time, or only someone who would help you now and then (for example, taking you to the doctor, or fixing lunch occasionally, etc.)?
    1 Someone who would take care of subject indefinitely (as long as needed)
    2 Someone who would take care of subject for a short time (a few weeks to six months)
    3 Someone who would help subject now and then (taking him to the doctor or fixing lunch, etc.
    – Not answered

  b. Who is this person?
    Name _____
    Relationship _____

Rating Scale

Rate the current social resources of the person being evaluated along the six-point scale presented below. Circle the *one* number that best describes the person's present circumstances.

1. *Excellent social resources*: Social relationships are very satisfying and extensive; at least one person would take care of him (her) indefinitely.

2. *Good social resources*: Social relationships are fairly satisfying and adequate and at least one person would take care of him (her) indefinitely, *or*
Social relationships are very satisfying and extensive, and only short-term help is available.

Table 4-4 (continued)

3. *Mildly socially impaired*: Social relationships are unsatisfactory, of poor quality, few; but at least one person would take care of him (her) indefinitely, *or*
   Social relationships are fairly satisfactory and adequate, and only short-term help is available.

4. *Moderately socially impaired*: Social relationships are unsatisfactory, of poor quality, few; and only short-term care is available, *or*
   Social relationships are at least adequate or satisfactory, but help would only be available now and then.

5. *Severely socially impaired*: Social relationships are unsatisfactory, of poor quality, few; and help would be available only now and then, *or*
   Social relationships are at least satisfactory or adequate, but help is not available even now and then.

6. *Totally socially impaired*: Social relationships are unsatisfactory, of poor quality, few; and help is not available even now and then.

Source: Adapted from Duke University Center for the Study of Aging and Human Development, *Multidimensional Functional Assessment: The OARS Methodology* (Durham, N.C.: Duke University, 1978).

Note: Italicized questions apply to those living in institutions.

heavy drinking, self-neglect, complaints about bodily aches and pains, and odd behavior. For each of the behaviors present, the extent of the patient's problem is rated as moderate or severe; the time of onset is rated on a five-point scale from "onset a week ago or less" to "always," and the informant's distress about the behavior is assigned to one of four categories ("none," "moderate," "severe," or "resigned"). A summary score for disturbed behavior is calculated by summing the twenty-two components; the authors argue that the items are discrete because 70 percent of the intercorrelations of items were less than 0.3 percent. The summary distress score is calculated by summing the distress items (giving a score of 0 for "resignation") and dividing by the numbers of behaviors that were present, making a possible range of 0 to 2.

3. *Patient's social performance.* Twelve areas of social performance are considered: household tasks, household management, child care, interest in child, discipline of child, spare time activities, informant–patient relationship/everyday conversation, support, affection/friendliness, sexual relationship (if applicable), work/study, and decision making. For each social-performance area deemed pertinent, the informant rates a diminished performance on a two-point scale for severity. Onset of the diminished performance and distress caused to the informant are rated the same way as in the patient-behavior section. The rate of change in the patient's performance of the social task is also rated on a five-point scale. The social-performance score is an aggregation of the scores on all items divided by

the number of applicable roles; this strategy is intended to avoid distorting the scores of those without children. A summary distress score is a mean created by summing the total score of items occasioning distress and dividing by the number of applicable items, making a possible range of 0 to 2.

4. *Adverse effects on others (burden).* Seventeen possible adverse effects on others are listed; eight of these apply to children of school age, eight apply to the informant, and the last is generalized disruption to others. For each item present, ratings are made of the onset, the severity, the likelihood that the problem is related to the patient (possibly or definitely), and the informant's distress over the problem. A summary objective-burden score is created, and a summary distress score (subjective burden) is created in the same way as are the other summary scores.

5. *Concurrent events.* Eleven concurrent events are considered: physical illness or injury; death; suicide attempts or overdoses; births, abortions, or miscarriages; unemployment; change of employment; financial problems; legal problems; changes in marital status; unexpected news; and disappointments. Each event present is rated for its time of onset and the likelihood that it is independent of the patient. No summary scores are described in this section.

6. *Support to informant.* The last section probes the help that the informant has received from other family members, friends, neighbors, or formal social services. In each instance, the relief is divided into that obtained through confiding and practical help received. Housing is also objectively assessed. No summary scores are provided for this section.

We have described the SBAS in such detail because it represents a comprehensive effort to separate the ingredients of social performance and its effect on the caregiver. Reliability tests to date have relied on recorded interviews only. Using this standard stimulus, four raters rating nine cases were able to demonstrate high correlations for each of the summary ratings—that is, the three objective-performance ratings and the three distress ratings. Item-by-item comparisons for each rater pair showed less congruence. Further analysis suggested that the raters were more likely to match on the objective ratings than on the distress ratings; the greatest confusion lay in distinguishing between resignation, on the one hand, and severe or moderate distress on the other.

Activities

Up to now we have emphasized the relationship side of social interactions. This is important from the perspective of gauging actual and potential sources of assistance and sources of social satisfaction. Another aspect of social interactions is activity per se. Logically, one would suppose that some level (and perhaps variety) of activity is conducive to life satisfaction and is perhaps linked to higher levels of physical and mental functioning. However, producing meaningful categories and interpreting information presents a major difficulty.

All activities are not equal; they range in energy expenditure from sedentary to strenuous and in terms of social involvement from solitary to congregate. Some activities are largely passive (watching television, attending a movie), whereas others require active intellectual or physical involvement (collecting stamps, taking walks). Simple listing of activities performed may not properly capture the social context or level of energy involved. If physical movement itself is the key variable, pedometer devices may be affixed to shoes or wheelchairs (Schulz 1976); unobtrusive measures of other activities may be more elusive, relying on self-report or observer information. The latter is hardly satisfactory in determining subjective enjoyment.

The type of frequency categories used in an activity measure logically depends on the kind of activity itself. In a study of the effects of moving on residents of multilevel accommodation for the elderly, Guttman (1977) developed a list of seventeen leisure-time activities. Respondents were asked how many times a year they went to movies, plays or concerts, or church services; how many times a month they attended meetings, played cards, visited friends, or ate meals out; and how many hours a day they spent on hobbies, reading, and watching television. For each grouping of questions, the time frame chosen obviously reflects common-sense judgments about increments that would be both compatible with the frequency of the event and fine enough to show improvement or deterioration of social functioning if such change were present. A tradeoff is also present between posing questions in terms of total frequency during a period, as opposed to asking about the last month (week, day) and extrapolating to a larger time frame. The latter strategy is more likely to provide an accurate accounting for the specific time period. However, seasonal variations and special circumstances may make the shorter, more-immediate frame of reference less useful. Caution is needed in measuring activities in institutions, especially if the measure will be used as a proxy for quality of life. If an interviewer happened to make the measure during the week of the institution's annual outing, for example, the activity level for an entire group would be distorted.

Furthermore, in institutional settings, certain activities may be built into the social program (movies, religious services, arts and crafts, bingo) so that participation is not a free choice among alternatives. To capture that distinction, an activity scale may ask, for each category of activity, whether the individual participates and whether that frequency of participation is perceived as too little, too much, or about right. The HRCA Reduced Activities Inventory (Sherwood et al. 1977) shown as item 15 in table 4–1, adopts that strategy. For eight listed activities (reading, watching television, listening to the radio or music, hobbies, receiving and reading mail, writing letters, taking rides, and informal group activities such as playing cards), the respondents indicate their interest on a five-point scale and their current participation level on a seven-point scale. The method for combining this information into a score is not explained. The type of activities included in the list are those considered appropriate to the scaled-down activity level feasible in the nursing home.

Just as the substitutability of social relationships is important, so too is the substitutability of social activities. To examine whether decrements in one kind of activity are compensated for by increases in others as an individual ages, some satisfactory measure of the spectrum of activities is needed. In general, we have been unable to locate many examples of activity scales for use in either community or institutional settings.

Graney and Graney (1974) have studied the substitutability of activities, especially with reference to communication behaviors. They viewed membership in voluntary or religious groups; reading newspapers, magazines, and books; listening to the radio and watching television; and conducting telephone and face-to-face conversations with friends, neighbors, and relatives as important communication activities. To test hypotheses that subjects experiencing decrements in some such activities (through physical, financial, or social losses) will compensate by increasing their participation in others, they did a longitudinal study using a nine-question activity scale (item 16 in table 4-1). Television viewing, reading, and listening to the radio were measured in "number of hours on a day like yesterday." Telephone calls made or received were measured by an actual count of yesterday's telephone calls. Visits to friends or neighbors in the immediate vicinity were measured by a four-point scale ("more than once a day," "daily," "less than once a day," "never"), whereas visits to friends and relatives in the city as a whole, religious attendance, and club or group attendance were tapped by a scale that used the month rather than the weeks as the unit of measurement. Maintenance of organizational memberships was scaled as "none," "one," or "two or more." In their analysis, Graney and Graney simply established cutoff points for a trichotomous measure of low, moderate, and high frequency in each of these activities. For example, two telephone calls or fewer per day was defined as "few," three to four as "moderate," and five or more as "frequent."

Another approach to measuring activity uses a log or diary format or gathers detailed retrospective information about a short time period. Assuming the cooperation of capable respondents, this is a precise method of determining how time is spent. Because it may not be feasible to collect detailed information over a lengthy period, such diaries would presumably be most useful when rare but significant events (such as a visit from an out-of-state child) are unimportant to the measure. Schonfield (1973) developed an approach to measuring the activities of the usual day (see table 4-1, item 17) that calls for totaling the number of hours typically spent in active pursuits and then dividing by the typical number of waking hours. Active pursuits include domestic activities and chores; active hobbies; and social activities requiring some preparation (receiving guests, going out); but exclude passive activities and hobbies. Passive activities include sitting and thinking, napping during the day, eating meals and snacks, reading, watching television, listening to the radio, and social activities requiring no preparation (such as sitting and talking to one's spouse or roommate). The interviewer gathers the factual information and then allocates the activities to the active or passive category. The final score is expressed as a percentage.

The future-activity score, listed as item 18 in table 4-1 (Schonfield 1973), is a variant of the usual-day score. Here the important concern is the number of hours in the week that have been committed to planned activities. The figure is derived by asking respondents to construct a future diary for the preceding week. The "committed hours" are defined as all special activities (appointments, visits, events, and traveling time to and from such events); the score is constructed by summing the committed hours and then dividing by the number of hours awake in a week. Again, the score is expressed as a percentage. The Future Activity Score is a tool for examining the theory that a planful, future orientation is associated with life satisfaction and successful aging. Using both the Future Activity and the Usual Day Scores, Schulz (1976) showed that predictable and controllable events (such as friendly visits whose timing was in control of the elderly person) had a positive effect on the well-being of the institutionalized aged. Note that the usual-day and the future-activity scores do not require specifying either the nature of the activity (beyond the distinction between activity and passivity) or the enjoyment that the activity occasions. If subjective enjoyment is important, then other measures are needed. Information is lacking on the reliability or stability of the future-activity score and the usual-day score.

Measures of Subjective Well-Being and Coping

Social functioning includes social outlook and attitudes. The practitioner is most interested in defining social attitudes when they illuminate positive or negative reactions to the current life situation rather than when they reflect relatively fixed personality traits. A positive constellation of attitudes could be an outcome of a propitious LTC plan, expeditiously implemented. From another perspective, a negative social outlook might be an important diagnostic key to reduced social functioning. Various terms have been used for scales measuring this quality of "oneness with the world" as it pertains to the elderly. These include subjective well-being, happiness, morale, life satisfaction, contentment, and personal adjustment. Carp (1977) provides a good statement of the underlying concept:

> . . . what we have been after in in measures of morale, life satisfaction, and the like is *the inner aspect of coping, the experiential facet of adaptation or adjustment.* [p. 19, emphasis ours]

However the variable is labeled, if it is an aspect of social functioning, it should be sensitive to the relationships, roles, and activities that are the objective aspects of social functioning. Indeed, some measures of subjective well-being systematically examine subjective attitudes about or satisfaction with specific areas of social life. Others contain a mix of items addressing objective reactions to specific social circumstances (for example, getting old, activities) and more-general "mood" questions. The more generalized the measure of subjective well-being, the more it overlaps with measures of mental states and resembles the measures of positive mental health that were considered in chapter 3. Affective status in particular—that is, mood, including depression—is correlated with measures of subjective well-being (Morris, Wolf, and Klerman 1975); indeed, some similar items are used to measure happiness and positive mental health. Several reviews, for example, include Bradburn's Affect Balance Scale in lists of morale measures (Sauer and Warland, forthcoming; Lawton 1977; Ware et al. 1979).

Coping also involves reactions to life conditions; but, in contrast to subjective well-being, coping is an active stance. In part, it is a skill requiring cognitive problem-solving abilities; the degree of effort required to cope is dependent on the amount of external pressure. Measurements of coping usually involve forms of projective testing or responses to hypothetical situations. We are not aware of studies validating whether coping strategies presented as hypothetical solutions are actually applied when the individual is presented with the stress. Furthermore, little longitudinal information is available to determine whether coping abilities and/or styles change over time. Scales relating to coping in geriatrics are, for the most part, in early experimental stages.

Measures of subjective well-being have been the subject of multiple reviews. Because the underlying concept is elusive, authors of review papers differ in the articles they include. For the Instrument Bank on Aging, Sauer and Warland (forthcoming) reviewed three single-item indicators and ten scales measuring "morale and life satisfaction"; they point out that all the measures suffer from a lack of consistent attention to the theoretical domains of the concept and from the propensity of those who borrow the measures to assume their reliability and validity under new conditions with new populations. Lohman (1977), studying the correlation among ten measures of life satisfaction, morale, and adjustment, found that, in general, the measures were related. In a paper summarizing the last thirty years of work on the "subjective well-being" of the elderly, Larson (1978) examined the correlation of well-being, however measured, to health, socioeconomic status, mental status, age, employment, and activity levels. This extremely helpful review paper, which summarized many studies, showed modest correlations in each area, although never enough to explain most of the variance in the particular domain. However, Larson reminds us that, even when the same test of subjective well-being is used in several different studies, we must be cautious in comparing scores across differing populations.

With the variety of approaches used to measure both subjective well-being and the comparison variables (such as health or activity levels), patterns could be different.

Linn (1979) reviews ways to assess "community adjustment" of the elderly. She perceives adjustment both as a state of equilibrium within the environment and as a process that reflects how a person satisfies needs and reduces tensions. Adjustment can be related to an individual's own expectations (personal adjustment) or to a societal context (social adjustment). For the elderly, ideal standards for social performance are unclear, statistical norms describing actual social functioning are largely unavailable, and clinically derived norms for "adjusted behavior" may not adequately address the aging experience because the elderly are underrepresented in psychotherapy. Because so many adjustment scales for the elderly inappropriately rely on activities or social-role performance, Linn suggests the merit of using measures of well-being, morale, or life satisfaction as proxies for adjustment in the aged. Because "the personal adjustment of older people depends largely on their present happiness, . . . feelings of inner satisfaction are perhaps a better index of adjustment than role performance in the aged p. 190." She then proceeds to review a number of rating-scale approaches to community adjustment, noting that investigators often must choose between using a scale that is not particularly designed for the elderly, on the one hand, and, on the other assembling a battery of more-discrete measures that together could signify community adjustment.

Another approach to measuring "adaptation" or "successful" coping is to use a composite of measures that tap characteristics defined as signs of good adaptation. Using this strategy in a study of frail elderly persons in New York, Adler, Cantor, and Johnson (1978) identified seven components of adaptation to the environment: knowledge of entitlements; activity levels; perceived life satisfaction; perceived income adequacy; perceived environmental safety; and attitude toward apartment and neighborhood. They did not address the questions of whether the concept of "community adjustment" is adequately depicted with these dimensions and of how the information on the seven variables should be combined for interpreting the data.

Table 4-5 lists selected measures of subjective well-being and coping. We have limited our examples to scales that have been used with elderly samples; even then, we make no claims to comprehensiveness. The Life Satisfaction Index (LSI) (Havighurst, Neugarten, and Tobin 1961) and the later Philadelphia Geriatric Center Morale Scale (Lawton 1972) are the two measures of subjective well-being that have received the most-serious attention from researchers. Because their properties have been examined more thoroughly than have those of other instruments on the list, and because the scales themselves have been refined on the basis of empirical observations, we give these two scales more attention in our discussion. We have omitted some measures pertinent to the elderly such as the Dean Morale Index (Cumming, Dean, and Newell 1958), the Cornell

Table 4-5

Overview of Selected Measures of Subjective Well-Being and Coping

1. Cavan Attitude Inventory (Cavan et al. 1949)	Seven statements in each of 8 areas (health, friendship, work, finances, religion, usefulness, happiness, and family); each of eight subareas has three statements requiring agreement, three requiring disagreement, and a neutral statement (dropped from score). Each sub-score is developed by adding the sum of the "agree" answers to the positive items and subtracting the sum of the "agree" answers to the negative items, making a range of –3 to +3. These scales are summed for a range of –24 to +24.
2. Kutner Morale Scale (Kutner et al. 1956)	Seven questions that concern positive thinking, with 1 point for each correct answer. Questions originally said to form a Guttman scale.
3. Life Satisfaction Index (LSI) (Havinghurst, Neugarten, and Tobin 1961)	The 22 questions were designed to tap 5 dimensions of life satisfaction: zest versus apathy; resolution and fortitude; congruence between desired and achieved goals; self-concept; and mood tone (see table 4-6 for items). Several versions have been developed. Validation against detailed interview information and judgment of clinical psychologist.
4. Oberleder Attitude Scale (Oberleder 1961)	Respondent given 25 statements about old age and asked to indicate agreement or disagreement on a 4-point scale. Statements reflect culturally accepted stereotypes of aging or antistereotypes. Respondent receives a point for each response that differs from aging stereotype. A score of 17+ is said to indicate an "adjustment problem" in nursing-home residents (see table 4-6 for items).
5. Contentment Index (Bloom and Blenkner 1970)	Ten items probed in interview (see table 4-6 for items). Interviewer probes and codes the response as favorable or not scorable (all other answers).
6. Tri-Scales (Schonfield 1973)	Respondent rates self on ten scales: happiness; financial situation; health; activities; family relationships; pleasure from companions; housing; clubs/organizations; transportation; and usefulness. On each subscale, respondent uses 9-point scale to make three self-ratings, comparing self at present to (1) the average American (x); (2) old people in general (o); and (3) his/her own best year (b). Each tri-score is created with formula $4x - 2b - o + 24$. The latter is a constant to ensure a minimum score of 1. A summary adjusted score is derived by adding all adjusted scores and dividing by 10.
7. PGC Morale Scale (Lawton 1972b)	The 22 questions are administered either in interview or self-completed questionnaire. Lawton (1972b) originally identified 6 factors in the scale: attitude toward own aging; agitation, lonely dissatisfaction; acceptance of status quo; optimism; and surgency. Morris and Sherwood (1975) dropped 5 items and found 2 factors, which they relabeled "tranquility" and "satisfaction with life progression." Lawton (1975) was able to reproduce only 3 factors: agitation, attitude toward own aging, and lonely dissatisfaction (see table 4-6 for items).

Table 4-5 (continued)

8. Geriatric Coping Schedule (Quayhagen and Chiriboga 1976)	Respondent is presented with 12 brief situations adapted for the elderly and representing loss or threat in five areas (health, finances, competency, self-concept, and interpersonal relations) and is asked what he would do, how he would have felt, and which of a list of 24 emotions would best describe his feelings. Finally, 11 questions are asked about problem-solving behavior; each is answered on a four-point scale ("always" to "never"). Information is not available on scoring. Open-ended responses on problems seem divided into at least three categories: resistance, compliance, and inaction.
9. Mode of Adaptations Patterns Scale (Sharma 1977)	An activity scale is compressed on 7 subscales for 7 roles: work (including volunteering); parent; relative; friend; neighbor; organizations; and solitary activities. Activity scores are dichotomized as high or low (scoring method unclear). A modified version of the PGC Morale Scale is administered with a possible scoring range of 0-19; a score of 11+ was dichotomized as high morale. From the four possible combinations of high and low activity and morale, four adaptation patterns were defined.
10. Geriatric Scale of Recent Life Events (Kiyak, Liang, and Kahana 1976)	The Recent Life Events Schedule of Holmes and Rahe (1967) was modified with 20 life events added to reflect events assumed relevant to an elderly sample. Weightings for the entire list of 55 events were derived from a study in which a sample of about 250 elderly persons were asked to provide stress scores based on their perceptions of the difficulty adapting to the event would create.

Personal Adjustment Index (Thompson, Streib, and Kosa 1960), and the Pierce and Clark Morale Scale (1973) because they neither illustrate unique approaches in the development of morale scales nor seem suited for current use.

The Cavan Attitude Inventory (Cavan et al. 1949) is an early example of an approach that keys satisfaction to designated areas of social functioning. In each of the eight subareas, seven statements are presented. For a respondent to receive maximum points for adjustment on a subscale, he must agree with the three positive statements and disagree with the three negative statements; an unscored "neutral" statement is included in each sequence. For example, on the "family" subscale, a positive statement is, "I am perfectly satisfied with the way my family treats me"; a negative statement is, "My family is always trying to boss me"; and the neutral statement is, "My family likes to have me around." In the "usefulness" subscale, positive statements are, "The days are too short for all I want to do," and, more strongly, "This is the most useful period of my life"; negative statements are, "I can't help feeling now that my life is not very useful," and, more strongly, "Sometimes I feel there's just no point in living"; the neutral statement is, "I am of some use to those around me."

The Cavan scales were widely used in the 1950s and 1960s, in the Duke Longitudinal Studies, among others, but have largely been replaced by less-cumbersome approaches. Reviewing overall experience with the Cavan Scales, Sauer and Warland (forthcoming) report a test-retest correlation of .72 based on a two-week to two-month time lapse and 110 subjects; a split-half reliability of .95 based on 200 persons; and some evidence that the subscales are consistently correlated with each other, even over time, in longitudinal studies. Validation of the overall score has been suggested by correlations with interview ratings of adjustment, and with the Cavan Activity Inventory. Lohman (1977) found that the correlation of the attitude inventory and ten other measures of subjective well-being ranged from .42 to .79; interestingly, it was correlated at .77 with the Philadelphia Geriatric Center Scale and at .799 with the Life Satisfaction Index (LSIA). Despite criticisms that the Cavan scale overemphasizes contentment with the status quo and perhaps wrongly assumes that high activity levels show positive adjustment, Lohman's findings led her to suggest further work to determine which aspects of morale are represented in the Cavan Attitude Inventory that are not represented in the other two scales. The complexity of the measure and the difficulty of administration with senile subjects militates against its use by most clinicians.

The Kutner Morale Scale, developed for a cross-sectional study of 500 persons over age 60, is a simpler approach, suitable for telephone administration (Kutner et al. 1956). The respondent is awarded one point for each correct answer to seven brief questions. The scale performs as a Guttman scale (coefficient of reproducibility of .9); the questions move from, "How often do you feel there's just no point in living?" (correct answer: "hardly ever") to, "As you get older, would you say things seem to be better or worse than you thought they would be?" (correct answer: "better"). Using this scale, Kutner and his colleagues were able to divide their sample roughly into thirds based on high, medium, or low morale. Sauer and Warland (forthcoming) review material that suggests that the Kutner scale does not measure morale as it has usually been defined but instead measures the "individual's world."

The Oberleder Attitude Scale (1961) may have become an anachronism in our present social context. It consists of twenty-five statements about old age with which the respondent indicates agreement or disagreement. The scoring key awards points when the response indicates acceptance of stereotypes of aging. A score of more than 17 is said to predict an "adjustment problem" for residents of nursing homes.

The scale was constructed empirically. The staff in a single nursing home selected a matched group of "well-adjusted" and "poorly adjusted" residents using the following criteria: the well adjusted should be cheerful; make few unreasonable demands; get along with others and seem to enjoy social participation;

Table 4-6

Four Examples of Scales Measuring Subjective Well-Being in the Elderly

Philadelphia Geriatric Center Morale Scale

1. Things keep getting worse as I get older. (No)[a]
2. I have as much pep as I did last year. (Yes)
3. How much do you feel lonely? (Not much)[b]
4. Little things bother me more this year. (No)
5. I see enough of my friends and relatives. (Yes)[b]
6. As you get older, you are less useful. (No)
7. If you could live where you wanted, where would you life? (Here)[b,c]
8. I sometimes worry so much that I can't sleep. (No)
9. As I get older, things are (better, worse, the same) than/as I thought they'd be. (Better)
10. I sometimes feel that life isn't worth living. (No)
11. I am happy now as I was when I was younger. (Yes)
12. Most days I have plenty to do. (No)[b,c]
13. I have a lot to be sad about. (No)
14. People had it better in the old days. (No)[b,c]
15. I am afraid of a lot of things. (No)
16. My health is (good, not so good). (Good)[b]
17. I get mad more than I used to. (No)
18. Life is hard for me most of the time. (No)
19. How satisfied are you with your life today? (Satisfied)
20. I take things hard. (No)
21. A person has to live for today and not worry about tomorrow. (Yes)[b,c]
22. I get upset easily. (No)

Life Satisfaction Index (LSI-A)

Here are some statements about life in general that people feel differently about. Would you read each statement in the list and, if you agree with it, put a checkmark in the space "agree." If you do not agree, put a checkmark in the space under "disagree." If you are not sure one way or the other, put a checkmark in the space "?."

1. As I grow older, things seem better than I thought they would be. (Agree)[d]
2. I have gotten more of the breaks in life than most of the people I know. (Agree)
3. This is the dreariest time of my life. (Disagree)
4. I am just as happy as when I was younger. (Agree)
5. My life could be happier than it is now. (Disagree)[e]
6. These are the best years of my life. (Agree)
7. Most of the things I do are boring or monotonous. (Disagree)
8. I expect some interesting and pleasant things to happen to me in the future. (Agree)[e]
9. The things I do are as interesting to me as they ever were. (Agree)
10. I feel old and tired. (Disagree)[e]
11. I feel my age, but it doesn't bother me. (Agree)[e,f]
12. As I look back on my life, I am fairly well satisfied. (Agree)
13. I would not change my past life, even if I could. (Agree)[e]
14. Compared to other people my age, I've made a lot of foolish decisions in my life. (Disagree)[e,f]
15. Compared to other people my age, I make a good appearance. (Agree)[e]
16. I have made plans for things I'll be doing a month or a year from now. (Agree)
17. When I think back over my life, I didn't get most of the important things I wanted. (Disagree)
18. Compared to other people, I get down in the dumps too often. (Disagree)
19. I've gotten pretty much what I expected out of life. (Agree)
20. In spite of what people say, the lot of the average man is getting worse, not better. (Disagree)

Table 4-6 (continued)

Contentment Index

1. In general, how satisfied are you with your present arrangements for housecleaning, laundry and shopping? (Satisfied, partly satisfied, or dissatisfied)
2. In general, how satisfied are you with your life today?
3. Has your health been a worry for you this past month?
4. Would you say you have been happy or unhappy this past month?
5. Would you agree or disagree with those people who say "things keep getting worse for me as I grow older"?
6. If you had a choice, would you prefer to live in your home here or some other place?
7. How do you feel about your neighborhood as a place to live?
8. Is your income adequate or inadequate?
9. How has your general mood been? Have you felt blue or like you were floating on air in the past month?
10. How do you feel about the future? What are you worried about in the future?

Total score = number of scorable (that is, favorable) responses.

Oberleder Attitude Scale[g]

1. The older you get, the more set in your ways you become.
2. Old age can be said to begin around 60 or 65.
3. Old people too often like to meddle in other people's business.
4. Older people become grouchy and stubborn with the years.
5. Old people can, and are, learning new things all the time.
6. Older people cannot expect to lead a completely full or satisfying life.
7. As you grow older, you become less and less useful.
8. People get shorter as they grow older.
9. You can't teach an old dog new tricks.
10. I would still prefer to have some kind of work to do.
11. Special housing projects for just old people are not a good idea, but the city should reserve apartments in the regular housing project for old people. That way, people of all ages are together.
12. I think it is usually a mistake for people over 65 to marry.
13. I believe a person is really glad to retire from work when he is 65 or 70.
14. Old people usually don't talk very much.
15. Old people are adjusting to new conditions all the time and doing it easily.
16. There should be special radio and TV programs for older folks.
17. I would like to enroll in a class for older people which trains them for a new kind of work.
18. Old people like to boss everybody.
19. At my age I say let the others do the work and get the credit.
20. As you grow older you must expect to depend on others.
21. A person should always try for something better no matter how old he is.
22. I prefer to be with people of my own age.
23. Older people need special foods.
24. Physical exercise of some kind is good for you as you grow older.
25. Trying to learn a new job at my age strikes me as a little silly.

Sources: For PGC: Adapted from M.P. Lawton, "The Dimensions of Morale," in *Research Planning and Action for the Elderly*, ed. D. Kent, R. Kastenbaum, and S. Sherwood (New York: Behavioral Publications, 1972). For LSI-A: Adapted from R.J. Havighurst, B.L. Neugarten, and S.S. Tobin, "The Measurement of Life Satisfaction," *Journal of Gerontology* 16(1961):134–143. For Contentment Index: Adapted from M. Bloom and M. Blenkner, "Assessing Functioning of Older Persons Living in the Community," *The Gerontologist* 10(1970):331–337. For Oberleder: Adapted from M. Oberleder, "An Attitude Scale to Determine Adjustment in Institutions for the Aged," *Journal of Chronic Disease* 15(1961): 915–923.

[a]The correct answer, shown in parentheses, is scored 1 point.

[b]Items dropped from scale in Morris and Sherwood's revision (1975).

[c]Items dropped from scale in Lawton's revision (1975).

[d]The correct answer, shown in parentheses, is scored one point.

[e]Items excluded from revision of Wood, Wylie, and Sheaffer (1969). They also score two points for the correct response and one point for an "uncertain" response.

[f]Items excluded from Adam's LSI-Z (1969).

[g]Answer in parentheses (A for agree or D for disagree) is awarded 1 point. The higher the score, the poorer the adjustment.

seem content with the facilities of the home; and accept annoyance, refraining from temper outbursts or excessive complaining. The poorly adjusted were chosen on the basis of inability to get along with others or to use the facilities of the home; excessive criticism; "overexaggerated ambitions interfering with realistic adjustment to institutional life; p. 916" or manifestations of a "disturbed" personality that is quarrelsome, selfish, and overdemanding with or without accompanying depression.

This sample completed a 176-item questionnaire with items representing stereotypes about old age (for example, "Old people cannot learn new things"); older values (for example, "I think it is usually a mistake for people over 65 to marry"); antistereotypes (for example, "Old people can and are learning new things all the time"); and younger values (for example, "I don't see anything wrong with people over 65 marrying"). The author had hypothesized that the maladjusted residents would concur with the antistereotypes and the young values and would thus have difficulty accepting the constraints of an institution. In fact, the opposite occurred; those who concurred with the antistereotypes and the young values and who rejected stereotypes of aging and old values were better adjusted.

The final scale, presented in table 4–6, consists of the twenty-five items that most predicted good and poor adjustment of the original sample. In validation studies with new samples, the scale continued to predict judgments of staff about patient adjustment (compared to blind ratings by staff). The scores tended to cluster between 12 and 16, with a range of 6 to 20. Any score exceeding 16 was interpreted as suggestive of poor adjustment and a likely management problem for the facility. Test-retest reliabilities with a one-month interval are reported for the summary scores on the four subcategories of items (that is, stereotypes, antistereotypes, old values, and young values), with coefficients of .87, .88, .88, and .75, respectively.

The Oberleder Attitude Scale represents an approach that seemed to work pragmatically, even though the underlying rationale for the results is unclear. The scale is based on the extent to which respondents accept and reject social attitudes; therefore, it may be expected to vary across culture and age cohorts, reducing its applicability. The last use of the scale that we were able to locate in the literature was in Silverstone and Wynter's (1975) study of the effects of heterosexual living arrangements on the adjustment of nursing-home patients of both sexes. In addition to the constant need to update and revalidate such a scale, one would also be concerned that it be a measure of the values that are rewarded by the nursing homes under study, rather than of the inherent adjustment of the residents.

The Tri-Scales (Schonfield 1973) require respondents to consider more than one reference point in rating satisfaction. This measure identifies ten subareas for self-rating, some tangible (such as transportation) and some more amorphous (such as happiness). The subject rates himself three times on a nine-point scale for each subscale: (1) present status compared to that of the average American; (2) compared to that of old people in general; and (3) compared to his or her own best year. A scoring system is used that gives most weight to the first rating but considers the others if they differ. Schulz (1976) used the Tri-Scales as his measure of adjustment in his study of predictability and control in nursing-home patients. The approach is subtle, picking up more than a simple rating. For example, a subject who rated himself below his "best year" in happiness would score less than another person who had the identical rating of present happiness compared to the "average American." The validity of including discrepancies between satisfaction with previous functioning and with current functioning is not clear.

The Contentment Scale (Bloom and Blenkner 1970) is an efficient approach to measuring well-being for the community-based elderly. Its authors were seeking an easily applied tool that would be sensitive to change and useful for measuring the effect of a community-based program. At the same time, they sought a measure that would be applicable to assessing the continuing status of contentment in subjects who moved to a nursing home. Bloom and Blenkner argue that contentment in one's clientele should be an important goal in LTC, despite the predominant value placed on usefulness in our society.

The items of the Contentment Scale are shown in table 4–6. A shorter form of the scale uses only the first five questions, which best predict the total scores. Reliability was tested through split-half reliability testing, with "acceptable" results. Validating was done by comparisons with the professional judgments of housing-project social workers who knew the clients. Later, as part of a study of the effects of protective services, the Contentment Index Scores were compared with ratings of the original research interviewer, those of service caseworkers who knew the patients, and those of the supervisor of the service workers. Interviewers who met with the respondent briefly, albeit intensively, were more likely to assess the client's contentment as the client did on the index, compared to the social workers, who, according to the authors, "took a longer-range behavioral view of the meaning of contentment in their ratings." (p. 35)

The Contentment Scale was used in a landmark experiment on the effects of protective service (Blenkner, Bloom, and Neilsen 1971) and in a survey of the effects of home-health aides on the rehabilitation of posthospital patients (Neilsen et al. 1972). The latter study used a four-question version, but the questions are not specified in the report. Changes in contentment were demonstrated over the course of a year; the group receiving the home health aides showed more positive change. The scale also differentiated those profiting most from the aides' help (arthritis and hip-fracture patients) from those whose contentment improved little (stroke patients). The five-question version of the Contentment Scale was used in the large-scale studies of day care and home care done as part of the demonstration of extended Medicare services permitted under Section 222 waivers of usual regulations (Weissert, Wan, and Livieratos 1980).

The Life Satisfaction Index (LSI) is the result of an effort to measure life satisfaction in a way "relatively independent of level of activity or social participation" (Neugarten, Havighurst, and Tobin 1961, p. 135). The study group analyzed its concept of subjective well-being theoretically and then applied its definitions against a series of detailed interviews with two panels of elderly subjects who were participating in a longitudinal study based in Kansas City. The initial theoretical analysis of the concept resulted in identification of five components: zest (as opposed to apathy); resolution and fortitude; congruence between desired and achieved goals; positive self-concept; and mood tone (that is, an optimistic attitude and mood). An anchored five-point scale for rating each of the five components was then developed. For 177 cases on which detailed information was available, judges performed Life Satisfaction Ratings (LSR) with a high degree of reported agreement among fourteen judges, with two judges rating each case. For this step the authors report that, with 885 paired judgments, 94 percent showed exact agreement or agreement within one step on the five-step scale.

Using the high scorers and the low scorers in the Kansas City samples as a validation, the authors then tested two short self-completed scales to measure life satisfaction; these instruments were administered to ninety-two respondents as part of the sixth interview in the longitudinal series. The first scale, known as LSIA, consisted of twenty-five items requiring agreement or disagreement. Five items were discarded as a result of the test, leaving the twenty items shown in table 4-6. The other approach (LSIB) contained open-ended questions and checklists to be scored on a three-point scale (see Neugarten, Havighurst, and Tobin [1961] for the twelve-question version of the LSIB that emerged after the test). The correlation between the final form of the LSIA scores and the original rating scores of the LSR was .55. The discrepancy is difficult to interpret. Because fourteen to twenty months elapsed between the wave of interviewing that yielded the LSI and the sixth wave, during which the LSIA was tested, the .55 correlation may understate the congruence between the two measures.

Wood, Wylie, and Sheafor (1969) restudied the instrument with a rural sample and, as a result, suggested that the index be reduced to thirteen items with a revised scoring system to give two points for affirmative responses and one point for uncertain responses, instead of the dichotomous scoring of the original scale. The items of this revision, known as the LSIA, are shown in table 4-6. Still later, Adams (1969) analyzed the performance of the full LSIA with 508 persons living in rural Missouri, using a discriminant analysis (to compare the responses on single items to the overall scores of high and low scorers) and a biserial correlation (comparing the mean of the affirmative-response group on each item to the LSIA mean score for the whole sample). Adams recommended deleting two items: "Compared to other people my age, I've made a lot of foolish decisions in my life," and, "I feel my age but it does not bother me." It is noteworthy that both these items are ambiguous on the face of it; he also recommended returning to the previous dichotomous scoring system. The latter recommendation was reinforced by Ray's (1979) analysis of the two methods of scoring based on data from 124 adults residing in Maryland.

The Adams version of the LSI was fielded in a large-scale study of aging in America (Harris 1975), using the eighteen original questions and a scoring system of 0 to 2 for each item. Out of the possible score of 36, connoting the greatest life satisfaction, means of 26.4 are reported for the population aged 18 to 64 years, compared to a mean of 24.4 for the sample of older persons. The median score for those aged 18 to 64 years was 24.4, compared to a more-positive median of 27.4 for those aged 65 to 69. The LSI median scores then drop with increasing age to a median of 25.7 for those aged 70 to 79 and of 23.8 for those age 80 and older. Mean LSI scores were significantly correlated with income and education; once income was controlled, differences by race disappeared. An item-by-item comparison of the public aged 18 to 64 to the public aged 65 and older showed that the percentage of persons agreeing with the statements was sometimes very similar for the two age groups. Questions reflecting on the life cycle tended to show small differences favoring the older group; for example, "I would not change my past, even if I could," elicited 56-percent agreement in the younger group and 62 percent in the older group; and, "As I look back on my life I am fairly well satisfied," prompted 85-percent agreement in the younger group and 87 percent in the older group. As might have been expected, "I feel old and somewhat tired" elicited much more agreement in the older age group (a difference of 25 percentage points); and, "These are the best years of my life" had much more disagreement among the elderly.

The LSIA may well represent an upper bound among scales measuring sub-jective well-being among the elderly. Nevertheless, we concur with Sauer and War-land (forthcoming), who question whether either reliability or validity has been adequately established.

The Philadelphia Geriatric Center (PGC) Morale Scale is the other major multidimensional measure of subjective well-being developed for the elderly. As originally constructed by Lawton (1972b), it contained twenty-two dichoto-mous items, yielding six factors ("surgency," "attitude toward own aging," "satisfaction with the status quo," "agitation," "optimism," and "lonely dis-satisfaction"). Test-retest reliabilities are reported for two samples with overall coefficients of .75 and .8; the test-retest reliabilities of some of the factors, especially those with only two or three items, were considerably lower.

Morris and Sherwood (1975) used the PGC Morale Scale with two samples (a group of 300 applicants to Hebrew Rehabilitation Center for Aged and 406 subjects in the Fall River Housing Study), identifying three factors ("agita-tion," "attitude toward own aging," and "lonely dissatisfaction"), but failing to replicate three of Lawton's factors. They suggested dropping five items ("Most days I have plenty to do," "My health is . . . ," "If you could live where you wanted, where would you live?" "How much do you feel lonely?" and "I see enough of my friends and relatives") because they lacked face validity as measures of morale. They then produced two factors, expanded versions of Lawton's "agitation" scale and "attitude toward own aging" scale, which, to avoid confusion, were relabeled "tranquility" and "satisfaction with life progression," respectively; fifteen of the seventeen remaining items fell into these two areas. Lawton (1975) applied the seventeen-item scale to a PGC population and to 824 subjects in a housing study, identifying three factors similar to those of Morris and Sherwood: "agitation," "attitude toward own aging," and "lonely dissatisfaction." Some items fell into more than one factor; in those cases, Lawton placed them in the subscale that seemed to make the most theoretical sense.

As a result of all the work across these multiple samples, the recommenda-tion of a seventeen-item scale emerged. The seemingly stable factors are made up of the following items

Agitation
  Little things bother me more this year.
  I sometimes worry so much I cannot sleep.
  I am afraid of a lot of things.
  I get mad more than I used to.
  I take things very hard.
  I get upset easily.

Attitude toward own aging
  Things keep getting worse as I get older.
  I have as much pep as I had last year.
  As you get older, you are less useful.
  As I get older, things are better/worse than I thought they would be.
  I am as happy now as when I was younger.

Lonely dissatisfaction
  How much do you feel lonely?
  I see enough of my friends and relatives.
  I sometimes feel that life isn't worth living.
  Life is hard for me much of the time.
  How satisfied are you with your life today.
  I have a lot to be sad about.

Lawton's revised version reinstated two items dropped by Morris and Sherwood ("How much do you feel lonely?" and, "I see enough of my friends and relatives") because they consistently fell into factors and because Lawton argued for their face validity as expressions of "an intrinsic aspect of overall life satisfaction" (Lawton 1975, p. 86). The three factors developed from seventeen-item scale have an advantage over the original six-factor version in that longer factors are likely to produce better test-retest-reliability scores.

Given the diversity of morale measures, as illustrated in our examples, what choices should be made? In 1975 the Gerontological Society sponsored a symposium on the subject. The proceedings of the meeting (Nydegger 1977) raise perplexing issues that are still unresolved. Lawton (1977) compared existing morale scales and offered some recommendations for users, namely, that the LSI should be used for "normally responsive subjects when the interest is in a single criterion of morale"; the PGC Morale Scale for "normally responsive and marginally comprehending subjects," (p. 14) especially when one is interested in the separate dimensions of morale. The Affect Balance Scale was tentatively suggested for use when a contemporary view of morale was sought.

At the same meeting, however, Carp (1977) questioned measurement of morale on two major counts:

1. The validation of the measures has relied heavily on professionals and care-givers with no input from the older persons themselves about components of the concept.
2. Using a comprehensive measure of morale as an indicator of program effectiveness is circuitous and perhaps irrelevant.

To take her example, a successful friendly visiting program might result in changed answers to Lawton's loneliness question but might not change rates of agreement with other questions (such as, "I do better work now than ever before," or, "I would not change my past life, even if I could"). Consequently, the omnibus measure waters down the evidence of program effect and may be most appropriate when one is comparing the effects of various programs in order to make decisions about where to make social investments.

Taylor (1977) took the argument even further, raising the question of whether morale is a legitimate expectation for participants in social programs:

> If a person says she is so worried that she cannot sleep nights, I think that we have some important information, whether or not it is seen to have anything to do with morale. If she lives in a neighborhood where forced entry and rape are common, the fact that she is unhappy about it is one of the last things that might occur to you. If she worries whether her social security check will come on time next month, the fact that it makes her unhappy seems almost impertinent. [p. 33]

In this spirit, Taylor urged that every researcher considering using morale as a variable should do so only if real losses would occur from the omission.

The several papers in the symposium also raised operational questions about measuring morale. Carp (1977) and Rosow (1977) pointed to the propensity to confound measures of morale by including within morale scales items about likely causes of poor morale such as health status or frequency of contact with relatives. Sherwood (1977) cited problems in ensuring that measures do not "bottom out" or "top out"—that is, ideally, very few persons should receive either the highest or lowest possible scores at an initial test if the instrument is to be capable of recording change in morale. Lawton (1977) cautioned against the use with elderly respondents of a lengthy instrument with too many response choices in each item. The positive-response set as a threat to validity was a common theme. Several commentators (for example, Bloom 1977) were concerned with the obtrusiveness of morale questionnaires, especially in a society where happiness is not regularly discussed. Taylor (1977) suggested that subjects may even form their impressions about the state of their own morale on the basis of the questions asked, perhaps inferring that they should be sad or feel life is meaningless because they are asked about it. If people do take their cues from the morale scales in this manner, then the measurement of morale poses ethical as well as practical problems.

Morale may be the internal manifestation of coping, but coping ability is in itself a useful variable to understand in an elderly client or population. Kahana, Fairchild, and Kahana (forthcoming) point out that ability to cope must depend in part on the extent and nature of the environmental demands for coping. At the same time, that coping ability may also be a personality trait, related to traits such as frustration tolerance, an internal locus of control, and flexibility.

They also remind us that coping behavior is generally learned as part of social-role modeling, so that individual responses to stress can be explained in part by societal norms without reference to the psychology of the individual.

The elderly are likely to be presented with successive environmental challenges that require coping at the very time they are undergoing changes in the social expectations associated with their roles and statuses. Although much research into coping is preoccupied with describing and classifying coping patterns, ultimately the clinician would be most interested in predicting ability to cope in order to make better allocation of protective or supportive resources. The measurement of coping with respect to the elderly is in an embryonic state; as Kahana, Fairchild, and Kahana point out, since most instruments have been developed for studies currently in progress, statements about their reliability, validity, or normal patterns are premature. Clearly, predictive ability is not yet achieved.

These authors reviewed thirteen instruments that they placed in the category of measures of coping. Some are projective tests, also used to assess general psychological well-being. They included in their review some projective tests (the GAT and the SAT) that were discussed in the section of the previous chapter on measures of general mental health. Many of the "coping" measures have the problems of reliability across testers associated with projective tests and, moreover, require extensive time and skill. Another category of tests is based on hypothetical problems; these are sometimes faulted for their reliance on reports of how one believes one would cope with a theoretical problem as evidence of how one actually would behave when confronted with the real problem. Table 4–5 includes as examples three of the measures discussed by Kahana, Fairchild, and Kahana (forthcoming).

The basis for many tests is the Coping Scale of Sidle and his colleagues (1969), which was not developed particularly for the elderly. The subject is presented with stories containing problems. For each story, the subject is asked to list all possible ways the problem could be handled. The subject is then presented with a list of ten possible coping strategies (for example, try to find out more about the situation, talk to others, see the humorous aspects of the situation) and asked, on a seven-point scale, how likely he or she would be to use the strategy for each story. The scoring for the open-ended section involves counts of numbers of tasks perceived, total number of strategies, number of kinds of strategies, and total number of words written. The ten strategy ratings for each story are also summed.

Using this general method, the Geriatric Coping Scale (Quayhagen and Chiriboga 1976) consists of twelve brief stories relevant to the elderly. For each story, subjects are asked what they would have done, how they would have felt, and which emotion from a list of twenty-four emotions would most closely describe their feelings. A list of eleven coping strategies is presented (ten of which are almost identical to Sidle's scale), and the subjects are asked to rate on a four-point scale (ranging from "always" to "never") how often they use each strategy to cope with problems.

The stories were designed to be suitable for elderly persons in congregate-living situations. For example, one concerns a woman watching her favorite television show when her roommate changes the station, and another depicts a man whose family has decided to take over his financial affairs. The method seems to have been simplified for use with the elderly in that the general coping strategies are related to all problems rather than to each individual one, and the response choices are reduced from seven to four points on the scale. No information is provided about how scores are derived. Considerable descriptive information could emerge from such a measure; for example, preliminary testing suggested that certain stories tended to be met with active resistance and others with depression. In another adaptation of the Sidle approach, the Elderly Care Research Scale, described by Kahana, Fairchild, and Kahana (forthcoming), a single story is presented. This depicts a 70-year-old man who finds out that his home is to be demolished and he will have to move. The subjects are asked how they would deal with the problem. Then the subjects are presented with a list of coping strategies consisting of Sidle's ten as well as twelve others, and are asked to rate their likelihood of using that strategy on a four-point scale.

Sharma's Modes of Adaptation Patterns Scale (1977) describes coping patterns according to the combination of activities across social roles and morale. This results in a fourfold classification of adaptive styles: namely, high activity plus high morale (conformist); high activity plus low morale (ritualist); low activity plus high morale (passive-contented); and low activity plus low morale (retreatist). The activity subscale consists of eighteen questions about social and recreational activities performed in the last month or acts of friendship and neighborliness performed in the past year. Morale is measured by the PGC Morale Scale. The result is an index of life coping as opposed to coping with a particular stress or problem. In one study, a sample of about 400 proved to be well distributed across the four cells, with differences in the prevalence of the adaptive strategies evident according to sex.

Finally, the Geriatric Scale of Recent Life Events (Kiyak, Liang, and Kahana 1976) is a revision of the Holmes/Rahe Recent Life Events Schedule (1967) that attempts to make it more appropriate to the changes experienced by the elderly. The items on the earlier scale were retained (with minor changes such as collapsing two items into one and subdividing six items into two). Twenty new items were added to reflect stressful events mentioned in open-ended interviews with elderly subjects. This produced a list of fifty items; the weightings for each item were determined by asking a sample of older persons to indicate the amount of readjustment that the particular event would require. The scale was cross-validated by two samples—an elderly community sample and a group of college students. The two groups were markedly similar in their average stress scores, although the elderly tended to avoid very high and very low stress scores, compared to the younger group. "Death of a spouse" received an average weighting of 79.5 from the elderly group; and, interstingly, "move to a home for the aged" received a stress score of 74.6. "Go to jail" (79.3), "victim of a crime" (73.1), and "friends and family turn away" (68.3) were among the highest weighted. So, too, was "stop driving," which received a weighting of 68.5. As far as we can determine, this scale has not been used to predict illness or exacerbations of health problems. Respondents are asked to indicate whether the events have occurred in the past three months, a variation on the time window usually used for the Holmes/Rahe schedule.

Measures of Person–Environment Fit

The third general category of measures that we are considering is relatively new in its application to the elderly. Recognizing that planning for LTC on either an individual or a societal basis implies at least some structuring of a life-style, the provider grapples with the variation in individual functional levels and preferences that would make an environment contribute to or detract from an older person's physical, emotional, or social well-being. In simple terms, we seek a way of predicting before the fact or describing after the fact whether a particular care environment is compatible with a particular individual. Using the language of Kahana (1974) and Coulton (1979), we have adopted the term *person–environment fit* to refer to this category of measures.

Lawton (1970) has made a distinction between *individual planning* (or *placement*), which involves matching an individual to one of several existing environments, and *social planning,* which entails designing environments to be compatible with a described community of individuals. Although his comments were addressed in particular to the challenge of matching the competencies of individuals to the demands of environments, the idea also applies to matching the expectations and preferences of the individual with the demands of the environment. At best, a measure of person–environment fit requires the examination of both the person and the environment and the construction of a measure of congruence.

We assume that, at some minimal threshold level, some characteristics of an adequate environment are universal. Thus environmental descriptors consistent with safety and comfort can be articulated, validated consensually, incorporated into evaluation tools, and used to form the basis for standards. We might also assume that some interpersonal components of a care environment (courtesy of staff, kindness, attention to physical needs) are also universally desired, even if they are difficult to define operationally and to measure. Such factors usually are monitored by ensuring the absence of overt abuse and the compliance with prescribed staffing ratios and minimum educational qualifications for staff; the dubious inference is that sufficient staff training and numbers can serve as a proxy for less-tangible but highly desired outcomes such as courteous, friendly, caring behavior.

Beattie and Bullock (1964) tried to capture the more-elusive aspects of the "emotional environment" of institutions for the aged. They devised a Social Responsibility Scale to measure staff concern for residents' needs above staff needs and a Social Climate Scale to measure the freedom of choice permitted to residents. Each scale had a format for nursing homes and one for homes for the aged. For example, the Social Climate Scale for nursing homes was considered positive if the institution permitted unrestricted visiting hours, if attempts were made to please residents who expressed dissatisfaction with the food or the living quarters, and if no permission was needed to leave the home for a day. These scales were completed by administrators of facilities, raising questions about the informants' capacity and motivation to provide valid answers. Assuming for the moment the reliability and validity of responses, this method measures the extent to which a social environment approaches an "ideal," and leaves aside differences in individual preferences.

Similarly, Bennett and Nahemow (1965) report an approach to measuring "institutional totality" based on ten criteria. High institutional totality was marked by: (1) permanence of the residents, (2) confinement of all activities within the institution, (3) sequentially scheduled activities for all residents, (4) formal indoctrination into rules and standards of conduct, (5) continuous observation of resident population by the staff, (6) standardized objective rewards and punishments, (7) absence of resident decision making about the use of their time or property, (8) removal of most personal property from residents, (9) involuntary recruitment of residents, and (10) congregate living. Each criterion is rated on a continuum of low, medium, or high totality with the midpoint representing a mixed situation (for example, when some residents are permanent and others are not). Questionnaires to administrators and/or observations seem to provide the basis for the ratings. The usefulness of such a scale is predicated on the idea that the total institution is, for the most part, degrading and dehumanizing and should be avoided except perhaps in circumstances of exceptional dependency.

With the growing awareness that subjective perceptions of the environment may be more important than the actual environmental descriptors in influencing well-being, the focus of measurement has shifted to the individual older person. Here, too, one could conceivably ask the respondent to react to a checklist of attributes deemed desirable in an environment (privacy, opportunity for friendship, flexibility of routines, and so on) and to identify whether these attributes are perceived as present. Whenever the large majority of elderly persons within a group share similar value preferences, such responses would indicate the extent to which the environment meets individual needs. Because of the likelihood that aspects of life-style are differentially valued, however, measures of an individual's perception of the environment usually probe both perceptions of reality (across selected dimensions) and perceptions of the importance or desirability of each dimension. Even then, the measures may omit some aspects of environmental satisfaction that may be important to substantial groups of people. To the extent that the original item pool is generated with input from a sizable representative sample of the population for whom the scale will be relevant, that hazard is minimized.

There is a catch-22 in determining the value preferences of elderly persons with respect to details of congregate living and institutional life. Without a frame of reference, a community-based person is unlikely to be able to make a valid response. On the other hand, evidence about "learned helplessness" in nursing homes suggests that those who have lost control over choices affecting their lives rather quickly lose the ability to make choices (Schulz 1976; Seligman 1975; Langer and Rodin 1976). Interviews with persons in highly institutionalized settings who perceive themselves as helpless and have lapsed into apathy cannot provide a fair guide to life-style preferences.

Research directed at describing the value preferences of elderly individuals is scanty, particularly when one considers a generalized social environment rather than an institutional setting. Reid and Ziegler (1977) report one such effort with a sample of 143 persons over age 65, 78 of whom lived in one of three church-owned homes in the Toronto area and 65 of whom lived independently. Taking great care not to guide the subjects, the study used open-ended questions about the meaning of happiness to the respondents; the specific aspects of everyday life that made them happy; specific changes that would make them happier; outcomes that they considered important for happiness (including reinforcements such as activities that they looked forward to or found rewarding); any major adjustments that were necessary as they became older; and, finally, the factors that made it easier or more difficult to adjust to becoming older. Answers were recorded verbatim, and content-analysis techniques were then used to develop categories. As might be expected, considerable diversity was evident, with only a few respondents contributing to some categories. On the other hand, common themes also appeared. Categories endorsed most frequently referred to involvement with other people; the category "helping others," for example, was included as a "reinforcer" of happiness by just as many people as was the category "having good health."

Eliciting information about what is valued in the environment is a complex and subtle task. Lawton (1980) reports fascinating efforts to determine the aspects of a housing environment that elderly persons might view as important. In one such approach, 200 community-dwelling persons were asked to state whether each of twelve items would be important in choosing a place to live. The items and the number of persons considering them important were as follows: a nice neighborhood (191), near help (190), privacy (189), a home or building that looks nice (184), near public transportation (183), near shopping (182), near hospital or doctor (167), absence of steps (152), near old friends

(146), near relatives (132), and availability of meal service (70). By this measure, privacy would seem an important attribute, mentioned by almost all respondents. When about half of these residents were interviewed a year later, they were asked to rank the importance of five criteria for choosing a place to live; the number of items was decreased for ease of ranking. Privacy emerged as the least-important criterion, trailing proximity to shopping, buses, church, and so on; proximity to friends and relatives; a nice neighborhood; and proximity to hospital, doctor, or people to help. Only 8 respondents ranked it first, and 57 ranked it last. In yet another approach with a different sample, respondents were asked to rank the five criteria against each other in pairs (for example, "Which would be more important, being close to shopping, buses, and churches, or being close to friends and relatives?"). The items were then ranked by frequency of being chosen in a pair, and this system yielded yet another ordering of value preferences. Thus three different methods produced a different hierarchy of preference, and perhaps an open-ended approach would have eliminated some of the variables and identified others.

Carp and Carp (1980) report a practical application of the person-environment fit concept. They found that persons identified in advance as likely to thrive in an "actively sociable situation" did, in fact, experience the greatest gains in social behavior and satisfaction in a move from an isolated living environment. At the same time, a small group of movers declined on these factors after the change. Thus the person-environment fit idea may have predictive utility.

Table 4-7 lists and briefly describes selected instruments that approach the question of person–environment fit. We have omitted measures that simply describe or rate an environment or that use provider indicators alone to determine the preferences on the elderly. Even then, the instruments differ in whether they focus primarily on the environment itself (its opportunities and constraints) or on the individual's perceptions. Only a few measures, still in their early stages of development, attempt to examine directly the congruence between environment and person. The instruments vary in their degree of concreteness, some focusing on specific observable items. There are five themes most often developed in these instruments:

1. The degree of perceived control, freedom, choice, autonomy, or individuality permitted to the individual by the environment.
2. Structure, rules, and expected behavior imposed by the environment on the individual.
3. Relationships between the individual and caregivers in the environment.
4. Perceptions of activity and stimulation levels.
5. Expressed satisfaction with various aspects of the environment.

The first three items on table 4-7 are unidimensional measures that tap perceived control in some manner. The Importance, Locus, and Range of Activities

Table 4-7
Selected Measures of Person-Environment Fit

Measure	Description	Comments
1. Importance, Locus, and Range of Activities Checklist (Hulicka, Morganti, and Cataldo 1975)	36 items (see table 4-8) representing elements of daily life; for each, respondent rates importance on 3-point scale (scored 3, 2, or 1) and amount of choice available regarding that item on a 3-point scale (score 3, 1, or -3). Each item's score is the product of the importance score and the choice score, a range of +9 to -9.	Test-retest reliability tested on group of college students only; validity checked by scores of those in restricted settings; that is, 10 men in the military compared with 20 civilians.
2. Locus of Desired Control (Reid, Haas, and Hawkins 1977)	Desirability of seven items rated on a 4-point scale (1-4) and the ability of the respondent to control that event is also rated on a 4-point scale. Each item is scored by multiplying the desirability and control scores (range is 1-16). Events are listed in table 4-8.	Alpha reliabilities of .64 and .66 were reported for a sample of 60 residents of a residential facility and for 147 persons from nursing homes and the community, respectively. No test-retest reliabilities or validity information is available.
3. Perceived Environmental Constraint Index (Wolk and Tellen 1976)	Respondents are given 6 statements to which they reply on a 5-point scale (from "not at all true" to "completely true"). See table 4-8 for statements. The six items are summed. Theoretical score range is 6-30. Self-completed questionnaire.	Developed for a study of the correlates of satisfaction in two kinds of retirement communities. No reliability or validity information.
4. Satisfaction with Nursing Home Scale (McCaffree and Harkins 1976)	Respondents asked about the importance of and their satisfaction with 22 items concerning nursing-home life (see table 4-8 for items). Importance and satisfaction are each rated on a 3-point scale of 0-2. Summary scores used the satisfaction data only.	Test-retest reliabilities within one week interval were .92 with the same interviewer and .69 with different interviewers. Alpha reliability with an N of 178 was .78. No information about validity.

Table 4-7 (continued)

Measure	Description	Comments
5. Home for the Aged Description Questionnaire (Pincus 1968)	Self-administered questionnaire to staff members and residents of nursing homes. Respondents agree or disagree with 36 items on a 5-point scale. Items were allocated to 5 dimensions of the institutional environment: privacy; freedom; resources; integration (as opposed to isolation); and personalization. Dimension scores are created by adding item scores on the dimension and dividing by the number of items.	No reliability or validity information.
6. Ward Atmosphere Scale (WAS) (Moos 1974)	100 true-false questions about ward completed by staff and residents. These divide into 10 subscales: involvement; support; spontaneity; autonomy; practical orientation; personal-problem orientation; anger and aggression; order and organization; program clarity; and staff control. A 40-question version consists of "best" 4 questions in each factor. Respondents can complete with reference to the real ward, the ideal ward, and the expectations held for the ward. One point is awarded for each correct answer.	Items were generated from observations of wards and intensive interviews with staff members and patients. The original larger item set was reduced in successive testing. Test-retest reliabilities calculated on 42 patients at one-week interval; reliability in subscales ranged from .83 to .68. Alpha reliabilities ranged from .82 to .6. Intercorrelations of dimensions showed that they were distinct.
7. Community-Oriented Programs Environment Scale (COPES) (Moos 1974)	Very similar in items and subscales to the WAS above. Adapted slightly so that they could be used in day-treatment programs, halfway houses, foster-care programs, and other community-based services.	Reliability and validity approached in the same way as in the WAS.
8. Sheltered Care Environment (Moos et al. 1979)	Self-administered questionnaire to staff and residents of 65 simple yes–no items. Like the WAS and COPES above, three forms exist—the real, the ideal, and the expected. Seven 9-question subscales are labeled cohesion, conflict, independence, self-expectation, organization, resident influence, and physical comfort.	Items narrowed down from larger pool. Each subscale had acceptable alpha reliability (range of .75–.61) and the intercorrelations among scales were moderate, suggesting independence of the seven scales.

9. Person-Environment Fit
    (Kahana 1974)

Interview with 90 items describing the institutional resident and 70 describing the environment (that is, activities, policies, behavior, and physical features). The resident and the staff member(s) each complete both parts

to give a "subjective" and "objective" view of both individual and environment. Four dimensions were produced by factor analysis: activity; stimulation; changeability versus sameness; impulsiveness versus impulse control; independence versus privacy. Trichotomous scores on each dimension are produced (high, medium, and low). The "fit" on the variable is the person score – the environment score.

No reliability or validity information.

10. Person-Environment Fit Scale
    (Coulton 1979)

Self-administered questionnaire of about 100 items. Item pool (originally much larger) was generated from semistructured interviews with 25 hospitalized adults to elicit specific statements about discrepancies experienced with their environments; 13 factors yielded for dimensions of fit: economic, physical, activity, information, order and control, family role, nonfamily role, affiliation/ acceptance, support, achievement, socioemotional, work aspirations, work demands.

Instrument designed to provide a measure of person–environment fit applicable to all environments and useful as outcome measure of social-work practice. Alpha reliabilities of 13 factors ranged from 94 to 61, with only 1 falling below 70. Construct validity and applicability of instrument still being tested.

Checklist (Hulicka, Morganti, and Cataldo 1975)—illustrated in table 4–8—lists thirty-six activities that would be particularly relevant in congregate-living situations but that also have more-general relevance. For each, the personal importance of the activity is scored, as is the amount of choice the individual perceives as available regarding it. (For example, one set of questions is, "How important is it to you who you sit with at meals?" and, "To what extent do you have a choice about who you sit with at meals?") The score on each item is derived by multiplying the importance score by the choice score. No information is available on summary scoring. The instrument was validated by a demonstration that young men in the military scored more poorly than a comparison group of civilians. The scores of a group of nursing-home residents showed them to have less choice about matters of perceived personal importance than did a group of community-dwelling elderly persons. In this latter test, the importance scores themselves differed, leading the authors to speculate that the nursing-home residents viewed as important what the others were taking for granted (for example, deciding when to take a bath, choosing what name to be called). The approach of weighting choice by importance seems theoretically sound, but little information is available to justify the selection of items or to ensure that items of likely importance are adequately sampled.

The Locus of Desired Control Scale (Reid, Haas, and Hawkins 1977) is shorter and simpler than the scale just discussed; it includes seven items that are rated in terms of their desirability and the perception of the respondent that he or she can control the event (see table 4–8). Again, the scores for desirability and for control are multiplied to derive each item score; and, again, no norms or information about reliability or validity are available.

The Perceived Environmental Control Scale (Wolk and Telleen 1976) is the most straightforward of the three. In that scale, six statements applicable to institutional life are presented for agreement or disagreement (see table 4–8). It is assumed that answers in the desired direction signify an absence of environmental constraint. (For example, agreement with "residents have free access to facilities and grounds" would be positive.) The scale was developed to permit study of the correlation between perceived environmental control and satisfaction; no information is available about the reliability or validity of the scale.

All three of these scales reflect the body of research that suggests that perceived choice and control is personally beneficial and that perceived lack of control is associated with morbidity and even mortality (Schulz 1976; Ferrari 1962; Langer and Rodin 1976). Once the association between perceived control and well-being is accepted, then any aspect of an environment that minimizes the opportunity for choice or decision making is potentially damaging to the individual.

The Satisfaction with Nursing Home Scale (McCaffree and Harkins 1976) was developed for a study of nursing-home outcomes. The authors indicated that they could not find an existing instrument to measure satisfaction. It

Table 4-8

Examples of Scales to Measure Person-Environment Fit

Importance, Locus and Range of Activities Checklist

For each activity, indicate its personal importance to you,[a] and the degree of choice you have regarding it.[b]

1. Who to sit with at meals.
2. What is served at meals.
3. What time to eat meals.
4. Who to have a snack or coffee with.
5. What time to go to bed.
6. What time to get up.
7. When to have a bath.
8. Where to see visitors or friends.
9. When to see visitors or friends.
10. When to watch TV.
11. What TV programs to watch.
12. Where to spend free time.
13. With whom to spend free time.
14. Who to have for friends.
15. What clothes to wear.
16. What type haircut to get.
17. What name to be called.
18. What hobbies to have.
19. What to spend money on.
20. Where to shop.
21. Whether to associate with other people or not.
22. Whether to offer suggestions to other people about how things are done.
23. Who to complain to.
24. Whether to attend religious service.
25. What papers or books to read.
26. How much personal privacy is available.
27. Whether to work.
28. Where to work.
29. What type work to do.
30. What personal possessions to have.
31. Who to live with.
32. Color of walls, pictures, etc. in living quarters.
33. Whether to have private room.
34. Whether to live at the same place or go elsewhere.
35. Whether to participate in certain activities (games, sports, meetings, etc.)

Perceived Environmental Constraint Index

Rate the following statements on a five-point scale from "not at all true" to "completely true."

1. The rules here keep one from doing the things one wants to do.
2. Living here makes one dependent on others.
3. Residents are asked for their advice when changes are planned and carried out by administrators.
4. Residents have free access to facilities and grounds.
5. The staff here respond to residents' requests.
6. If a resident has a problem, he can solve it by taking the initiative.

Table 4-8 (continued)

Satisfaction with Nursing Home Scale

Items[c]

1. Have a place to be alone.
2. Be close to family.
3. Have activities of interest to you.
4. Have good food.
5. Have a clean room and surroundings.
6. Have personal belongings allowed in your room.
7. Provide for your own self-care.
8. Have frequent contact with a doctor.
9. Make new friends in the home.
10. Have staff who care about you.
11. Have a flexible meal and bedtime schedule.
12. Be able to leave the home to shop or visit.
13. Be able to close your door and not be disturbed.
14. Be able to have alcohol when you want it.
15. Be able to smoke when you want to.
16. Be close to friends.
17. Have attention from the staff.
18. Have a good roommate.
19. Be around staff with a good attitude.
20. Be independent.
21. Have quiet.
22. Get along with other residents and patients.

Locus of Desired Control Scale

How desirable or important is it for you . . .[d]

1. to receive regular visits from your friends or relatives?
2. to be able to decide on your own what your daily activities will be?
3. to be able to place your possessions where you want to place them?
4. to receive attention or recognition from those around you?
5. that your doctor come to see you when you ask for him?
6. to be able to find privacy from others?
7. to be with your friends who live at (name of nursing home) when you want to be?

Expectancies:

1. To what extent can you cause friends or relatives to come and visit regularly?[e]
2. How often can you yourself decide what your daily activities are going to be?[f]
3. I am able to place my possessions where I want to place them.[g]
4. How often can you acquire attention from those around you?[f]
5. To what extent do you think you can cause your doctor to come and see you whenever you ask for him?[e]
6. How often can you give yourself privacy when you want it?[f]
7. How often can you be with your friends who live in (name of nursing home)?[f]

Sources: For Range of Activities: Adapted from I. Hulicka, J. Morganti, and J. Cataldo, "Perceived Latitude of Choice of Institutionalized and Non-Institutionalized Elderly Women," *Experimental Aging Research* 1(1975):27–39. For Constraint Index: Adapted from S. Wolk and S. Telleen, "Psychological and Social Correlates of Life Satisfaction as a Function of Residential Constraint," *Journal of Gerontology* 31(1976):89–98. For Satisfaction: Adapted from K.M. McCaffree and E.M. Harkins, *Final Report for Evaluation of the*

Table 4-8 (continued)

Outcomes of Nursing Home Care (Seattle, Wash.: Battelle Human Affairs Research Centers, 1976. For Locus: Adapted from D. Reid, G. Haas, and D. Hawkins, "Locus of Desired Control and Positive Self-Concept of the Elderly," *Journal of Gerontology* 32(1977):441–450.

[a]Importance is scored as: very important (3), somewhat important (2), and unimportant (1).

[b]Choice is scored as: free choice (3), some choice (1), and no choice (–3). Each item is scored by multiplying the importance and choice scores, producing a range of +9 or –9.

[c]Respondents are asked the personal importance of each item; choices are: Not important (0), somewhat important (1), or very important (2). Then the respondent is asked about satisfaction with that item; choices are: Not at all satisfied (0), somewhat satisfied (1), or very satisfied (2).

[d]Response choices: Not important, somewhat important, generally important, very important.

[e]Response choices: Cannot cause, can cause somewhat, can cause quite a bit, can cause a great deal.

[f]Response choices: Never, sometimes, quite often, always.

[g]Response choices: Disagree, agree somewhat, agree, agree strongly.

supports that contention that the only analogous instrument we could locate is Bennett's Evaluation Index, described by Anderson and Patten (forthcoming) and consisting of twelve open-ended questions asking the residents "what do you think" about selected items such as the nurses, the neighbors on the floor, or the people in the dining room. Apparently the interviewer categorizes the answer as positive, mixed, or negative (2 to 0 points). Indeed, this approach would seem to create problems for inter-rater reliability.

The McCaffree and Harkins scale serves us well as an illustration of generic problems in measuring satisfaction—an extremely important outcome for evaluating nursing-home care. The twenty-two-item scale (shown in table 4-8) includes specific aspects of the location, amenities, services, routines, and privileges (the latter including the right to have an alcoholic beverage when one wishes and to smoke when one wishes). Each item was rated in terms both of personal importance to the respondent and of satisfaction. The authors scored the scale by summing the satisfaction items. They decided not to weight importance with satisfaction, arguing that in a pilot test, simple satisfaction scores were correlated with satisfaction scores weighted by importance at .96 for the first test and .84 for the retest; however, no information is given about the way the weightings were done. With a checklist approach, weighting importance into the equation seems necessary lest items that the respondents consider least important contribute most to their satisfaction score. On the face of it, one might expect such a relationship to exist; if a person considers, for example, that the opportunity to play golf is unimportant, he or she would also be likely to express complete satisfaction with that opportunity as provided by the nursing home, thus earning full points for the item. Test-retest reliability dropped considerably (from .92 to .69) when a different rater did the interviews.

Measuring patient satisfaction in a nursing-home setting is fraught with problems. An immediate practical issue is establishing the climate of trust and privacy that would permit disclosure of negative comments. For example, interviewers have found themselves asking for an opinion of a roommate while the roommate was present, or for opinions about staff members when a nurse was passing by; this problem is exacerbated when the respondent is hard of hearing and the interviewer finds it necessary to shout. Actual wording of items is important too; we note that "satisfaction" can sometimes be viewed in terms of compatibility with expectations (which may have been low) and sometimes in terms of whether the object in question is intrinsically satisfying. If we ask, "Are you satisfied with the food?" we are more likely to be answered in terms of initial expectations than if we ask, "Do you like the food here?" Nevertheless, however the question is phrased, the additional comments of respondents indicate that some will reply in terms of expectations and others in terms of positive likes or dislikes.

For a Rand Corporation study of nursing-home patients' outcomes, we tested an approach to measuring patient satisfaction that uses several true-or-false statements and a single global question about satisfaction (The Rand Corporation 1979). The true-or-false statements were designed so that agreement with some and disagreement with others signify satisfaction. Examples of items are: "The food is good here"; "You don't have enough privacy here"; "There is nothing a resident can do about changing the rules of the home"; "When you need help, someone will come within a reasonable time"; "The amount of noise here bothers you." Respondents answer each question as "mostly true," "mostly false," or "sometimes true, sometimes false"; the latter designation recognizes fairly common mixed patterns (for example, some of the staff are perceived as pleasant and some not). The global question, "Summing it all up, how well do you like living here?" was also answered on a three-point scale; our analysis will determine whether the overall scale scores will correlate well with the global question. Although each true-or-false statement was intended to be as clear as possible, pretesting revealed areas of unsuspected ambiguity. For instance, in response to the question, "Your personal belongings are safe here," several residents replied that they are safe because they are locked up. Thus a simple "yes" answer to the question may not be a valid indicator of satisfaction. On the other hand, an instrument that depends on probing and requires judgment about the "real meaning" of each answer will be difficult to use reliably.

Pincus (1968) has used a thirty-six-question Home for the Aged Description Questionnaire (HDQ) for his studies of the environments of nursing homes. Nursing-home environments are described along four dimensions: public/private (that is, the ability of residents to maintain a personal domain); structured/

unstructured (that is, the degree to which the resident must adjust his life to rules and discipline and, conversely, the flexibility and initiative permitted); resource sparse/resource rich; and isolated/integrated (that is, the degree to which the environment affords opportunities for interaction with the larger community in which it is located). The thirty-six statements fit into a matrix that uses these four dimensions of institutional life as one axis and three aspects of the institutional setting (the physical plant, the rules and the program, and the staff behavior) as the other. Initially, the HDQ was administered to staff members of three nursing homes; factor analysis apparently yielded five factors: privacy, freedom, resources, integration, and personalization. Use of the instrument with residents as respondents has demonstrated the incongruence between resident and staff perceptions. Seemingly, the score on the privacy dimension best predicts the general satisfaction score, leading the authors (Pincus and Wood 1970) to suggest that perhaps privacy is a commodity that can be appreciated across a variety of functional abilities, in contrast to resource richness, freedom, or integration with the community, environmental qualities that may require a level of functional ability before a resident can profit from them. It does not appear that the HDQ has been tested for reliability or used with minimally responsive residents.

The Ward Atmosphere Scale (WAS) and the Community-Oriented Programs Environment Scale (COPES), which are described as items 6 and 7 of table 4-8, were both developed by Moos (1974) and apply particularly to mental-health-treatment programs. The WAS contains 100 true/false questions in its long form and 40 in a shorter version; ten subscales are derived relating to various dimensions of ward life. Of special methodologic interest is the use of the WAS in three contexts: form C (which refers to actual life on the ward); form I (which refers to respondents' views of an ideal ward); and form E (which refers to initial expectations of the ward). Various combinations of these measures permit analysis of discrepancies between initial expectations and perceived reality, discrepancies between perceived ideals and realities, congruence of individual perceptions and group perceptions, or congruence of staff perceptions and patient perceptions. The COPES is very similar to the WAS, but is modified to apply to day programs and other community-based services.

The Sheltered Care Environment Scale (SCES) (Moos et al. 1979) is perhaps the most relevant to geriatrics of the three scales produced by Moos and his colleagues that are discussed here. The SCES is part of a Multiphasic Environmental Assessment Procedure (Moos and Lemke 1979) that also uses four instruments: a Physical and Architectural Features Checklist, a Policy and Program Information Form, a Resident and Staff Information Form, and a Rating Scale to capture observer impressions of the facility. The SCES is the only one of the five instruments that polls residents and staff as individuals; the other instruments codify information about the setting, the policies, and the staff and residents as a group.

The SCES was developed to be usable at a fifth-grade literacy level. Its subscales tap constructs that the authors believe relevant to congregate settings. *Cohesion* is defined in terms of how helpful and supportive staff members are toward residents and residents toward each other (sample question: "Do residents get a lot of individual attention?")[a] *Conflict* is defined as the extent to which residents express anger or criticism (sample question: "Do residents complain a lot?"). *Independence* is the amount of self-sufficiency and responsibility encouraged (sample question: "Do residents set up their own activities?"). *Self-exploration* is the characteristic of an environment that encourages expressiveness (sample question: "Do residents ever talk about illness and death?"). *Organization* refers to the importance of order and routine and the clarity of expectations (sample question: "Do residents always know when the staff will be around?"). *Resident influence* refers to the ability of residents to control the setting (sample question: "Would a resident be asked to leave if he/she broke a rule?"). Finally, *physical comfort* is self-explanatory (sample question: "Does it ever smell bad here?"). The items retained in the questionnaire all had reasonable variance in the first fielding. Like the WAS and the COPES, the SCES permits comparison of contrasting staff and resident perceptions or of initial expectations, ideal expectations, and perceived reality. It also provides a mechanism for determining whether changes in the setting are associated with changes on any of the SCES dimensions.

We note, however, that the authors acknowledge the difficulty in achieving good response rates among residents. A minimum of a 10-percent response rate was attainable in SNFs, with the majority of SNFs yielding a 20-percent response rate.

Kahana (1974) has focused attention on person–environment fit within institutions for the elderly. She speculates that different individuals will have different expectations of the environment and that the congruence between environment and person will be highly associated with morale. In a paper outlining the concept of congruence between person and institutional environment (1974), Kahana suggested seven dimensions: segregate, congregate, institutional control, structure, stimulation/activity, affect, and impulse control. In a study of three homes for the elderly, she measured the environment and the individual's preferences, finding that the congruence concept accounted for a large proportion of the variance in morale among the residents. Unfortunately, that paper does not provide information about how the measurements were made. Also, since physically or mentally inform residents were omitted from the study, the concept has been studied only with regard to fitter residents.

For information about the person–environment-fit instrument itself, our source is the review by Anderson and Patten (forthcoming). They indicate that

---

[a]The full scales are available on request from Dr. Rudolf Moos, Department of Psychiatry and Behavioral Science, Stanford University, Stanford, California 94305.

the measure of the environment consists of seventy items describing the activities, policies, staff behavior, and physical aspects, and that the individual measure is a structured interview with ninety questions modeled partly after the Pincus HDQ, described previously. Factor analysis identified four dimensions that appeared on both the individual and the environmental scales (activity/stimulation; changeability versus sameness; impulse versus control; and independence versus privacy). A high, medium, or low score is created on each dimension for both environment and individual, and the congruence is calculated by subtracting the individual scores from the environment score. Information about reliability or validity is not readily available. Nevertheless, the avenue of study represented by this beginning effort to measure person–environment fit in institutions seems important and worthy of further attention.

Coulton's exploratory search for a measure of person–environment fit (1979) was motivated by the social-work profession's need for a measure that responds to the overriding goal of social-work practice: to help individuals function better within their social environments. The target of change may be the individual, the environment, or both; but the resultant outcome should be a better person–environment fit. In contrast to Kahana's approach, Coulton was seeking a measure that social workers could use in many different settings with different types of clients. To identify appropriate items for such a scale, Coulton interviewed twenty-five hospital patients about discrepancies that they had experienced between their needs or desires and their environment. The large number of items thus identified was administered to another sample, and the results were factor analyzed. The person–environment-fit measure consists at present of 100 items, each of which is answered on a Likert-type scale. Thirteen subscales are suggested. For example, the economic-fit subscale contains items such as, "I have enough money to buy those little extras, those small luxuries," "My expenses are so heavy that I . . . (cannot meet payments at all, occasionally cannot meet payments, can barely meet payments, meeting payments is no problem)." To take another example, the activity-fit subscale asks whether the respondents would like more organized activities, more things to do in their leisure time, have people visit more often, go to parties more often, go to nightclubs more often, or have more-important things to do to keep busy. The order-and-control-fit subscale contains fifteen items dealing with respondents' reactions to the amount of privacy, peace and quiet, change, and orderliness within their life.

Coulton's line of research is equally important to Kahana's because, in many instances, one will wish to assess the fit between an individual and the current environment but will not have access to the environment for purposes of measurement. Therefore, an instrument that contains an element of perceived environmental adequacy in each item would permit measurement of person–environment fit for community-based clients. This work, too, is acknowledged to be in its early stages. Because the items for the pool were generated by hospital patients prior to discharge and may be weighted toward the aspects of environmental fit that would occur particularly to hospital patients, Coulton indicates that the revised 100-item instrument is now being tested in several other settings and that these results are awaited before the instrument is further refined.

Measures of Social Functioning of the Cognitively Impaired

Finally, we turn to techniques for measuring social behavior, including relationship skills and coping abilities, among persons who are so cognitively impaired that they cannot be expected to respond to a questionnaire approach. Essentially, the only recourse left is to structure a situation and observe the responses. Three such approaches are the Scale for Measuring Minimal Social Behavior (Farina, Arenberg, and Guskin 1957); the Greeting Behavior Scale (Main and Bennett 1972); and the more-elaborate VIRO (for *V*igor, *I*ntactness, *O*rientation, and *R*elationship) scale (Kastenbaum and Sherwood 1972).

The Minimal Social Behavior Scale was constructed for use with chronic deteriorated mental patients. Its originators described their motivation as a response to a need for some instrument to evaluate the impact on the severely deteriorated patient of the psychoactive drugs becoming prevalent in the 1950s.

The context of the administration is an interview with the examiner in the latter's office. The patient receives points for responding to the greeting, taking a seat when offered, and other similar behavior. The interview contains a number of events that the examiner stages in order to score the patient's responses. For example, he drops a pencil and awards points if the patient picks it up; he offers a cigarette and awards points for an intelligible acceptance or refusal; he busies himself with paperwork, offering the subject a magazine, and scores a point if any pages are thumbed; he simulates a headache and watches for a response; he places matches in view of the subject and then searches for a match, awarding a point if the subject shows him the matches. When the examiner terminates the interview by rising from his chair, he scores a point if the patient rises and then leaves the room. Immediately after the interview, the examiner scores additional points for the absence of a number of antisocial phenomena (disarranged clothing, drooling, failure to meet the examiner's eye, and so forth). Inter-rater reliability of this scale was tested by simultaneous ratings by an observer behind a screen (the correlation was .95 in a sample of 35 subjects). One wonders, however, about the validity of an approach that requires the examiner to engage in illogical behavior and then rates the logic of the subject's responses.

The Greeting Behavior Scale (Main and Bennett 1972) was used as part of a larger study of nursing-home residents. Social behavior was measured by responses to the interviewer's seven initial statements, which were tape recorded for future analysis. The answers were scored, according to response amount, relevance, coherence, and length, on cooperation, self-confidence, giving and returning deference, and responding ritually. The statements were as follows: (1) "How do you do. I am ____"; (2) "Thank you for agreeing to see me"; (3) "I'm doing a survey about the opinions of people who live in nursing homes"; (4) "I would like to ask you a few questions if that's all right with you"; (5) "It shouldn't take much time"; (6) "But before I begin, how are you feeling today?"; and (7) "Do you have any questions before I begin the interview?"

The total score a resident could obtain on the Greeting Behavior Scale was 52. On each statement other than (2) and (5), 1 point was awarded for response amount if any response was made, 1 point was awarded for relevance if the response was related to the statement, 2 points were awarded for each completely coherent response. For all responses, a length score was calculated based on the number of words, (0 points for one to three words, 2 points for eight to ten words, 3 points for twelve to fifteen words, and 4 points for more than fifteen words). Cooperation scores consisted of 1 point for indicating a willingness to be interviewed in response to statement (4) and 1 point for indicating that time didn't matter in response to statement (5). Self-confidence was scored 1 point each if statements (4) and (5) were answered without showing anxiety or doubt. Giving and receiving deference were scored by responses to the first two statements; in response to the first statement, the resident was expected to say something on the order of, "I am fine, thank you; how are you?" for a full 5 points. To the second statement, a response of, "You are welcome," would earn a full 5 points. Finally, a ritual response to the question about health ("I'm fine") earned 2 points, any other response received 1 point, and no response earned a 0.

The authors acknowledge that the scoring procedure would need to be simplified to make the scale more practical. They viewed it as an indicator of the extent to which the resident was socialized at the time the interview was administered. We would again question the assumptions of the scale, particularly if the expectations for responsive behavior in the institution were minimal and if the respondent lacked interest in the interview. We were unable to locate any further uses of this scale in the literature.

The VIRO scale (Kastenbaum and Sherwood 1972) is the best-known and most carefully studied measure of social behavior among the minimally impaired. Unlike the Farina Minimal Social Behavior Scale, it does not set up artificial situations. Rather, the interviewer rates the subject based on the interview behavior during a short, open-ended assessment. The VIRO MSQ (see chapter 3) is administered to calculate the orientation score. The "vigor" score is a combination of the rating of the initial impression of the client (vigorous versus feeble) and a rating of the energy levels. "Intactness" variables are fluency of speech, attentiveness, controlled versus tangential thought, and self-perspective versus self-engrossment. The "relationship" score consists of the initial impression of the individual as receptive or closed, the enthusiasm of the subject's participation, the engrossment in the relationship, and the eagerness displayed to see the interviewer again. Each individual variable is rated on a four-point scale.

Detailed instructions are given for rating, and the authors claim that reliable results can be achieved. The interviewer training emphasizes that the interviewers must base their ratings on observations rather than on their expectations. Other instructions clarify that full points are given for responses that pass a minimal threshold; for example, the same score for fluency would be earned by someone whose verbal ability approximated that of a normal adult and by a person of great eloquence. The initial "first-impression" ratings are made within the first sixty minutes of the contact, permitting analysis of whether a first impression is compatible with the results of the full interview.

The VIRO approach appears to require considerable self-discipline from the interviewer, as well as a certain amount of judgment. The authors argue that VIRO profiles of the four dimensions can reveal patterns of behavior with clinical significance; for example, an individual who is disoriented for time and place may still be socially intact. They also suggest that interview behavior is, after all, an example of social behavior and, in some screening situations, is the only example available to the caregiver. The VIRO permits taking advantage of this opportunity. The authors suggest that the VIRO could be used to establish baseline behavior and monitor change as well as to show the outcomes of treatment. We are skeptical, however, of the VIRO's use other than in specialized settings where a considerable investment is made in training of interviewers and interpretation of results. Furthermore, this investment would need to be ongoing in nature.

Conclusion

For many of the variables discussed in this chapter, it is difficult to recommend specific instruments for specific purposes. Measures of social interaction, contacts, activities, and intergenerational exchanges are surely necessary; but the state of the art does not yet support clear criteria for which tools should be used by geriatric specialists as opposed to those working with persons of all ages. Nor are we ready to suggest which scales are most appropriate for screening as opposed to full assessment. Similarly, the measurement of coping abilities or person–environment fit in the elderly is still in its early stages. More-cohesive work has been done in measurement of morale; here too, however, questions remain about how to interpret results, especially because our basis for understanding changes over time in morale scores of individuals is quite weak.

Part of the problem in advancing our ability to measure social functioning lies in the diversity of conceptualizations. Perhaps more than any of the other areas covered in this book, social functioning is a product of both our intellectual and our moral heritage. Measures of social functioning are used as outcomes of care received by individuals or as evidence of the need for services for a community group. The measure takes on great importance—becoming the looking glass of the professional into the world of the consumer. The goal is to describe that world accurately rather than merely to reflect the image cast by our own measuring tools.

The potential for intellectual refraction can be illustrated with an example outside the field of geriatrics. After the Three Mile Island nuclear-reactor accident of 1979, behavioral researchers became interested in the effect of the incident on the citizens of the area. According to an account in *Behavior Today* (1980), a Pennsylvania State University College of Medicine Task Force studied demoralization of the citizenry, and its results were reported in *The New York Times* of 17 April 1980 under the headline "Long Distress Found Over Atom Incident." At about the same time, the Behavioral Task Force of the President's Commission on the Accident at Three Mile Island suggested that the stress effects of the accident were transitory and short term. The Pennsylvania researcher assured the reporter that the results of the studies were not inconsistent; both groups found evidence of a dramatic rise in demoralization, which then dropped off sharply. But the two studies used different measures, tapping slightly different constructs. "What many commentators have failed to grasp . . . is the distinction between short-term demoralization and long-term distress—and the extent to which the latter can only be detected if one is asking the right questions in the right way ("TMI-Type Disasters" 1980). The remainder of the report describes the distinctions between the two instruments in terms of items included and analysis techniques (for example, one researcher dichotomized "often," "sometimes," and "never" into "often" versus the other two choices).

It is all too likely that conflicting statements about the world of the elderly and their social needs are produced by similar inconsistencies in measurement. Increased attention focused on LTC makes congressional and other budgeteers, politicians, popular health reporters, and representatives of various provider industries all avid consumers of data about the social well-being of the elderly. Few will take the time to do the careful backtracking needed to determine how "support systems," "isolation," "morale," and other variables were defined.

In our concluding chapter, we offer some general recommendations for research in measurement; the comments apply particularly to the measures of social functioning. Among the important agenda items are:

1. Identification of clinically significant thresholds for interpreting social information about strength of social-support systems, social stimulation and activity, and social relationships.
2. Determination of how best to acquire valid information in the all-important area of client satisfaction, particularly among persons who are dependent on the care given.
3. Development of longitudinal information about the stability of perceived social well-being over time and its sensitivity to changed social circumstances.

In the interim, we urge that practicing geriatricians and case managers move cautiously ahead. Just as with package inserts for drugs, they should read the instructions carefully before using. They should not be afraid to apply the tests of common sense: Are these really the important issues for my patients/clients? They should test screening devices to identify those persons at social risk from among the very large group of persons who experience a decline in social contacts and stimulation with advancing years. Similarly, they should develop and test strategies for monitoring social functioning. So many observations are possible under the general rubric of social functioning that it is crucial for us to narrow them down to those that are most important as indicators of social well-being or as social predictors of need for service.

5 Multidimensional Measures

So far we have discussed measurement of functional status in specific domains: cognitive, affective, and social. These, in turn, lend themselves to further subdivision. We have underscored repeatedly the interdependence of the various domains. In this chapter we consider those aggregate measures that provide an overview of patient or client status. In long-term-care (LTC) vernacular, this general class of instrument is known as a *multidimensional measure.*

Multidimensional measures serve several purposes. The clinician needs information about functioning across a variety of domains in order to construct a "snapshot" of the individual's current status. Similarly, a program evaluator who wishes to examine the effects of LTC service on more than one functional domain also requires a multidimensional measure. Some multidimensional measures venture beyond simply assembling scales and subscales. Rather, they synthesize the information into one or more summary statements about the client's status. Such summaries enable one to compare individuals and groups. Theoretically, such comparisons permit more-rational allocation of services. Summary scores facilitate equitably applied eligibility criteria for program benefits. The idea of reducing a vast amount of data into a scoring formula is therefore appealing, but it is also fraught with difficulties.

Consider an analogy to the financial statement. An enormous amount of information about assets and liabilities and the circumstances attached to each can be summarized in a "bottom-line" figure that defines the individual's net worth. This figure is used by decision makers; lenders use it to allocate loans to the best credit risks; scholarship committees, to grant awards to the neediest. But even in the fact-oriented world of business, such summary statements may distort reality by emphasizing the wrong aspects of a person's financial circumstances. A similar bottom-line summary of the well-being of an elderly individual requires documentation in the more-ambiguous areas of physical, mental, and social assets and liabilities. Formulas for weighting the information, however, are rudimentary and relatively untested. Constructing multidimensional measures requires decisions about the kind of information to put in each column as well as about the relative importance of the selected items.

Multidimensional measurement is both a theme and a goal for LTC in the 1980s. It has taken on a positive aura, almost as if a comprehensive assessment itself represents a service for the client. Case-management programs, many designed in a demonstration mode, have been built on the cornerstone of multidimensional assessment. The Long-Term Care Geronotology Centers, originated by the Administration on Aging (AoA) in 1979 as "centers of excellence" for LTC, are developing comprehensive-assessment techniques as a model for students of various disciplines. Monitoring agencies for LTC such as PSROs or state Medicaid agencies also specialize in comprehensive assessment; the assessment provides the data base on which to judge both the appropriateness and the quality of care. Hospital discharge planners and social-service workers also pay homage to the multidimensional assessment for elderly patients with multiple care needs. At this writing, proposed legislation sponsored by Congressmen Pepper and Waxman would assert the legitimacy of a multidimensional assessment as a community-based LTC benefit under Medicaid.

Multidisciplinary measures are legion. After reviewing many examples, we note that they usually have a core of common content, yet also vary markedly in content (that is, the mix of items and types and numbers of borrowed or new scales); length; administration protocols; and scoring. Reliability and validity information is not readily available for most multidimensional measures. Some instruments were developed for a single study, demonstration, or fact-finding mission (the latter often known as a *needs assessment*). Others were designed to meet the information needs and guide the decisions of case-management demonstrations such as TRIAGE in Connecticut (Hodgson and Quinn 1980); ACCESS in Monroe County, New York (Eggert, Bowlyow, and Nichols 1980); or the Iowa Gerontology Model Project (Hageboeck 1979).

Unpublished instruments are circulated (for example, at professional meetings) and stimulate yet other developers, who may modify them for their particular purposes. To illustrate the variation available, consider the three quite different approaches to multidimensional assessment exemplified by the Pennsylvania Domiciliary Care Program Social Adjustment Assessment Form (Philadelphia Geriatric Center, n.d.); the Enquiry Into the Welfare of Old People with its companion Medical Questionnaire and Examination Record (Goldberg 1970); or the Assessment Instrument of the Sepulveda Veterans Administration Geriatric Assessment Unit (Rubenstein, Romano, and Abrass 1980). The differing emphases are not surprising when one considers that these batteries were developed, respectively, to screen for admission to a domiciliary home, to demonstrate the effects of professional social work on a community-based population of frail elderly in England, and to measure the impact of an inpatient geriatric-assessment program on the well-being of a veteran population. To some extent the items and the analysis rules are dictated by an understanding of the kind of program options that are available to the respondents and to the professional decision maker on behalf of the particular clientele.

In the latter part of this chapter we discuss four multidimensional instruments in some detail: the Sickness Impact Profile (SIP); the Older Americans Research and Service Center Instrument (OARS); the Comprehensive Assessment and Referral Evaluation (CARE); and the Patient Appraisal and Care Evaluation (PACE). They were selected because together they represent serious, systematic, and ongoing efforts to develop multidimensional-measurement capacity. At the same time, the distinct differences in the four approaches provide an excellent illustration of issues.

General Issues

Before turning to these selected instruments, we raise some general issues facing those who make multidimensional measurements of the elderly.

Who Does the Measurement?

Multidimensional assessment, by its very nature, requires measurement in diverse areas. Multidisciplinary teamwork, a highly valued modality in LTC, assembles persons with diverse training and expertise within single programs. Perhaps for this reason, multidisciplinary teamwork and multidimensional assessment have often been linked in some sort of mutual justification for each other's existence. In the most-circular expression of this reasoning, a multidisciplinary team is justified by the need for multidimensional assessments, and multidimensional assessments are advocated to give each team member a perspective on the problem and a contribution to the management plan. Disentangling teamwork and assessment is important for determining who should actually make the multidimensional measures.

Two separate but related questions emerge: (1) What level of expertise is required to perform the multidimensional assessment? (2) Should the assessment be performed by one data-gatherer or by a team?

Skill Level. Some multidimensional measurements rely heavily on professional judgment because they require quasi-diagnostic classifications of physical- and mental-health status. If decision rules for such judgments are not explicit or if the individual observations also require professional judgment (for example, ratings of depression or of environmental "adequacy"), higher levels of training are required than if the items are observable and specific. Even when direct observation is used, considerable training may be necessary. If, for example, drug use is assessed by checking the supplies of medications, one might argue that some medical sophistication is required to obtain accurate and complete information. (Knowledge about the particular drugs prescribed might make apparent the need for different probes about use patterns or about related medications.) Others argue that a skilled measurer with superior interviewing and relationship skills can elicit cooperation from the subjects and, therefore, increase the validity of the information. It has also been suggested that "hands-on" evaluation of physical status is required for measuring the status of some patients; and this, in turn, requires duly licensed personnel.

On the other hand, data collection by professionals imposes constraints. Physicians, nurse practitioners, psychologists, clinical social workers, and other professional data gatherers drive up costs. Although some instances justify an assessment tool that depends on such an elite cadre, more often the goal is to refine an instrument so that it can yield reliable and valid data in the hands of less-well-educated persons. The budgets of most service organizations or monitoring agencies cannot accommodate the high cost of expertise. Furthermore, often nonprofessional personnel are in the best position to make the observations (for example, nursing-home attendants, home-health aides) and must be equipped with tools that they can handle.

Team or Solo. Team measurement represents the Cadillac of professional assessment. It permits the various disciplinary representatives (nurse, social worker, occupational therapist, nutritionist, pharmacist, and so on) to make systematic observations. The PACE system, discussed later on, is predicated on the premise that the whole team should be involved in both assessement and care planning. Little systematic information is available to compare an assessment made by a single interviewer examining several domains with an assessment conducted by a team of experts. Theoretically, the team members should be able to generate or validate the important items within their own fields of competence and, in that way, contribute to instrumentation without being involved in actual measurement.

Recommendations for specialized assessments could certainly follow from multidimensional measures made by a single interviewer. Especially in clinical contexts, those who need an evaluation by a particular expert (such as a dentist, a hearing specialist, a psychiatrist, a prosthetist, or a dietician) should be identifiable from their initial assessment. Unless the decision rules are clear, however, referrals for specialized assessments may be made on the basis of vague impressions rather than of clear indications.

No hard and fast laws can be advanced about who should do the measurement. This depends on the purpose of the measurement, the variables included, the population involved, and the number of persons to be assessed. As a general guide, however, we would advocate that the educational level be kept as low, and the number of contributors to the single assessment as few, as will be possible to collect the information needed. The multidimensional assessment is meant to be a tool to organize disparate information and, in clinical contexts, to serve as a resource for the professional. For a truly gifted professional with abundant time, the best instrument might be a piece of blank paper. In view of the large numbers of persons in the population at risk for LTC and the scarcity of trained care given, so unstructured a strategy seems particularly inappropriate.

Length

Because multidimensional measures cover so many areas of dysfunction, they tend to be lengthy. Those applying such assessment instruments in a clinical situation quickly become concerned with the respondent burden implied. This burden is especially apparent when the subject is infirm and when the information has no immediate bearing on the care plan. Furthermore, one suspects an inverse relationship between quality and quantity of data. Burden affects the data collector as well as the informant. Enthusiasm and diligence tend to flag, especially if the data collector does not perceive the importance of particular items or does not see how the information can be used.

Given the virtue of relative brevity, the user is faced with deciding whether it is preferable to sample items to represent the various domains of behavior or to explore each in considerable detail. One compromise position is to develop a relatively brief set of core questions that probe critical areas. This can be accompanied by an optional package to explore in greater detail any areas where initial probing suggests dysfunction. The latter, for example, is the approach taken in the CARE instrument. In part, the decision about how thoroughly to sample within a domain depends on the purpose of the instrument. As we discuss in the concluding chapter, a program evaluator may be best served by a few well-chosen and reliable items to represent each domain; in that case the challenge is to select those items that might best serve as markers. By contrast, the clinician who uses the instrument to observe and manage an individual client needs more-detailed information on any item with practical significance to the particular respondent. Often, on the current LTC scene, a multidimensional tool is inappropriately expected to do double duty as a research and a clinical measure.

The Iowa Comprehensive Assessment Profile (Hageboeck 1979) is an example of an extremely long measure; full administration can take four hours and usually requires two sittings. The original version of this assessment contained almost 1,000 variables. Even though many variables were eliminated after a period of use, the assessment team judged that other relevant dimensions (in that particular case, items that would indicate neglect or abuse) had to be added. Proponents of the approach argue that the front-end investment of a detailed team assessment, although costly, is justified by the ability to detect remediable problems and to defer or prevent a highly vulnerable group from entering an institution. Assuming for the moment that this assertion is true, a more-streamlined approach to multidimensional assessment would surely be necessary to screen from among the many "old-old" individuals in the community those whose vulnerability merits the full-scale four-hour assessment.

One useful test of instrument length is to ask how the information gathered will be used. There is an overwhelming temptation to gather exhaustive (and exhausting) data, in case it may be useful in the future. In most instances, however, the clinician can manage only a handful of relevant items. Much of the detailed information is either ignored or greatly summarized.

Multidimensional Rating Techniques

Three of the four instruments described in detail later in this chapter require direct collection of information from the patient (the SIP is a self-completed questionnaire, and the OARS and CARE are interview schedules). The fourth method, the PACE system, involves professional ratings but depends on well-trained professionals who have had ample opportunity for specialized observations. Another stream of multidimensional assessment, developed largely in the geriatric units of state mental hospitals, illustrates an attempt to produce instruments that could be used by nursing aides and attendants to rate the functional status of all patients, including those who cannot respond to direct questions. Among such scales are the Stockton Geriatric Rating Scale (Meer and Baker 1965), the Plutchik Geriatric Rating Scale (Plutchik, Conte, and Lieberman 1971); the Parachek Geriatric Rating Scale (Miller and Parachek 1974), and the Physical and Mental Impairment-of-Function Evaluation Scale (PAMIE) (Gurel, Linn, and Linn 1972).

These rating scales reflect in part the needs of the times. The geriatric wards in the mental hospitals of the 1950s and 1960s were a grab bag of patients, some long term, with great variation in diagnosis and with varying mixes of physical, mental, and social problems. The community-mental-health movement of the mid-1960s, combined with the advent of Medicare and Medicaid, prompted a new look at these patients. After 1965, many elderly persons institutionalized at state expense became eligible for Medicaid-sponsored nursing-home placement with its generous federal match. Staffs of state hospitals needed to make determinations of the likelihood that both long-term residents and new admissions might be suitable for community placement; this, in turn, required some objective method of assessing the functional abilities of a large group of people. Multidimensionality was needed at the very least to distinguish physical and mental dysfunction.

The Stockton Geriatric Rating Scale (SGRS) was based on daily patient behavior; its developers attempted to include all behavior relevant to the patient's leaving the hospital as improved. The final version of the scale consists of thirty-three items of patient performance, each rated on a scale of 0 to 2 ("never," "sometimes," or "frequently"). Factor analysis yielded four factors: physical disability, apathy, communication failure, and socially irritating behavior. The ten physical-disability items include: "The patient needs protection from falling out of bed or chair," and, "The patient is incontinent." The ten apathy items include: "The patient does not socialize with other patients," "The patient does not start conversations," and, "The patient does not know any of the personnel by name." The factor labeled communication failure had only four items: "The patient does not understand others," "The patient does not make himself understood," "The patient does not respond to his name," and "The patient expresses no interest in leaving the hospital." The nine items under socially irritating behavior include, for example, "The patient makes repetitive vocal sounds," "The patient accuses others of harming him," or, "The patient is often awake at night."

The SGRS was validated by comparisons with patient outcomes, measured in terms of one-year mortality rates and number of days out of the hospital. Changes on the scale scores were also compatible with clinicians' views of those who showed improvement after electric-shock therapy. The authors of the SGRS adopted a strategy of having two independent ratings done for each patient; the patient's final score is an average of both ratings. They argue that this is necessary because the behavior evoked in the geriatric patient by one staff member may be different from that evoked by another, even if both staff members are making valid observations of the behavior. This strategy makes inter-rater reliability testing impossible and, in some ways, irrelevant.

As indicated by Skinner et al. (1976), the SGRS seems to represent an internal state of the individual less than it does the multiple demands placed on the external environment. The items are ambiguous and open to interpretation; this problem is compounded by the strategy of "averaging" conflicting ratings rather than reconciling them.

The Plutchik Geriatric Rating Scale (Plutchik et al. 1971) was developed at the Bronx State Hospital. It has thirty-three items, with a three-point continuum; areas rated include physical ability, verbal communication, self-care, and social behavior. The scale is very similar in content and format to the Stockton rating form, with a similar emphasis on ease of administration and lack of dependence on a cooperative patient.

Seeking an even briefer geriatric rating scale as a screening device, Miller and Parachek (1974) tested the Parachek Geriatric Behavior Rating Scale (PGBRS), which consists of ten multiple-choice items adapted from the Plutchik scale; each item has five possible categories. Included on the PGBRS are three items on physical condition (ambulation, eyesight, and hearing); four items on general self-care (toilet habits, eating, hygiene, and grooming); and three items on social behaviors (helpfulness on the ward, responsiveness in individual relationships, and involvement in group activities).

The Plutchik and Parachek scales were both administered (each by a different tester) to a sample of 150 geriatric patients at the Arizona State Hospital. The correlations between the two tests were high both before treatment (.88) and after treatment (.85) for a group of thirty-nine patients receiving post-tests. The authors therefore concluded that the shorter form is more efficient.

The Physical and Mental Impairment-of-Function Evaluation (PAMIE) is a more detailed approach to gaining a comprehensive picture of an institutionalized geriatric population (Gurel, Linn, and Linn 1972). It contains seventy-seven yes-or-no items. The authors indicate that they were striving for items that would focus on overt observable behavior and would minimize inference about that behavior. PAMIE ratings were made on the basis of the previous week's behavior. Ten reliable subscales were generated by factor analysis: self-care dependency, belligerent/irritable, mentally disorganized/confused, anxious/

depressed, bedfast/moribund, behaviorally deteriorated, sensimotor [sic] impaired, paranoid/suspicious, withdrawn/apathetic, and ambulatory. The PAMIE scores or subscores have been correlated with one-year survival, physical disability as measured by the Cumulative Illness Rating Scale (see chapter 2), professional prognoses, and professionals' views about appropriate placement goals.

We have described the Stockton, Plutchnik, Parachek, and PAMIE scales for the sake of completeness. Generally speaking, such rating scales rely so much on the judgment of the caregivers that their use is contraindicated if any self-report, systematic observation, or combination would substitute. In contrast, Johnston and Stack (1980) argue that when the Stockton Geriatric Rating Scale is used by nurses, the results are highly correlated with OARS scale, and they advocate the former for reasons of efficiency. Their findings, however, were based on only thirty-two cases in a test situation.

Using Existing Instruments

One way to characterize multidimensional instruments is by the extent to which they represent anthologies as opposed to integrated works. Some multidimensional measures are composite instruments, consisting of a number of established instruments that represent particular concepts and domains. The multidimensional aspect is represented by the aggregation of the discrete instruments into a single battery that is applied at one point in time, permitting comparisons of dysfunction across the different domains. The format may therefore be quite inconsistent from one part of the battery to another (for example, the time frames or the response choices may differ). Such inconsistency complicates interpretation of the relationship among the domains.

The alternative approach is to create a single instrument that covers a variety of domains at one time. In its most-integrated version, the particular domain or concept being measured by a given set of questions is not readily apparent. Instead, questions are grouped to enhance the flow of data collection and to minimize halo effects, rather than for ease of analysis. The developers of the CARE instrument argue strongly that the quality of data gathered from older subjects is improved with this type of approach. They therefore strive to maintain a normal flow of conversation. For example, questions on hallucinations are in sequence with questions on visual acuity, and data on drug abuse are covered in a section on medications. The development of specific domain scores is then left for the analysis phase, where more-complex instruction is required about how to interpret the information from the highly integrated instrument.

The OARS instrument is, in part, an example of an anthology approach. The developers endeavored to locate the best of existing instruments, which they further refined to make more appropriate to the elderly population. (For example, the mental-health questions are derived from the Minnesota Multiphasic Personality Inventory, and the ADL questions bear an affinity to Katz scales and other Likert-type ADL questions.) The resulting instrument is arranged in topical sections. The consistent theme tying the instrument together is the summary ratings made in five general domains; for these ratings, the data collector is instructed to use similar six-point anchored scales; but the questions on which those summary scales are based differ markedly in format and content from one domain to another.

Aggregating Information

As the foregoing discussion indicates, multidimensional measures require decisions about how to aggregate diverse kinds of information. For example, a multidimensional measure may provide a single summary score that incorporates the contributions of various dysfunctions on the different dimensions into one measure of dysfunction. In contrast, another approach simply offers profiles in which the individual level of functioning in each dimension is kept separate. The first approach requires some kind of weighting system that allows for the relative value of each deficiency in contributing to the total deficit in well-being. The latter skirts this problem in presenting the data but leaves the issue unresolved for those who then must interpret the implications of the profiles.

Often the distinction between the two approaches is blurred. For example, as our discussion of the OARS instrument will illustrate, the original profile approach was later adapted to generate summary impairment scores based on the number of disabilities encountered. Such summaries, although attractive as a means of condensing voluminous information about a client and comparing groups of clients, make certain assumptions that are not always justifiable. An impairment in the economic area, for instance, is not necessarily equivalent to an impairment in the physical or cognitive area. Because information about the appropriate weightings to apply to different kinds of problems or combinations is lacking, one cannot readily calculate the level at which one type of impairment may be held equivalent to another. In the absence of definitive information, we may be tempted to hold them all as equivalent. Although this approach is seductive in its simplicity, it may be misleading.

Reliability

Achieving reliable data has been flagged as a problem in each section of this book. The issues are no different for multidimensional measures but are exacerbated by the volume of information typically collected, the usual context of a multidimensional assessment, and the several levels of abstraction involved in reaching the summary score or scores.

As always, we are interested in intertemporal reliability (that is, the likelihood that, barring real change, the findings will be the same on successive administrations); inter-rater reliability (the likelihood, barring real change, that the findings will be the same across different interviewers); and interitem reliability (the consistency of items that purport to measure the same concept or domain). The first two forms of reliability testing create most of the practical problems for data collection, whereas the last is a statistical maneuver.

The complexity and length of multidimensional batteries and their use in clinical contexts where personnel turnover means that more than one data collector is likely to be involved combine to make concern over inter-rater reliability critical. The term is used loosely to refer to a variety of approaches. The multidimensional measures that we have reviewed report inter-rater reliability, but one cannot always determine how those data were collected. Furthermore, the samples for inter-rater reliability testing are often small.

Table 5-1 illustrates several different approaches to testing the inter-rater reliability of a long and complex instrument. We can consider reliability at three levels of activity: (1) eliciting the information; (2) recording the responses; and (3) making judgments and summary ratings. Two interviewers may elicit a very different quantity and quality of information because of their interviewing style or personal qualities. If the instrument requires probes in response to cues from the respondent, then the differential decision to probe and the framing of the probes may indeed affect the responses. At another level, assuming that identical responses (both verbal and nonverbal) are offered, interviewers may differ in how they record the item responses. These differences may be a function either of incomplete understandings of the standard protocol or of genuine disagreements about the meaning of what has been said or observed. Finally, at the highest level of abstraction, the interviewers may differ in how they interpret a constellation of items into a summary score depicting functional status in one of the domains. Ironically, agreement may be quite poor at the level of the individual items recorded but may be substantially better at the more-abstract level of the summary ratings. This is particularly true if the scale for summary ratings has only a few points, each of which is defined by at least one observable dimension.

A special problem for inter-rater reliability is created if the instrument depends, in part, on the abstraction of material from a secondary source such as a medical record. Although it is possible to measure the agreement of two or more abstractors who fill out the instrument from the same chart, the reliability of the original information can rarely be tested.

Leaving aside inter-rater reliability, the multidimensional measures raise problems for intertemporal reliability. Many factors might yield differences over repeated administrations, even if the interviewer were held constant. Here the following considerations are relevant:

1. The instruments are lengthy, often requiring more than one sitting. The timing of the administration, the way it is broken into segments, and

Table 5-1
The Advantages and Disadvantages of Different Methods of Testing Inter-rater Reliability of Multidimensional Measures

Method	Advantages	Disadvantages
1. Two or more interviewers administer instrument independently and results on items, scales, and global ratings are compared.	Enables comparison of the effects of inter-viewer differences (such as age, sex, per-sonality, skill) on the responses elicited.	Impossible to distinguish whether incongruence is a result of interviewer or respondent factors. Respondent burden may affect data quality the second time. A selection bias is created by the limitation to respondents willing or able to have two tests.
2. Two or more interviewers are present; one conducts the interview and all record responses and make judgments.	Minimizes respondent burden. Tests ability of more than one interviewer to record items and make judgments con-gruently when stimulus is held constant.	Interviewer differences in eliciting responses will not be picked up. The group interview may inhibit responses.
3. The interview is video- or audiotaped. Additional interviewers record infor-mation and make ratings on the basis of the tape.	Same as no. 2 with the added advantage that many people can be involved in testing their inter-rater reliability. A tangible stimulus remains for use in trying to improve reliability.	Same as no. 2. Videotaping may be particularly obtrusive and introduces the element of the cameraman's focus. Audiotapes provide an incomplete record.
4. The interview is conducted with one or more observers behind a one-way mirror.	Same as nos. 2 and 3 but less obtrusive than group interviews or tapes.	Same as no. 2 but depends on interview taking place in a well-equipped office.
5. One interviewer administers battery, records data, and performs ratings. Additional interviews use that recorded data to do their own ratings.	Minimizes respondent burden. Is less manpower intensive, making larger reliability samples possible.	Does not permit testing of inter-rater reliability in eliciting information or recording it.
6. Inter-rater reliability of parts of the instrument tested in sections. (This can be done in the method outlined in 1, 2, 3, or 4.)	Method is more convenient for interviewer and respondent.	Component parts of a battery may not behave the same way separately as they do when embedded in a longer instrument. Inter-rater reliability of summary scoring is more difficult to test.
7. Inter-rater reliability as established pre-viously is accepted for component of the battery.	Minimizes startup time.	Same as no. 6. Also requires assumption that inter-rater relia-bility achieved with other subjects and other interviewers will pertain.

the inconveniences to the respondent in terms of foregone opportunities all may affect responses.

2. The instruments typically require eliciting information about social support and family relationships from a significant other. If the selection of that significant other is left to convenience and judgment, the data may differ qualitatively, depending on which relative is interviewed.

3. The data gatherer is required to decide whether a cognitively impaired individual is capable of providing information. This places a large burden of judgment on the interviewer and determines whether or not he obtains the rest of the data.

4. Data are often collected in a setting where the interviewer has little control over the context of the interview and/or must make many small decisions about managing the interview. For example, one might logically suppose that a respondent interviewed at home, in the presence of relatives, would answer questions about feelings and family support differently than if he were alone. Similarly, a relative might speak differently about the capacity of a parent, depending on whether the parent is present. In the same way, distractions in settings like the nursing home can make complex tasks even more difficult to assess.

5. The selection bias for completing lengthy interviews is unclear. We know that potential subjects may decline or postpone an assessment if they are fatigued, ill, or depressed; yet those might be the very dimensions that are being measured. (This problem is most marked if the instrument requires observations or asks about the last day or two, less so if the respondent is asked to reflect back over a longer period in the recent past.) For community surveys, it may be that scheduling the interview at the convenience of the respondent, although necessary, affects the data.

Most of these questions affecting intertemporal reliability are amenable to empirical investigation, but such studies are laborious to execute and not particularly attractive to fund.

Validity

Reliability, of course, is a necessary component of validity; on that score alone, many of our multidimensional measures are on shaky ground. Reliability, on the other hand, is not in itself sufficient for validity. The classic example involves highly reliable judgments about the social well-being of nursing-home patients made by attendants who have firmly held biases about a patient or family. Here the high reliability is due to the presence of stereotyped ideas about the capabilities and characteristics of the patients.

Validity testing of multidimensional measures presents a paradox. The rationale for multidimensional measures is the advantage of more-comprehensive data in order to provide more-comprehensive care. Yet our supreme test of truth for such instruments has tended to be the extent to which they emulate the very clinical judgment that they are designed to improve. Validation against clinical judgments has worked best in terms of mental-health measures. It is less satisfactory in the areas of physical health, pain and discomfort, or functional abilities. In the social area, validation against clinical judgment seems misguided, considering that the instruments are meant particularly to redress the propensity of office-bound clinicians to ignore social functioning in their evaluations. Comparisons with clinical judgment are perhaps worst in those socioeconomic areas where authorities are unclear as to what specific observations to make from the clinical perspective and are thus even more dependent on the employment of adequate measures.

In the absence of a clinical standard, we rely on predictive validity (for example, the extent to which scores from such instruments can predict the patient's likelihood of entering an institution) or discriminant validity (that is, the ability of one set of scores to tap a domain discrete from other domains tapped by other sets of scores within the overall instrument).

Discriminant validity, however, is open to statistical exploitation. As has already been pointed out in this book, most efforts to derive meaningful scores for individual concepts have depended on statistical analysis. In some cases, items developed or modified from previous instruments are pooled with items specifically derived from clinical experience or intuitively felt to be relevant to the population of immediate concern. The statistical relationships observed among those items are used as a justification for creating new measures. These measures (for example, factor scores) are then labeled to conform with the domain they seem to be tapping. Although in many cases such statistically derived scores may prove practically useful, in other instances they may be little more than statistical artifacts. Although we speak rather glibly of face validity and convergent and discriminate validity, we have too little experience with most of these measures to be confident either that they function effectively in the practical clinical setting or that they have an ability to discriminate among clients with sufficient precision to predict accurately their course over time. Predictive validity is perhaps the best standard of all, with one caveat: Measurement may become a self-fulfilling prophecy with regard to such events as institutional placement unless it is tested by a group independent of those responsible for allocating care.

Validity is threatened when the respondent believes that important decisions will be made or that desired benefits will be allocated on the basis of the information provided. Just as a college application measures the candidate's ability to make a good impression, the responses of the elderly respondent may be an indicator of his or her beliefs about the most personally advantageous response. A very special problem for validity is created in the case of dependent respondents within institutions. In some domains, such as patient satisfaction, valid information may be almost impossible to collect.

We now turn to a dicussion of the four selected instruments. In describing them we will not repeat our discussions of individual sections of these instruments (for example, sections of OARS and PACE) that appeared earlier in the book. Rather, we concentrate on the instruments as composite measures and emphasize in particular the ways in which large amounts of information are collapsed.

Sickness Impact Profile

The Sickness Impact Profile (SIP) is a multidimensional measure designed to measure sickness-related dysfunction in a population. It was initially intended to assess health status as an outcome measure of health care (Bergner et al. 1976b; Gilson et al. 1975); however, it covers a broad range of dimensions within its fourteen categories of items (see table 5-2). Compared with other instruments, it is more nearly an authored work than an anthology.

The scale was developed to be inclusive. Items were culled from the literature and nominated by providers, consumers, and lay persons until no new items could be identified. The revised profile exists in both a long form (235 questions) and a short form (146 questions). Substantial work has gone into developing scales based on equal-appearing intervals (Carter et al. 1976). A panel of twenty-five judges (composed of physicians, nurses, and health-administration students) rated each item for the degree of dysfunction it represented on an eleven-point scale. Further ratings within and across categories and normalizing procedures were used to create scales that could yield both an overall disability score and individual-scale scores for each category. These initial scale values were then tested by independent ratings by 108 prepaid group-practice enrollees stratified by age, sex, and type of membership. Again, there was high reliability of scale values. Correlation between the mean scale values from the two groups was .92; there was a consistent trend across all categories for the consumer

Table 5-2
The Fourteen Behavior Categories in the Sickness Impact Profile

A Social interaction	H Movement of the body
B Ambulation	I Communication
C Sleep and rest	J Pastimes, recreation
D Taking nutrition	K Intellectual function
E Usual daily work	L Family interaction
F Household management	M Emotions, sensations
G Mobility/confinement	N Personal hygiene

Source: W.B. Carter, R.A. Bobbitt, M. Bergner, and B.S. Gilson, "Validation of an Interval Scaling: The Sickness Impact Profile," *Health Services Research* 11(1976): 516-528.

group to assign higher (more-disabled) values than did the professionals. The SIP can be reported as a total score, as a profile score compared with a scale of 100, or as individual category scores.

The SIP was designed for both oral and written administration. It has been subjected to a large series of reliability and validity tests. Initial test-retest data from the early pilot studies on thirty-one nonelderly subjects suggest a reliability of .8 to .88 for the long form. A more-elaborate test-retest reliability study with 119 patients (36 rehabilitation, 22 speech pathology, and 61 outpatients with chronic problems) showed even more encouraging results (Pollard et al. 1976). A variety of replications and comparisons of the long versus the short form and of interviewer versus self-administration (long form only) were made across a twenty-four-hour period. Correlation coefficients for overall scores ranged from .85 (interviewer-administered long form both times) to .95 (self-administered long form and interviewer-administered long form). Individual category correlations ranged from .62 (household management) to .90 (personal hygiene). However, when a more-stringent test of agreement percentage (AP) [number of agreements/(number of agreements + number of disagreements)] was applied, the overall rate was only .50 and the mean AP for each subject was .47. Overall APs for each category ranged from .32 (interaction with family members) to .63 (usual daily work). Looking for effects of age on reliability, the authors concluded that respondent age was not an important factor.

In an effort to establish the validity of the scale, 278 patients drawn from four groups (75 rehabilitation patients, 48 speech and hearing patients, 80 outpatients with chronic disease, and 75 elderly group-practice enrollees[a]) were given the SIP (Bergner et al. 1976a). Corresponding professional groups were then asked to rate each individual and a variety of comparisons were made. Overall the SIP did distinguish the four subgroups of patients in the predicted order (that is, the rehabilitation and speech and hearing inpatients were at higher scores than the outpatients with chronic disease, who, in turn, had higher scores than the group-practice enrollees. When the respondents were asked to give a self-assessment of their own health, the correlation was on the order of .54. Similarly, a self-assessment of their level of dysfunction had a correlation of .52, and a measure of disability drawn from a series of questions in the National Health Interview Study (NHIS) correlated at .61. Assessments of the speech pathology correlated at only .27 and .32 with professional assessments by speech pathologists. Clinical assessment and dysfunction for outpatients with chronic problems correlated at .49 overall, but the correlation coefficient varied inversely with the training of the physician observer.

Although it was not intended particularly as a tool for geriatric populations, the SIP has been used in that context. Abrahams and his colleagues report using ten scales of the SIP (A, B, C, D, G, H, I, K, M, and N) to look for differences over a fifteen-week period among twelve subjects in a nursing-home setting,

---

[a]Sixty-three percent aged 55 to 74 and 17 percent aged 75 and over.

aged 62 to 99 years, who had undergone active psychosocial rehabilitation (Abrahams, Wallach, and Divens 1979). Comparisons of before-and-after scores revealed statistically significant differences in three scales (social interaction, sleep and rest activity, and mobility and confinement). We note with interest that the subscales omitted—E, J, and L—deal with usual daily work, pastimes and recreation, and family interaction, respectively. Although the investigators judged that the SIP items on these subscales were judged inappropriate for an institutionalized population, we maintain that the omitted concepts are among those most relevant to the well-being of nursing-home residents.

OARS Instrument

The OARS instrument is a multidimensional-assessment tool developed to fulfill at least three separate functions. It was intended to be useful for the clinician, for the researcher, and for the program analyst. The initial version, often referred to as the community-survey questionnaire (CSQ), was modified and shortened to produce the multidimensional functional-assessment questionnaire (MFAQ). The revised questionnaire contains 105 questions and is designed to be administered in approximately one hour.[b] The questionnaire yields information about functional activity in five domains:

1. *Social resources:* Quantity and quality of relationships with friends and family; availability of care in time of need.
2. *Economic resources:* Adequacy of income and resources.
3. *Mental health:* Extent of psychiatric well-being; presence of organicity.
4. *Physical health:* Presence of physical disorders; participation in physical activities.
5. *ADL:* Capacity to perform various instrumental and physical (or bodily care) tasks that permit individuals to live independently.

From the responses to the questions in each domain, a rater (either the interviewer or an independent, trained rater) makes a judgment of the functional status in each dimension along a six-point scale where 1 = excellent functioning and 6 = totally impaired. These five ratings (one for each domain) can then be combined in a variety of ways. The six-point scale can be collapsed to a dichotomous scale where individuals rated 1 to 3 are considered to be functioning adequately and those rated 4 to 6 are considered to be impaired for that dimension. A cumulative impairment score (CIS) can be derived by adding the

---

[b]Training and technical assistance in the use of the OARS instrument is available from the staff of the Older Americans Resources and Services Group, Duke University Center for the Study of Aging & Human Development, Durham, North Carolina, 27710.

impairment points for each of the five domains to yield a range from 5 (no impairment on any dimension) to 30 (all dimensions totally impaired).

In another study of a community population, the Cleveland GAO study (U.S. Comptroller General 1977), an overall assessment of well-being was developed with eight intervals from unimpaired to extremely impaired. (The Cleveland categories are shown in table 5-3). Yet another way of arraying the MFAQ data is to display the various combinations of dichotomous patterns (impaired, unimpaired) for each of the five variables. Such a display results in 2^5 or 32 different possible combinations. Because of the various ways in which data from this instrument can be combined, it offers versatility but also great confusion. Careful interpretation is required to determine the basis for the specific combination of ratings. Moreover, it is important to appreciate that, whatever the scaling used, the measures of impairment are derived from ratings based on judgments of either the interviewer or an independent rater. No explicit rules for aggregating answers to particular questions have been used.

Reliability

The studies on the reliability and validity of the OARS instrument were done on the larger parent instrument. In a examination of test-retest reliability, thirty

Table 5-3
OARS Impairment Classification Schema Used in Cleveland GAO Study

Unimpaired:
  Excellent or good in all five areas of human functioning.
Slightly impaired:
  Excellent or good in four areas.
Mildly impaired:
  Mildly or moderately impaired in two areas, or mildly or moderately impaired in one area and severely or completely impaired in another.
Moderately impaired:
  Mildly or moderately impaired in three areas, or mildly or moderately impaired in two and severely or completely impaired in one.
Generally impaired:
  Mildly or moderately impaired in four areas.
Greatly impaired:
  Mildly or moderately impaired in three areas, and severely and completely impaired in another.
Very greatly impaired:
  Mildly or moderately impaired in all five areas.
Extremely impaired:
  Mildly or moderately impaired in four areas and severely or completely impaired in the other, or severely or completely impaired in two or more areas.

Source: W.F. Laurie, "The Cleveland Experience: Functional Status and Services Use," in *Multidimensional Functional Assessment: The OARS Methodology*, Duke University Center for the Study of Aging and Human Development (Durham, N.C.: Duke University, 1978).

community residents described as representative of those aged 65 and over in the Durham area were retested over a three- to six-week interval (mean = five weeks). One-third had experienced a major event in the interim. These reinterviews provided 240 pairs of discrete items. In some cases, scale-score differences of one point on three-point or greater scales were considered equivalent if the investigators felt that no real distinctions were being blurred. Some of the item pairs consisted of scale scores and some of individual items. Of the 240 pairs of items, 92 percent of the responses were identical, and changes were noted in 11 percent of the subjective and 7 percent of the objective items. The correlation coefficient for each domain ranged from .32 for mental health to .82 for physical health and ADL.

A test of inter-rater reliability of the ratings was done with data from seventeen community-survey questionnaires. Eight of the questionnaires were rated by ten different raters and nine by eight raters. The coefficient of concordance ranged from a low of .38 for economic resources to a high of .88 for physical health; all correlations were .65 or better with the exception of the one already cited. Disagreements that would result in a different placement in an impaired category (ratings 4 to 6), as opposed to an unimpaired category (ratings 1 to 3), occurred only about 7 percent of the time.

Intra-rater reliability was assessed by having the eight CSQs rerated twelve to eighteen months later by seven of the original ten raters. The product–moment correlation for these ratings ranged from .47 to 1.0; the majority had correlations greater than .85.

Validity

Validation of the OARS instrument took a variety of forms. At the most-basic level, the authors claim consensual validity on the basis that the instrument contains only those items on which experts agreed. More-active attempts to establish validity included a comparison of ratings derived from the instrument with clinical interview data. A research technician interviewed twenty-two clients using the OARS instrument. The same clients were then interviewed in a clinical situation by seven clinicians (social workers and psychiatrists). The clinicians rated the data derived from the instruments for all patients, including both those they did and those they did not personally interview. The clinicians' ratings were compared with their own clinical assessments using paired T-tests. The only statistically significant difference was that the clinicians identified a poorer level of ADL functioning than did their ratings based on the OARS form.

A subset drawn from a large community sample was reinterviewed using the CSQ and then examined by relevant professionals to compare professional judgments with the ratings derived from the CSQ. This study included eighty-two clients. They were seen by ten different psychiatrists to assess their mental functioning clinically and by four physician assistants to assess their physical functioning. The psychiatrists had also rated some of the CSQ data. The Spearman rank-order correlations for the agreement between the psychiatrists' clinical assessment and the mental-functioning section of the CSQ was .62. For physical functioning, the correlation was .70.

The validity of the OARS instrument is argued on the basis of its ability to discriminate among different populations. Information in table 5-4 compares data drawn from a random sample of 997 community residents aged 65 and over, 98 consecutive clients aged 50 and over referred to the clinic because of age-related problems, and a random sample of 102 persons aged 65 and older living in institutions. The authors claim discriminate validity by the comparison of means for the three populations. They demonstrate the expected progressive direction, where the community residents would be the most functional and the institutional residents the least.

The OARS questionnaire provides information on functioning and services. Questions about services cover both a set of prescriptions for services needed and a description of services actually received by the individual. A set of twenty-four generic classes of services was developed, as shown in table 5-5. These service categories were used in the Cleveland GAO study (U.S. Comptroller General 1977). Although no formal reliability or validity studies have been conducted, the authors report good provider acceptance of the categories. The interviewers in the Cleveland study reported no problems in applying these categories. Efforts to compare data from agency records with those from individual-client reports are described as having produced "satisfactory" agreements in the Cleveland study.

Table 5-4
Comparison of OARS Ratings on Five Dimensions for Community, Clinic, and Institutionalized Subjects

	Community		Clinic		Institution	
	Mean	Standard Deviation	Mean	Standard Deviation	Mean	Standard Deviation
Social resources	2.24	1.00	3.26	1.18	4.20	1.13
Economic resources	2.79	1.08	2.91	1.02	3.26	.84
Mental health	2.79	1.06	4.13	.87	4.53	1.22
Physical health	3.04	1.02	3.60	.91	3.74	.98
ADL	2.36	1.42·	3.64	1.48	5.31	.91
N	997[a]		98		102	

Source: Extrapolated from G.G. Fillenbaum, "Validity and Reliability of the Multidimensional Functional Assessment Questionnaire," in *Multidimensional Functional Assessment: The OARS Methodology*, Duke University Center for the Study of Aging and Human Development (Durham, N.C.: Duke University, 1978).

[a]Because of insufficient data, some subjects did not receive ratings. The number receiving ratings was: social, 980; economic, 971; mental, 970; physical, 994; ADL, 996.

Table 5-5
OARS Categories of Services

Service	Unit of Measure
A. *Basic maintenance services*	
Transportation	Passenger round trips
Food, groceries	Dollars
Living quarters (housing)	Dollars
B. *Supportive services*	
Personal-care services	Contact hours
Continuous supervision	
Checking services	
Meal preparation	Meals
Homemaker-household services	Hours
Administrative, legal, and protective services	Hours
C. *Remedial services*	
Social/recreational services	Sessions
Employment services	Number of times such assistance was provided
Sheltered employment	Hours of employment
Educational services, employment related	Training session hours
Remedial training	Sessions
Mental-health services	Sessions
Psychotropic drugs	
Nursing care	Contact hours
Medical services	Number of visits
	Drugs: Dollars
	Procedures: Dollars
Supportive devices and prostheses	Dollars
Physical therapy	Sessions
Relocation and placement services	Moves
Systematic multidimensional evaluation	Number of hours spent in evaluation
Financial assistance	Dollars
Coordination, information, and referral services	Hours

Source: Duke University Center for the Study of Aging and Human Development, *Multidimensional Functional Assessment: The OARS Methodology* (Durham, N.C.: Duke University, 1978), app. B.

The OARS approach is amenable to streamlining. Pfeiffer's Functional Assessment Inventory is a thirty-minute version of the OARS instrument that nevertheless contains the same key components and yields ratings on the same five domains. In a test of the Functional Assessment Inventory with clients in four different service settings (that is, nursing homes, adult congregate-living facilities, adult day-care programs, and senior centers), the instrument yielded different profiles for the four groups with variation in the expected direction (Pfeiffer, Johnson, and Chiofolo 1980). The shorter instrument seemed to be well received, with refusal rates held to 10 percent. As in the case of the longer OARS instrument, the authors indicate that reliability and validity cannot be assumed unless users undergo training.[c]

CARE Instrument

As its title suggests, the Comprehensive Assessment and Referral Evaluation (CARE) instrument was designed as a tool to replicate clinical judgments. It was developed for the United States–United Kingdom Cross-National Project, which was attempting to measure the functioning of elderly community residents in two cultures. The American developers were associated with the New York State Psychiatric Institute.

CARE uses a semistructured-interview guide to be administered by well-trained interviewers. It contains both discrete items and an inventory of defined ratings that taps psychiatric, medical, nutritional, economic, and social problems. It has been carefully and deliberately organized to utilize a style and flow that was constructed to maintain participation of geriatric patients in a relatively lengthy interview. The authors estimate that the average length of an interview is approximately ninety minutes, but describe a range of forty-five minutes to two and one-half hours. The instrument includes self-report items, specific test items, observation items, and global-judgment items. It was designed to generate data that could replicate clinical syndromes, as well as to provide information on functional levels of activity.

The initial purpose of the CARE technique was to generate a set of cross-national comparative longitudinal data about urban-community residents in New York and London. However, it was also intended to provide a method to examine changes in symptoms, complaints, and functioning over time in order to assess the effectiveness of therapy and to provide a basis by which multidisciplinary teams could use a common data base to share their assessments and examine their effectiveness. As shown in figure 5-1, the instrument reflects a strong psychiatric concern.

The mental-status schedule is largely derived from two earlier instruments: the Measure of Present Psychiatric State developed by Wing et al. (1967) and the Mental Status Schedule of Spitzer et al. (1967). The resulting Geriatric Mental Status Schedule was derived from a number of clinical and statistical manipulations, including the addition of a specific mental-status questionnaire, the Bender Face–Hand Test, and a number of items deemed clinically appropriate for elderly psychiatric patients. To this psychiatrically oriented battery then were added a specific medical segment and a social segment. These several

---

[c]Information about training for the abbreviated OARS instrument is available from Dr. Eric Pfeiffer, Division of Geriatric Psychiatry, 12901 North 30th Street, Tampa, Florida 33612.

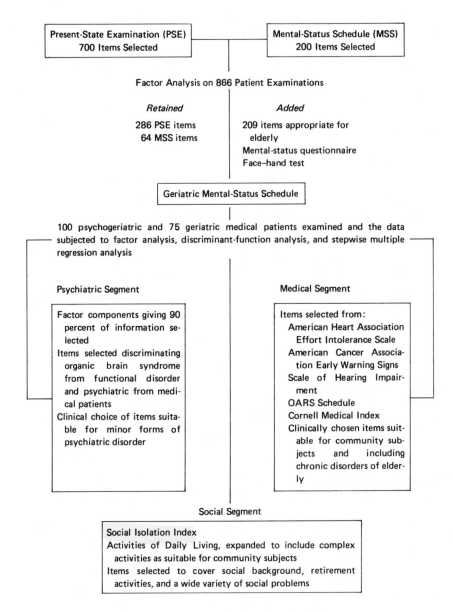

Source: B. Gurland, J. Kuriansky, L. Sharpe, R. Simon, P. Stiller, and P. Birkett, "The Comprehensive Assessment and Referral Evaluation (CARE)—Rationale, Development and Reliability: Part II. A Factor Analysis," *International Journal of Aging and Human Development* 8(1977):9–42.

Figure 5-1. Development Steps Taken to Produce the CARE

segments have been highly integrated to produce a naturally flowing interview that consists of a core set of mandatory items and a subset of contingent items that are used to elucidate information triggered by the responses to the mandatory items. The actual distribution of items is shown in table 5-6. It is noted that these include both specific questions and ratings made by the interviewer. They have been organized under the three types of information—self-report or test items, observations, and global ratings—and across three categories of problem ratings. It is further noted that, in several instances, the same item can be used to cover more than one problem area.

The authors of the CARE instrument take pains to emphasize the desirability of organizing the interview in such a way as to reduce stress for both the interviewer and the interviewee. The CARE instrument has been constructed to be as interesting and understandable to the interviewee as possible and to avoid any embarrassment arising from sustained failure at specific tasks such as cognitive functions. These items are thus scattered throughout the interview. Similarly, obvious questions regarding psychiatric symptoms are merged with those concerning medical symptoms or with questions about social problems. The way that this has been achieved in the CARE instrument is illustrated in table 5-7 (Gurland et al 1977), which provides a listing of the topic areas covered and the order in which they appear.

At present, the scores from the CARE instrument have been derived in several ways. Some represent global judgments made by the interviewer on the basis of clinically intuitive combinations of items; others used semistructured guidelines within which the interviewee is rated. The development team is

Table 5-6
CARE Items

Problem Areas	Self-Report/Test		Observation Ratings	Global Ratings
	Questions	Ratings		
Psychiatric		252	79	
Medical/physical/ nutritional		272	57	
Social		265	39	
Total	565(280)[a]	731(368)[b]	81[b]	30[b]
Number of Duplications		58	74	

Source: Extrapolated from B. Gurland, J. Kuriansky, L. Sharpe, R. Simon, D. Stiller, and P. Birkett, "The Comprehensive Assessment and Referral Evaluation (CARE)—Rationale, Development and Reliability: Part II. A Factor Analysis," *International Journal of Aging and Human Development* 8(1977):9–42, table 1, figure 6.

[a]Figure includes mandatory and contingent items; latter in parentheses. Totals do not add up because of duplicate counting.

[b]Duplications; one item may touch on more than one problem area.

Table 5-7
A General List of the Topic Areas in CARE, in the Order in Which They Appear

Identifying data/Dementia I: Census type data/country of origin/race/length of time spoken English

Dementia II: Error in length of residence/telephone number
General enquiries about main problems
Worry/depression/suicide/self-deprecation
Elation
Anxiety/fear of going out/infrequency of excursions
Referential and paranoid ideas
Household arrangement/loneliness
Family and friendly relationships/present- and past-isolation index/closeness
Emergency assistance
Anger/family burden on subject
Obsessions/thought reading
Weight/appetite/digestion/difficulties in shopping and preparing food/dietary intake/ alcohol intake
Sleep disturbance
Depersonalization

Dementia III: Subjective and objective difficulty with memory/tests of recall
Fits and faints/autonomic functions/bowel and bladder
Slowness and anergia/restlessness
Self-rating of health
Fractures and operations/medical and nonmedical/attention/examinations/medicines or drugs/drug addiction
Arthritis/aches and pains
Breathlessness/smoking/heart disease/hypertension/chest pain/hoarseness/fevers
Limitation in mobility/care of feet/limitation of exertion/simple tests of motor function
Sores, growths, discharges/strokes/hospitalization and bed rest
Hearing/auditory hallucinations
Vision/visual hallucinations
Hypochondriasis
Disfigurement/antisocial behavior
Loss of interests/activities list
History of depression
Organizations and religion/educational and occupational history
Work and related problems/retirement history
Income/health insurance/medical and other expenses/handling of finances/shortages
Housing facilities and related problems
Ability to dress/do chores/help needed or received
Neighborhood and crime
Overall self-rating of satisfaction/happiness/insight
Mute/stuporous/abnormalities of speech
Additional observations of subject and environment/communication difficulties

Source: Extrapolated from B. Gurland, J. Kuriansky, L. Sharpe, R. Simon, D. Stiller, and P. Birkett, "The Comprehensive Assessment and Referral Evaluation (CARE)–Rationale, Development and Reliability: Part II. A Factor Analysis," *International Journal of Aging and Human Development* 8(1977):9–42, table 1, figure 6.

currently pursuing statistical approaches to developing factor scores for still other items.

The reliability of the several sections of the instrument has been tested in various ways. An early test was performed on the 1974 version of the instrument. In that test, four interviewers (two psychiatrists and two social scientists) each interviewed two female patients. The remaining three interviewers rated the videotape of each interview, thus providing four ratings of eight patients. Six ad hoc dimensions were identified—two each from the psychiatric, medical, and socioeconomic domains. A score for each of these six dimensions was established by summing the number of positive responses. Table 5-8 summarizes the inter-rater-reliability coefficients from such a comparison of ratings only. Levels of agreement with the psychiatric dimensions tended to be good, agreement with the medical/physical dimensions relatively poor, and agreement with the social dimensions acceptable.

Work originally went into the tests of reliability and validity of the geriatric mental-state schedule from which CARE was partly derived. In a comparison of twenty consecutive hospital admissions using the schedule to generate a four-digit ICDA diagnostic code, when the interviewer's rating was compared to that of someone observing the interview, there was complete agreement in twelve cases and at least partial agreement in seventeen cases. When the results of the initial interview were compared with those of an independent second interview, there was complete agreement in eleven cases and partial agreement in seventeen.

Table 5-8
Mean Inter-rater Reliability Correlations from 1974 CARE Study

Psychiatric dimensions	
Memory disorientation (21 items)	.88
Depression-anxiety (48 items)	.92
Medical-physical dimensions	
Immobility-incapacity (19 items)	.48
Physical-perceptual difficulty (41 items)	.61
Social dimensions	
Isolation (24 items)	.72
Poor housing-income (15 items)	.79

Source: Extrapolated from B. Gurland, J. Kuriansky, L. Sharpe, R. Simon, D. Stiller, and P. Birkett, "The Comprehensive Assessment and Referral Evaluation (CARE)—Rationale, Development and Reliability: Part II. A Factor Analysis," *International Journal of Aging and Human Development* 8(1977):9–42, table 1, figure 6.

The second study, done in both the United Kingdom and the United States on twelve and ten patients, respectively, using a more-definitive version of the interview schedule and comparing only interviewer and observer ratings, found complete agreement in 38 percent of the U.K. patients and 35 percent of the U.S. patients, and at least principal-category agreement in 73 percent and 69 percent, respectively (Copeland et al. 1976).

When individual items were studied, the interitem correlations for the initial 20 percent comparing observer and interviewer was .73; for interview/reinterview, the correlation fell to .48. For the pool of U.S./U.K. patients, the mean correlation between observer and interviewer was .71. Using a more-stringent test of agreement (the Kappa statistic), which in turn was weighted for the seriousness of the discrepancy, the investigators found a marked difference in the rate of agreement between ratings and independently derived information, as shown in table 5-9. The reports on items in the main body of the schedule were generally consistent when those of the observer were compared with those of the interviewer, but much less so when data from two independent interviews were compared. The overall rate of agreement was reduced by the relatively low level of agreement on items dealing with the patient's behavior, appearance, and speech.

In the main, most of the claims for validity of the measures have been addressed to the basic validity of the sources from which the items within the CARE instrument were derived. Claims were also made for face validity on the basis of expert review. For the geriatric mental-state schedule, an effort was made to establish validity by comparing the results of diagnostic classifications derived from the schedule to thirty geriatric patients and comparing those results with the diagnosis obtained after a more-complete psychiatric history was obtained independently. In 20 percent of the cases there was a change in diagnosis; 7 percent of these changes occurred within the first three digits of the ICDA diagnostic code.

Table 5-9
Weighted Kappa Scores (for Seriousness of Discrepancy for Geriatric Mental State Schedule [CARE])

	Main Part of Schedule	Behavior, Appearance, and Speech	All Items
Interviewer-observer	.84	.46	.78
Interview-reinterview	.48	.34	.45

Source: Adapted J.R.M. Copeland, M.J. Kelleher, J.M. Kellett, and A.J. Gomlay, with B.J. Gurland, J.L. Freiss, and L. Sharpe," A Semi-Structured Clinical Interview in the Elderly: The Geriatric Mental State Schedule: I. Development and Reliability," *Psychological Medicine* 6(1976):439–449.

In a test of a variant of the CARE instrument (the INCARE system intended for institutionalized persons), the validity of the performance of the activities of daily living (PADL) was tested. The results on 100 consecutive admissions to psychiatric wards in New York and London suggested that the PADL corresponded much more closely to the report of a knowledgeable informant than did patient self-report of functioning. More importantly, the PADL measures predicted a favorable outcome of hospitalization more effectively than did either the patient's self-report or the informant report (Kuriansky et al. 1976).

Patient Appraisal and Care Evaluation (PACE)

The assessment system generally known by the acronym PACE has gone through a number of iterations in its evolution. The original work was undertaken by a consortium of four universities (Case Western Reserve University Medical School, Harvard University, Johns Hopkins University School of Hygiene and Public Health, and Syracuse University Research Corporation). In the early 1970s this group developed the Patient Classification Form (PCF), which was intended to serve various ends: managing individual patients, administration of long-term care within the institution and within the community, policymaking, epidemiologic research, and education.

The items or patient descriptors were chosen to be patient oriented, multidimensional, objective (rather than subjective or interpretive), and relevant in terms of their significance for patient outcomes. The PCF has been criticized on the ground that these descriptors, shown in table 5-10, underrepresent psychosocial components. The PCF offered a uniform terminology for long-term care and a method by which standardized coverage of materials could lead to more-consistent decisions about patients. No specific scoring algorithms were developed, although a coding system for each of the items was prepared. The classification system was to be used in multidisciplinary-team conferences for patient-care planning in which decisions about appropriate placement of individuals and review of their progress could be made (Jones, McNitt, and McKnight 1974; Abdellah 1978).

A subsequent version of the PACE system, referred to alternatively as PACE II or Patient Care Management (PCM), evolved from the PCF. As shown in table 5-11, the purposes of the PCM were slightly different from those of the PCF. More emphasis was placed on quality-of-care assessment and client placement and less on the more-academic goals of epidemiologic research, education, and policymaking. The basic components of the PCM system build on those of the PCF, with several additions (see table 5-12). Although more attention is paid to the psychosocial factors (including the client's adjustment and social interaction, as well as specific behaviors), the emphasis remains medical. PACE II does not contain enough psychosocial data to guide a community-placement decision. A patient-care section identifies the need for a variety of nursing

Table 5–10
PCF Classification Descriptors

Identifying and sociodemographic items:
    Date of classification
    Interviewer or classifier
    Program or project identification
    Patient's record or study number
    Social-security number or health-insurance-benefit number
    Birth date
    Birthplace
    Sex
    Race
    Marital status
    Religious preference
    Residence address
    Patient's location at time of assessment
    Length of time at location
    Usual living arrangements
    Number of living children
    Education
    Usual occupation
    Employment status
    Total family income
    Health-care coverage

Functioning-status items:
    Mobility level
    Transferring
    Walking
    Wheeling
    Stair climbing
    Bathing
    Dressing
    Eating/feeding
    Toileting
    Bowel function
    Bladder function
    Communication of needs
    Orientation as to place, time, person
    Behavior pattern

Impairment items:
    Sight impairment
    Hearing impairment
    Speech impairment
    Fractures and dislocations
    Joint motion disorders
    Joint pain and swelling
    Dentition
    Missing limbs
    Paralysis/paresis

Medical status—risk factor measurements:
    Height
    Weight
    Blood pressure
    Blood cholesterol
    Kidney function measurement: BUN

Table 5-10 (continued)

Medical status (continued)
    Albuminuria
    Cigarette smoking
Certain medically defined conditions:[a]
    Alcoholism
    Anemia
    Angina and/or myocardial infarction
    Arthritis
    Cardiac arrhythmias
    Congestive heart failure
    Diabetes mellitus
    Drug abuse
    Hypertension
    Malignancy
    Mental illness
    Neurologic disorders
    Respiratory disease, chronic

Source: Adapted from E. Jones, B. McNitt, and E. McKnight, *Patient Classification for Long-Term Care: User's Manual*, DHEW Publ. No. HRA 75-3107 (Washington, D.C.: U.S. Government Printing Office, 1974).

Table 5-11
Comparison of PACE I (PCF) and PACE II (PCM)

	PCF (PACE I)	*PCM (PACE II)*
Purposes:	1. Individual-patient care	1. Individual-client data
	2. Resource management with institution or program	2. Resource management and resource allocation
	3. Community-resource allocation	3. Quality of care–appropriateness and outcomes
	4. Policymaking for LTC; program planning and evaluation	4. Appropriate client placement and continuity of care
	5. Epidemiologic research on course of illness	
	6. Education and training of professionals and others for LTC field	
Components:	1. Identifying and sociodemographic items	1. Admission data
	2. Functional-status items	2. Functional capacity
	3. Impairments	3. Impairment record
	4. Medical-risk factors	4. Medical data
	5. Medically defined conditions	5. Patient-care data

Table 5-12
PCM (PACE II) Classification Descriptors

Admission data
   Provider identification
   Client identification
   Provider location
   Provider type
   Date of latest admission to provider
   Date of first admission to provider
   Date of latest discharge from provider
   Number of prior admission(s) to provider
   Last principal provider
   Physician's prognosis on admission
Demographic data
   Date of birth
   Sex
   Race/ethnicity
   Current marital status
   Usual residence
   Residence location
   Usual living arrangement
   Court-ordered constraints
Psychosocial factors
   Client's adjustment to care plan
   Client's social interaction and adjustment
      to facility
   Behavioral problems
Medical data
   Medically defined conditions
      Neoplasms
      Endocrine, nutritional metabolic
         diseases and immunity disorders
      Disease of the blood and blood-
         forming organs
      Organic psychotic conditions
      Other psychotic conditions
      Neurotic personality disorders
      Mental retardation, mild
      Mental retardation, moderate
      Mental retardation, severe
      Mental retardation, profound
      Mental retardation, level unspecified
      Diseases of the nervous system and
         sense organs
      Stroke, including late effects
      Atherosclerosis
      Diseases of the circulatory system other
         than stroke and atherosclerosis
      Diseases of the respiratory system
      Diseases of the digestive system
      Diseases of the genitourinary system
      Diseases of the skin and subcutaneous
         tissue
      Diseases of the musculoskeletal system
         and connective tissue

Patient care
   Special procedures
      General nursing care
      Rehabilitation/restorative
      Teaching
      Psychosocial
   Professional visits
      Attending physician
      Consultant physician
      Dentist
      Optometrist/ophthalmologist
      Audiologist/speech pathologist
      Psychologist
      Podiatrist
      Other
   Medications
Discharge data
   Date of discharge
   Status on discharge
   Discharged to:

Medical data (cont'd)
   Impairments
      Skin
         Decubitus ulcer
         Skin abnormalities
      Extremities and trunk
         Missing limbs
         Prosthesis
         Hip prosthesis
         Fracture
         Dislocations
      Sensory/communication status
         Vision
         Hearing
      Expressive communication
      Receptive communication
      Bowel and bladder status
   Physical function
      Upper extremities
      Lower extremities
      Head and trunk
   Strength, balance, and coordination
   Activities of daily living
      Mobility
         Goes outside
         Walking
         Climbing stairs
         Transferring
         Wheeling

Table 5-12 (continued)

Medically defined conditions (cont'd)	Activities of daily living (cont'd)
Symptoms, signs, and ill-defined conditions	Personal care
	Bathing/showering
Injury and poisoning	Toileting
Other	Dressing
Medical-status measurements	Grooming
Height	Eating
Weight	Dental/oral status
Blood pressure	Nutritional status
Pulse rate	Diet
Respiratory rate	Intake problems
Blood sugar	Output problems
Blood urea nitrogen	Food likes and dislikes
Hemoglobin	
Hematocrit	
Urine albumin, sugar, acetone	
Stool test for occult blood	

Source: Adapted from U.S. Department of Health, Education, and Welfare, *Working Document on Patient Care Management* (Washington, D.C.: U.S. Government Printing Office, 1978a).

procedures, special procedures, rehabilitative and restorative care, teaching, and psychosocial therapies. There is a section for indicating the rate at which the professional attention has been provided to the client. Recording of medication goes beyond the type and frequency of drug to consider side effects, drug interactions, and drug dependence. Medical conditions have been expanded to cover the full range of International Classification of Diseases (ICD-9 CM) categories. The PCM thus represents an expanded version of the PCF, designed to lead the appraisers more directly through the patient-care-planning process.

With both the PCF and PCM, the data gatherers are given general rules with definitions but are left to use a variety of sources from which the data might be collected. These would include records, direct observations, and the patient himself. As with the PCF, no specific scoring algorithms are provided for the PCM. It is intended that teams collectively assess needs and that a set of priorities and treatment goals be established in conjunction with the client and his family to the extent possible.

Because of the nature of the multiple sources of data, no estimates of reliability are possible for either the PCF or the PCM. In a study of seven nursing homes in the Boston area, Densen and his colleagues tested the rate at which PCF data could be abstracted from the several sources and recorded in a reliable fashion (Densen and Jones 1976). They report agreement ratios generally in the range of .95 or better for sociodemographic items. For functional-status items, the agreement ratio ranged from .64 to .98; for impairment items, from .80 to 1.0. For risk-factor measurements, all were better than .85. For visitors and other social contacts, the range was from .52 to .86. A crude test of predictive validity was applied by looking at the survival rates using a life-table analysis for patients according to their status at the time of initial assessment for several variables (see table 5-13). In general, each of the four characteristics (age, ADL status, number of medically defined conditions, and the presence of a diagnosis of cancer) contributed to the overall prediction of mortality in the anticipated direction.

Under funding from the W.K. Kellogg Foundation, Falcone (1978, 1979) has carried out tests of reproducibility using a form based essentially on the PCF. Comparing independent recording for eleven individuals assessed at the time of referral for LTC from three acute-care hospitals, she found high levels of agreement between the two raters, generally on the order of .9 or better. She went on to develop a set of algorithms by which the information from the PCF could be translated into service needs. In this way, Falcone identified twenty assessment items, drawn primarily from the PCF (eighteen PCF items plus medication administration and noninstitutional living space) with which to develop a set of simple algorithms to identify the need for services in specific categories. The assessment items and the corresponding service categories are shown in table 5-14.

A sample of those algorithms is shown in figure 5-2. In that example, dependency in up to one area of activities of daily living is presumed to need no nursing services. Dependency in up to three is presumed to require the assistance of either a lay person or an aide. Dependency in four or more functions would presumably require the services of either a licensed or a professional nurse. Only those patients who needed to be fed intravenously or by clysis would require professional nursing. A similar decision tree was developed for medication administration, as shown in the figure. In that case, the indications for administration by trained individuals tend to drive the model, although persons who need monitoring of drug taking more often than once a week will almost always require either a licensed or a professional nurse. In order to test the accuracy of predictions using the translation model, Falcone used the records from the earlier Densen study and selected a stratified sample of fifty patient records. Ten professionals (five nurses and five social workers) reviewed the PCF data to develop their recommendations for the need for services.

In those cases where there was general agreement among raters as to the need for a service (the exception was housekeeping), the translation model agreed with the recommendation at a high level of statistical significance. Agreement between the translation model and professional judgment was highest for audiology and speech therapy, followed closely by that for emotional and social assessment and treatment, physical therapy, ophthomology and optometry, and nursing service. The linking of data from the PCF (or PCM) to such a decision-making algorithm shows great promise for providing relatively simple assessments in the field. It is currently being tested in a number of additional settings.

Conclusion

In this chapter we presented several models of multidimensional measures. Although these measures have varied in their aspirations, they have consistently demonstrated the types of problems one faces in attempting to compile a broad composite measure. The problems of the whole are not merely equal to the sum of those of the parts. Additional problems are faced in multidimensional measurement.

Perhaps the most-difficult challenge in multidimensional assessment is to choose the appropriate criterion for validation. Each of these measures has been the subject of some effort at validation. In almost every case, the criterion chosen was clinical judgment. Unfortunately, however, clinical judgment in these areas is not well developed. Furthermore, there is evidence of problems in establishing inter-rater reliability even when well-trained and experienced judges are available.

In the last analysis, the choice of a multidimensional instrument or the mixing and matching of existing scales to provide measures across a variety of domains must depend on the purpose of the instrument. Perhaps too many expectations are laid on a single instrument—that it provide a data base; that it yield the information for clinical decision making; that it be useful for monitoring individual change; that it serve as a vehicle for program evaluation; that it illuminate societal trends. These concerns return us to the issues laid out at the beginning of this book, when we explored the appropriate role of measurement in long-term care.

Having reviewed the state of the art, we are left with the practical question of what a practitioner or researcher should do. In the last chapter we draw a distinction between clinical and research assessment and present some criteria for measures in each. We also use the last chapter to examine ways in which assessment data about impairments and resources have been used to develop practical LTC strategies.

Table 5-13
Probabilities of Surviving to Specified Time Periods After Admission to Nursing Homes, for Patients in Selected Categories at Initial Classification

Category[a]	Number of Patients in Category	Probability of Surviving After Admission to:					
		One Month	Two Months	Three Months	Six Months	One Year	Two Years
All patients admitted	1,745	0.815	0.755	n.a.	n.a.	n.a.	n.a.
Patients with initial assessment, total	1,534	0.854	0.792	0.754	0.681	0.602	0.501
Age:							
Under 80 years	813	0.870	0.814	0.773	0.695	0.638	0.562
80 years or over	720[b]	0.836	0.767	0.732	0.664	0.560	0.425
ADL Status:[c]							
A	161	0.950	0.944	0.918	0.847	0.741	0.599[d]
B	53	0.943	0.925	0.867	0.806	0.747	0.747[d]
C	93	0.914	0.892	0.869	0.806	0.762	0.711[d]
D	72	0.912	0.870	0.855	0.825	0.762	0.556[d]
E	325	0.923	0.892	0.865	0.812	0.770	0.685[d]
F	349	0.854	0.786	0.737	0.651	0.558	0.503[d]
G	481	0.744	0.633	0.586	0.498	0.401	0.275[d]
Number of medically defined conditions:							
None	145	0.883	0.819	0.797	0.773	0.658	0.589[d]
1	550	0.862	0.795	0.761	0.701	0.627	0.572[d]
2	529	0.843	0.780	0.740	0.657	0.583	0.451[d]
3 or more	310	0.845	0.796	0.744	0.643	0.564	0.391[d]

Diagnosis of cancer:

All patients with cancer	260	0.746	0.625	0.536	0.397	0.303	0.238[d]
A or B status	35	0.829	0.800	0.655	0.525	0.427	0.284[d]
C, D, or E	70	0.757	0.685	0.625	0.415	0.294[d]	0.294[d]
F or G	155	0.723	0.558	0.468	0.360	0.275	0.193[d]

Source: Adapted from P.M. Densen, *An Approach to the Assessment of Long-Term Care: Final Report* (Boston: Harvard Center for Community Health and Medical Care, 1976).

Note: n.a. = not available

[a] All sub-categories in the table are of patients remaining in nursing homes at least one week and having an initial assessment.

[b] One patient excluded from tabulation in error.

[c] ADL = activities of daily living: bathing, dressing, going to toilet, transferring, continence and feeding. A = no assistance with any of the activities, B = assistance with one, C with 2, D with 3, E with 4, F with 5, and G = assistance with all 6 activities.

[d] Fewer than ten person-months of observation in final month of period.

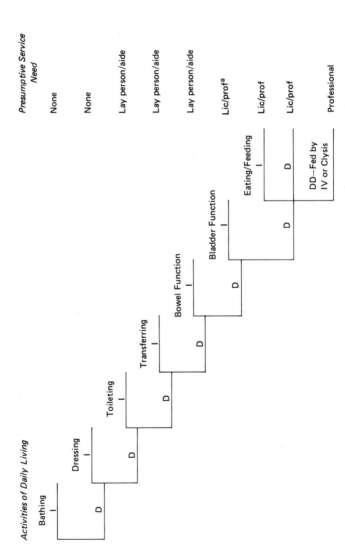

Activities of Daily Living

Presumptive Service Need

I—Independent; D—Dependent; DD—Special case indicating the need for highest level of nursing skill

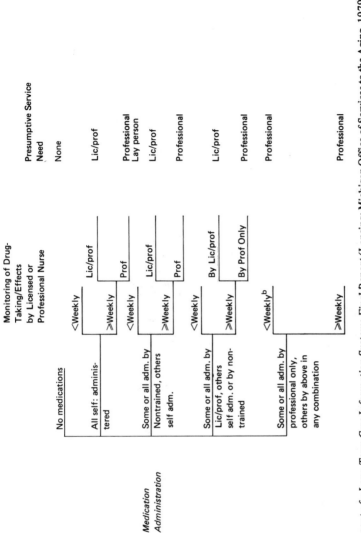

Source: A.R. Falcone, *Development of a Long-Term Care Information System: Final Report* (Lansing: Michigan Office of Services to the Aging, 1979).

[a]Lic/prof refers to the skills of a licensed or professional nurse to perform the service, as distinguished from a professional nurse only. The highest level of nursing skill required is predicted as needed, but it does not negate the need for the services of persons with fewer skills as well, which would be specified in a care plan.

[b]Note that monitoring information for this last category is not required to indicate that professional nursing is needed.

Figure 5–2. Examples of Translation Model Predicting the Need for Nursing Care

Table 5-14
Items in LTCIS Translation Model

Assessment Items	Service Category
Dependency in seven ADL areas (bathing, dressing, transferring, toileting, bowel function, bladder function, eating/ feeding)	Assistance by lay persons/aides Licensed nursing Professional nursing Housekeeping Meal preparation
Medication administration[a]	Licensed or professional nursing
Mobility level	Shopping
Joint motion	Professional nursing or physical therapy
Hip fracture	Physical therapy
Paralysis/paresis	Physical therapy
Missing limbs	Physical therapy
Sight	Ophthalmology/optometry
Hearing	Audiology
Speech	Speech therapy
Dentition	Dental care
Behavior pattern	Supervision by lay persons/aides Emotional and social assessment/ treatment
Orientation	Supervision by lay persons/aides Emotional and social assessment/ treatment
Noninstitutional living space[a]	Home-finding services

[a]Not from Patient Classification Form

Choosing and Using Measurements in Geriatrics: Recommendations and Conclusions

We recognize that at times the level of discussion in this book has been abstract. Often we have been preoccupied with the sometimes subtle threats to validity inherent in the various measures. Occasionally we have gone off on tangents to explore the rationale behind a particular instrument or approach. In this concluding chapter we refocus our attention on the practical needs of geriatric providers—those health and social-service personnel who plan, deliver, or evaluate services. It is they who must answer the "who," "where," "when," "how," "what," and "why" of measurement in long-term care and must emerge, sometimes rather rapidly, prepared to act with the best tools available.

We are also aware that much of this book has been critical. This criticism is directed at the state of the art and not at the many investigators have who taken up the conceptual challenges of developing instruments. It is much easier to criticize measures than to construct them. Despite our criticisms, we strongly support more action within the limits of our knowledge rather than perpetual hesitation at the threshold. At this stage in the practice of geriatrics, more harm is done by failure to measure than by measuring with inadequate instruments. Although users should be aware of the risks associated with various available measures, they should apply the best of those measures despite their inadequacies. This position is no more inconsistent than is advocating the use of the scalpel despite the fact that it is sharp and could injure. Our goal is that newly educated physicians, psychologists, and others who specialize in geriatrics respect the possible pitfalls and dangers of instruments that classify, but that, at the same time, they emerge with a recognition of the importance of systematic measurement as an integral part of their clinical practice.

After reviewing so many instruments, we return to themes raised in the introduction. There we drew distinctions on the basis of the potential user (that is, the geriatric practitioner in a variety of disciplines, the generalist practitioner who deals with clients across a wide age spectrum, the case manager, or the researcher and evaluator); the function of the measurement (screening, description, assessment, monitoring, or prediction); and the focus of analysis (the elderly person or groups of elderly people). The types of information collected, the stringency of the data-collection protocol, the amount of detail required, and the approach to analysis must differ according to the purpose of the instrument, the nature of the target population, and the capabilities of the users.

The implications of these tenets are explored in the following sections.

Clinical Assessment Versus Research Assessment

Commonly, a single instrument is expected to do double or triple duty. This is particularly true when a comprehensive client assessment is designed to serve clinical decision makers, to provide the verdict on the effectiveness of a program, and to offer basic information on longitudinal changes that occur in the dependent elderly. An all-purpose instrument can rarely be produced. For example, evaluators or researchers rightly emphasize data-collection modes that ensure a consistent approach to each patient, uniform recording of information, and standardized rules for interpreting responses. By contrast, flexibility might be encouraged in the clinical settings, allowing practitioners to pursue seemingly relevant items in greater depth and to use whatever interview strategies they judge best to cement a working relationship.

The criteria for an assessment instrument and those for a research instrument differ in a number of ways. Choice of a client-assessment instrument involves the following considerations:

1. The instrument must yield comprehensive information about the client and the client's situation so that it forms the basis for an individualized understanding of the problem areas.
2. It must assist providers in making decisions with and on behalf of a client by providing information about functional abilities and suggesting the etiology of the observed dysfunction and how it might be remedied.
3. It must be sensitive to changes in functional status over time; in long-term care, a change in status may be more important than an actual observation at any one point in time.
4. It must be keyed to thresholds with clinical significance for the client's well-being or independence.
5. It must provide a justifiable way of defining eligibility for services, so that benefits can be applied equitably.
6. It must distinguish sufficiently small increments of change to permit differentiation of functioning at the lower end of the continuum, where slight improvement or worsening might be very significant for the client.
7. It must cover both regular performance and capability. Performance is influenced by motivation and opportunity (for example, in many nursing homes, residents are not permitted to bathe themselves). But a case manager or caregiver needs to determine actual capabilities, apart from environmental constraints, in order to make a plan that permits achievement of functional potential.
8. It must be an acceptable procedure for the client, so that the assessment enhances rather than harms a positive relationship between providers and clients.

9. It must be acceptable to the providers. The purposes of the questions should be clear to them if they are to be motivated to use the instrument. To achieve this end, the instrument should be as streamlined as is consistent with the need for comprehensive data. If the user is a case manager with background in the social-service field, rather than a health specialist, then any health observations or judgments required in the assessment must be feasible for a person of that background.

10. It must not rely on costly on bulky equipment.

11. It requires a branching procedure so that the assessment tool is appropriate for clients whose functional status varies widely without requiring persons to respond to questions that are obviously too difficult, too simple, or inappropriate to their functional or social limitations.

12. It must produce categories of need that satisfy requirements for equity in the initiation and discontinuance of services across clients.

13. The assessment procedures need a branching approach, which permits the case manager to explore areas of particular importance for individual clients. (For example, employment might be important for chronically ill clients of preretirement age.)

14. The assessment package should be supplemented with a brief screening procedure to determine need for full-scale assessment. The initial comprehensive assessment at intake can be streamlined, with branching for reassessments and monitoring procedures that emphasize collection of specific information at specific intervals, depending on the nature of the problem being monitored.

15. Practical decision rules are needed to determine when the client is an appropriate informant and when reliable information on a particular domain needs to be sought elsewhere, especially for that proportion of the population at risk who are cognitively impaired.

In contrast, choice of an instrument for research and evaluation purposes may need to involve some of the following criteria:

1. The tool should minimize judgment and maximize objective indicators of functional status. This is particularly important if the study design is such that caregivers are supplying data about their clientele or if many data collectors will be involved in collecting client-centered information. In both cases, bias due to personal interest of data collectors and inter-rater-reliability problems will be minimized if specific observable indicators are used.

2. Related to the foregoing, the procedures should be free from bias due to data-collector involvement in care and consequent vested interest in the client outcomes.

3. It must assess the client on the dimensions emphasized in the goals of the program or service system. This permits providers to monitor the way specific decisions tie into the overriding goals and to use such information to refine the care process.

4. The procedures should minimize bias due to reliance on clients as informants; if clients' benefit structure or eligibility status is at stake (or is perceived to be jeopardized) as a result of responses, validity is threatened.

5. Consistent procedures should govern the frequency of information gathering, the choice of informant, the time frame used as a reference point, the amount and nature of probing for additional information, the amount of clarification and interpretation of questions, and all aspects of data collection, even including the wording of questions.

6. Data collection should be as unobtrusive as possible, so as not to influence the phenomenon measured.

7. Measures used to evaluate the quality of care through patient outcomes can safely emphasize those outcomes without consideration of etiology (if the case mix is equivalent). For example, if a desired outcome of a particular program is patient self-care, this can be measured and compared with findings for a control group without finding out whether the failure to perform is due to incapacity, poor motivation, lack of opportunity, or institutional regulations.

8. Items measured for research or program evaluation must have stability over time. If, for instance, affect is so unstable for some segment of the LTC population that it changes on a weekly basis, then it may be inappropriate for inclusion as an outcome measure for a study with infrequent data collection. It is all too possible that a "before" measure would capture one mood and an "after" measure capture the opposite mood; therefore, neither measure would describe the habitual state of the client.

9. Scales used should generate good variance for the subject population.

10. Client measures used for studying the quality of care or the quality of life in an LTC program should focus on actual performance rather than on hypothetical capabilities. For example, if institutional rules prohibit self-care, then the nonperformance rather than the inherent ability of the patient is the important variable.

Figure 6-1 summarizes clinical and research requirements for LTC measurements. As the figure indicates, reliable, valid, and practical tools are always wanted, regardless of whether they are to be used for clinical or for research purposes. The distinctions are a matter of emphasis and priority rather than clear-cut differences.

The conflict occurs when, as often happens, a clinical-assessment tool is developed and is then used for program evaluation as well as for clinical decision-making. This is an inherently attractive strategy because duplicate information

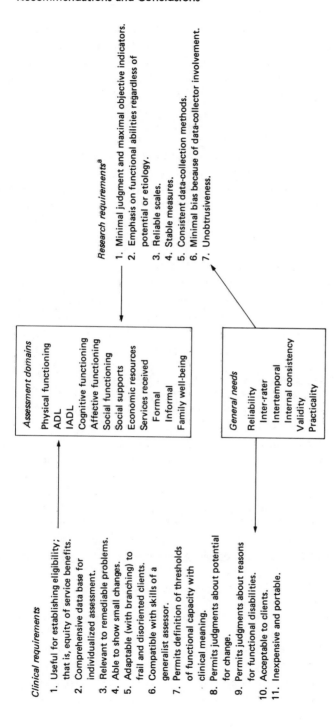

Clinical requirements

1. Useful for establishing eligibility; that is, equity of service benefits.
2. Comprehensive data base for individualized assessment.
3. Relevant to remediable problems.
4. Able to show small changes.
5. Adaptable (with branching) to frail and disoriented clients.
6. Compatible with skills of a generalist assessor.
7. Permits definition of thresholds of functional capacity with clinical meaning.
8. Permits judgments about potential for change.
9. Permits judgments about reasons for functional disabilities.
10. Acceptable to clients.
11. Inexpensive and portable.

Assessment domains

Physical functioning
ADL
IADL
Cognitive functioning
Affective functioning
Social functioning
Social supports
Economic resources
Services received
Formal
Informal
Family well-being

General needs

Reliability
Inter-rater
Intertemporal
Internal consistency
Validity
Practicality

Research requirements[a]

1. Minimal judgment and maximal objective indicators.
2. Emphasis on functional abilities regardless of potential or etiology.
3. Reliable scales.
4. Stable measures.
5. Consistent data-collection methods.
6. Minimal bias because of data-collector involvement.
7. Unobtrusiveness.

Figure 6-1. Schematic Presentation of Criteria for Assessment Instrument for Case Management and Evaluation

[a]for those variables used in evaluation.

gathering is inefficient. A virtue is sometimes made of this necessity; some suggest that practitioners can be motivated to collect high-quality data routinely for the sake of research. Yet surely measurement in clinical practice is necessary to document change in individuals and does not require additional justification. Equating systematic data collection with an external research purpose can be counterproductive; such data may be collected casually and readily ignored. Certainly the quality of data is often compromised when they are collected by busy clinicians with other agendas.

In quasi-experimental or experimental studies that compare program clients to untreated controls, the strategy may be to use the existing clinically derived data to describe the experimental group, whereas the control-group information is collected by an evaluator. Frequently, all the information generated from a detailed management-information system is evoked to describe the experimental group. This situation complicates the interpretation of results because the two sources of data are not comparable. In the clinical context, observations of the treatment group are made by observers who are in a good position to verify and amplify information at a frequency demanded by the clinical needs. Even if the clinician makes formal measurements at intervals dictated by research protocols, he can neither readily ignore the detail gleaned through the service relationship nor avoid being influenced by that relationship. In contrast, the research-data collector is limited to the timing and method of observation permitted by the research protocol. For clinical purposes, all information should be used, regardless of source and timing; but for research purposes, any differences between experimental and control groups must be real differences rather than artifacts of the measurement process.

A specialized problem occurs when a case-management program is being evaluated. Case management is a rational service-delivery approach that includes screening, comprehensive multidimensional assessment, case planning based on assessed resources and needs, and implementation of coordinated care. A comprehensive assessment is thus a pivotal process in case management; in itself, the assessment is designed to highlight remediable problems for both provider and consumer. But in some evaluation designs, the assessment is both an independent variable being tested for effectiveness and the source of information about the dependent variable—for instance, functional abilities, affect, satisfaction. We encounter a pardox: If one dismisses the effect of assessment, then what is the treatment being studied? If one hypothesizes that a comprehensive assessment is a powerful change agent, then the experiment is compromised if the same assessment is offered to a control group. The mere act of participating in a detailed assessment may suggest to a respondent the nature of problems and possible solutions. Yet, as already stated, bias is introduced if the information used for a control group is less detailed than that for an experimental group.

The best solution to this dilemma is to use clinically generated data for clinical purposes and to collect evaluative data independently on both experimental and control-group members. These latter data may be limited to a few well-chosen measurable variables that might be markers of functional status in each domain. If separate evaluation data cannot be gathered, then another strategy is to select for evaluation purposes a subset of measures and scales composed of specific and observable items. Experimental and control groups could be compared on those selected variables alone. This method is less satisfactory because it does not eliminate potential invalidity resulting from the relationship between provider and client. Independent observers, however, could validate the measures on a sample of the experimental group.

Clinical Assessment, Screening, and Monitoring

Just as distinctions between measurement for research and those for clinical purposes are required, so too are distinctions among various types of clinical measurement. Again, the purpose of the measurement suggests the selection criteria. In geriatrics and LTC today, the salutary emphasis on multidimensional assessment has come at the cost of some oversimplification and perhaps overroutinization of the process. As the previous chapter suggested, developing a multidimensional-assessment tool is painstaking and slow; perhaps this accounts for the tendency to make a single tool fit multiple purposes of screening, assessment, and monitoring. This practice is wasteful at best and, at worst, misleading.

Screening

Screening itself has at least two distinct purposes, which are easily confused and which have implications for the screening tools. It is imperative to distinguish between screening for case finding and screening for population descriptions. The two forms of screening require different strategies for sampling, for choosing tests, and for interpreting results.

When the purpose is to describe the population, a representative sample is needed and the instrument must depict the continuum of functional categories needed to capture the phenomenon. When the purpose is case finding, the instrument should be keyed to the appropriate thresholds for identifying cases and the sampling should concentrate on likely populations at risk. A common error is to use information derived from screening clinics as a source of information about the prevalence of a problem in a population. A different kind of pitfall is to make many more distinctions than are necessary with clinical case-finding tools. A clinical screen should not be concerned with the distribution above the threshold that has been deemed important. Moreover, the clinician should hesitate to screen unless useful actions are possible when findings are positive.

Clinical case finding is sometimes construed in terms of eligibility testing. This is true when an entitlement is involved and all those who meet specified criteria are eligible for a given service. Screening for eligibility is thus dictated by the relevant laws and regulations, often involving admittedly arbitrary but usually specific criteria (such as age, income, or residence). Eligibility determinations are generally directed toward establishing whether an individual has crossed a given threshold. One rarely speaks of one client as being more eligible than another. Once a client has crossed that threshold, there is seldom any emphasis on examining the degree of impairment. In contrast, clinical case finding can also be construed in terms of identifying those individuals likely to require service on a priority basis—a triaging function. Again, screening for eligibility and for identification of those who should be assessed for services are complementary but not identical functions. Many persons could be eligible for a service who would not appropriately require it. (Consider, for example, that more individuals are eligible for the GI Bill than invoke its benefits.) Similarly, some individuals may present a profile suggesting high need for service, even though they are not currently eligible for any readily identifiable service packages. For that reason, case-finding techniques usually must go beyond simple eligibility screens to identify those with high-priority needs.

Objective screening for entry into program caseloads is essential if the cost effectiveness of these programs is to be examined later. Much information in geriatrics and gerontology is plagued by nonequivalent target groups (Kane and Kane 1980). Without an assurance that the groups receiving service are comparable, two service strategies cannot usefully be compared. Similarly, program participants cannot be compared with nonparticipants (in the absence of randomization) without a test of equivalence in the dimensions deemed important.

Such screens to establish equivalence of targets are difficult to construct. For example, in testing the effectiveness of an emergency-alarm system, Sherwood and Morris (1980) isolated three target groups: the severely functionally impaired and socially isolated, the severely functionally impaired and not socially isolated, and the socially isolated and either medically vulnerable or moderately functionally impaired. Social isolation was defined as having no regular daily contact with anyone either in person or by telephone. Medical vulnerability was judged to occur if any of the following were present: dizziness, seizures, chest pains, passing out, medicine prescribed for a heart condition, hypertension, diabetes, age 80 or over, or a history of falls. On the other hand, the allocation to severe or moderate functional-impairment categories was made on the basis of a clinical judgment by a nurse or social worker, albeit with the provision of some empirical reference points. Generally, those who were housebound, severely limited in mobility, or in need of extensive personal care went into the "severe" category; and those who could not cook, clean, or shop, or who were considered to put themselves at risk of accident when doing so, were placed in the "moderate" category. This method of allocating persons to target groups can be criticized, but the process is absolutely crucial to assessing effects.

Regardless of whether the screening is designed to describe the population or to form the basis for case finding, certain considerations are relevant in choosing the screening tool. The instrument should be brief, inexpensive, and capable of administration by personnel who have little or no professional training. Self-screening tools are also appropriate; geriatrics as yet has no equivalent of the "seven warning signs of cancer," yet such well-publicized screeners that could be used by patients and their relatives would be helpful.

Sensitivity (that is, the extent to which the screen captures all of the real cases) and specificity (the extent to which false cases are screened out) are always concerns with any screening tool. In the medical field, the question of how sensitive a test should be is raised with each diagnostic measure. Usually the decision is conservative, based on the principle that it is better falsely to include some persons than to miss a single case of a serious treatable disease (for example, breast cancer, hypertension). However, in this book we are not concerned with laboratory tests for diagnostically identifiable syndromes but with screening measures to identify those who would profit by that mix of sociomedical services known as long-term care. In some instances (for example, screening to identify senility or to determine need for institutionalization), the legal maxim that it is better to risk that the guilty go free than to punish the innocent may be more germane than the medical emphasis on catching all treatable problems. If so, specificity may need to take priority over sensitivity.

Another criterion for setting sensitivity thresholds is the anticipated prevalence of the condition. If the condition is common, then the sensitivity thresholds should be high lest the majority of the population screened fall into the net. This observation is especially important in geriatrics and LTC. Recent rhetoric has emphasized that vulnerable groups such as physically frail, old-old individuals who are recently bereaved may benefit from counseling and environmental assistance and therefore should be screened for depression. However, given the very large number of persons who would fall into that category and the likelihood that most recently bereaved persons will be at least mildly depressed, a useful screening tool must be specific enough to pick up the high-priority cases. For more information about the tradeoffs between sensitivity and specificity, see McNeil, Keeler, and Adelstein (1975).

Screening usually triggers further assessment. Certainly screening questions can be literally incorporated into an assessment instrument, utilizing a branching design. In that case, assessors first complete the screening measure and then determine eligibility and/or need for further assessment, which they continue to perform if the screen is positive. As a practical matter, however, it may be neither economical nor advisable to incorporate screening and assessment as a single procedure. The cost effectiveness is in doubt if highly paid clinical personnel are involved or if consumers are transported at considerable expense to undergo screening.

More importantly, the two-stage approach consisting of brief screening and later assessment seems to respond better to the sequence of events from the perspective of an individual or a relative who becomes concerned with a problem. The first recourse is usually to telephone a physician, social agency, or some other resource and ask whether the problem should be followed up. Therefore, it is important to have developed screening questions that will provide a proper basis for such advice. Often a receptionist will be applying the screening. In other instances, it may be highly desirable to develop a series of screening questions that a professional can use on the telephone with an elderly individual or a concerned relative.

Considerable thought is needed to develop useful screening questions and to differentiate screening procedures depending on whether the primary contact is by telephone or in person and whether it is made by the elderly person, a family member, or a professional referral source. For example, if a potential client presents himself or telephones to ask for service, a brief mental-status screening would indicate the intrinsic reliability of the informant, whereas social-screening questions would elicit information about others who should be involved in supplying assessment information. If, on the other hand, the inquiry emanates from a relative, then screening questions that yielded information about the reason for concern, the nature and severity of problem, the reported mental status of the potential client, and the social circumstances would also indicate the extent to which the situation is an emergency and give guidelines for decisions about how to proceed with the assessment (who should do it, where and when it should take place, or which persons should be involved as informants).

Assessment

Criteria for selecting a clinical-assessment tool have already been discussed in this chapter and have been contrasted to criteria for selecting an assessment tool for research and evaluation. Here, then, we will proceed to the issue of future monitoring after an initial assessment is complete. We do emphasize, however, that the assessment strategy should be based on an understanding of the population being targeted by the particular program. Preparatory discussion about the expected range of functional characteristics within the clientele and the frequency expected for the various patterns is well worthwhile. The reward is an assessment instrument with content and categories that are more likely to describe meaningful changes in the clients being served.

Monitoring

Monitoring proceeds on two fronts: (1) following changes in areas targeted for intervention or viewed as a problem and (2) rescreening in areas not targeted for intervention. The frequency and intensity of the observations made in the monitoring mode depend on whether the area was originally pinpointed as a problem area. In either case, a complete reassessment using the original measurement tool may be inappropriate. Even in an area where treatment is occurring, the original assessment delineates and restricts the range within which change can be expected.

Choice of the intervals for monitoring ideally should be based on the nature of the problem, the expected frequency of change, and the nature of the intervention used. Unfortunately, despite the dynamic and variable nature of the client situation, many current regulations mandate a fixed periodicity for monitoring. A classic example is the recertification of nursing-home patients. Here the regulations drive the care system and ensure that physician reexaminations will occur at fixed intervals for all nursing-home patients. In reality, the monitoring intervals are better dictated by the predictable expectations of change or by early indications of such change. We urge that more research be directed toward determining the natural history of various conditions associated with aging and the range of expected changes under various treatments and conditions.

Ideally, the content of monitoring devices should be based on knowledge about the predictable course of improvement or deterioration in the various domains. Specific objective markers of such changes are most desirable so that the elderly person, the family member, or paraprofessional personnel can carry out the monitoring function. The concern with paraprofessional personnel is critical because persons with remarkably low levels of formal education and literacy are often in the best position to make the necessary observations. Consider, for example, the typical nursing-home aide or homemaker. Such staff may be in regular contact with the elderly person but will need systematic tools to make observations that are keyed to the assessed problems and the treatment plans for the individual.

A problem-oriented monitoring system can facilitate useful observations. One such system, developed for semiliterate nursing-home attendants, keyed the observations to the presenting problem and, for each problem, instructed the aide about the frequency of each observation, the signs of change that might be worrisome, and the degree of urgency with which to take actions when adverse early changes were detected (Woolley et al. 1974). (See table 6-1 for an example of the system as applied to the problem of a broken hip.) Flow charts permit nursing-home attendants to enter observations with almost no writing. Such devices have the additional advantage of making clear to the

Table 6–1
The Benchmark Approach to Monitoring the Status of Nursing-Home Patients: Fractured Hip as an Example

For Fractured Hip: Observation Made by Aides or Attendants	Frequency of Observation[a]	Benchmark for Action	Action[b]
1. Independence Scale Score	Every 2 weeks	Decreased score or no change in 6 weeks after therapy begun	Inform nurse practitioner (NP)
2. Behavioral Scale Score	Every 2 weeks	Decreased score or no change in 6 weeks after therapy begun	Inform NP
3. Soreness in either calf (Use –, R = right soreness; L = left soreness)	Daily–check by pushing foot up with knee extended	Present	Place patient on bedrest, notify NP
4. Temperature (°F)	prn increased hip pain, calf pain, malaise	Above 100°F orally for 8–16 hours	Notify NP. Take temperature every 4–8 hours if elevated
5. Contracture or stiff joint especially foot drop, hip flexion, knee flexion, hip abducted or turned out (+ or –)	Daily	Present	Continue to position properly and give ROM to tolerance. Inform NP. Chart location of contracture.
6. Distance walked at one time (in yards)	Daily	Decrease over 3 days or no improvement in 1 week after therapy begun	Inform NP
7. Pain in hip (+ for pain)	prn	No relief by medication for 24 hours of administration	Notify NP

Source: G.A. Pepper, L.B. Jorgensen, R.L. Kane, and J.K. Devenport, "Problem-Oriented Process: Nurses' Manual" (Mimeographed, 1972).

[a]Below is a flow sheet showing how the monitoring could be displayed for a hypothetical patient with broken hip.

FLOW SHEET

DATE	8/12	8/13	8/14	8/15	8/16	8/17	8/18	8/19	8/20	8/21	8/22	8/23	8/24	8/25	8/26	8/27
Hip Fracture 1. Independence Scale Score	20	✕	✕	✕	✕	✕	✕	✕	✕	✕	✕	✕	✕	✕	✕	✕
2. Behavior Scale Score	✕	✕	✕	✕	✕	✕	✕	40	✕	✕	✕	✕	✕	✕	✕	✕
3. Soreness in either calf (-, R or L)	-	-	-	-	-	-	-	* R	R							
4. Contracture (+ or -)	-	-	C +	+	+	* +	+	+	-	-	-	-	-	-	-	-
5. Distance Walked (yds.)	10	10	11	12	13	14	15	C	N							
6. Temperature (°F) prn								101° F	F							

[b]In this system, "inform nurse practitioner" could be done at next regular meeting, and "notify nurse practitioner" was to be done sometime during the day the benchmark observation was made. Another possible action, "call nurse practitioner immediately," does not occur in this particular example.

staff the purposes of the observations. Very little work has been done, however, to develop problem-oriented monitoring systems for psychosocial problems. The Colorado Foundation for Medical Care has made beginnings in this area, developing outcome-based audits for problems such as depression, isolation, or aggression in institutional settings (Kane et al. 1979). The purpose of that system was regular monitoring of the quality of care received by patients with identifiable conditions; to develop the auditing tool, observable markers suggesting the need for action were defined. Retrospective review tools cannot be extrapolated to indicate the frequency and nature of the observations needed to monitor the course of the problem, although the techniques are translatable to monitoring measures. Ideally, however, one would expect the systems for reviewing quality of care to follow rather than precede the systems developed by providers to monitor that same care.

Using Measurements to Make LTC Decisions

On one level, clinical assessment provides the necessary descriptive information about clients who are being observed or treated. If the art and science of assessment is to reach its full potential, however, then the data derived should guide the care system and suggest intervention strategies. Translating assessments into service packages is a challenge that needs further systematic attention. The question is how to make efficient use of the sometimes voluminous information to assist in clinical decision making or, in LTC parlance, *care planning*.

Using Algorithms

Clinical decisions are made in two general ways: (1) by professional judgment based on knowledge and experience and (2) by predetermined decision rules. The bulk of the work in LTC assessment has been geared toward making the status of "client" more explicit; the assumption is that a systematic and detailed data base will enhance the effectiveness of professional judgments. The actual prescriptive decisions in such a method are left to the interpretations of the clinician. Although less highly trained individuals may make the observations and complete assessment instruments, the professional (or the team) must review the material and make the plan.

In contrast, predetermined decision rules (or algorithms) tell how to make a treatment plan based on the information and scores generated from the assessment data. If an algorithm model is used, and assuming that the professional team has produced the original decision rules, then individuals with less training may generate care plans. In practice, however, the highly trained professional sometimes continues to collect the information (despite objective assessment forms) and continues to make the care plans (despite decision algorithms). We must become better able to distinguish when personal involvement of the professional is necessary. It is true that some of the individual items in many multidimensional scales require judgments and that such judgments later become incorporated into the algorithms. If the assessment uses judgments as data (for example, ratings of client happiness, environmental safety, or the likelihood that the client has been the victim of abuse), then professional personnel are needed to collect information, even if the decision rules are later applied by personnel with less training.

Extrapolating from medical experience with algorithms, we suggest that, when they can be made explicit, they perform well in producing accurate decisions. They do, however, provoke resistance among clinicians who either dismiss the procedure as simplistic or resent infringements on practice. The algorithms eventually become internalized so that they are incorporated into professional judgment.

At this stage, we lack the knowledge necessary to create algorithms for the complex medical-social decisions in LTC planning. This is an important and promising area of development, however, and is enhanced by the information generated from systematic assessment procedures. Some steps have been taken in the direction of refining decision-making capabilities. As discussed in the previous chapter, Falcone (1979) has developed relatively simple algorithms for translating the Patient Care Classification, analogous to the PACE system, into service decisions. On another front, investigators at Duke University (Dellinger 1978; Burton, Damon, and Dellinger 1978) have explicated a conceptual model for making resource-allocation decisions based on the OARS functional assessment and the classification of services that constitutes part B of the OARS instrument. The OARS methodology has the added advantage of permitting comparisons of the relative costs of different "service packages" for similarly impaired individuals. Such comparisons have been made both in North Carolina and with the larger data set from the Cleveland GAO studies (Burton et al. 1978; Laurie 1978). Future analyses promise to fill in the blanks in a "technology matrix," which requires information about the distribution of expected outcomes given a particular functional status and a particular service package.

Our ability to create algorithms is limited by our clinical skills. When Sager (1979) presented standardized case "scenarios" to professionals, who, in turn, were asked to prescribe appropriate home-care service packages, he found a great discrepancy across providers. Algorithms can be developed only after clinical consistency is achieved.

Decision algorithms could be developed theoretically and then tested for effectiveness in terms of client outcomes. More commonly and perhaps more practically, decision algorithms are constructed in the opposite fashion, using deductive reasoning; that is, studies are conducted to make explicit the decisions of clinicians or the kinds of service packages received by different individuals, and rules are modeled after this reality. One problem with this approach is that clinicians are limited in their prescriptions both by availability of resources and by their imaginations. Consequently, both the range of services used and the variety of combinations may be constrained.

When decision rules are developed to replicate clinical choices, such predictive models should be based on the best-available care settings; for example, those with skilled personnel and a range of resources, or those that produce favorable results in terms of client outcomes or satisfaction. The standard of all practice is elevated when successive modeling efforts are based on the best available examples and, in the interim, decision rules are widely popularized. Over time, this repeated process, theoretically at least, drives the distribution of decision making upward to greater effectiveness. Finally, if models are developed on the basis of extant reality and interventions are made to change those circumstances (for example, if new resources and options for care are generated), remodeling is necessary.

Decisions About Institutionalization

The gravest decisions that LTC providers currently make involve recommending institutional placement. Such decisions are usually professional judgments, aided by an instrument (such as the PACE methodology) that inventories impairments as perceived by the professional. Practically speaking, the instruments reflect the categories of eligibility under Medicare and state Medicaid regulations. For example, instruments developed by the Professional Standards Review Organizations, charged with monitoring the appropriate use of the federal health-care dollar, are geared toward establishing the eligibility threshold for institutional care rather than assisting planners in determining whether institutional placement is the best plan.

Nevertheless, it is widely believed that, for every person in institutional care, two persons with equal physical and mental impairment reside in the community. Home care is possible for anyone if the resources are available. We have only to evoke the image of the late Howard Hughes the millionaire recluse who, despite renal failure and apparently delusional status, spent his last years receiving long-term care in the penthouse suites of various luxury hotels. It appears that socioeconomic factors are pivotal in determining whether an institutional placement will be necessary; these factors include the income and housing of the elderly person and the availability of care (either paid for by the LTC patient or family, or provided by relatives, friends, or public programs).

Grauer and Birnbom (1975) developed a Geriatric Functional Rating Scale to determine the need for institutional care. In so doing, they took cognizance of the social factors associated with placement decisions. In their strategy, physical and mental condition are rated, with impairments contributing to a negative score. Functional abilities, support from the community, living quarters, relatives and friends, and finances are all rated, contributing to a positive score. The final score is calculated by subtracting the total negative score from the total positive score.

Table 6-2 shows the items used for the Geriatric Functional Rating Scale and the scoring attached. Note that professional judgment is needed to rate the physical and mental condition and that a substantial loss of points occurs if the individual depends on a wheelchair or support other than a cane for mobility. The items on the community-support side of the equation are of particular interest. Points are awarded for ethnic compatibility of the individual with the neighborhood (an item often overlooked), the availability of delivery services from local shops, and the availability of various recreational opportunities and of health and social services. Living quarters earn positive points if they are on the ground floor or if the building has an elevator. Finally, note that the scale makers have made some decisions about relatives and friends; an individual who lives with an able and compatible spouse receives 10 points are given. If he lives with any other able and compatible individual, he receives only 5 points; and living with an incompatible spouse, friend, or relative gives no points on the social-support side. Clearly, deciding that the live-in relative or friend is either not able or not compatible requires considerable inference.

The Grauer Functional Rating Scale has been criticized for its seemingly arbitrary scoring system (Anderson and Patten, forthcoming). On the other hand, its major advantage is that it was shown (in the Canadian context) to have predictive ability. In a follow-up of 130 persons originally assessed with this method, 83 percent of those earning a score below 20 were either dead or institutionalized; in contrast, 90 percent of those earning a score of 40 or more were residents in the community. The scale is currently being used by the Wisconsin Community Care Organization; it will be interesting to determine whether it also predicts institutionalization in this country.

We view the Grauer scale less as a formal instrument with good measurement properties than as an approach to weighting information to determine risk of institutionalization. We are not aware of reliability testing for the scale; surely the amount of judgment and, therefore, of expertise, required to complete it is great. In addition, to be able to assess mental and physical status and the amicability of the relationship with support people, the rater would also need to be aware of or obtain information about recreational opportunities (such as parks and libraries) and more-formal services. But the approach is particularly interesting because it includes practical variables relating to the community and the care system as well as to the individual's needs and his family's supportiveness. If such an approach could be refined and proved reliable and valid, then one could try systematically to alter the outcome by changing the predictors—arranging for stores to deliver, providing a janitor who can be called on in emergencies, adding recreational and other services, and so forth.

Table 6–2
Geriatric Functional Rating Scale

	Observation	Score	Observation	Score	Observation	Score
1. Physical Condition						
A. Eyesight	Good, Watches TV, Reads, Needlework	0	Distinguishes faces	-3	Sees light only	-10
B. Hearing	Good	0	Loud voice	-3	Deaf	-5
C. Mobility	Fully Mobile, Dresses, Carries Parcels, Rides bus	0	Uses cane or should use one, Dependent on railings	-3	Requires cane and other support, Wheelchair	-15
D. Pulmocardiovascular function	No restrictions	0	One flight of stairs, One city block	-3	Partly or totally bedridden	-20
E. Diet	No restrictions	0			Yes	-3
2. Mental condition						
A. Disorientation	None	0	Time	-3	Person and/or place	-15
B. Delusions	None	0	Mild–severe suspiciousness	-3	Overt	-10
C. Memory loss	None	0	Benign	-3	Malignant	-20
D. Energy and drive	Normal	0			Hypoactive or hyperactive	-5
E. Judgment	Intact	0			Impaired	-5
F. Hallucinations	None	0			Auditory and/or visual	-10
3. Functional abilities						
A. Reads and writes letters.						+2
B. Able to use telephone.						+5
C. Able to bank and shop.						+5
D. Able to prepare simple meals and bake.						+7
E. Washes, dresses, and toilets self without assistance.						+5
F. Uses public transportation.						+7
G. Able or would be able to take own medication and follow diet.						+10

4. *Support from the community*
   A. Ethnic compatibility. + 2
   B. If living alone, can get support and help from a reliable relative, friend, neighbor, janitor. +10
   C. Able to shop at reliable grocer's (willing to deliver when necessary). + 5
   D. Available supportive and recreational facilities:
       Clubs geared to aged + 2
       Church, synagogue + 1
       Library + 1
       Park, shopping center, restaurant, movies + 1
   E. Geographic availability of:
       Public-health nurses + 2
       Meals-on-Wheels service + 2
       Homemaker services + 2
       Friendly visitor + 2
       Hospital with emergency and clinic facilities + 2
       Public transportation + 2

5. *Living quarters*
   Elevator service or living on ground floor or basement. + 3

6. *Relatives and friends*
   A. Not married but lives with compatible and helpful relative or friend. + 5
   B. Lives with incompatible relative, friend, or spouse. 0
   C. Lives with able and compatible spouse. +10

7. *Financial situation*
   A. Totally independent. + 5
   B. Dependent on helpful relative. + 3
   C. Dependent mainly on old-age pension and/or other community resources. 0

Total plus score ——
Total minus score ——
Final score ——

Source: Adapted from H. Grauer and F. Birnbom, "A Geriatric Functional Rating Scale to Determine the Need for Institutional Care," *Journal of the American Geriatrics Society* 20(1975): 472–476.

Considering Time Dependency

LTC services are directed toward maintaining independence among the frail elderly. Care planning involves assisting individuals toward maximum independence while, at the same time, making sure, their needs are met This requires striking a balance between overprotectiveness (discouraging independence) and underservice (risking inadequate care). In developing formulas to determine how many and what kind of services to order, the case manager or provider takes into account the client's functional status and personal and familial resources.

A useful way of estimating the need for care is based on the amount of time that an individual actually needs the assistance of another person. Gurland and his colleagues (1978) use *personal-time dependency* (PTD) to refer to the characteristic of "requiring time-consuming help from another person in coping with the demands of the environment." (p. 1) In a random sample of 450 New York City community dwellers aged 65 and over, 30 percent were deemed to have personal-time dependency. This designation was made by determining the formal and informal care already received by the individual and making a professional judgment about whether the subject could manage in that setting without those services. In a review of the records of 104 cases, two raters reached 90-percent agreement. The investigators pointed out that PTD was not prevalent in those under age 85 but was almost universal in the group over age 90. Persons living alone and single or divorced individuals were underrepresented in the PTD group, suggesting that they were already in institutions. Depression was closely associated with PTD, both in the subject with PTD and in other household members.

The CARE instrument was used to pinpoint variables associated with the overall judgment of PTD. Difficulty with chores, grooming, laundry, shopping, doing business, and getting out for excursions was correlated with PTD. Problems in ambulation or bathing without assistance were also frequent. The large number of problems related to the need for help with chores suggested to the authors that relatively small amounts of nonprofessional assistance might make a sizable difference in the ability of persons with PTD to sustain themselves at home.

Taking a more-specific approach to evaluating the need for care, Isaacs and Neville (1975) developed the related concepts of "solitude ratings" and "interval needs." Solitude ratings are simply determinations of the amount and pattern of time that the subject is alone. Several categories of solitude were developed, including "diurnal" solitude (characteristic of those who live with or near working relatives), and "nocturnal" solitude (characteristic of those who live alone but have resources, attendants, or activities during the day). The interval need is the frequency with which the individual requires personal attention in order to manage personal care, that is, to attend to health, safety, and cleanliness needs. (Discounted in this system is the time required or desirable for emotional support.) Discrepancies between the solitude ratings and the interval needs require an adjustment from the care system, which could either be a strengthening of informal help or a provision of formal services.

Our prescriptive acumen would be enormously enhanced were we able to refine further the ideas of personal-time dependency toward an understanding of the minimum increments of service required to maintain an individual in the community. Home-care services in the United States may have established guidelines for care at too frequent intervals and may have depended too much on professional personnel. This, in turn, drives up the costs in comparison with those for congregate settings and makes institutional placement more appealing financially. Also because personal time seems pivotal, the factors contributing to willingness to provide personal time need much more study. The New York study already cited (Gurland et al. 1978) showed that "perceived inconvenience" was most associated with decisions to consider an institution. This finding, in blunt terms, is almost tautological; what is now needed is specification of the circumstances under which inconvenience is perceived to be greatest and least.

A Matter of Values

As we use measurements to compare and contrast LTC outcomes or to make allocations for care, we confront many value-laden issues. Sometimes value weightings are reflected in the very questions we ask and the way we score our results; these value weights, intrinsic to the instruments, may even go unnoticed by the user. Values are also involved when results are interpreted and interventions are selected to maximize the likelihood of improvement in one or another domain. Because maximizing more than one outcome simultaneously is a literal impossibility, difficult choices must be made. Values may be considered in relation to measurement in two ways: (1) values are involved in the measure of each domain; and (2) values are involved when one domain is weighted against another in multidimensional measures.

We cannot avoid values. The more we focus on outcomes, the more critical values become. Perhaps the best course of action is to make them explicit. One aspect to consider in producing scales and batteries is whose values the measurement should reflect. Are the individual values of the particular elderly person most important? Or are we acting on the collective values of older persons or of society in general? Given the truism that the elderly are a heterogeneous group, any weighting based on aggregate value preferences will risk distorting the preferences of the individual in question.

Value choices are necessary in decisions about whether to measure actualities or perceptions. The answer may vary with the type of item being measured or with the context. Measurement of eating habits or abilities probably rightly focuses on the actuality of whether the subject is able to prepare meals, feed himself, and remember to do so. Satisfaction with those meals or contentment with life in general, however, would seem to be so subjective that the perception would be equivalent to the reality. If a person believes he is happy, he is happy. Other variables such as social contacts are more problematic. If the purpose of measuring social contacts is to gauge loneliness, then the perception of being surrounded by friends and family may be as good as the reality. If, however, the purpose is to assess the availability of a support system to provide care, then the factual existence or lack of social contacts is more important than the individual's perceptions.

Various options are open. One strategy is to design measures that incorporate value weights. The very act of aggregating items under a title such as "happiness" or "social activity" implies a value judgment. Score weightings also place additional value on some items as opposed to others. (For example, most ADL scores consider that dependence on equipment is a lesser degree of dependency than dependence on a person and score it accordingly.) Another strategy is to incorporate measures of preference internally into measures, either within or across domains; for example, the respondent is asked to choose preferences among alternatives.

As we focus attention on outcomes, we must consider how to value one set of outcomes against another. Is one pair of events (for example, pain and mobility) preferable to another (no pain and immobility)? Techniques are available by which such value preferences can be measured (Mushkin and Dunlop 1979; Berg 1973; "Health Status Indexes" 1976).

In the context of decision algorithms and care planning, we must ask when we value an outcome sufficiently to risk untoward events to achieve it. For example, the confused person at home must weigh the chances of a mishap at home against the loss of quality of life in an institution prepared to offer close supervision. The case manager process confronts these kinds of tradeoffs on a regular basis, but decision-making algorithms have not achieved the complexity to adjust for value preferences of the clients.

Recommendations

1. *Use measurements systematically and routinely in LTC practice.* At the present time, not enough measurement is being done. Despite the constraints delineated in this book, we are not utilizing what we do know. Progress requires a continuous effort. A framework is needed within which to confront and reconceptualize the dilemmas posed by elderly patients. Measurement offers this framework.

It is not enough to deplore the multiple problems presented by the elderly client. A method for delineating those problems and their interactions is necessary. Without such a system, the overwhelming burden of problems threatens to terrify rather than inspire the caregiver. The ability to separate the problems, to reduce them to manageable proportions, and to identify increments of potential change that offer some expectation of accomplishment can serve as a motivating force for greater attention.

Medical students particularly and professional students in general have ambivalent reactions to aged clients. Compassion is offset by despair of ever being able to alter a generally bleak picture. Exhortations cannot change attitudes. The physician and others need tools to measure states and observe meaningful increments of change. By measuring small changes, one notes that they do in fact occur. The very act of measuring emphasizes the need to consider areas beyond the bounds of any one profession. It provides a means of recognizing the client's strength as well as his deficits and thereby of illustrating to young professionals the enormous coping capacity of the elderly. In this capacity, measuring offers the neophyte practitioner a set of tools, albeit rudimentary ones, with which he can take up the challenge of geriatric care. Without such an armamentarium, he is more likely to avoid such patients, imbuing them with negative characteristics consistent with his feelings of impotence. (This syndrome has been described as "the innocent victim' —a tendency to feel negative toward persons in need whom we feel impotent to help.)

2. *Avoid casual diagnostic labels.* More-precise description should militate against premature labeling and the inherent dangers of the self-fulfilling prophecy. Much has been written about the poor correspondence between traditional taxonomies (especially medical diagnoses) and the complex functional condition of the elderly patient with multiple problems. The carelessly applied label of senility, for example, can set in motion a chain of virtually irreversible events, leading the person so labeled to be placed in an environment in which he would be likely to exhibit symptoms of senility. Similarly, a person labeled as disabled may begin to behave as if he were disabled.

In the face of the labeling phenomenon, the clinician should be wary of diagnoses that offer little benefit. As a rule, functional diagnoses based on the types of measures are more likely to indicate specific courses of action than are more-traditional diagnostic labels. This statement is not meant to denigrate the importance of a careful clinical assessment and close medical supervision of chronic illnesses; it is at least as dangerous to dismiss the treatable medical condition as it is to label the untreatable. Rather, we wish to emphasize the critical role of functional multidimensional assessment using existing measures as an intrinsic part of the management of the geriatric patient. Such measurements have an important role in the initial assessment and an equally vital role in the continued care of each patient. These measures provide useful parameters by which to assess progress and serve as a basis for anticipating further change.

3. *Be consistent.* Because measurement in geriatrics is a growth industry, new measures and refinements of old measures are bound to appear within the life span of many projects. At the same time, the field is typified by large numbers of rarely used measures. Progress depends on our ability to accumulate substantial experience with the best of the measures available. Having chosen wisely from among those available, one should avoid changes in midstudy. If the newest technique just reported is continually adopted, such fluctuations will make it difficult to interpret real change and to separate it from the artifacts induced by meandering measurement. At a time when we need data bases that will permit testing of predictive models, such fickleness is intolerable. Once a decision has been reached about which measures are most suitable for the context, firm resolution is needed. Each addition of a new battery, each tiny tampering, creates a new context and potential noise in the system.

4. *Report experience honestly and completely.* One of the great frustrations in social research and its application is the difficulty in reproducing results. Too often the restrictions of information dissemination and the desire to share good news obscure the full range of experience an investigator or a clinician has had with a particular instrument. Useful and important aspects of the performance of a given measure in a particular setting are thus lost, as are, consequently, important distinctions about using the measures.

Whenever results are reported, basic information is needed about how the measure was used. These would include information on the sample—not only descriptive statistics but also information on possible selection biases such as preselection and refusal rates, the setting in which the data were gathered, tests of reliability (what types and how done). Finally, each report should include recommendations on how the measure might be better used the next time. What lessons were learned? Which approaches worked well and which need improvement? This type of cumulative data on experience from the field will do a great deal to advance the state of our art, particularly if the measures are applied consistently.

5. *Support methodologic research.* To facilitate systematic collection of naturalistic data from the field, careful research is needed on the way various factors affect reporting and how validity of the measures might be established. Such studies require controlled manipulation of variables in experimental situations where redundant data can be collected. In this way we can begin to understand the effect of data-collection techniques on results. Another variant of methodologic research would examine the congruence and discrepancies among various informants (for example, the elderly person, the significant other, and the caregiver). We cannot simply assume that these respondents are interchangeable. Anecdotal clinical experience suggests that patients and their families often present contradictory information to caregivers.

Unfortunately, methodologic studies are not appealing to funding agencies, which favor demonstrations of service. More typically, the investigator is encouraged to apply his measure on some "real world" problem with more-apparent relevance. The methodologic work, if any, is wedged into a "pretest" period. Such a policy is shortsighted, and these conditions favor the promulgation of poorly tested measures. There is great pressure to pull something off the shelf, to shop through the measurement catalog. Unquestionably, we need much more applied work. But we also need careful and deliberate investigations of how the measures perform and what they measure. An ounce of conceptualization and testing may well be worth at least a pound of application.

Final Thoughts

We have come full circle now, back to our beginning. Geriatrics and gerontology are evolving as applied disciplines. Their development as branches of clinical care will depend in substantial part on an ability to demonstrate an effective grasp of the problems of the elderly and their solutions. It has been said that the cornerstone of a new specialty is the availability of a technology. Measurement may serve that purpose for geriatrics. Even a casual glance at the demographic forecasts suggests that any effort to improve the science of geriatrics will benefit both students and practitioners. Measurement carefully done can foster exciting improvements in the care of the elderly and, at the same time, a better understanding of our own human condition.

References

Abdellah, F.G. "Long-Term Policy Issues: Alternatives to Institutional Care." *Annals of the American Academy of Political and Social Science* 438: (1978):28-39.

Abrahams, J.P.; Wallach, H.F.; and Divens, S. "Behavioral Improvement in Long-Term Geriatric Patients During an Age-Integrated Psychosocial Rehabilitation Program." *Journal of the American Geriatric Society* 27: (1979): 218-221.

Adams, D.L. "Analysis of a Life Satisfaction Index." *Journal of Gerontology* 24: (1969):470-474.

Adler, A.; Cantor, M.; and Johnson, J.L. "Toward a Typology of Frailty." Paper presented at the Gerontological Society Meeting, Dallas, Texas, 18 November 1978. (Mimeographed.)

American Psychiatric Association. *Diagnostic and Statistical Manual of Mental Disorders*, 3d ed. Washington, D.C.: Task Force on Nomenclature and Statistics, 1978.

Ammons, R.B., and Ammons, C.H. "The Quick Test (QT): Provisional Manual." *Psychological Reports* 11 (1962):111-161.

Anderson, N.N., and Patten, S.K. "The Effectiveness of Long-Term Care." In *Research Instruments in Social Gerontology,* ed. D.J. Mangen and W.A. Peterson. Vol. 3. Minneapolis: University of Minnesota, forthcoming.

Anderson, W.F. *Practical Management of the Elderly*. Oxford: Blackwell Scientific Publications, 1971.

_____. "Modern Trends in Geriatric Medicine." *Maryland State Medical Journal,* May 1974.

Arling, G. "The Elderly Widow and Her Family, Neighbors, and Friends." *Journal of Marriage and the Family* 38 (1976):747-768.

Aydelotte, M.K. "Use of Patient Welfare as a Criterion Measure." *Nursing Research* 11 (1962):10-14.

Beattie, W., and Bullock, J. "Evaluating Services and Personnel in Facilities for the Aged." In *Geriatric Institutional Management,* ed. M. Leeds and H. Shore. New York: G.P. Putnam's Sons, 1964.

Beck, A., and Weissman, A. "The Measurement of Pessimism: The Hopelessness Scale." *Journal of Consulting and Clinical Psychology* 42 (1974):861-865.

Beck, A.T.; Ward, C.H.; Mendelson, M.; Mock, J.; and Erbaugh, J. "An Inventory for Measuring Depression." *Archives of General Psychiatry* 4 (1961):53-63.

Bellak, L., and Bellak, S.S. *Manual for the Senior Apperception Technique*. Larchmont, N.Y.: CPS, 1973.

Bennett, R. "Living Conditions and Everyday Needs of the Elderly with

Particular Reference to Social Isolation." *International Journal of Aging and Human Development* 4 (1973a):179-198.

———. "Social Isolation and Isolation-Reducing Programs." *Bulletin of the New York Academy of Medicine* 49 (1973b):1143-1163.

Bennett, R., and Nahemow, L. "Institutional Totality and Criteria of Social Adjustment in Residences for the Aged." *Journal of Social Issues* 21 (1965):44-78.

Berg, R.L. *Health Status Indexes.* Chicago: Hospital Research and Educational Trust, 1973.

Berger, E.Y. "A System for Rating the Severity of Senility." *Journal of the American Geriatric Society* 28 (1980):234-236.

Bergner, M.; Bobbitt, R.A.; Pollard, W.E.; Martin, D.P.; and Gilson, B.S. "Sickness Impact Profile: Validation of a Health Status Measure." *Medical Care* 14 (1976a):57-67.

Bergner, M.; Bobbitt, R.A.; Kressel, S.; Pollard, W.E.; Gilson, B.S.; and Morris, J.R. "The Sickness Impact Profile: Conceptual Formulation and Methodology for the Development of a Health Status Measure." *International Journal of Health Services* 6 (1976b):393-415.

Binstock, R.H., and Shanas, E. *Handbook of Aging and the Social Sciences.* New York: Van Nostrand Reinhold, 1976.

Birren, J.E. "Increment and Decrement in the Intellectual Status of the Aged." *Psychiatric Resident Report* 23 (1968):207-201.

Birren, J.E., and Sloane, R.B. *Handbook of Mental Health and Aging.* Englewood Cliffs, N.J.: Prentice-Hall, 1980.

Birren, J.E.; Butler, R.N.; Greenhouse, S.W.; Sokoloff, L.; and Yarrow, M.R., eds. *Human Aging: A Biological and Behavioral Study.* Bethesda, Md.: National Institute of Mental Health, 1963.

Blazer, D. "Diagnosis of Depression in the Elderly." *Journal of the American Geriatrics Society* 28 (1980):52-58.

Blenkner, M.; Bloom, M.; and Neilsen, M.A. "A Research and Demonstration Project in Protective Services." *Social Casework* 52 (1971):483-489.

Blessed, G.; Tomlinson, B.E.; and Roth, M. "Association Between Quantitative Measures of Dementia and of Senile Change in the Cerebral Grey Matter of Elderly Subjects." *British Journal of Psychiatry* 114 (1968): 797-811.

Bloom, M. "Evaluation Instruments: Tests and Measurements in Long-Term Care." In *Long-Term Care: A Handbook for Researchers, Planners and Providers*, ed. S. Sherwood. New York: Spectrum, 1975.

———. "Alternatives to Morale Scales." In *Measuring Morale: A Guide to Effective Assessment,* ed. C.N. Nydegger. Washington, D.C.: Gerontological Society, 1977.

Bloom, M., and Blenkner, M. "Assessing Functioning of Older Persons Living in the Community." *The Gerontologist* 10 (1970):331-337.

Blumenthal, M.D. "Measuring Depressive Symptomatology in a General Population." *Archives of General Psychiatry* 32 (1975):971-978.

Botwinick, J. "Intellectual Abilities." In *Handbook of the Psychology of Aging*, ed. J.E. Birren and K.W. Schale. New York: Van Nostrand Reinhold, 1977.

Bradburn, N.M. *The Structure of Psychological Well-Being*. Chicago: University of Chicago Press, 1969.

Britton, P.G., and Savage, R.D. "A Short Form of the WAIS for Use with the Aged." *British Journal of Psychiatry* 112 (1966):417-418.

———. "The Factorial Structure of the Minnesota Multiphasic Personality Inventory from an Aged Sample." *Journal of Genetic Psychology* 114 (1969):13-17.

Brocklehurst, J.C.; Carthy, M.H.; Leeming, J.T.; and Robinson, J.M. "Medical Screening of Old People Accepted for Residential Care." *Lancet*, 1978, pp. 141-143.

Brodman, K.; Erdmann, A.J.; Jr., Lorge, I.; and Wolff, H.G. "The Cornell Medical Index—Health Questionnaire: II. As a Diagnostic Instrument." *Journal of the American Medical Association* 145 (1951):152-157.

Brody, E.M. "A Million Procrustean Beds." *The Gerontologist* 13 (1973):430-435.

Brody, E.M., and Spark, G.M. "Institutionalization of the Aged: A Family Crisis." *Family Process* 5 (1966):76-90.

Brody, E.M.; Kleban, M.H.; Lamont, M.P.; and Moss, M. "A Longitudinal Look at Excess Disabilities in the Mentally Impaired Aged." *Journal of Gerontology* 29 (1974):79-84.

Brown, B.F. The Impact of Confidants on Adjusting to Stressful Events in Adulthood. Paper delivered at the Annual Meetings of the Gerontological Society of America, San Diego, November 1980.

Burton, R.M.; Damon, W.W.; and Dellinger, D.C. "A Conceptual Model for Resource Allocation: The OARS Model." In *Multidimensional Functional Assessment: The OARS Methodology*, Duke University Center for the Study of Aging and Human Development. Durham, N.C.: Duke University, 1978.

Burton, R.M.; Damon, W.W.; Dellinger, D.C.; Erickson, D.J.; and Peterson, D.W. "Nursing Home Cost and Care: An Investigation of Alternatives." In *Multidimensional Functional Assessment: The OARS Methodology*, Duke University Center for the Study of Aging and Human Development. Durham, N.C.: Duke University, 1978.

Carp, F.M. "Morale: What Questions are We Asking of Whom?" In *Measuring Morale: A Guide to Effective Assessment*, ed. C.N. Nydegger. Washington, D.C.: Gerontological Society, 1977.

Carp, F.M. and Carp A. "Person-Environment Congruence and Sociability." *Research on Aging* 2 (December 1980):395-415.

Carter, W.B.; Bobbitt, R.A.; Bergner, M. and Gilson, B.S. "Validation of an

Interval Scaling: The Sickness Impact Profile." *Health Services Research* 11 (1976):516-528.

Cavan, R.S.; Burges, E.W.; Havinghurst, R.J.; and Goldhamer, H. *Personal Adjustment in Old Age.* Chicago: Science Research Associates, 1949.

Coblentz, J.M.; Mattis, S.; Zingesser, D.H.; Kasoff, S.S.; Wisniewski, H.M.; and Katzman, R. "Presenile Dementia: Clinical Aspects and Evaluation of Cerebrospinal Fluid Dynamics." *Archives of Neurology* 29 (1973):299-308.

Cohen, C.I., and Sokolovsky, J. "Clinical Use of Network Analysis for Psychiatric and Aged Populations." *Community Mental Health Journal* 15 (1979): 203-213.

Copeland, J.R.M.; Kelleher, M.J.; Kellett, J.M.; and Gourlay, A.J.; with Gurland, B.J., Fleiss, J.L.; and Sharpe, L. "A Semi-Structured Clinical Interview in the Elderly: The Geriatric Mental State Schedule: I. Development and Reliability." *Psychological Medicine* 6 (1976):439-449.

Coulton, C. "Developing an Instrument to Measure Person-Environment Fit." *Journal of Social Service Research* 3 (1979):159-173.

Crook, T.; Ferris, S.; and McCarthy, M. "The Misplaced-Objects Task: A Brief Test for Memory Dysfunction in the Aged." *Journal of the American Geriatric Society* 27 (1979):284-287.

Cumming, E.; Dean, L.; and Newell, D. "What is Morale? A Case History of a Validity Problem." *Human Organization*, 1958, pp. 3-8.

Currie, G.; MacNeill, R.M.; Walker, J.G.; Barnie, E.; and Mudie, E.W. "Medical and Social Screening of Patients Aged 70 to 72 by an Urban General Practice Health Team." *British Medical Journal* 2 (1974):108-111.

Cutler, N. "Age Variations in the Dimensionality of Life Satisfaction." *Journal of Gerontology* 34 (1979):573-578.

Dellinger, D.C. "The Concept of a Service Package: Prescribing, Measuring, and Costing Services." In *Multidimensional Functional Assessment: The OARS Methodology*, Duke University Center for the Study of Aging and Human Development. Durham, N.C.: Duke University, 1978.

Deniston, O.L., and Jette, A. "A Functional Status Assessment Instrument: Validation in an Elderly Population." *Health Services Research* 15 (1980): 21-34.

Densen, P.M. *An Approach to the Assessment of Long-Term Care: Final Report.* Boston: Harvard Center for Community Health and Medical Care, 1976.

Densen, P.M. and Jones, E.W. "The Patient Classification for Long-Term Care Developed by Four Research Groups in the United States." *Medical Care* 14 (1976, suppl.):126-133.

Derogatis, L.R.; Lipma, R.A.; Rickels, K.; Uhlenhuth, E.H.; and Covi, L. "The Hopkins Sympton Checklist (HSCL): A Measure of Primary Symptom Dimensions." *Pharmacopsychiatry* 7 (1974):79-110.

Doherty, N. *TRIAGE Research Group Annual Report.* Farmington, Conn.: University of Connecticut Health Center, 1976.

Donald, C.A.; Ware, J.E., Jr.; Brook, R.H.; and Avery, A.D. *Conceptualization and Measurement of Health for Adults in the Health Insurance Study*, vol. IV. *Social Health*, (R-1987/4-HEW). Santa Monica, Calif.: Rand Corporation, 1978.

Donaldson, S.W. *Donaldson ADL Evaluation Form*. Boston: Tufts University School of Medicine, n.d.

Donaldson, S.W.; Wagner, C.C.; and Gresham, G.E. "A Unified ADL Evaluation Form." *Archives of Physical Medicine and Rehabilitation* 54 (1973):175-185.

Drachman, D.A. "An Approach to the Neurology of Aging." In *Handbook of Mental Health and Aging*, ed. J.E. Birren and R.B. Sloane. Englewood Cliffs, N.J.: Prentice-Hall, 1980.

Duff, R.W., and Hong, L.K. "Quality and Quantity of Social Interactions in the Life Satisfaction of Older Americans." *Sociology and Social Research*, forthcoming.

Duke University Center for the Study of Aging and Human Development. *Multidimensional Functional Assessment: The OARS Methodology*. Durham, N.C.: Duke University, 1978.

Dye, C.J. "Personality." In *Research Instruments in Social Gerontology* Vol. I, ed. D.J. Mangen and W.A. Peterson, Minneapolis: University of Minnesota, forthcoming.

Eggert, G.M., and Bowlyow, J.E. *Preliminary Findings: The ACCESS Model*. Rochester, N.Y.: Monroe County Long-Term Care Program, 1979.

Eggert, G.M.: Bowlyow, J.E.; and Nichols, C.W. "Gaining Control of the Long-Term Care Systems: First Returns from the ACCESS Experiment." *The Gerontologist* 20 (1980):356-363.

Eisdorfer, C., and Friedel, R.O., eds. *Cognitive and Emotional Disturbance in the Elderly: Clinical Issues*. Chicago: Year Book Medical Publishers, 1977.

Erickson, R.C., and Scott, M.L. "Clinical Memory Testing: A Review." *Psychological Bulletin* 84 (1977):1130-1149.

Ernst, M., and Ernst, N.S. "Functional Capacity." In *Research Instruments in Social Gerontology*, ed. D.J. Mangen and W.A. Peterson. Vol. 3. Minneapolis: University of Minnesota, forthcoming.

Ernst, P.; Badash, D.; Beran, B.; Kosovsky, R.; and Kleinhauz, M. "Incidence of Mental Illness in the Aged: Unmasking the Effects of a Diagnosis of Chronic Brain Syndrome." *Journal of the American Geriatric Society* 25 (1977a): 371-375.

Ernst, P.; Bera, B.; Badash, D.; Kosovsky, R.; and Kleinhauz, M. "Treatment of the Aged Mentally Ill: Further Unmasking of the Effects of a Diagnosis of Chronic Brain Syndrome." *Journal of the American Geriatric Society* 25 (1977b):446-469.

Falcone, A.R. *Long-Term Care Information System Assessment Process*. Lansing: Michigan Office of Services to the Aging, 1978.

———. *Development of a Long-Term Care Information System: Final Report.* Lansing: Michigan Office of Services to the Aging, 1979.

Farina, A.; Arenberg, D.; and Guskin, S. "A Scale for Measuring Minimal Social Behavior." *Journal of Consulting Psychology* 21 (1957):265-268.

Ferrari, N. "Institutionalization and Attitude Change in an Aged Population: A Field Study in Dissonance Theory." Unpublished dissertation, Case Western Reserve University, Cleveland, 1962.

Ferraro, K.F. "Self-Ratings of Health Among the Old and the Old-Old." *Journal of Health and Social Behavior* 21 (1980):377-383.

Fillenbaum, G.G. "Validity and Reliability of the Multidimensional Functional Assessment Questionnaire." In *Multidimensional Functional Assessment: The OARS Methodology,* Duke University Center for the Study of Aging and Human Development. Durham, N.C.: Duke University, 1978.

———. "Comparison of Two Brief Tests of Organic Brain Impairment: The MSQ and the Short Portable MSQ." *Journal of the American Geriatrics Society* 28 (1980):381-384.

Fillenbaum, G.G., and Pfeiffer, E. "The Mini-Mult: A Cautionary Note." *Journal of Consulting and Clinical Psychology* 44 (1976):698-703.

Fink, M.; Green, M.; and Bender, M.B. "The Face-Hand Test as a Diagnostic Sign of Organic Mental Syndrome." *Neurology* 2 (1952):46-59.

Fishback, D.B. "Mental Status Questionnaire for Organic Brain Syndrome, with a New Visual Counting Test." *Journal of the American Geriatric Society* 25 (1977):167-170.

Flanagan, J.C. "A Research Approach to Improving Our Quality of Life." *American Psychologist* 33 (1978):138-147.

Folstein, M.F.; Folstein, S.; and McHugh, P.R. "Mini-Mental State: A Practical Method for Grading the Cognitive State of Patients for the Clinician." *Journal of Psychiatric Research* 12 (1975):189-198.

Froland, C.; Brodsky, G.; Olson, M.; and Stewart, L. "Social Support and Social Adjustment: Implications for Mental Health Professionals." *Community Mental Health Journal* 15 (1979):82-93.

Gaitz, C.M., and Scott, J. "Age and the Measurement of Mental Health." *Journal of Health and Social Behavior* 13 (1972):55-67.

Gallagher, D.; Thompson, L.W.; and Levy, S.M. "Clinical Psychological Assessment of Older Adults." In *Aging in the 1980's: Selected Contemporary Issues in the Psychology of Aging,* ed. L. Poon. Washington, D.C.: American Psychological Association, 1980.

Gendreau, L.; Roach, T.; and Gendreau, P. "Assessing the Intelligence of Aged Persons: Report on the Quick Test." *Psychological Reports* 32 (1973): 475-480.

George, L.K. "The Happiness Syndrome: Methodological and Substantive Issues in the Study of Social Psychological Well-Being in Adulthood." *The Gerontologist* 19 (1979):210-216.

George, L.K., and Bearon, L.B. *Quality of Life in Older Persons: Meaning and Measurement.* New York: Human Sciences Press, 1980.

Gilson, B.S.; Gilson, J.S.; Bergner, M.; Bobbitt, R.A.; Kressel, S.; Pollard, W.E.; and Vesselago, M. "The Sickness Impact Profile: Development of an Outcome Measure of Health Care." *American Journal of Public Health* 65 (1975):1304-1310.

Glassman, J.J.; Tell, R.L.; Larrivee, J.P.; and Helland, R. "Toward an Estimation of Service Need." In *Community Planning for an Aging Society,* ed. M. Lawton et al. Stroudsberg, Pa.: Dowden, Hutchinson, and Ross, 1976.

Goga, J.A., and Hambacher, W.O. "Psychologic and Behavioral Assessment of Geriatric Patients: A Review." *Journal of the American Geriatric Society* 25 (1977):232-237.

Goldberg, E.M. *Helping the Aged: A Field Experiment in Social Work.* London: George Allen Unwin, 1970.

Good, M.J.D.; Smilkstein, G.; Good, B.J.; Shaffer, T.; and Arons, T. "The Family APGAR Index: A Study of Construct Validity." *Journal of Family Practice* 8 (1979):577-582.

Goran, M.; Crystal, R. Ford, L.; and Tebbutt, J. "PSRO Review of LTC Utilization and Quality." *Medical Care* 14 (1976):94-98.

Graney, M.J., and Graney, E.E. "Scaling Adjustment in Older People." *International Journal on Aging and Human Development* 4 (1973):351-359.

———. "Communications Activity Substitutions in Aging." *Journal of Communication* 24 (1974):88-96.

Granger, C.V. *Medical Rehabilitation Research and Training Center No. 7 Annual Progress Report.* Boston: Tufts University School of Medicine, 1974.

Granger, C.V., and Greer, D.S. "Functional Status Measurement and Medical Rehabilitation Outcomes." *Archives of Physical Medicine and Rehabilitation* 57 (1976):103-109.

Granger, C.V.; Greer, D.S.; Liset, E.; Coulombe, J.; and O'Brien, E. "Measurement of Outcomes of Care for Stroke Patients." *Stroke* 6 (1975):34-41.

Grauer, H., and Birnbom, F. "A Geriatric Functional Rating Scale to Determine the Need for Institutional Care." *Journal of the American Geriatrics Society* 20 (1975):472-476.

Gross-Andrew, S., and Zimmer, A. "Incentives to Families Caring for Disabled Elderly: Research and Demonstration Project to Strengthen the Natural Support System." *Journal of Gerontological Social Work* 1 (1978):119-135.

Gurel, L.; Linn, M.W.; and Linn, B.S. "Physical and Mental Impairment-of-Function Evaluation in the Aged: The PAMIE Scale." *Journal of Gerontology* 27 (1972):83-90.

Gurland, B.J. "The Assessment of the Mental Health Status of Older Adults." In *Handbook of Mental Health and Aging,* ed. J.E. Birren and R.B. Sloane. Englewood Cliffs, N.J.: Prentice-Hall, 1980.

Gurland, B.J.; Fleiss, J.L.; Goldberg, K.; Sharpe, L.; Copeland, J.R.M.; Kelleher, M.J.; and Kellett, J.M. "A Semi-Structured Clinical Interview for the Assessment of Diagnosis and Mental State in the Elderly: The Geriatric Mental State Schedule." *Psychological Medicine* 6 (1976):451-459.

Gurland, B.; Kuriansky, J.; Sharpe, L.; Simon, R.; Stiller, P.; and Birkett, P. "The Comprehensive Assessment and Referral Evaluation (CARE)— Rationale, Development and Reliability: Part II. A Factor Analysis." *International Journal of Aging and Human Development* 8 (1977):9-42.

Gurland, B.; Dean, L.; Gurland, R.; and Cook, D. "Personal Time Dependency in the Elderly of New York City: Findings from the US-UK Cross-National Geriatric Community Study." In *Dependency in the Elderly of New York City: Policy and Service Implications of the US-UK Cross-National Geriatric Community Study,* Community Council of Greater New York. Report of a Research Utilization Workshop held on 23 March 1978.

Gurland, B.J.; Dean, L.; Copeland, J.; Kelleher, M.; Gurland, R.; and Golden, R. "Criteria for the Diagnosis of Dementia in the Community Elderly" July 1979. (Mimeographed.)

Gutkin, C.; Morris, J.N.; Sherwood, S.; and Stone, R. "A Mathematical Function to Predict Potential of Transfer to a Community Care Home for Level II Nursing Home Patients in Vermont." Draft paper, 30 January 1979.

Guttman, D., ed. *The Impact of Needs, Knowledge, Ability and Living Arrangements on Decision-Making of the Elderly.* Washington, D.C.: National Catholic School of Social Services, Catholic University, 1977.

Habot, B., and Libow, L.S. "The Interrelationship of Mental and Physical Status and Its Assessment in the Older Adult: Mind-Body Interaction." In *Handbook of Mental Health and Aging,* ed. J.E. Birren and R.B. Sloane. Englewood Cliffs, N.J.: Prentice-Hall, 1980.

Hageboeck, H. *Iowa Comprehensive Assessment Profile for the Assessment of Functional Dependence of Older Persons and Adult Disabled.* Iowa City: Iowa Gerontology Project, University of Iowa, 1979.

Harris, Louis and Associates. *The Myth and Reality of Aging in America.* Washington, D.C.: National Council on Aging, 1975.

Havighurst, R.J., and Albrecht, R. *Older People.* New York: Longmans, Green, and Company, 1953.

Havighurst, R.J.; Neugarten, B.L.; and Tobin, S.S. "The Measurement of Life Satisfaction." *Journal of Gerontology* 16 (1961):134-143.

"Health Status Indexes—Work in Progress." *Health Services Research,* Special Issue. Chicago: Hospital Research and Educational Trust, 1976.

Hersch, E.L.; Kral, V.A.; and Palmer, R.B. "Clinical Value of the London Psychogeriatric Rating Scale." *Journal of the American Geriatric Society* 26 (1978):348-354.

Hill, R. *Family Development in Three Generations: A Longitudinal Study of Changing Family Patterns of Planning and Achievement.* Cambridge, Mass.: Schenkman Publishing Company, 1970.

Hodgson, J.H., and Quinn, J.L. "Impact of the TRIAGE Health Care Delivery System on Client Morale, Independent Living and the Cost of Care." *The Gerontologist* 20 (1980):364-371.

Hodkinson, H.M. "Evaluation of a Mental Test Score for the Assessment of Mental Impairment in the Elderly." *Age and Ageing* 1 (1972):233-238.

Holmes, T.H., and Rahe, R.H. "The Social Readjustment Rating Scale." *Journal of Psychosomatic Research* 11 (1967):219-225.

Honigfeld, G.; and Klett, C.J. "Nurses' Observation Scale for Inpatient Evaluation: A New Scale for Measuring Improvement in Chronic Schizophrenia." *Journal of Clinical Psychology* 21 (1965):65-71.

Horn, J.L. "Organization of Data on Life-Span Development of Human Abilities." In *Life-Span Developmental Psychology: Research and Theory,* ed. L.R. Goulet and P.B. Baltes. New York: Academic Press, 1970.

Hulicka, I.; Morganti, J.; and Cataldo, J. "Perceived Latitude of Choice of Institutionalized and Non-Institutionalized Elderly Women." *Experimental Aging Research* 1 (1975):27-39.

Isaacs, B., and Akhtar, A.J. "The Set Test." *Age and Ageing* 1 (1972):222-226.

Isaacs, B., and Kennie, A.T. "The Set Test as an Aid to the Detection of Dementia in Old People." *British Journal of Psychiatry* 132 (1973):467-470.

Isaacs, B., and Neville, Y. *The Measurement of Need in Old People* (Scottish Health Service Studies No. 34). Perth: Milne, Tannahill & Methuen, 1975.

Isaacs, B.; Livingstone, M.; and Neville, Y. *Survival of the Unfittest: A Study of Geriatric Patients in Glasgow.* London: Routledge & Kegan Paul, 1972.

Jette, A.M., and Deniston, O.L. "Inter-Observer Reliability of a Functional Status Assessment Instrument." *Journal of Chronic Disease* 31 (1978): 573-580.

Johnston, J.C., and Stack, T.F. "A Comparison of the Effectiveness of the OARS Multi-Demensional Assessment Tool and the Stockton Geriatric Rating Scale as a Means of Evaluating Functional Ability in the Hospitalized Elderly Client." Paper presented at the meeting of the Gerontological Society of America, San Diego, Calif., 20-25 November 1980.

Jones, E.; McNitt, B.; and McKnight E. *Patient Classification for Long-Term Care: User's Manual.* DHEW Publication No. HRA 75-3107. Washington, D.C.: U.S. Government Printing Office, 1974.

Kahana, B. "Use of Projective Techniques in Personality Assessment of the Aged." In *Clinical Psychology of Aging,* ed. M. Storandt, I.C. Siegler, and M.F. Elias. New York: Plenum Press, 1978.

Kahana, E. "Matching Environments to Needs of the Aged: A Conceptual Scheme." In *Late Life Communities and Environment Policy*, ed. J.F. Gubrium. Springfield, Ill.: Charles C. Thomas, 1974.

Kahana, E.; Fairchild, T.; and Kahana, B. "Adaptation." In *Research Instruments in Social Gerontology,* ed. D.J. Mangen and W.A. Peterson. Vol. 1. Minneapolis: University of Minnesota, forthcoming.

Kahn, R.L.; Goldfarb, A.I.; Pollack, M.; and Gerber, I.E. "Relationship of

Mental and Physical Status in Institutionalized Aged Persons." *American Journal of Psychiatry* 117 (1960a):120-124.

Kahn, R.L.; Goldfarb, A.I.; Pollack, M.; and Peck, A. "Brief Objective Measures for the Determination of Mental Status in the Aged." *American Journal of Psychiatry* 117 (1960b):326-328.

Kane, R.A.; Kane, R.L.; Kleffel, D.; Brook, R.; Eby, C.; Goldberg, G.; Rubenstein, L.; and VanRyzin, J. *The PSRO and the Nursing Home*, R-2459/1-HCFA. Santa Monica, Calif.: Rand Corporation, 1979.

Kane, R.L., and Kane, R.A. "Alternatives to Institutional Care of the Elderly: Beyond the Dichotomy." *The Gerontologist* 20 (1980):249-259.

Kane, R.L.; Solomon, D.H.; Beck, J.C.; Keeler, E.; and Kane, R.A. *Geriatrics in the United States: Manpower Projections and Training Considerations.* Lexington, Mass.: Lexington Books, D.C. Heath and Company, 1981.

Kastenbaum, R. "The Realm of Death: An Emerging Area in Psychological Research." *Journal of Human Relations* 13 (1965):538-552.

Kastenbaum, R., and Sherwood, S. "VIRO: A Scale for Assessing the Interview Behavior of Elderly People." In *Research, Planning and Action for the Elderly,* ed. D.P. Kent, R. Kastenbaum, and S. Sherwood. New York: Behavioral Publications, 1972.

Katz, S.; Ford, A.B.; Moskowitz, R.W.; Jackson, B.A.; and Jaffee, M.W. "Studies of Illness in the Aged. The Index of ADL: A Standardized Measure of Biological and Psychosocial Function." *Journal of the American Medical Association* 185 (1963):94ff.

Katz, S.; Hedrick, S.; and Henderson, N. "The Measurement of Long-Term Care Needs and Impact." *Health and Medical Care Services Review* 2 (1979):2-21.

Kay, D.W.K. "Epidemiology and Identification of Brain Deficit in the Elderly." In *Cognitive and Emotional Disturbance in the Elderly: Clinical Issues,* ed. C. Eisdorfer and R.O. Friedel. Chicago: Year Book Medical Publishers, 1977.

Keller, T.W. "Epidemiology of Depression Among the Elderly," 1979. (Mimeographed.)

Kendell, R.E. *The Role of Diagnosis in Psychiatry.* London: Blackwell Scientific Publications, 1975.

Kent, D.; Kastenbaum, R.; and Sherwood, S., eds. *Research Planning and Action for the Elderly.* New York: Behavioral Publications, 1972.

Kerckhoff, A.C. "Nuclear and Extended Family Relationships: A Normative and Behavioral Analysis." In *Social Structure and Family: Generational Relations,* ed. E. Shanas and G. Streib Englewood Cliffs, N.J.: Prentice-Hall, 1965.

Kincannon, J.C. "Prediction of the Standard MMPI Scale Scores from 71 Items: The Mini-Mult." *Journal of Consulting and Clinical Psychology* 32 (1968):319-325.

Kiyak, A.; Liang, J.; and Kahana, E. "Methodological Inquiry into the Schedule of Recent Life Events." Paper presented at the American Psychological Association Meetings, New York, August 1976.

Kleban, M.M., and Brody, E.M. "Prediction of Improvement in Mentally Impaired Aged: Personality Ratings by Social Workers." *Journal of Gerontology* 27 (1972):69-76.

Klonoff, H., and Kennedy, M. "Memory and Perceptual Functioning in Octogenarians and Nonagenarians in the Community." *Journal of Gerontology* 20 (1965):328-333.

Kochansky, G.E. "Psychiatric Rating Scales for Assessing Psychopathology in the Elderly: A Critical Review." In *Psychiatric Symptoms and Cognitive Loss in the Elderly: Evaluation and Assessment Techniques*, ed. A. Raskin and L. Jarvik. Washington, D.C.: Hemisphere Publishing Company, 1979.

Kovar, M.G. "Elderly People: The Population 65 Years and Over." In *Health, United States, 1976-1977*, DHEW Publication No. HRA 77-1232. Washington, D.C.: U.S. Government Printing Office, 1977a.

_____. "Health of the Elderly and Use of Health Services." *Public Health Reports* 92 (1977b):9-19.

Kramer, N.A., and Jarvik, L.F. "Assessment of Intellectual Changes in the Elderly." In *Psychiatric Symptoms and Cognitive Loss in the Elderly: Evaluation and Assessment Techniques*, ed. A. Raskin and L.F. Jarvik. Washington, D.C.: Hemisphere Publishing Company, 1979.

Kulys, R., and Tobin, S.S. "Older People and Their 'Responsible Others.'" *Social Work* 25 (1980):138-145.

Kuriansky, J.B., and Gurland, B. "Performance Test of Activities of Daily Living." *International Journal of Aging and Human Development* 7 (1976):343-352.

Kuriansky, J.B.; Gurland, B.J.; Fleiss, J.L.; and Cowan, D.W. "The Assessment of Self-Care Capacity in Geriatric Psychiatric Patients." *Journal of Clinical Psychology* 32 (1976):95-102.

Kutner, B.; Fanshel, D.; Togo, A.; and Langner, T. *Five Hundred Over Sixty.* New York: Russell Sage Foundation, 1956.

Laird, C. *Limbo*. Novato, Calif.: Chandler and Sharp, 1979.

Langer, E., and Rodin, J. "Effects of Choice and Enhanced Personal Responsibility for the Aged." *Journal of Personality and Social Psychology* 34 (1976):191-198.

Langner, T.S. "A Twenty-two Item Screening Score of Psychiatric Symptoms Indicating Impairment." *Journal of Health and Human Behavior* 3 (1962): 269-276.

Larson, R. "Thirty Years of Research on the Subjective Well-Being of Older Americans." *Journal of Gerontology* 33 (1978):109-125.

Laurie, W.F. "The Cleveland Experience: Functional Status and Services Use." In *Multidimensional Functional Assessment: The OARS Methodology*,

Duke University Center for the Study of Aging and Human Development. Durham, N.C.: Duke University, 1978.

Lawton, M.P. "Psychological Well-Being Interview." (Mimeographed, n.d.)

———. "PGC Mental Status Questionnaire." (Mimeographed, 1968.)

———. "Assessment, Integration, and Environments for Older People." *The Geronotologist* 10 (1970):38-46.

———. "Assessing the Competence of Older People." In *Research Planning and Action for the Elderly*, ed., D. Kent, R. Kastenbaum, and S. Sherwood. New York: Behavioral Publications, 1972a.

———. "Dimensions of Morale." In *Research Planning and Action for the Elderly*, ed. D. Kent, R. Kastenbaum, and S. Sherwood. New York: Behavioral Publications, 1972b.

———. "Social Ecology and the Health of Older People." *American Journal of Public Health* 64 (1974):257-260.

———. "The Philadelphia Geriatric Morale Scale: A Revision." *Journal of Gerontology* 30 (1975):85-89.

———. "Morale: What are We Measuring?" In *Measuring Morale: A Guide to Effective Assessment*, ed. C.N. Nydegger. Washington, D.C.: Gerontological Society, 1977.

———. *Social and Medical Services in Housing for the Aged,* DHHS Publication No. ADM 80-861. Washington, D.C.: U.S. Government Printing Office, 1980.

Lawton, M.P.; Ward, M.; and Yaffe, S. "Indices of Health in an Aging Population." *Journal of Gerontology* 22 (1967):334-342.

Lawton, M.P.; Whelihan, W.M.; and Belsky, J.K. "Personality Tests and Their Uses with Older Adults." In *Handbook of Mental Health and Aging*, ed. J.E. Birren and R.B. Sloane. Englewood Cliffs, N.J.: Prentice-Hall, 1980.

Lee, G. "Children and the Elderly: Interaction and Morale." *Research on Aging* 1 (1979):335-380.

Lee, G., and Ihinger-Tallman, M. "Sibling Interaction and Morale: The Effects of Family Relations on Older People." *Research on Aging* 2 (1980):367-391.

Leering, C. "A Structural Model of Functional Capacity in the Aged." *Journal of the American Geriatric Society* 27 (1979):314-316.

Lemke, S., and Moos, R. "Assessing the Institutional Policies of Sheltered Care Settings." *Journal of Gerontology* 35 (1980):96-107.

Levine, N. "Validation of the Quick Test for Intelligence Screening of the Elderly." *Psychological Reports* 29 (1971):167-172.

Levitt, E., and Lubin, B. *Depression: Concepts, Controversies and Some New Facts*. New York: Springer Publishing Company, 1975.

Libow, L.S. "Pseudo-senility: Acute and Reversible Organic Brain Syndrome." In *Cognitive and Emotional Disturbance in the Elderly: Clinical Issues*, ed. C. Eisdorfer and R.O. Friedel. Chicago: Year Book Medical Publishers, 1977.

Lin, N.; Dean, A.; and Ensel, W.M. "Constructing Social Support Scales: A Methodological Note." Paper presented at the Conference on Stress, Social Support, and Schizophrenia, Burlington, Vermont, 24 September 1979.

Linn, B.S., and Linn, M.W. "Objective and Self-Assessed Health in the Old and Very Old." *Social Science and Medicine* 14 (1980):311-315.

Linn, B.S.; Linn, M.W.; and Gurel, L. "Cumulative Illness Rating Scale." *Journal of the American Geriatric Society* 16 (1968):622-626.

Linn, M.W. "A Rapid Disability Rating Scale." *Journal of the American Geriatric Society* 15 (1967):211-214.

———. "Assessing Community Adjustment in the Elderly." In *Psychiatric Symptoms and Cognitive Loss in the Elderly: Evaluation and Assessment Techniques,* ed. A. Raskin and L.F. Jarvik. New York: Hemisphere Publishing Company, 1979.

Linn, M.W.; Gurel, L.; and Linn, B.S. "Patient Outcome as a Measure of Quality of Nursing Home Care." *American Journal of Public Health* 67 (1977): 337-344.

Linn, M.W.; Sculthorpe, W.B.; Evje, M.; Slater, P.H.; and Goodman, S.P. "A Social Dysfunction Rating Scale." *Journal of Psychiatric Research* 6 (1969): 299-306.

Lohman, N. "Correlations of Life Satisfaction, Morale, and Adjustment Measures." *Journal of Gerontology* 32 (1977):73-75.

Lopata, H.Z. *Widowhood in an American City.* Cambridge, Mass.: Schenkman Publishing Company, 1972.

———. "Support Systems of Elderly Urbanites: Chicago of the 1970's." *The Gerontologist* 35 (1975):41.

Maddox, G.L. "Some Correlates of Differences in Self-Assessments of Health Status among the Elderly." *Journal of Geronotology* 17 (1962):180-185.

Mahoney, F.I., and Barthel, D.W. "Functional Evaluation: The Barthel Index." *Maryland State Medical Journal* 14 (1965):61–65.

Main, S., and Bennett, R. "Greeting Behavior and Social Adjustment in Aged Residents of a Nursing Home." In *Research Planning and Action for the Elderly,* ed. D. Kent, R. Kastenbaum, and S. Sherwood. New York: Behavioral Publications, 1972.

Mancini, J.A. "Family Relationships and Morale Among People 65 Years of Age and Older." *American Journal of Orthopsychiatry* 49 (1979):292-300.

Mangen, D.J., and Peterson, W.A., eds. *Research Instruments in Social Gerontology.* Vol. 1-vol. 3. Minneapolis: University of Minnesota, forthcoming.

McCaffree, K.M., and Harkins, E.M. *Final Report for Evaluation of the Outcomes of Nursing Home Care.* Seattle, Wash.: Battelle Human Affairs Research Centers, 1976.

McNeil, B.J.; Keeler, E.; and Adelstein, S.J. "Primer on Certain Elements of

Medical Decision Making." *New England Journal of Medicine* 292 (1975): 211-215.

Meer, B., and Baker, J.A. "Reliability of Measurements of Intellectual Functioning of Geriatric Patients." *Journal of Gerontology* 20 (1965):410-414.

Melzack, R. "The McGill Pain Questionnaire: Major Properties and Scoring Methods." *Pain* 1 (1975):227-299.

Mercer, S.O., and Kane, R.A. "Helplessness and Hopelessness in the Institutionalized Aged: A Field Experiment." *Health and Social Work* 4 (1979): 91-116.

Miller, E. "Cognitive Assessment of the Older Adult." In *Handbook of Mental Health and Aging,* ed. J.E. Birren and R.B. Sloane. Englewood Cliffs, N.J.: Prentice-Hall, 1980.

Miller, E.R., and Parachek, J.F. "Validation and Standardization of a Goal-Oriented, Quick-Screening Geriatric Scale." *Journal of the American Geriatric Society* 22 (1974):278-281.

Miller, M. "Geriatric Suicide: The Arizona Study." *The Gerontologist* 18 (1978):488-495.

Milne, J.S.; Maule, M.M.; Cormack, S.; and Williamson, J. "The Design and Testing of a Questionnaire and Examination to Assess Physical and Mental Health in Older People Using a Staff Nurse as the Observer." *Journal of Chronic Disease* 25 (1972):385-405.

Mitchell, R.E., and Trickett, E.J. "Social Networks as Mediators of Social Support: An Analysis of the Effects and Determinants of Social Networks." *Community Mental Health Journal* 16 (1980):27-44.

Monroe, R.T.; Whiskin, F.E.; Bonacich, P.; and Jewell, W.O. III. "The Cornell Medical Index Questionnaire as a Measure of Health in Older People." *Journal of Gerontology* 20 (1965):18-22.

Moos, R.H. *Evaluating Treatment Environments: A Social Ecological Approach.* New York: John Wiley and Sons, 1974.

Moos, R.H., and Lemke, S. *Multiphasic Environmental Assessment Procedure.* Palo Alto, Calif.: Stanford University School of Medicine, 1979.

Moos, R.H.; Grauvain, M.; Max, S.W.; and Mehren, B. "Assessing the Environments of Sheltered Care Settings." *The Gerontologist* 19 (1979):74-82.

Moriwaki, S.Y. "The Affect Balance Scale: A Validity Study with Aged Samples." *Journal of Gerontology* 29 (1974):73-78.

Morris, J.N., and Sherwood, S. "A Retesting and Modification of the Philadelphia Geriatric Center Morale Scale." *Journal of Gerontology* 30 (1975): 77-84.

Morris, J.N.; Wolf, R.S.; and Klerman, L.V. "Common Themes Among Morale and Depression Scales." *Journal of Gerontology* 30 (1975):209-215.

Moskowitz, E., and McCann, C.B. "Classification of Disability in the Chronically Ill and Aging." *Journal of Chronic Disability* 5 (1957):342-346.

Mossey, J.M., and Tisdale, W.A. "Measurement of Functional Health Status of the Institutionalized Elderly: Rationale for and Development of an 'Index.'" Working Paper No. 4, Georgetown University, Washington, D.C., 1979. (Mimeographed.)

Mushkin, S.J., and Dunlop, D.W. eds. *Health: What is it Worth? Measures of Health Benefits.* New York: Pergamon Press, 1979.

Nahemow, L., and Bennett, R. "Attitude Change with Institutionalization of the Aged." Unpublished final report, Biometrics Research, New York State Department of Mental Hygiene, 1967.

Neilsen, M.; Blenkner, M.; Bloom, M.; Downs, T.; and Beggs, H. "Older Persons After Hospitalization: A Controlled Study of Home Aide Service." *American Journal of Public Health* 62 (1972): 1094-1101.

Neugarten, B.; Havighurst, R.; and Tobin, S. "The Measure of Life Satisfaction." *Journal of Gerontology* 16 (1961):134-143.

Nydegger, C.N., ed. *Measuring Morale: A Guide to Effective Assessment.* Washington, D.C.: Gerontological Society, 1977.

Oberleder, M. "An Attitude Scale to Determine Adjustment in Institutions for the Aged." *Journal of Chronic Disease* 15 (1961):915-923.

Ogren, E.H., and Linn, M.W. "Male Nursing Home Patients: Relocation and Mortality." *Journal of the American Geriatric Society* 19 (1971):229-239.

Pepper, G.A.; Jorgensen, L.B.; Kane, R.L.; and Devenport, J.K. "Problem-Oriented Process: Nurses' Manual." (Mimeographed, 1972.)

Perlin, S., and Butler, R.N. "Psychiatric Aspects of Adaptation to the Aging Experience." In *Human Aging: A Biological and Behavioral Study,* ed. J.E. Birren et al. Bethesda, Md.: National Institute of Mental Health, 1963.

Peterson, W.A.; Mangen, D.J.; and Sanders, R. *The Development of an Instrument Bank: Assessment of Available Instruments and Measurement Scales for the Study of Aging and the Elderly: Final Report.* Kansas City, Mo.: Midwest Council for Social Research in Aging, 1978.

Pfeiffer, E. "A Short Portable Mental Status Questionnaire for the Assessment of Organic Brain Deficit in Elderly Patients." *Journal of the American Geriatrics Society* 23 (1975):433-441.

Pfeiffer, E.; Johnson, T.M.; and Chiofolo, R.C. "Functional Assessment of Elderly Subjects in Four Service Settings." Paper presented at the Annual Scientific Meeting, Gerontological Society of America, San Diego, Calif., 21-25 November 1980.

Philadelphia Geriatric Center. "The Pennsylvania Domiciliary Care Program Social Adjustment Form." (Mimeographed, n.d.)

Pierce, R., and Clark, M. "Measurement of Morale in the Elderly." *International Journal of Aging and Human Development* 4 (1973):83-101.

Pincus, A. "The Definition and Measurement of the Institutional Environment in Homes for the Aged." *The Gerontologist* 8 (1968):207-210.

Pincus, A., and Wood, V. "Methodological Issues in Measuring the Environment in Institutions of the Aged and Its Impact on Residents." *Aging and Human Development* 1 (1970):117-126.

Platt, S.; Weyman, A.; and Hirsch, S. "Social Behavior Assessment Schedule (SBAS): Training Manual and Rating Guide," 2d ed. (Mimeographed, 1978.)

Platt, S.; Weyman, A.; Hirsch, S.; and Hewett, S. "The Social Behavior Assessment Schedule (SBAS): Rationale, Contents, Scoring and Reliability of a New Interview Schedule." *Social Psychiatry* 15 (1980):43-55.

Pless, I.B., and Satterwhite, B. "Family Function and Family Problems." In *Child Health and the Community*, ed. R.J. Haggarty, K.J. Roughman, and I.B. Pless. New York: John Wiley and Sons, 1975.

Plutchik, R.; Conte, H.; and Lieberman, M. "Development of a Scale (GIES) for Assessment of Cognitive and Perceptual Functioning in Geriatric Patients." *Journal of the American Geriatric Society* 19 (1971):614-623.

Pollard, W.E.; Bobbitt, R.A.; Bergner, M.; Martin, D.P.; and Gilson, B.S. "The Sickness Impact Profile: Reliability of a Health Status Measure." *Medical Care* 14 (1976):146-155.

Quayhagan, M.P., and Chiriboga, D. "Geriatric Coping Schedule: Potential and Problems." Paper presented at the 29th Annual Meeting of the Gerontological Society, New York, October 1976.

Rand Corporation. "Prognosing the Course of Nursing-Home Patients," Proposal No. 79-090. Submitted to National Center for Health Services Research, 21 March 1979.

Raskin, A., and Jarvik, L.F. *Psychiatric Symptoms and Cognitive Loss in the Elderly: Evaluation and Assessment Techniques.* Washington, D.C.: Hemisphere Publishing Company, 1979.

Ray, R.O. "The Life Satisfaction Index-Form A As Applied to Older Adults: Technical Note on Scoring Patterns." *Journal of the American Geriatric Society* 27 (1979):418-420.

Reid, D.W., and Ziegler, M. "A Survey of the Reinforcements and Activities Elderly Citizens Feel Are Important for Their General Happiness." *Essence* 1 (1977):5-24.

Reid, D.; Haas, G.; and Hawkins, D. "Locus of Desired Control and Positive Self-Concept of the Elderly." *Journal of Gerontology* 32 (1977):441-450.

Rosencranz, H.A., and Pihlblad, C.T. "Measuring the Health of the Elderly." *Journal of Gerontology* 25 (1970):129-133.

Rosow, I. *Social Integration of the Aged.* New York: Free Press, 1967.

_____. "Morale: Concept and Measurement." In *Measuring Morale: A Guide to Effective Assessment,* ed. C.N. Nydegger. Washington, D.C.: Gerontological Society, 1977.

Rosow, I., and Breslau, N. "A Guttman Health Scale for the Aged." *Journal of Gerontology* 21 (1966):556-559.

Rubenstein, L.Z.; Romano, J.; and Abrass, I. "Effectiveness of an Inpatient Geriatraic Evaluation Unit." Paper presented at the Annual Meeting of the Gerontological Society of America, San Diego, California, 21-25 November 1980.

Sager, A. *Learning the Home Care Needs of the Elderly: Patient, Family, and Professional Views of an Alternative to Institutionalization.* Waltham, Mass.: Brandeis University, Levinson Policy Institute, 1979.

Salzman, C.; Shader, R.T.; Kochansky, G.E.; and Cronin, D.M. "Rating Scales for Psychotropic Drug Research with Geriatric Patients: I. Behavior Ratings." *Journal of the American Geriatrics Society* 20 (1972a):209-214.

Salzman, C.; Kochansky, G.E.; Shader, R.L.; and Cronin, D.M. "Rating Scales for Psychotropic Drug Research with Geriatric Patients: II. Mood Ratings." *Journal of the American Geriatric Society* 20 (1972b):215-221.

Salzman, C.; and Shader, R.I. "Clinical Evaluation of Depression in the Elderly." In *Psychiatric Symptoms and Cognitive Loss in the Elderly: Evaluation and Assessment Techniques,* ed. A. Raskin and L. Jarvik. Washington, D.C.: Hemisphere Publishing Company, 1979.

Sarno, J.E.; Sarno, M.T.; and Levita, E. "The Functional Life Scale." *Archives of Physical Medicine and Rehabilitation* 54 (1973):214-220.

Sarton, M. *As We Are Now.* New York: Norton, 1973.

Sauer, W., and Warland, R. "Morale and Life Satisfaction." In *Research Instruments in Social Geronotology,* ed. D.J. Mangen and W.A. Peterson. Vol. 1. Minneapolis: University of Minnesota, forthcoming.

Savage, R.D., and Britton, P.G. "A Short Scale for the Assessment of Mental Health in the Community Aged." *British Journal of Psychiatry* 113 (1967): 521-523.

Schaie, J.P., and Schaie, K.W. "Psychological Evaluation of the Cognitively Impared Elderly." In *Cognitive and Emotional Disturbance in the Elderly: Clinical Issues,* ed. C. Eisdorfer and R.O. Friedel. Chicago: Year Book Medical Publishers, 1977a.

Schaie, K.W., and Schaie, J.P. "Clinical Assessment and Aging." In *Handbook of the Psychology of Aging,* ed. J.E. Birren and K.W. Schaie. New York: Van Nostrand Reinhold, 1977b.

Schoening, H.A.; Anderegg, L.; Bergstrom, D.; Fonda, M.; Steinke, N.; and Ulrich, P. "Numerical Scoring of Self-Care Status of Patients." *Archives of Physical Medicine and Rehabilitation* 46 (1965):689-697.

Schoening, H.A., and Iversen, I.A. "Numerical Scoring of Self-Care Status: A Study of the Kenny Self-Care Evaluation." *Archives of Physical Medicine and Rehabilitation* 49 (1968):221-229.

Schonfield, D. "Future Commitments and Successful Aging: I. The Random Sample." *Journal of Gerontology* 28 (1973):189-196.

Schulz, R. "Effects of Control and Predictability on the Physical and Psychological Well-Being of the Institutionalized Aged." *Journal of Personality and Social Psychology* 33 (1976):563-573.

Seligman, M. *Helplessness: On Depression, Development, and Death.* San Francisco, Calif.: W.H. Freeman and Company, 1975.

Shader, R.I.; Harmatz, J.S.; and Salzman, C. "A New Scale for Clinical Assessment in Geriatric Populations: Sandoz Clinical Assessment—Geriatric (SCAG)." *Journal of the American Geriatric Society* 22 (1974):107-113.

Shanas, E. *The Health of Older People.* Cambridge, Mass.: Harvard University Press, 1962.

Shanas, E.; Townsend, P.; Wedderburn, D.; Friis, H.; Milhoj, P.; and Stehouwer, J. *Old People in Three Industrial Societies.* New York: Atherton Press, 1968.

Sharma, S. "Adaptation Patterns of Urban and Ethnic Aged." Ph.D. dissertation, Wayne State University, Detroit, Michigan, 1977.

Sherwood, S. *Long-Term Care: A Handbook for Researchers, Planners and Providers.* New York: Spectrum, 1975.

_____. "The Problems and Value of Morale Measurement." In *Measuring Morale: A Guide to Effective Assessment,* ed. C.N. Nydegger. Washington, D.C.: Gerontological Society, 1977.

Sherwood, S., and Feldman, C.S. "The Use of Easily Obtained Precoded Data in Screening Applicants to a Long-Term Care Facility." *The Gerontologist* 10 (1970):182-188.

Sherwood, S., and Morris, J.N. *A Study of the Effects of Emergency Alarm and Response System for the Aged: A Final Report.* Boston, Mass.: Hebrew Rehabilitation Center for Aged, 1980.

Sherwood, S.J.; Morris, J.; Mor, V.; and Gutkin, C. "Compendium of Measures for Describing and Assessing Long Term Care Populations." Boston: Hebrew Rehabilitation Center for Aged, 1977. (Mimeographed.)

Sidle, A.; Moos, R.; Cady, P.; and Adams, S. "Development of a Coping Scale." *Archives of General Psychiatry* 20 (1969):226-232.

Silverstone, B., and Wynter, L. "The Effects of Introducing a Heterosexual Living Space." *The Gerontologist* 15 (1975):83-87.

Skinner, D.E.; Charpentier, P.R.; Wissmann, K.G.; Foose, A.C.; and Soliz, R. *Evaluation of Personal Care Organizations and Other In-Home Alternatives to Nursing Home Care for the Elderly and Long-Term Disabled,* Interim Report No. 4: Major Experimental Design Considerations of a Prospective Study of Clients Served by Alternatives to Institutional Care. Silver Spring, Md.: Applied Management Sciences, 1976.

Sloane, R.B. "Organic Brain Syndrome." In *Handbook of Mental Health and*

Aging, ed. J.E. Birren and R.B. Sloane. Englewood Cliffs, N.J.: Prentice-Hall, 1980.

Smilkstein, G. "The Family APGAR: A Proposal for a Family Function Test and Its Use by Physicians." *Journal of Family Practice* 6 (1978):1231-1239.

Spitzer, R.L.; Fleiss, J.L.; Endicott, J.; and Cohen, J. "Mental Status Schedule: Properties of Factor-Analytically Derived Scales." *Archives of General Psychiatry* 16 (1967):479-493.

Steuer, J.; Bank, L.; Olsen, E.J.; and Jarvik, L.F. "Depression, Physical Health and Somatic Complaints in the Elderly." *Journal of Gerontology* 35 (1980): 683-688.

Stewart, A.L.; Ware, J.E., Jr.; Brook, R.H.; and Davies-Avery, A. *Conceptualization and Measurement of Health for Adults in the Health Insurance Study,* vol. II. *Physical Health in Terms of Functioning,* R-1987/2-HEW. Santa Monica, Calif.: Rand Corporation, 1978.

Taylor, C. "Why Measure Morale?" In *Measuring Morale: A Guide to Effective Assessment,* ed. C.N. Nydegger. Washington, D.C.: Gerontological Society, 1977.

Tec, N., and Granick (Bennett), R. "Social Isolation and Difficulties in Social Interaction of Residents of a Home for the Aged." *Social Problems* 7 (1960):226-232.

Thompson, W.; Streib, G.; Kosa, J. "The Effect of Retirement on Personal Adjustment: A Panel Analysis." *Journal of Gerontology* 15 (1960):166-169.

Tissue, T. "Another Look at Self-Rated Health Among the Elderly." *Journal of Gerontology* 27 (1972):91-94.

"TMI-Type Disasters May Require New Psychological Instruments." *Behavior Today* 11, May 1980.

Tulloch, J. *A Home Is Not a Home.* New York: Seabury Press, 1975.

U.S. Comptroller General. *The Well-Being of Older People in Cleveland, Ohio,* DHEW Publication No. HRD 77-70. Washington, D.C.: U.S. Government Printing Office, 1977.

_____. *Conditions of Older People: National Information System Needed,* DHEW Publication No. HRD 79-95. Washington, D.C.: U.S. Government Printing Office, 1979.

U.S. Department of Commerce. Bureau of the Census. *1976 Survey of Institutionalized Persons: A Study of Persons Receiving Long-Term Care,* Current Population Reports Special Series P-23, No. 69. Washington, D.C.: U.S. Government Printing Office, 1978.

U.S. Department of Health, Education, and Welfare (DHEW). *Working Document on Patient Care Management.* Washington, D.C.: U.S. Government Printing Office, 1978a.

_____. *Long-Term Care Minimum Data Set,* Preliminary Report of the Technical Consultant Panel on the Long-Term Care Data Set, U.S. National Committee on Vital and Health Statistics. Washington, D.C.: U.S. Government Printing Office, 1978b.

Ware, J.E., Jr.; Johnston, S.A.; Davies-Avery, A.; and Brook, R.H. *Conceptualization and Measurement of Health Status for Adults in the Health Insurance Study,* vol. III. *Mental Health,* R-1987/3-HEW. Santa Monica, Calif.: Rand Coporation, 1979.

Wechsler, D. "A Standardized Memory Scale for Clinical Use." *Journal of Psychology* 19 (1945):87-95.

Weinstock, C., and Bennett, R. "From 'Waiting on the List' to Becoming a 'Newcomer' and an 'Oldtimer' in a Home for the Aged: Two Studies of Socialization and Its Impact on Cognitive Functioning." *International Journal of Aging and Human Development* 2 (1971):46-58.

Weiss, R.W. "The Fund of Sociability." *Trans-Action* 6 (1969):36-43.

Weissert, W.G.; Wan, T.T.H.; and Livieratos, B.B. *Effects and Costs of Day Care and Homemaker Services for the Chronically Ill: A Randomized Experiment,* DHHS Publication No. PHS 79-3258. Hyattsville, Md.: Department of Health and Human Services, 1980.

Wing, J.K.; Birley, J.L.T.; Cooper, J.E.; Graham, P.; and Isaacs, A.D. "Reliability of a Procedure for Measuring Present Psychiatric State." *British Journal of Psychiatry* 113 (1967):499-515.

Wolk, R.L. "Refined Projected Techniques with the Aged." In *Research, Planning and Action for the Elderly,* ed. D.P. Kent, R. Kastenbaum, and S. Sherwood. New York: Behavioral Publications, 1972.

Wolk, S., and Telleen, S. "Psychological and Social Correlates of Life Satisfaction as a Function of Residential Constraint." *Journal of Gerontology* 31 (1976):89-98.

Wood, V.; Wylie, M.; and Sheafor, B. "An Analysis of a Short Self-Report Measure of Life Satisfaction: Correlation with Rater Judgments." *The Gerontologist* 6 (1969):31. (Abstract.)

Woolley, F.R.; Warnick, R.; Kane, R.L.; and Dyer, E.D. *Problem-Oriented Nursing.* New York: Springer, 1974.

Wylie, C.M. "Gauging the Response of Stroke Patients to Rehabilitation." *Journal of the American Geriatric Society* 15 (1967):797-805.

Zeman, F.D. "The Functional Capacity of the Aged: Its Estimation and Practical Importance." *Mt. Sinai Hospital Journal* 14 (1947):721-728.

Zung, W.W.K. "A Self-Rating Depression Scale." *Archives of General Psychiatry* 12 (1965):63-70.

_____. "Depression in the Normal Aged." *Psychosomatics* 8 (1967):287-292.

Index

Social interactions and resources, measures of, 135–137, 151–154; activities, 169–172; intergenerational support and role performance, 156–162; rating scales, 163–169; social networks, 154–156

Social and mental well-being, relationship of, 73

Social networks, 154–156; defined, 136, 154–155

Social Networks Assessment Questionnaire (SNAQ), 156

Social Responsibility Scale, 190

Social support system, defined, 155

Societal-role expectations, lack of, for elderly, 144–145

Socioeconomic and cultural determinants, 144

Sokolovsky, J., 155

Solitude ratings, 266–267

Specificity, degree of, 148

Spitzer, R.L., 229

Stack, T.F., 216

Steuer, J., 111, 116

Stewart, A.L., 25

Stockton Geriatric Rating Scale (SGRS), 128, 214–215, 216

Streib, G., 176

Studies, longitudinal or cross-sectional, 21–22

Subjective component, 143–144

Subjective well-being and coping, measures of, 137–139, 172–174, 185–187; Cavan Attitude Inventory, 176–177; Contentment Scale, 181–182; Geriatric Coping Scale, 187–188; Geriatric Scale of Recent Life Events, 188; Kutner Morale Scale, 177; Life Satisfaction Index, 174, 177, 182–184, 185; Modes of Adaptation Patterns Scale, 188; Oberleder Attitude Scale, 177–181; omission of, 174–176; Philadelphia Geriatric Center Morale Scale, 174, 177, 184–185, 188; Tri-Scales, 181

Suicide, among elderly, 72

Survey of Institutionalized Persons, 53–54

Syracuse University Research Corporation, 235

Taylor, C., 186

Tec, N., 162

Telleen, S., 196

Tests: intelligence, 78–80; projective, 128–129; psychological, 78–80

Thematic Apperception Test (TAT), 129

Thompson, L.W., 6, 107, 109, 117

Thompson, W., 176

Three Mile Island nuclear-reactor accident, 207

Time dependency, considering, 266–267

Time window, choice of, 147–148

Tisdale, W.A., 53

Tissue, T., 29

Tobin, S.S., 149, 174, 182

Tomlinson, B.E., 97

TRIAGE Quality of Life Scale, 12–13

TRIAGE system, 4, 210

Trickett, E.J., 155

Tri-Scales, 181

Tulloch, J., 151

Usual Day Scores, 171–172

Validity, 11–12; of multidimensional measures, 220–222; of OARS instrument, 226–229

Values, 267–268

Variable, interactive nature of, 142

Veterans Administration, 37, 49

VIRO Orientation Scale, 91–94, 204, 205–206

Visual Counting Test, 97

Wagner, C.C., 54

Wallach, H.F., 224

Wan, T.T.H., 179

Ward, M., 30–31

Ward Atmosphere Scale (WAS), 201, 202

Ware, J.E., Jr., 173

Warland, R., 173, 177, 184

Wechsler Adult Intelligence Scale (WAIS), 73, 98; shortened version of, 99

Wechsler Memory Test, 99–100

Weinstock, C., 73, 162

Weiss, R.W., 145

Weissert, W.G., 179

Weissman, A., 117

Weyman, A., 165

Whelihan, W.M., 80

Wing, J.K., 229

Wisconsin Community Care Organization, 263

Wolf, R.S., 111, 138, 173

Wolk, S., 196

Wood, V., 183, 201

Woolley, F.R., 257

Worcester Home Care Study, 45, 51

Wylie, C.M., 48

Wylie, M., 183

Wynter, L., 181

Yaffee, S., 30–31

Zeman, F.D., 58

Ziegler, M., 144, 191

Zimmer, A., 59

Zung Self-Rating Depression Scale (SDS), 111–116, 132

About the Authors

Rosalie A. Kane, D.S.W. is a social-work researcher, author, and educator. Formerly a faculty member at the University of Utah School of Social Work, she has been affiliated with The Rand Corporation since 1977. She is a lecturer at UCLA School of Social Welfare, where she is developing curriculum in health and long-term care. Dr. Kane is also the editor of *Health and Social Work*.

Robert L. Kane, M.D., is professor of Geriatric Medicine and Public Health at UCLA and a senior researcher at The Rand Corporation. A holder of a Geriatric Medicine Academic Award from the National Institutes of Health, he has conducted a series of research projects on long-term care, including an early demonstration of the use of geriatric nurse practitioners to provide primary care to nursing-home patients. Dr. Kane is the author or editor of ten books and over 100 articles. He is the editor of the *Journal of Community Health*.

List of Selected
Rand Books

Armor, David J.; Polich, J. Michael; and Stambul, Harriet B. *Alcoholism and Treatment.* New York: John Wiley and Sons, 1978.

Brewer, Garry D., and Kakalik, James S. *Handicapped Children: Strategies for Improving Services.* New York: McGraw-Hill Book Company, 1979.

Bruno, James E., ed. *Emerging Issues in Education: Policy Implications for the Schools.* Lexington, Mass.: Lexington Books, D.C. Heath and Company, 1972.

Carpenter-Huffman, P.; Kletter, R.C.; and Yin, R.K. *Cable Television: Developing Community Services.* New York: Crane, Russak and Company, 1975.

Comstock, George; Chaffee, Steven; Katzman, Natan; McCombs, Maxwell; and Roberts, Donald. *Television and Human Behavior.* New York: Columbia University Press, 1978.

Dalkey, Norman C. *Studies in the Quality of Life: Delphi and Decisionmaking.* Lexington, Mass.: D.C. Heath and Company, 1972.

Greenwood, Peter W.; Chaiken, Jan; and Petersilia, Joan. *The Criminal Investigation Process.* Lexington, Mass.: Lexington Books, D.C. Heath and Company, 1977.

Kane, R.L.; Solomon, D.H.; Beck, J.C.; Keeler, E.; and Kane, R.A. *Geriatrics in the United States: Manpower Projections and Training Considerations.* Lexington, Mass.: Lexington Books, D.C. Heath and Company, 1981.

McLaughlin, Milbrey Wallin. *Evaluation and Reform: The Elementary and Secondary Education Act of 1965/Title I.* Cambridge, Mass.: Ballinger Publishing Company, 1975.

Park, Rolla Edward. *The Role of Analysis in Regulatory Decisionmaking.* Lexington, Mass.: D.C. Heath and Company, 1973.

Quade, E.S. *Analysis for Public Decisions.* New York: American Elsevier Publishing Company, 1975.

Sackman, Harold. *Delphi Critique: Expert Opinion, Forecasting, and Group Process.* Lexington, Mass.: D.C. Heath and Company, 1975.

Smith, James P. *Female Labor Supply.* Princeton, N.J.: Princeton University Press, 1980.

Timpane, Michael, ed. *The Federal Interest in Financing Schooling.* Cambridge, Mass.: Ballinger Publishing Company, 1978.

Wirt, John G.; Lieberman, Arnold J.; and Levien, Roger E. *R&D Management: Methods Used by Federal Agencies.* Lexington, Mass.: D.C. Heath and Company, 1975.

Yin, Robert K.; Bateman, Peter M.; Marks, Ellen L.; and Quick, Suzanne K. *Changing Urban Bureaucracies: How New Practices Get Routinized.* Lexington, Mass.: LexingtonBooks, D.C. Heath and Company, 1979.

Yin, Robert., and Yates, Douglas, *Street-Level Governments: Assessing Decentralization and Urban Systems.* Lexington, Mass.: Lexington Books, D.C. Heath and Company, 1975.